A Post-Liberal Peace

MW00356371

This book examines how the liberal peace experiment of the post-Cold War environment has failed to connect with its target populations, which have instead set about transforming it according to their own local requirements.

Liberal peacebuilding has caused a range of unintended consequences. These emerge from the liberal peace's internal contradictions, and from its claims to offer both a universal normative and epistemological basis for peace, and a technology and process which can be applied to achieve it. When viewed from a range of contextual and local perspectives, these top-down and distant processes often appear to represent power rather than humanitarianism or emancipation. Yet, the liberal peace also offers a civil peace. These tensions enable a range of hitherto little understood local and contextual peacebuilding agencies to emerge, which renegotiate both the local context and the liberal peace framework, leading to a local-liberal hybrid form of peace. This might be called a post-liberal peace. Such processes are examined in this book in a range of different cases of peacebuilding and statebuilding since the end of the Cold War.

This book will be of interest to students of Peacebuilding, Peacekeeping, Peace and Conflict Studies, international organisations and International Relations/ Security Studies.

Oliver P. Richmond is a Professor in the School of International Relations, University of St. Andrews, UK, and Director of the Centre for Peace and Conflict Studies. His publications include *The Transformation of Peace* (2005), *Peace in International Relations* (Routledge, 2008) and *Liberal Peace Transitions* (with Jason Franks, 2009).

Routledge Studies in Peace and Conflict Resolution
Series Editors: Tom Woodhouse and Oliver Ramsbotham,
University of Bradford

A Post-Liberal Peace

Oliver P. Richmond

Routledge
Taylor & Francis Group

LONDON AND NEW YORK

First published 2011
by Routledge
2 Park Square, Milton Park, Abingdon, Oxon, OX14 4RN

Simultaneously published in the USA and Canada
by Routledge
711 Third Avenue, New York, NY 10017

Routledge is an imprint of the Taylor & Francis Group, an informa business

British Library Cataloguing in Publication Data
A catalogue record for this book is available from the British Library

Library of Congress Cataloging-in-Publication Data
Richmond, Oliver P.
    A post-liberal peace / Oliver P. Richmond.
    p. cm.
    1. Peace-building. 2. Conflict management. I. Title.
    JZ5538.R527 2011
    303.6'6--dc22
    2010053566

ISBN13: 978-0-415-66782-1 (hbk)
ISBN13: 978-0-415-66784-5 (pbk)
ISBN13: 978-0-203-81026-2 (ebk)

Typeset in Baskerville by Fakenham Prepress Solutions, Fakenham,
Norfolk NR21 8NN

Printed and bound in Great Britain by
CPI Antony Rowe, Chippenham, Wiltshire

To Beatrice, who represents the present and the future. For Eric and Joyce Richmond, and Bernard Nesden, from a generation who knew both war and peace.

Let us give the term genealogy to the union of erudite knowledge and local memories which allow us to establish a historical knowledge of struggles and to make use of this knowledge tactically today.[1]

---

1 Michel Foucault, 'Two Lectures', *Power/Knowledge*, London: Pantheon, 1972, p.83.

Contents

Acknowledgements

So many people have given their time and patience to this book, often in adverse circumstances and relatively difficult locations. These adversities range from the pressures of work and politics in international institutions, state institutions, politics, development/donor agencies, human rights organisations, a wide range of NGOs, social movements, local associations, and so forth. But more important are those that exist in the contours of often barely visible everyday life in its most marginal locations in my view. I would like especially to thank local researchers, assistants, translators, interviewees, and focus group participants in my field sites during visits to Cambodia, Timor Leste, Kosovo, Bosnia, Liberia, Namibia, Mozambique, Guatemala, and the Solomon Islands. I am grateful to them all and hope that I have done their contributions some justice. The problems faced by them in these intertwined projects of peace place my own mundane issues with university bureaucracy, the rigours of travel, and the polite debates of Western academia into a proper perspective. More importantly, I hope that this study mirrors a growing realisation that the politics and struggles of everyday life in conflict and post-conflict settings might now be more actively represented in the new interdisciplinary debates surrounding IR and peace and conflict studies. It is perhaps time to acknowledge the politics at stake in these debates and related practices.

I would like to thank in particular colleagues at Kulterstudier in Pondicherry, The School of IR and ACPACS, at the University of Queensland, the Department of Politics and International Relations, University of Oxford, Koc University, Istanbul, The Centre for Peace Studies, University of Coimbra, Portugal, and Pontificia Universidade Catolica of Rio de Janeiro, all of which provided me with tranquil locations for stimulating discussions about the issues in this book. I would like to thank my colleagues and partners at GTZ, Timor Leste: The Ministry for Peace and Reconciliation, Solomon Islands; Centre for Interdisciplinary Studies, Sarajevo; PRIO in Oslo; The Centre for Human Security, Sciences Po, Paris; and the Centre for Peace and Conflict Studies and the School of IR at the University of St Andrews. In particular I would like to thank Roland Bleiker, Morgan Brigg, Stefanie Kappler, Zeliha Kashman, Roger MacGinty, Necati Polat, Mike Pugh, Nick Rengger, Shahrbanou Tadjbakhsh, Yiannis Tellidis, Rob Walker, Alison Watson, and several reviewers for commenting in detail on parts of the text. I would like to thank my partners on an EUFP7 project on a 'Just And Durable Peace', particularly Annika Bjorkdahl and Karin Aggestam at Lund University, who tolerated my being spread too thinly. I would also like to thank those who attended various presentations of this study over the last few years for their contributions, at the University of Oxford: University of Bath; University of Bradford; University of Westminster; University of Exeter; University of Nicosia (where I presented the first attempt in 2007); University of Coimbra, Portugal; Phillips Universitat, Germany; Max Planck Institute, Halle, Germany; George Mason University, Washington; Sciences Po, Paris; PRIO, Oslo; Khung Hee University, Korea; Koc University and Sabanci University, both in Istanbul; University of Liberia; Trinity College, Dublin; University of Tubingham, Germany; University of Queensland; Autonomous University of Madrid; PUC University, Rio de Janiero; as well as the ISA conferences in New York and San Francisco, and the Millennium Conference at LSE in 2009. Funding for the fieldwork was in part made available by the Nuffield Trust, The Carnegie Trust, the University of St Andrews, a Visiting Professorship at the University of Queensland, and an EUFP7 grant for a project on a 'Just And Durable Peace' (specifically Part I, grant no. 217488). Last of all thanks and apologies to friends and loved ones for their patience with my 'work ethic' and frequent invitations to 'visit' awkward places.

Introduction[1]

> ... a genealogy should be seen as [an ...] attempt to emancipate historical knowledges from [...] subjection, to render them, that is, capable of opposition, and of struggle against the coercion of a theoretical, unitary, formal and scientific discourse. It is based on the reactivation of local knowledges [...] in opposition to the scientific hierarchisation of knowledges and the effects intrinsic to their power.[2]

Beyond the liberal peace?

The liberal peace has become a model through which Western-led agency, epistemology, and institutions, have attempted to unite the world under a hegemonic system that replicates liberal institutions, norms, and political, social, and economic systems.[3] It has been deployed in something like fifty to sixty post-conflict and fragile states over the last twenty years. Peace in these terms is seen not as an international gift, or as a local production, but as a contract. Emancipatory thinking about peace has collapsed into conditionality and governmentality. This has the attraction for international planners of a number of dynamics, including state pacification and regional stabilisation, transformation, normative legitimacy, civil emancipation, the bringing into being of a social contract, opening markets and validating the liberal state as a universal framework for emancipation. This has also often been an attractive proposition for many of this broad project's recipients outside of the West, in the developing, conflict, and post-conflict world. Sometimes this agreement has been honest and at other times it has been more devious, as has the development of the liberal peace project itself. This framework has been persuasive and intelligible at global, state, and local levels, despite its own bounded and contextual provenance. It emanates from Western experiences of development, peacebuilding, society, sovereignty, institutions, and the state. Since the end of the Cold War and until recently, it has remained without challenge, at least in mainstream international fora.

This is also perhaps the reason why the liberal peace has appeared in some contexts – often from the perspective of local recipients (or to be precise the political *subjects* of peacebuilding, statebuilding, modernisation, and development) to be insensitive, parochial, narrow and even complacent. This perspective claims it engenders ethnocentrism, cultural biases, and a narrow set of interests,[4] bounded by Hobbes and Locke.

It might be said that in its various iterations and broadest characterisation the liberal peace has been in crisis since the first intervention in Somalia by the UN and the US in the early 1990s. The responses to UNOSOM I and II, and to UNITAF (United Nations Task Force) were seen at the time by many as an extreme expression of state and citizen dysfunctionalism and anarchic violence, and little was written about what these events meant for the new, more confident version of the liberal peace in the post-Cold War environment. Despite these interventions, almost twenty years later, Somalia is still seen as a failed state. Many of the other interventions, whether peacebuilding, statebuilding, or 'peace-enforcement' have had unintended consequences or failed to meet their ambitious goals: Timor Leste and its ever-fragile state; in the Pacific, Sub-Saharan Africa, Cambodia and Central America where hybrid political regimes have emerged, often combining authoritarian rule and democracy, or custom and indigeneity; Kosovo where peacebuilding was co-opted into a nationalist project; Bosnia Herzegovina where political deadlock still prevents the reforms necessary for EU accession as the ultimate guarantee of peace; and finally Afghanistan and Iraq, where even the most basic form of security has failed to emerge despite (or perhaps partly because of) liberal interventionism. In these latter cases – perhaps the biggest peace project since the Marshall Plan – ironically a form of 'liberal state' has emerged which is fortified, militarised, spends most of its revenue on security, provides massive public sector employment to avoid humanitarian emergency, and is underpinned by quickly rotated international personnel (often US military or advisors).[5] These are at best parodies of the liberal state.

Many scholars have criticised the liberal peace and liberal statebuilding project from a wide variety of perspectives (often concentrating on the problems raised because of its co-option by ideological neoliberalism, which denies many of the rights the liberal peace proposes, its focus on statehood and territorial sovereignty, and its incapacity in connecting with local contextual issues). Others have defended the liberal peace, claiming that there is no real alternative or modification. The former arguments have been empirically proven time and time again in a wide range of post-conflict or post-violence examples,[6] yet are widely ignored by the mainstream who prefer the latter narrative (often for methodological, ideological or professional reasons). The defensive claim that there is 'no real alternative' is, on the other hand, a liberal fantasy, derived from crypto-colonial claims of cosmopolitan universalism. In fact there are alternatives and significant modifications to the liberal agenda already intellectually available and empirically observable.

Interesting dynamics have emerged in terms of local responses in post-conflict[7] peacebuilding, statebuilding, modernisation, and development environments. These have been at community (or customary, or other identity forms) or elite levels (politicians, business, and state elites), and do not indicate complete antipathy or complete acceptance. It has often been thought that there is little capacity for peace (or at best it is of a small scale), at the local level, but increasingly it appears that this is not the case. Local peacebuilding has more agency, and international peacebuilding, perhaps less than is often assumed.

Though my examples and cases in this study often focus on local agency derived from custom and community or the adoption of modernisation, I should point out that there has been a long-standing discussion of other dynamics of agency, including class, inequality, neopatrimonialism, gender, and socio-economic issues as forming the basis of local agency for peacebuilding, in both African and Central or South American settings.[8] These various dynamics have also been used to indicate tensions with the liberal peace system, as well as the salience of local actors in determining a sustainable peace. Yet, local failures to implement the liberal peace model are mainly blamed on local actors, political elites, predatory and pathological behaviour, and a lack of understanding of the benefits of the liberal peace infecting the target state. This inability of analyses framed by, supporting, propagating, or based on the liberal peace model to engage with context beyond their own occurs for a number of reasons. These range from its internal intellectual tensions, its material limitations, its methodo-logical inability to move beyond its universal prescriptions derived from a narrow Western experience, and its architectural priorities in security, economics, rights, and institutional terms. The most significant limitation has been its many failures in engaging with local actors (from the state to the community level), and to comprehend the perspectives, influences, cultures, customs, histories, or political, economic, social systems that exist, or to engage these in interwoven international and local peace projects. This has arisen because the liberal peace represents the biases of a specific set of actors, a knowledge system and epistemic community, allied to a narrow set of interests, norms, institutions and techniques, developed from these.[9] Yet, its subjects have resisted, exposed local ownership as external regulation, and have fragmented the hegemony of the liberal peace.

A localised perspective of peacebuilding – the view from below but also transversally and transnationally connected to the global – is the starting point for a reassessment of the liberal peace project, in keeping with emancipatory discourses of peacebuilding, and provides the basis for the approach this study adopts. Sites of resistance in the context of peacebuilding, with a view to emancipation and empathy with others ultimately lead to hybrid forms of peace. They require a reconsideration of who and what peace is constructed for, how it is negotiated and renegotiated by the strong and the weak (or then subaltern), what is to be included in its parameters, and how its emancipatory objectives develop. It involves engaging with alternative, resistant or critical agencies for peace, in tension with the liberal model, and perhaps hidden to it. It also requires understanding of the sorts of politics, systems, and hybridity that are produced, when such forms of agency come into contact with alternative, transformative projects in everyday contexts, as well as the sorts of emancipation, empathy, and care provided by the liberal peace versus that required in contextual terms. An emancipatory peace, in such terms, might be thought of as an everyday form of peace, offering care, respecting but also mediating culture and identity, institu-tions, and custom, providing for needs, and assisting the most marginalised in their local, state, regional and international contexts. It represents the provocation or creation of local peacebuilding agency, allows it space to contest the liberal peace and represent its own contextual dynamics, and ultimately through a local and transnational political process, leads to hybrid forms of peace. In broader terms, the local context in peacebuilding raises the issue of the roles and capacities of local agencies in reformulating international relations, especially in the liberal guise of cosmopolitanism, rights, institutions, and markets and their varied consequences for local contexts.

The remainder of this introduction provides the basis for this argument and sketches out its path.

The liberal peace framework

While the liberal peace project is in disarray many of its supporters correctly argue, usually via quantitative methodologies, that the number of inter-state and civil wars have reduced in the last ten years or so, as have the number of deaths (perhaps with the exception of the heavily disputed figures of civilian deaths for the war in Iraq). The number of durable negotiated settlements also appears to have increased.[10] This is significant but it also masks a widespread, local dissatisfaction with what the liberal peace actually represents for its subjects in post-violence environments. This is very evident in local and qualitative, social, economic, and political terms, as much contemporary, methodologically and theoretically sophisticated and locally grounded research now illustrates.[11] This contradicts the orthodox, institutional and elite level, state-based approaches often deployed, and reflects the events that have unfolded in situations as diverse as Timor Leste, Bosnia, Kosovo, or Cambodia.[12]

In many post-violence environments local perceptions of the liberal peace project and its statebuilding focus indicate it to be ethically bankrupt, subject to double standards, coercive and conditional, acultural, relatively unconcerned with needs, social welfare, or public services, and unfeeling and insensitive towards its subjects. Indeed, these deficiencies may even have incited resistance, reflecting the common emergence of a local post-colonial narrative about liberal peacebuilding's endorsement of an international-local relationship, configured as managers and subjects. So far the liberal peace project has not been subject to a concerted ethical consideration. Instead its legitimacy tends to rest on the praxis of already peaceful liberal polities, derived from the international level. This is exemplified by the often slavish focus on mandates, Security Council resolutions, international policy frameworks, or donor priorities over context.

To summarise my earlier work on this matter, the liberal peace framework rests upon conceptions of liberal-internationalist thought, on liberal-institutionalism, on the democratic peace hypothesis and free trade, on international law, and the balance between individual freedoms and regulations. These are embedded in liberal thinking and in the state, via a liberal social contract. It draws heavily on the Western philosophical and political debates that emerged from the writings of Hobbes, Machiavelli, Abbé St Pierre, Kant, Rousseau, Locke, Paine, Penn,

Cobden, Mill, Bentham, and Grotius, among others, in the context of cycles of war, diplomacy, statebuilding, imperialism, and colonialism.[13] In academic and policy writings related to peacebuilding and statebuilding it is normally taken to signify, in Wilsonian terms,[14] the processes, actors, and 'technologies' associated with humanitarian intervention, with security sector reform (and DDR), with institution building, good governance, democratisation, rule of law programming, human rights, reconstruction, development, and free market reform.[15]

There are four main strands of thought contained within the liberal peace framework from which these components are derived. These include the 'victor's peace', the 'institutional peace', the 'constitutional peace', and the 'civil peace'.[16] These combine to form the liberal peace model, each contributing to a different area of governance, relating to security, institutions, governance and constitutions, rule of law, human rights, development and marketisation, and civil society. The liberal peace is differentiated from the liberal democratic peace in that it offers a broader focus, not just on domestic political institutions and their international implications, but on the character of peace in civil and societal, political, economic, security, and international spheres. This has been the model and loose 'consensus' that internationals have attempted to apply in UN peace operations – from Cambodia in the early 1990s to Timor Leste and Afghanistan more recently – and also via other international and regional organisations since the end of the Cold War.[17] In practice, the first three strands of the liberal peace framework dominate peacebuilding, with a focus on security, institutional and constitutional reform. These dictate the significance of international regimes, organisations, and law, and democracy, the rule of law, human rights and the free market. Liberalism is understood to be aspirational, aimed at the freedom of individuals, and the liberal peace is always framed by the state and the market.

The civil peace is a key part of this agenda as it supports the liberal peace's overall emancipatory claims, which approach a version of social justice, and offer grounded legitimacy, being derived from local agency as well as international liberal norms. The civil peace is derived from the phenomena of direct action, of citizen advocacy and mobilisation, and from the attainment or defence of basic human rights and values. Within the liberal peace context it indicates individual agency within an international organisation, donor, agency, or, NGO (non-governmental organisation) context or within the market, rather than community agency. This latter concept is deemed to carry problematic ideological and cultural baggage. It also represents and underlines the old contractual dilemmas between the state and the citizen, of self-government, self-determination, and pluralism.

These intellectual strands offer different levels of engagement with local contexts, the 'everyday' and with 'care'.[18] They indicate conservative, orthodox, and emancipatory graduations of the liberal peace. The conservative graduation offers basic security and state level order, but little more. The orthodox graduation attempts to go further, while the emancipatory graduation offers social transformation. The conservative graduation of the liberal peace is associated with top-down and heavily externalised approaches to peacebuilding. These have been widely accepted as a transitional necessity in most post-war environments. Often, illiberal transitions (multilateral humanitarian intervention or even unilateral invasion) towards liberal institution building are key to this approach[19] (as have been seen in Somalia, the Balkans, Afghanistan, and Iraq). Conservative graduations of the liberal peace may offer basic everyday or state security but little care.

The *orthodox* graduation of the liberal peace focuses on top-down institution building. Bottom-up approaches engaging with civil society are relatively widespread, but international actors focus on the development of the liberal state, its institutions, and a neoliberal economy. This is rights-based and developed through conditionality. It tends to be justified by the argument that security, order, and institutions always come first. These are derived from the praxis of internationals not local actors, for whom ownership of the liberal peace is eventually envisaged.[20] This model is exemplified by the UN family's practices of peacebuilding and governance reform, which started at the end of the Cold War and in particular culminated in the Kosovo mission and UN sovereignty for a time over Timor Leste. The orthodox gradation offers significantly more engagement with its subjects over a broader range of issues denoting potential for an everyday peace. Assuming security matters have been assuaged by this point, this establishes institutions that provide care, relating to governance and public services but within the confines dictated by neoliberal marketisation.

The final gradation represents a more critical form of the liberal peace. This *emancipatory* model is concerned with needs as well as rights (and a blurring of the line between these categories), and a much closer relationship between custodians and subjects, implying local ownership. This is a bottom-up approach with a stronger concern for social welfare and justice. It equates with the civil peace and generally is not state-led but shaped by NGOs, trade unions, advocacy and social movements as well as to some regional and international actors. Here the everyday and care become the major concerns of peacebuilding, though this treads a fine line between providing what external actors believe to be suitable versions of these according to their external understandings of the everyday, and what recipients may want according to contextual dynamics. However, this comes closest to engaging with the notion of an everyday ethic of peace.

The liberal peace framework and its graduations converge on a notion of *peace-as-governance*, to make use of a pertinent concept (with due regard for its origin in Western political contexts).[21] This is both biopolitical and governmentalising in the Foucaultian sense of these terms, reordering state and society via the alphabet soup of agencies, organisations, and institutions. The framework relies on the concepts of territorial statehood and sovereignty, and on dominant states in the international community. These assume that the epistemology, ontology, and methods associated with the liberal peace are on ethically firm ground and should be contained within the modern sovereign state. Its parameters suggest an end to violence and, through the liberal state formulation, an everyday form of peace, which engages with the local, its cultural dynamics, welfare needs, and environment. Thus, it leads to the social contract inherent in a liberal state. This has been extended into a claimed, automatically ethical blueprint for its transferral to non-Western, often undeveloped, and often regarded as non-liberal polities. Yet, it is also a disciplinary framework that often rests on coercion, a lack of consent, conditionality, and the prioritisation of elites over the interests of the many. As such criticisms emerged in the 1990s, the more recent 'light footprint' approach in Afghanistan has been interpreted as a scaling back of the governmental claims of the liberal peace, but similar values remain in the internationals' approach even there.[22]

The ethics of liberalism suggest the 'good life' where individual privileges denote freedom to act politically, economically and socially, within a liberal governance framework which constitutionally guarantees human rights. Yet, the governmental and institutional imbalance in the very highly specialised context of post-conflict states undermines this ethic of engendering autonomy and agency. It often stifles local voices and their concerns about peace.[23] Many of the subjects of recent statebuilding experiments regard the liberal peace as an ideology whose universal aspirations are not mirrored on the ground.[24] This results in the re-securitisation of the post-conflict state whereby politics is deemed to start from security and institutions, rather than from social justice, community and everyday life. Thus, the politics of the liberal peace are perceived to represent the maintenance of existing normative and political hierarchies at the local, national, and global levels. This also makes some or many of its participants and subjects complicit in anti-democratic and anti-self-determination processes. These are tied to the state and to institutions that do not necessarily represent the local as either a civil society or in an everyday context.[25]

This is particularly exaggerated in the liberal peace's most conservative, militarised forms – as praxis in Afghanistan or Iraq has illustrated. It is also the case to some degree even in its orthodox, more institutionalised forms as in Kosovo, Timor Leste, or Bosnia.[26] This has diverted attention away from a search for more contextually legitimate alternatives, for hybrid forms of peace, for empathetic strategies through which the liberal blueprint for peace that has loosely emerged at the international level might coexist with local alternatives.[27] This is not to argue, as Barnett and Zuercher have already shown, that 'cooptive peacebuilding' (where international normative projection, conditionality and local elite requirements for survival produce an uneasy local compromise)[28] is without benefit, especially compared to the often violent alternatives, but this should not lead to complacency with respect to the critical development of the field, or the contextual legitimacy of intervention, liberal peacebuilding and statebuilding.

Developing a critical account of the record of liberal peacebuilding

Experience and data from a range of UN and UNDP (United Nations Development Programme) thematic or country focused reports has shown liberal peacebuilding to have less impact on everyday life than is often claimed by its institutional proponents, the donor and development communities, and particularly the International Financial Institutions (IFIs). One example among many can be found in the context of Timor Leste after the crisis of 2006. A UN report conceded that despite a lengthy and costly UN involvement there since 1999,

> … poverty and its associated deprivations including high urban unemployment and the absence of any prospect of meaningful involvement and employment opportunities in the foreseeable future, especially for young people have also contributed to the crisis.[29]

Yet there was little sense of a need to reflect on the underlying liberal peace paradigm that allowed a 'peace' to be built in Timor Leste which ignored these issues. In a more recent example, a report on Afghanistan by the UN Secretary General ignored any direct engagement with such issues in favour of traditional political and security concerns, with the exception of one telling reference:

> The failure of development actors to ensure that quieter provinces in the north and west receive a tangible peace dividend has played into the latent north-south fault line within Afghanistan …[30]

This report's later sections on development, human rights, and humanitarian issues or human security, focused on orthodox issues relating to institution-building or emergency problems.[31] In the conclusion to the report the full litany of liberal peacebuilding discourse is repeated in seeming ignorance of the lessons of Timor Leste, or indeed of Afghanistan itself. Accordingly, the transition in Afghanistan is under '… increasing strain owing to insurgency, weak governance and the narco-economy'. The government needs to '… restore confidence to the population in tangible ways' but this is conceptualised as being derived from,

> … stronger leadership from the Government, greater donor coherence — including improved coordination between the military and civilian international engagement in Afghanistan — and a strong commitment from neighbouring countries, [without which] many of the security, institution-building and development gains made since the Bonn Conference may yet stall or even be reversed.[32]

This list of priorities, focusing on security, terrorism, narcotics, and then the orthodoxy of the liberal peace as a subsequent priority (governance, development, reconciliation, and human rights abuses in this order) effectively places a local peace dividend in everyday terms for communities and individuals as a distant and lesser priority. It is disconnected from the conduct of democratic politics and the legitimacy of the state.[33] This is because the liberal peace's primary goal in its intervention into the local is actually aimed at stability in international order between sovereign states. This is to be achieved ideally through the construction of a liberal social contract to produce domestic, regional, and international order.

The ethical and policy metanarratives about liberal peace derive from the founding myths of Westphalia, its state-centric elitism, its focus on territorial boundaries and sovereignty, its proto-institutional and its disciplinary nature. This is a 'moment of exclusion', essentially.[34] The concept of peace has generally been subject to utopian or dystopian assumptions, and the notion of the liberal peace has emerged as an 'auto-ambivalent' compromise.[35] It has been imbued with a specific set of interests, partly through the de-contextualisation of classical political theory and history which supports inherency arguments about conflict, or confirms liberal norms of market-democracy, all of which are supposed to represent inclusiveness and plurality. This informs a propensity to try to transform rather than engage with non-liberal others, introducing instead exclusivity and liberal enclosure. It also validates territorial state sovereignty and a social contract skewed in favour of the state, free markets, and the eradication of the indigenous or a locally more authentic polity (often through property rights),[36] identity, and needs, among other tendencies.[37] This has been used to promote a culture of governmental and securitised institutionalism[38] rather than promoting an everyday peace.[39] It has supported the classical view that liberal states and peoples are effectively superior in rights and status to others, and has extended these arguments to allow for the justification of direct or subtle forms of colonialism, interventionism, and local depoliticisation to occur.[40] A civil and emancipatory peace might arise through liberalism, but it may also lead to violence of a structural or direct nature in post-conflict contexts.[41] In practice it also may have negative effects on self-determination and agency.[42]

In this context an ethical evaluation of the liberal peace beyond the West underlines its tendency to be flimsy: denying self-determination and self-government, and depoliticising. This is as opposed to the potential of peace being empathetic and emancipatory, resting upon an ontological agreement and hybridity (meaning the development of an ontology that is not exclusive but is open to difference in everyday settings).[43] These latter qualities imply that the agents and recipients of the liberal peace are able to relate to each other on an everyday, human level, rather than merely through problem-solving institutional frameworks that dictate or negate lived experience. They indicate the need for a deep negotiation of peace even by the agents of the liberal model, and for a willingness to see the Western model itself modified by its engagement with its own 'others'.

What has emerged from more critical literatures, as a result, is a focus on local ownership, human rights, human security, culture, social and grass-roots resources for self-government, local capacity or agency, even resistance, as significant even in relation to the priorities of security or institutional capacities and international order. This infers an engagement with the everyday, to provide care, to empathise, and to enable emancipation.[44] These objectives are integral to the liberal peace in theory, but in practice asymmetries inherent in its top-down nature, elite governance and complicity with local elites, are more visible. This insight enables an investigation of modifications to the liberal peace without necessarily calling for its abandonment (though post-structural work indicates continuing dissatisfaction with the inherent biases of even a moderated liberal form of peacebuilding).

Serious problems arise, however, with any attempt to retain while modifying the core of the liberal peace. The neoliberal co-option of the liberal peace, its lack of needs or social welfare frameworks (that give meaning to liberal rights and state institutions), failure to mediate cultural difference or recognise non-secular or traditional sites of politics and power, and tendency towards assimilation rather than local cultural engagement, means that it is often exceptionally abrasive when transplanted. It might be said that the conservative end of the liberal peace spectrum, as with liberal imperialism, has become an exercise in hubris and wishful thinking for the internationals, Western states, donors, agencies and NGOs that propagate it, mainly because it lacks contextual sensitivities. Ethically, moving beyond these limitations, this would amount to an ontological commitment to care for others in their everyday contexts, based upon empathy, respect and the recognition of difference. This commitment to care has instead been displaced by a parsimonious orthodoxy that offers its participants the unproblematic right of interpreting and making policy for others, normally defined as states rather than peoples or communities. This is why the liberal peace is mainly focused on an international or regional peace and the state's place therein, rather than an everyday form of peace, care, empathy, or emancipation.

From the perspective of attempting to reform the liberal peace model, what needs to be considered is how to identify the rights, resources, identity, welfare, cultural disposition, and ontological hybridity, that would make liberal states, institutionalism, and governance viable in everyday contexts where others reside. This requires an engagement with not just the currently fashionable and controversial issues of local ownership or local participation,[45] but the far deeper 'local-local' (i.e. what lies beneath the veneer of internationally sponsored local actors and NGOs constituting a 'civil' as opposed to 'uncivil' society), which allows for genuine self-government, self-determination, democracy and human rights.

Yet, because theory often fails when it attempts to present a truth as anything other than a 'historically specific spatial ontology'[46] the paradox of thinking about peace is that governance and statebuilding require essentialism and instrumentalism. This need for theory and practice is supposed to offer progress from a war system to peace system in advance of its engagement with a specific conflict context. This means that great care must be taken to separate this intention with a historical or ideological blueprint approach to peace that is then transplanted into conflict zones.[47] This raises the broader question of how developing an account of peace can engage with the other without falling into an Orientalist and coercive syndrome, disregarding or discounting local context. Thus 'peace' as a concept offers a contradiction – it requires a method, ontology, and epistemology which is negotiated locally, but prompted externally by agents who must engage with the contextual other, but cannot comprehend context fully (at least in a short time and at the depth of detail required for such ambitious relationships). It may well be that the Enlightenment-derived discourse of liberal peace is not sophisticated enough for contemporary ethical requirements for a sustainable peace.

This does not mean that elements of the liberal peace may not be broadly applicable, but that the assumption that they are should not be made a priori. The negotiation of a single and universal concept of peace may be a worthy goal but it also may be as much a chimera as Einstein's 'unified theory'. A permanent modernity of the post-civil war environment that Hobbes was familiar with would not be an acceptable peace to many today. Neither would a hegemonic peace that was predetermined, equally permanent, and not reflective of the myriad of groups, interests, cultures, and dimensions of the local, or of international relations. Yet, the liberal peace has become an intervention in local discussions about peace, often replacing them entirely with the views of a transnational peacebuilding class and the institutions they are part of. This is indicative of a deeper contest over interpreting and governing the other.

The liberal peace is predicated upon the disciplinary enterprise of constructing rights for its epistemic communities of policymakers, analysts, academics, officials, and other personnel, to interpret and make policy on their behalf. Much of this move has been predicated upon the desire of this community to emancipate the other from war, violence, and unstable political, social and economic structures, to set an example, as well as to govern.[48] The orthodoxy has been to accept mainly rationalist approaches, and certainly not to question this privilege.[49] Questioning this tendency – as has already occurred in some disciplines such as sociology and anthropology[50] – illustrates and underlines the problem of IR (International Relations), perhaps now the dominant discipline in the consideration of peace-building and statebuilding as a potentially 'Orientalist', neo-colonial discipline, and its main methodological problems in dealing with others, difference, and the everyday. A growing of literature points to the problems of liberalism in this context.[51]

Consequently, if the liberal peace is to be salvaged in mainstream terms it would have to offer a more pluralist debate on its own modifications or alternatives, a *via media* between itself and them. It would also have to offer a technology of governance that is broadly representative of all actors at multiple levels, public and private, gendered and aged, and of multiple identities. This would mean it would adopt a potentially hybrid localised identity to counterbalance its global or governmental metanarrative of cosmopolitanism, with commensurate implications for its claimed boundaries, rules, rights, freedoms, and norms. This might mean it would accrue more everyday legitimacy, which might be then formalised in governmental, institutional or constitutional structures and legal frameworks, which would rest primarily upon a 'new' social contract. This legitimacy would rest upon its provision of social, cultural, economic and political resources sufficient to meet the demands made upon it by its local, everyday, constituencies, and an international community of which the former should be a stakeholder, part owner, and able to co-constitute. It would also rest upon an international social contract, while not displacing indigenous legitimacy with preponderant institutions that are inflexible or even unintentionally obscure the local and the everyday. Such a framework should not then be set in stone but instead must be seen as an evolving form, focusing on an everyday peace, and the necessary emancipatory and empathetic structures and institutions this may require.

The difficulty with this ethical repositioning of the liberal peace is that it no longer represents the 'really-existing' liberal peace in contemporary post-conflict environments. Instead these have come to rest upon biopolitics, the administration of life, and governmentality.[52] Peacebuilding in this liberal sense represents the ways donors, governments, and institutions produce political subjects or citizens best suited to fulfil their policies, agendas, interests and ideologies. Practices, discourses, and rationalities are organised around these, to produce governmentality, or as I described it in an earlier work, 'peace as governance'.[53] This has very significant implications for the local, for locality, context, and peacebuilding agency, especially therefore for the sustainability of any peace which arises from liberal peacebuilding strategies.

This points to the problems inherent in universal frameworks for peace, engaging with others while avoiding Orientalism, neo-colonialism, or an over-reliance on predatory institutional frameworks at the expense of everyday life. Thus, liberal peace elevates elites and institutions over societies and everyday life. This is often seen as representative of dominant Western interests, culture and ideology. A broader social justice is perceived to be absent, and it fails to achieve acceptable levels of care in everyday contexts, even by distant liberal humanitarian standards.[54] It is unable to communicate across cultures, rests upon a legalistic framework, disassociates law from local norms, attempts to preserve the pre-existing Western liberal order, and claims a problematic universality.[55] As a result, it fails to provide even thin recognition let alone mutual consent. What is missing is local legitimacy, and international-local peacebuilding contract, reconciliation, dialogue and communication – indeed a discourse ethic of empathetic self-emancipation in an everyday context. The liberal concept of 'toleration' over difference, as the word implies, is too limited to produce pluralism or hybridity, and liberalism's link with sovereignty, markets, and the state, as well as its homogenising tendencies provide significant constraints. Issues such as needs and culture are ignored as a result, meaning that the liberal peace is not an everyday peace.

Because of the ethical ambitions of enabling emancipation *after* achieving security and building institutions, the liberal peace is increasingly seen as caught up in a securitised and governmental praxis, being ideological, and deploying a metanarrative which provokes resistance amongst what it portrays as powerless local agents.[56] This post-colonial critique doubts the claims of even the emancipatory graduation of liberal peace but rather sees its use to legitimate its conservative and orthodox graduations. This challenges the liberal peace's implied claim that progress from a conservative version, based upon military and diplomatic processes (equated with a negative peace), to an orthodox liberal statebuilding process and then to an emancipatory version of the liberal peace (positive peace) will occur. The liberal social contract endeavours to accrue legitimacy for the regulatory institutions of governance required by offering mainly political rights to individuals as sufficient enticement for them to acquiesce to the liberal state project. Legitimacy emanates from above, often from the UN or from donors, rather than from local consent. This works on the assumption that the freedoms derived from political rights are more significant than culture, needs or material gain for individuals in post-conflict situations. The emancipatory graduation of liberal peace does offer the potential for reflection on the ethical implications of this but it is in this top-down, institutional format, that liberal peacebuilding fails to adequately consider the requirements for a social contract beyond political rights for grass-roots actors in their everyday context. As a result their consent is often lacking and the legitimacy of the liberal peacebuilding project is undermined.

There must be a response to the moral hazards of liberal peacebuilding, which lies in its reflection of the 'coldness' (i.e. its concern with elites and states rather than society, community, and everyday experience) of just war thinking, democratic and market oriented institutionalism, and justice oriented, mainly Western ontologies – from which arise its related epistemology and methodologies. These sacrifice the local needs, welfare, culture, and care of peoples according to institutionalised modes of political, social, and economic governance, some of which work in developing a social contract while others do not. In fact, in this enormous area of societal issues, the liberal peace offers little, because it is mainly aimed at the ethical frameworks arising from remedying inter-state conflict, rather than the sociopolitical dynamics of any breakdown into conflict. This reflects the fact that liberal peacebuilding itself is an institutional framework derived from the logic of stabilising the Westphalian system and its positivist ontologies of security and strategy. This points to a need to return the everyday to the praxis of an emancipatory form of peace.

The Local, the Everyday and the Infrapolitics of Peacebuilding

It is hardly surprising that from below, and according to the 'infrapolitics of peacebuilding' (meaning its hidden, fragmented, often disguised and localised agencies and capacities) such an approach seems to its subjects to be overbearing, perhaps even colonial, and not representative of local, contextual notions of peace and politics in their multiple, heterogeneous, and transversal characters. It is these that produce 'locality' (which includes local-global relations)[57] and legitimacy in actual fact.[58] As Appadurai has argued, locality, 'the local', or even deeper, more contextual 'local-local', depicts that which lies beneath the often artificial and externalised 'civil society') represents a

> ... complex phenomenological quality, constituted by a serious of links between the sense of social immediacy, the technologies of interactivity, and the relativity of contexts ... expressed in certain types of agency, sociality, and reproducibility ....[59]

It is not essentialisable in an easily instrumentalised manner (as many internationals often assume), nor it is necessarily representative of a fixed geographical space (as many assume the terms local/locality indicate). It resists the 'enclavisation' which these may lead to, especially in the context of the broader processes of deterritorialisation which are occurring. It is most importantly representative of forms of agency which reproduce locality and subjectivity, often through a struggle to maintain social, economic, political and cultural continuity and autonomy, whilst adapting and developing, of which the most important for this study are those aimed at peacebuilding. Internationals do not see them easily because of dominant methodologies and epistemology. Even if these are visible to the liberal gaze, they tend to be regarded as incapable of the sorts of large-scale political mobilisation required for liberal notions of statehood, peace and development.

Henceforth, I use the term 'the local' to denote what international actors normally perceive as a range of actors and terrains spanning their non-Western and 'non-liberal' partners for liberal peacebuilding and statebuilding at the elite level (whilst also acknowledging that many local actors may have extensive trans-national and transversal experience of liberal politics), and civil society. I use the term 'local-local' to indicate the existence and diversity of communities and individuals that constitute political society beyond this often liberally projected artifice of elites and civil society, who may also have transnational and transversal exposure. This latter is where the everyday is at its most powerful as a critical tool. I do not equate the everyday/local with illiberalism or liberalism necessarily.[60] Nor do I want to exaggerate a local-international binary: such categories inevitably capture only part of the political tensions within peacebuilding.

The local is often 'evacuated' from social science analysis[61] on a number of grounds, ranging from its banality, its superficiality, its analytical vagueness, its apparent binary opposition with other priorities (such as the international or the state), and its arbitrary boundaries, to the risk of its essentialisation and instrumentalisation. Such positions on the 'evacuation of the local' connect with Foucaultian arguments about governmentality and biopolitics,[62] where agency is passed to states and governments to renegotiate citizen's rights and more dangerously, their biology, while also mobilising them for wealth, rights, and representation. Foucault's response to this danger was to focus on the 'technology of the self' and 'self-care',[63] where individuals found ways of reclaiming the agency that had been usurped by states (or in the case of liberal peacebuilding, internationals). This can also be connected with the relationship between states and civil society, the local (or local-local), where the latter are both subservient to but constitute the state.

Thus, the 'infrapolitics of peacebuilding' imply significant agency at the local level, sometime oppositional and sometimes not, even amongst supposedly marginalised actors, or amongst those 'not yet liberal'. This is reclaimed agency, or critical agency which exists in spaces liberal peacebuilding and statebuilding cannot reach. It indicates the hermeneutic, diverse, fluid, transnational and transversal aspect of the local, its everyday agencies, its extensions into the international, the liberal peace, and a range of dynamics – cultural and otherwise – which transcend reductive analysis. It indicates also that peacebuilding is contested, and is not just a terrain that international actors occupy or are able to engage in.

Such insights require ethical, ethnographic, and active research methodologies, in order to allow an understanding of the local, locality, context, and their interactions with and against the liberal peacebuilding architecture that has developed. This would show how the infrapolitics of peacebuilding emerge and create or provoke new peacebuilding agencies, modifying both the local and the liberal frameworks, nudging each to move beyond their tradition categorisations and essentialisations. This requires an 'ethnoscape'[64] as part of the framing of peace-building and statebuilding, allowing an understanding of the dynamics of local agency, of context, but also of the colonial impulses that seem to be the unintended consequence of the development of the architecture of liberal peacebuilding.

This somewhat ambitious study sets out to examine what this means for contemporary peacebuilding and for IR, drawing on extensive fieldwork from several recent post-conflict peacebuilding sites around the world, and develops a theoretical response which may inform new thinking about such situations, in the 'autocritical' mode as described by Spivak. She points out that the 'subaltern cannot speak' unless 'resistance' is recognised.[65] For IR, and those working on the multidisciplinary debates surrounding peacebuilding, this means moving away from the notion that the discipline's role is to support the interests of a 'security establishment', or the West, the developed, or enlightened in general. Instead it should be concerned with the wide range of conditions and experiences of everyday life and politics in peace and war, and the emancipatory and trans-formative projects that are elucidated in these contexts.

This realisation requires a pluralist reflection on who peace is for, and what it means in the modern global context. 'This is investigated in critical, genealogical mode, conscious of the need for methodological approaches that do not evacuate the local, nor disguise marginal agencies, perhaps akin to the experimental eclecticism I have earlier outlined.'[66] This reflection follows on from my previous work on four generations of thinking about peace: from first generation conflict management approaches; to second generation conflict resolution and trans-formation approaches; to third generation liberal peacebuilding/statebuilding approaches; and a fourth generation approach that transcends the limitations of liberalism and aims for an empathetic and emancipatory form of peace with intimations of hybridity. It also extends my later interrogation of the liberal peace.[67] This enables an exploration of the *everyday* nature of any sustainable peace, focused on a culturally appropriate form of individual or community life and care, and the critical and often resistant agencies which emerge and constitute contextual legitimacy. This points either to the need for a form of liberal peace with a broader social contract, or more ambitiously, one that transcends liberal and neoliberal, Western biases, enabling everyday peacebuilding agencies to mediated the liberal peace through transnational processes.

Such a search, via critical research agendas for peace[68] termed here '*eirenist*', indicates the need for an ethical re-evaluation of the liberal peace.[69] Eirenism was a term used by Erasmus as a call against religious chauvinism after the Reformation.[70] In a modern context it provides a lens through which one can evaluate the claims, apparent or hidden, of a particular epistemology, concept, theory, method, or ideology pertaining to making peace. The failure to apply such a tool so far has led liberal peacebuilding approaches into a paradoxical situation. They have reinstated social and economic class systems, undermined democracy, and caused downward social mobility. Yet, liberal peace's Renaissance and Enlightenment underpinnings make clear that the states-system of territorial sovereignty, the approximation of democracy, of human rights and free trade, also carries a humanist concern with social justice and wide-ranging pluralism (often to be guaranteed by an international organisation).[71] Ironically, this is where its failings are most obvious. Its focus has been on security and institutions, rather than developing an engagement with the everyday life of post-conflict citizens. It has sometimes been built on force rather than consent, and more often conditionality, and it has failed to recognise local cultural norms and traditions. It has created a 'virtual peace' in its many theatres, meaning the empty shell of a state with little relevance to the everyday lives of most of its peoples.[72] This is not to say that narrow security issues have not been somewhat assuaged through peace-keeping and statebuilding, and that this has not been without benefit. It should not be taken that the Enlightenment rationalism, which has created the liberal peace system, is not without its benefits or contributions to peace. But it should not monopolise conceptions of peace. Indeed, the liberal peace is not the product of merely Western, European, interactions, but has been more widely informed in a post-colonial context.[73] Thus, the infrapolitics of peacebuilding have arisen as a way of representing the local, everyday context.

Informed by Foucault's revealing words (in the epigraph above) the analysis developed in this study represents more than a 'mere' critique designed to restore the liberal peace. It aims to enable the political contestation of externalised and contextual notions of peace, of governmentality,[74] not to mention of biopolitics,[75] in order to reconstruct a process of peacebuilding that enables local peace-building agencies to represent themselves, and the liberal peace to encounter and respect other political systems and other versions of peace. Yet, just in the same way that the notion of (and also the word) liberalism came into being in the context of the paradoxes of imperial and colonial rule[76] so too a genealogy of IR and peace shows how both relate to power, war, violence, and order, in generally uncomfortable ways. Out of the meeting of the liberal peace in the post-Cold War period with other versions of peace (however limited) and other forms of politics and society, a sort of hybrid version of peace[77] appears to be emerging if only slightly visible through the fog produced by liberal prescriptions that now claim a near ontological status and difficult local contexts.

So, in these terms everyday life is representative of agency, of compliance, of resistance, and so often of hidden capacities. These can be termed critical agencies for peacebuilding, drawn from contexts which include custom, identity, culture, needs provision, and other dynamics which mount a political challenge, even in marginal terms to the liberal peace. It is also a space in which social, political, economic, cultural, religious, identity, spiritual, and other forms of agencies, expressions, and relations exist, in local-local, civil society, state, trans-national and transversal terms. Peace and war are experienced most acutely in the everyday context, which includes the personal, the family, community, custom, work, class, leisure, politics, culture, society, and economics, as well as the state, the public, and the nation – as they are imagined by their subjects. It includes survival, alienation, mystification, compliance, and resistance, as de Certeau and Lefebvre have shown.[78] Ultimately, the infrapolitics of peacebuilding are having unanticipated effects on the liberal peacebuilding and statebuilding project.

Hybridity and post-liberalism

As a potential alternative, hybridity in terms of peace represents both the capacity of international liberal and local peacebuilding actors and projects to engage with each other, perhaps even to the benefit of the 'local' version of peace. It is also cognisant of the possibility that hybridity represents the powerful rather than the local. It is important to note that hybridity is an inevitable outcome of the liberal peace and its contextual engagements. The question is more whether hybridity offers a transformation and an emancipatory version of peace, especially when it represents partially at least, the agency of local actors recently engaged in conflict and international actors recently involved in instrumental forms of peacebuilding and statebuilding? How might international actors enable such local processes?

Such a search opens up a discussion of a post-liberal peace as a logical outcome of the meeting of infrapolitics and liberal peace. This study develops such an account drawing on the liberal peace framework, but engaging with critical agency, discussions about governmentality, biopower, biopolitics, emancipation, self-care, and with alternative debates on empathy and the everyday, on resistance and hybridity, to begin to imagine the possibility of a post-liberal peace that does not collapse into a grand narrative of ideology masquerading as ontology. Critical agency emerges from this study as a crucial concept for peacebuilding, related to and with an understanding of the local, context, and resistance as a fundamental component of international and social theory, where it operates as a key dynamic of human security, representation, and peace. This occurs not through the channels, or with the impact, that IR expects. It occurs in hidden and fragmented ways rather than via the formal institutions of liberal political mobilisation. This represents critical agency, implying a local, contextual and subaltern (meaning civil society and the local-local beneath it) capacity to mobilise non-violently, either visibly and in a coordinated manner, or in hidden and fragmented ways. Both are effective in different ways, especially in view of contextual resonance and the construction of legitimacy, order, and peace. Such understanding utilises the work of a range of authors sensitive to critical methodological and theoretical matters (such as the everyday, empathy, identity, ethnography, culture, custom, welfare, gender, arts and emotions, agonism, and post-colonialism). It does not use these concepts in tight conceptual forms, but instead (in an effort to avoid yet more oppressive metanarratives of 'peace'), retains a degree of ambiguity in their meaning. Many chapters draw on fieldwork, focus groups and interviews, in order to reflect subaltern critiques of the current hegemonic paradigm that has sought to capture peacebuilding (but in recognition of the transversality of such labels), and to develop a contextual discussion of what a post-liberal peace might look like. Its aim is to engage with local forms of politics, society, and economics, in post-conflict environments, in terms of both how conflict has been replicated and also how emancipatory projects for peace might emanate from them in ways which also transform the liberal peace project, perhaps even unbeknownst to itself. It is in this relationship between the local and the liberal peace project that local, contextual, critical agency moves into view or restarts and hybrid possibilities for the transformation of both the liberal and the local emerge.

What have already emerged in theory and practice are hybrid forms of the liberal peace, which are modified by their contact with the very local context that it claims does not exist, is mistaken or insignificant, or romanticises and mythologises. This represents the birth of a post-liberal peace. A 'local-liberal hybrid' is emerging, which constitutes, as this study will illustrate, post-liberal forms of peace. The local is named as 'local' not to essentialise it, but with the acknowledgement that until its context and dynamics are understood in their complexity, its character cannot be captured in one word. The international is characterised as 'liberal' because, at least in peacebuilding terms, it follows the varieties of liberalism currently in circulation, in institutional, political, social, and economic terms. Peacebuilding thus represents the interface between the local and the liberal (in broad terms), and rather than imposing the liberal normative system on the local, should facilitate a new mediation between the two in each context. This realisation necessitates a rethink of dominant paradigms of peace, and of course the development of a clearer understanding of what constitutes the local and the liberal, how the interface between the liberal and the local operates, and with what consequences. Of course, these are general terms and dynamics, sketching patterns rather than essentialising such dynamics.

This raises the question of whether the local and the liberal repulse each other, meaning that the emergent hybrid is inevitably based on internal contradictions, or whether they are attracted to each other – in which case, it is based on the production of new political cultures and institutional paradigms. Both can occur, and indeed, have occurred, from Cambodia to Afghanistan and the Solomon Islands. One of the most interesting aspects of this post-liberal form of peace is that it may rescue and reunite both the liberal and the local rather than encouraging them to reject each other (as is the case with the current liberal peace paradigm). This would entail the recognition that liberalism is actually a form of customary political community, derived from the Western experience (i.e. the West's own 'local'). Most non- or partially liberal environments have emerged from their own authentic customary experience, which has survived colonialism, war, and poverty, often because they enable social support and resilience, as well as norms and institutions, despite such experiences. They normally have remained more relevant to peoples' everyday lives than their often predatory or failing states or the virtual states that liberal peacebuilding has reproduced. Thus, understanding the 'everyday' is crucial for the local-liberal hybrid.

A local-liberal hybrid can represent either a combination of very negative political practices (for example, rigorously determined liberal institutionalism and market development solutions with patriarchal, feudal, communal, or sexist, practices) or it can be more positive (in that it connects complementary practices related to democracy, self-determination, agency, autonomy, solidarity, human rights and needs, and a rule of law, with customary social support networks, customary forms of governance and political order). Or it can connect both negative and positive practices (meaning that both the liberal and the local develop elements of attraction and rejection). Though the problem posed here might be that liberalism and customary forms of governance impede each other, this is not always the case. Indeed, liberalism, more specifically, is less likely to recognise the local, the contextual, customary order, than the local is to marginalise the liberal. This is partly due to the power relations between liberalism and the local which inevitably favours liberal political order, but it is also due to an inherent blind-spot of liberalism towards the local. Yet, there is a mutual attraction between the liberal and the local, which in many conflict and post-conflict zones, influences the process of producing a hybrid peace.

This hybridity is emerging in diverse locations where the liberal has 'met' the local despite such difficulties since the end of the Cold War, from El Salvador, Guatemala, Namibia, Cambodia, to Bosnia, Kosovo, Sierra Leone, Liberia, Uganda, Timor Leste, Solomon Islands, Afghanistan, and Iraq. This is not necessarily an emancipatory form of peace, as theorised in my earlier (2005) work. Sometimes it is a relatively conservative form of peace, but it also may carry the seeds of local agency and a future, more contextually legitimate form of peace-building. A better understanding of this hybridity may enable the emergence of more emancipatory versions of peace than so far has occurred, which engage with alterity rather than marginalise it, and liberate both local and international from conflict. This hybridity, though not without its pitfalls, offers greater potential for an emancipatory form of peace to emerge than simply transplanting the liberal peace onto post-colonial, post-conflict development settings, as has been the recent approach. The emergence of hybridity is the result of the clash and connection of fundamentally different forms of political organisation and community. It should not be taken that liberalism will emerge predominant as difficult compromises on values and norms as well as institutions need to be negotiated by the liberal and the local. It is as likely that the local will shape the liberal in each context as the liberal will shape the local. In this way, the local-liberal hybrid represents a long-term process of political evolution towards a post-liberal form of peace, representing both hegemony and the local in complex ways.

A brief chapter outline

The first part of this study examines how the liberal peace and associated state-building processes 'romanticise the local', distance context, needs, and culture in order to transform what Pugh has called unruly subjects, or what Duffield has called uninsurable, surplus populations.[79] This enables unfortunate and methodologically and ethically indefensible, non-consensual forms of 'peacebuilding' reliant on external actors and alliances with often predatory local elites. These problems and unintended consequences are discussed in Chapters 1 and 2.

Chapter 3 examines these processes in the context of Cambodia, Bosnia Herzegovina, Kosovo and Timor Leste, as well as some responses from a range of local actors, from grass roots, civil society, and elites. Chapter 4 begins to develop a theoretical response to this unintended and problematic outcome of liberal peacebuilding.

In the second part of the book, I examine the range of what might be called critical, post-structuralist, and post-colonial theories, which can be deployed in order to understand such processes and also to aid in the shift from a liberal to a post-liberal form of peace most likely to be internationally and contextually legitimate and sustainable. Chapter 5 examines peacebuilding 'agency' as a process of resistance, especially in its contextual and critical form (as opposed to the more usual concentration on international and eternal agency along with local compliance), and what this means for peacebuilding in general. It examines how it responds to the processes of the liberal peace, with what effect, particularly in terms of the production hybridity.

Chapter 6 places this debate into a number of empirical contexts, focussing mainly on Timor Leste and the Solomon Islands where recent statebuilding attempts have produced very interesting processes of peacebuilding, both locally and internationally driven.

In the Conclusion, I argue that critical agency, even resistance to externality, represents the birth of a post-liberal peace – a contextual process of peace-building with more prospects for international and local legitimacy (even if this is a fraught and tense, perhaps agonistic, relationship), sustainability, and in emancipatory form, liberation.

A note of caution

There are, I have discovered in the course of working on this book (which I began in 2006), many methodological and ethical traps in attempting to bring the local, context, custom, political subjectivity, and agency, 'back' into a discussion of peacebuilding. I have struggled with questions such as what is, who are, or form, the local, context, and where does agency come from? How can we understand agency when we do not have the methodological tools to uncover it? How can we engage with context without exposing it to harm, and indeed what does harm mean in such discussions? I have found issue with the simplifications and dichotomies of thinking in terms and local and international, liberal and non-liberal, and so forth. I have become very concerned with the tendency of even critical thinking to reduce the local, context, the non-liberal, undemocratic, or non-developed in imagined, fixed political and geographical spaces, such as the 'global south', failed states, or even the 'liberal' and 'international'. Even a post-colonial move is often effectively reduced to discussions of state foreign policy and the approaches of the 'BRICs' or the emerging donors (again, as state actors).

It is clear that the sorts of muscular social science common to the North and to Western based research are biased towards fixing (in several senses of the word) the local, context, custom, and agency in particularly negative, often romanticised, and enclosed spaces: the local is not fluid, transnational or transversal and it is 'non-liberal'; custom is backward and cannot provide mobilisation for peace; agency is an Enlightenment concept and cannot be thought of where political subjects cannot mobilise on a grand scale for reasons of poverty, institutions, or resources, and many more. Peace is often consolidated through the application of a fragile and only narrowly representative blueprint (however much this is denied) for liberal international institutions and liberal state-based governance in the context of a global and state level, neoliberal, economic system which makes little pretence of engaging with inequality and needs even where conflicts over both have long destabilised societies and had negative implications for rights, identity, culture and a range of institutions.

I have done my best to navigate through such problems in what follows, though it is inevitable that I have not been fully – or even partially – successful. I hope though, that it is clear that there is emerging an understanding of the agency, language, discourses, and practices, for peace which is situated right at the limits of Northern liberalism and social science. They may enable a far more represent-ative, sensitised, contextual and empathetic understanding of what peacebuilding could entail in its most emancipatory, consensual, fourth generation forms. This might begin to uncover intimately connected local and global dynamics of peace, whether personal or institutional, and their complex but inevitable interactions. Indeed, this is a project that began long ago when social, political, economic, civil movements began to coalesce around an understanding that they had the capacity to mobilise for identity, rights and needs, and could influence their leaders, states, and institutions to such ends – from their community to the inter-national. The terrain for such agency for peace may have shifted from large-scale political confrontation and mobilisation, but it is nonetheless fundamental to the development of new and peaceful political orders.

Part I

The romanticisation of the local

1 Civil society, needs and welfare

Chapter 22
Everyone, as a member of society, has the right to social security and is entitled to a realization, through national effort and international co-operation and in accordance with the organisation and resources of each State, of the economic, social and cultural rights indispensable for his dignity and the free development of his personality.

Chapter 23
Everyone has the right to work, to free choice of employment, to just and favourable conditions of work and to protection against unemployment.

Chapter 25
Everyone has the right to a standard of living adequate for the health and well-being of himself and of his family, including food, clothing, housing and medical care and necessary social services, and the right to security in the event of unemployment, sickness, disability, widowhood, old age or other lack of livelihood in circumstances beyond his control.

Chapter 27
Everyone has the right freely to participate in the cultural life of the community, to enjoy the arts and to share in scientific advancement and its benefits.

UN Universal Declaration of Human Rights, 1948

Introduction

In the introduction to this study I argued that a post-liberal form of peace is emerging. This rests partly upon often hidden forms of local, critical agency, which is often resistant to external intervention, sometime compliant, but may question the sources of legitimacy. Such critical agency for peacebuilding, attempts to modify the liberal peace framework and also exploits some of its more emancipatory potential. In part it is provoked by specific weaknesses of the liberal peace, particularly in its needs and cultural awareness of others in post-conflict environments. Such agency is a response to the distancing and governmentalising project liberal peace has become.

It has long been argued that peacebuilding praxis should address issues of social justice, needs, welfare, and culture, and that such issues have represented major gaps in mainstream theoretical and policy agendas. Liberal peacebuilding has often distanced and marginalised its post-conflict subjects by contrast. Ironically, it is these subjects it has set out to 'save'. Such distancing strategies maintain the legitimacy of the liberal peace model, often by preventing a sustained engagement with local context, needs and culture, and focusing on security, rights, institutions, and markets – with contradictory and controversial outcomes. Needs are supposed, in contemporary praxis, to be dealt with by trickle-down processes, both direct and indirect: as are norms, law, and institutional reform. Yet this often has produced an artificial form of civil society, disconnected from local political, social, culture, customary, and economic processes and expectations. This means any peace arising from such an approach cannot be locally owned or self-sustaining, but instead produces the very dependency on international actors that, it is often argued, should be avoided at all costs. A needs or welfare oriented model might therefore be more appropriate than one aimed solely at rights, though as the following chapters illustrate, this is also not without its problems.

The key feature of the dominant liberal approach to peacebuilding, which has been mainly responsible for its recent elision with statebuilding, represents a neoliberal marketisation of peace, rather than engagement with the agents and subjects of this peace, even on more traditional liberal terms. This elision has both ignored but also underlined the tension in the relationship between peace, post-conflict subjects and their state, and the international community. Its legitimacy is derived from its claim of an emancipatory social contract, which is to be produced externally in the exceptional circumstances of post-conflict polities. This production of legitimacy is a specifically Western- and Enlightenment-derived, problem-solving discourse of peace. It is the result of a long evolution of thought derived from the dominant, mainly Western promoted concern with security, reconstruction, development, modernisation, conflict resolution and transformation, peacebuilding and statebuilding. Yet, there is a major question as to whether it is culturally and socially appropriate or sensitive in all contexts.

This has implications for whether the liberal peace framework, loose as it is, has a chance of establishing a locally self-sustaining peace – as recent praxis in diverse locations has queried to a large degree. In this context, difference is only acceptable when it operates within the liberal framework of tolerance, and only becomes apparent if it moves into this context (i.e. difference converts itself into sameness). This is dangerously close to an external rejection of local, contextual processes of peace and politics: a 'romanticisation of the local' where only international agency is deemed capable of making peace. This is often for methodological and ontological reasons, for expediency and strategic goals. It reflects the liberal culture of peacebuilding, and its relatively hegemonic engagement with the local rather than an equitable engagement and concern with everyday life and local legitimacy. This propagates specific liberal-institutionalist and neoliberal practices, and defers responsibility for the needs and welfare of the local (the space where capacity is probably least in liberal eyes). Its cultural and needs engagement is therefore little more than instrumental and is often designed to maintain distance between the local and the international, denying local agency, so that the local can be governed in liberal ways irrespective of the complexity of context or a local legitimacy for such transformation. Liberal peacebuilding rests upon cultural assumptions that legitimate governance over the socio-economic wellbeing of a territories' inhabitants, as well as over any contextual cultural dynamics, thus denying the very local agencies it seeks to enable.

This chapter explores theses weaknesses in the context of liberal peace's neoliberal turn, versus a potentially more needs or welfare oriented version of peacebuilding. This may be taken to have as its aim a social form of peace, in which civil society and culture is fully engaged with by internationals in both rights and needs terms. It examines the role of civil society, culture, and welfare in peacebuilding.

Civil society, needs and culture

Recent attention amongst IR theorists, the development, peace and conflict studies communities, as well as many practitioners and policymakers in the peacebuilding and statebuilding community, has focused upon the problem of creating a self-sustaining, civil peace in post-violence, post-conflict environments. This focuses attention at the local level of analysis, which in realist-liberal terms (meaning the state as the aim of liberal peacebuilding which combines security, rights, and institutions)[1] denotes that of civil society. This is an artificial construct which introduces checks and balances, accountability, and representation between citizens and elites which tend to control the different aspects of the state, even in liberal form.

It has become clear that the challenge of understanding the politics of peacebuilding is far greater when the local, civil society, culture, class, gender, and needs are incorporated as key areas of concern. This is perhaps the reason why they are often relegated to lower (or localised) priorities than security or institution-building by internationals. Thus, the 'local' (in IR and political science) and for most international peacebuilding, statebuilding, and development actors indicates an acultural denotation of a general context, in which 'civil society' is created by internationals. Alternatively, it is a pre-modern sphere, which is non-liberal and not marketised, in an abrasive relationship with liberal notions of civil society. It is also often seen as apolitical (as opposed to the complex social institutions, needs, political traditions, identities, implied by the term 'culture'). In fact, civil society from the perspective of most international actors, represents a method of privatising the service provision often associated with the state. Yet most members of civil society see it as denoting a political space through which citizens construct and control their political subjectivity and institutions (even though internationals resort to fairly directive means to induce the creation of a civil society). This enables them to hold the state accountable for their representation, rights, and needs.

Via such externalised strategies, local needs and welfare are removed from the statebuilding process, and culture is marginalised in a rights, security and markets version of liberal peacebuilding. Yet, to paraphrase Clifford, both culture and welfare are concepts that are difficult to understand and define, are deeply compromised, but yet cannot be ignored.[2] The fact that they often have been ignored is partly due to the widespread adoption of problem-solving rights oriented approaches into IR and for peacebuilding, and the subsequent bias introduced by its related methodologies. These have the unintended consequence of obscuring everyday aspects of political, social, economic, and cultural life in local contexts.

The term civil society now denotes a compliant and transformed social grouping, able to hold the state accountable, and to create wealth. This is to be enabled externally import conflict environments via a self-legitimating range of interventionary strategies to support formal and informal groups that are both part of, and relatively, independent from the state.[3] Civil society holds the state and its elites accountable. It plays an essential role in a liberal state, and one that cannot be done without, if the state is not to become predatory. However, because it has been so externalised in post-conflict states, and dependent on donors' rather limited support (though they have great ambitions for it) civil society in practice has often become an engineered artifice that floats above and substitutes for the 'local' and for context.

This is despite the fact that it is also generally assumed that civil society asserts historical and natural indigenous dynamics, represents a local synthesis or community of reconciled peoples, and their interested and disinterested mediation of rights and needs: it is '… not humanitarian but communitarian'.[4] It consequently legitimates conservative liberal governance and enforcement strategies, is defined by international actors and donors according to their own 'scripts' of engagement with context, and is brought into being by externally funded NGOs and other organisations. It represents a liberal veneer over the local; it endeavours to assist, transform, and normalise it into the mould of a professional, corporate middle class.

Such strategies are clearly not contextually designed, but rest on liberal, cosmopolitan assertions of common norms and institutions. They are unconsciously designed to distance and marginalise uncomfortable and authentic local voices, their needs, expectations, and practices in favour of transnational liberal agents of peacebuilding. In this sense, while purporting to promote local ownership of peace and the liberal state which is coming into being, these strategies actually rhetorically marginalise context, needs, culture, and the material aspects of a peace dividend required to give rights substance – especially for the citizen and the subaltern. It removes these from international normative and material processes of responsibility, so peacebuilding can instead turn to promoting and developing the liberal version of what is civil.[5]

Foucault links civil society, as it is constructed in terms of liberal governmentality, to the need to be complicit with and support the neoliberal thesis: '… a space of sovereignty which for good or ill is inhabited by economic subjects …'. These subjects find the 'good life' in the liberal shell of the state and in the market.[6] In this sense it is a 'governmental technology'[7] designed to depoliticise the really existing context and the local in its supposedly pre-modern, or undeveloped, and passive condition, while it learns about liberal civil society.[8] The agency often associated with civil society is therefore negated by governmentality, which in neoliberal form enables distant government of post conflict spaces, according to Western rational forms of problem-solving, often without local support.[9]

As Foucault argues even from his relatively Eurocratic perspective we should be cautious about arguments that rhetorically confirm the importance of civil society while at the same time undermining it.[10] This sleight of hand is the essence of the 'liberal civil society' putatively installed in post-conflict zones. This externalised form is not constitutive of the liberal social contract but instead is driven by donor agendas, and deterritorialised by the market. The resultant focus on state level institutions, often on governance, corruption, and on elite relationships, means civil society becomes an afterthought for peacebuilding. This ironically returns the focus of local communities and elites to power, territory and sovereignty, by way of reaction. The liberal social contract – which one would expect to be crucial to the liberal state – is caught between paradoxical pressures, meaning that the needs of post-conflict individuals, communities, and societies are directly addressed by international peacebuilders and statebuilders, who instead adopt a strategic focus on security, rights, and institutions, as well as trickle-down wealth. Paradoxically, as a result, the 'local' has become a new site of contestation, whether to enable, emancipate, include, exclude, self-determine, marginalise, silence, or govern.

Civil society, thus fragmented and essentialised, has become a rather super-ficial melange of externally visible and supported normative advocates for liberal peacebuilding's core values, rights, institutions, and processes. It holds back 'uncivil society', the barbarians, the traditional or customary, and the non-secular which it is feared lurk behind local politics and await an opportunity to undermine the liberal state. It has been elided into the very problematic liberal project of statebuilding,[11] which is assumed would supply the necessary security and institu-tions, not to mention material resources, to achieve the 'good life'. Yet, civil society is supposed to be vibrant, play a key role in advocacy, make the state accountable and improve human rights and development, while also meeting material needs. It is through these paradoxical international expectations that the local is perceived as apolitical, in that culture and needs and often identity are made invisible. Civil society in such processes becomes relatively disconnected from its own local, and more connected to the Western, liberal ideal of civil society and its own context. Indeed, recently donors have begun talking about shifting funds from civil society to the market and the stimulation of private enterprise and to the state through budgetary support, because they cannot see discernable effects from previous civil society funding. This is due to their expectations and methodological biases.[12]

Lockean liberalism, aimed at the social contract between subjects and rules over the preservation of life, liberty, and property, is heavily reflected in the intel-lectual discourses of liberal peacebuilding and statebuilding.[13] These processes have lent themselves to this interpretation via the intellectual and policy commu-nities which support statebuilding practices as have emerged in Iraq, Afghanistan, and earlier in East Timor, Kosovo, or Bosnia. In reality, statebuilding, and its association with peacebuilding, is now focused on how to connect the technocratic institutions of the liberal state, which it is believed can be built by external actors, with or without local consent. Yet, with some form of social contract, a liberal state would actually be illiberal and illegitimate, possibly at best a trusteeship in which the local's rights and needs are indefinitely deferred and any legitimacy mainly stems from donors, Security Council resolutions, international actors, and elite complicity or co-optation. Such legitimacy is often now constructed exter-nally, through the support of international actors, and their aspirations towards international humanitarian norms and norms of liberal governance. This has the effect of marginalising the need for local engagements with peacebuilding and for reconciliation, which the liberal state might have better addressed through its more sweeping, but also more intrusive, older, social democratic position on equality and resource distribution.

States, institutions, and governmental practices have displaced some aspects of human needs in order to provide an emphasis on political rights as a result. Societies, groups, identities, cultures, and needs are only rhetorically part of this discourse. Yet, a civil peace, and its offshoots of local ownership and participation, has come to preoccupy the Western dominated peacebuilding consensus[14] being employed in conflict and post-conflict environments around the world. This has generally focused upon institutional versions of the state and individualist Oakshottian 'civil association' in instances where context is extremely varied.[15]

Thus, it is widely accepted that where peacebuilding or statebuilding occurs it must both create and promote a vibrant civil society. It also expects to receive much of its legitimacy on the ground from civil society and local actors, so the notion of a civil society also acts as a crucial validation of liberal peacebuilding strategies and objectives. Yet, while the civil peace might be taken to denote the indigenous character of peace within local culture and traditional social frameworks, the concept of civil society is mainly used to represent a Western view of non-governmental actors, citizens, subjects, workers, consumers, and institutions which are empowered from above and outside in order to adopt neoliberal modes of statehood. On the surface this is politicising, and represents a process of self-determination and self-government. But in practice this has proven to be depoliticising, partly because it often rests upon the conflation of welfare and cultural needs and rights in similar, but secondary, rhetorical categories. This means that needs are not met and cultural agency is ignored, making it difficult for local ownership to be meaningful and for civil society to transcend the narrowness of international visions of what it may entail in a particular context.

Empowerment and emancipation in this version of peacebuilding therefore must be carried out in the shadow of 'security'; and political rights and institutions are pre-eminent over human needs and structural problems within the liberal-realist [read neoliberal] conceptualisation of statebuilding now dominant. This favours security apparatus, individualism, economic freedom and interdependence, and access to politically representative institutions. It produces a prioritisation that intrinsically undermines the most basic of human needs necessary for day-to-day survival and also marginalises identity, unless it is a political identity. In this system, rights and institutions are effectively meaningless to the post-conflict citizen, who is preoccupied with everyday survival. A vibrant civil society is unlikely to emerge in such conditions except in subsistence mode, either in customary terms and so hidden from the international view or heavily dependent on donor support and direction. This probably explains why internationals often argue that there is 'little or no local capacity' in the field.

It is somewhat ironic that despite all of this, the civil peace and the 'vibrant civil society it signifies' is often said to be the most significant component of the liberal peacebuilding and statebuilding project. After all, what good are institutions if the general population of a state does not take part in them, or they do not represent a contract between individual, representatives, and the state? The civil peace is often virtual, a charade, referred to by international actors only to legitimate the new institutional reforms they sponsor. At best it is recognised only as a dependent entity in a relationship of conditionality with international actors, who act benevolently but according to their own interests and norms. In practice, then, the civil peace is not a space of empathy, emancipation and agency. Rather, the notion of a civil society is a Western concept predicated on social and political rights, which are divorced through a neoliberal sleight of hand from basic needs. Instead, civil society is now seen as a cultural, social, and political arena in which individuals and communities are supposed to become liberal, but without having access to interim economic resources, or retaining their identities and culture.

Welfare and development

While the concept of culture has received limited attention, one of the biggest gaps that has emerged in peacebuilding has been the question of needs, inequality, and social welfare. It has been assumed that marketisation and liberalisation would be adequate to provide material substance to the liberal peace for its recipients. It is common that conflict, development, needs and inequality are seen to have a loose connection, but it is rare that culture or welfare are seen as positive contributions to peacebuilding. Yet, this recognition can be found as far back as the Declaration of Human Rights (Chapters 22, 23, and 25, and the International Covenant on Economic, Social and Cultural Rights (Chapters 6, 9, 11 and 13). One of the early success stories of modern statebuilding, the Marshall Plan, provided an early example of how reconstruction might work. It endeavoured in a Keynesian context to provide employment and assistance through massive investment to produce a peaceful, liberal, modernity, even if it did not acknowledge local culture or custom for the most part. It is particularly perplexing that there is so little on culture, needs and welfare that had been written in contemporary IR, or peace and conflict studies. It might be expected that welfare could even be seen as an instrument to empower (positive) or co-opt (negative) 'culture', subjects, and workers for the purposes of the liberal peace. Liberalism is more comfortable with an institutional and productive identification of the other, and less so with its capacity to understand and support the identity and agency of the other, even in the context of liberalism's own assertion of the need for peaceful states to be based upon a social contract.

While the liberal state encourages a balance in the distribution of all resources (not just political) the neoliberal state emphasises rights, institutional checks and balances, and free trade (effectively endorsing a class system given existing local and international inequalities and hierarchies). One might say that the former liberal justifications for *res nullius* are echoed by such strategies (as Locke himself was aware). The resulting practice has been in line with a neoliberal state, one in which the market dictates politics and the social distribution of resources. But the idea that the market may drive peace, and lead to a widespread adoption of the state's liberal institutions is based on the belief that internationals have sufficient capacity to ensure this occurs, and that local elites and civil society will support such a move, rather than see it as undermining or misdiagnosing their perceived requirements or their interests. It also is based on the idea that economic peace emerges naturally, is self-regulating, and is of a higher importance than a social or civil peace (though perhaps slightly lesser than institutional or constitutional forms of peace).

In the most recent attempt to build the liberal state in Iraq, efforts to engage with civil society have coincided with a purposive introduction of a market economy, even though there was a clear preference amongst civil society, local communities, and trade unions for a welfare-oriented state model.[16] This, in genealogical terms, can be traced back to the principle of *res nullius*, through which unoccupied land should be put to productive, commercial use, despite possible customary uses, justifying both colonialism and later private property and enterprise.[17] This illustrates how liberal peacebuilding, and its progeny, statebuilding, reflect a certain ideological position – or a certain culture. It ignores local voices, which might if given the choice make decisions that would from the local perspective provide the state with more legitimacy than the particular neoliberal model that is often now projected. Customary, social democratic, or welfare forms of state might be locally chosen as a preferred form of modernisation. Indeed, given the lack of apparent concern of the statebuilding model with human needs or with human life that such denial apparently represents, these practices actually appear from the local perspective to represent occupation and neo-colonialism rather than a liberation from conflict, oppression, inequality, poverty, contests over institutions, identity, and territory.

One of the key features of these dynamics has been the way neoliberal development thinking and marketisation has supplanted discussions about local needs and welfare, often emanating from the logic of freestanding rights. Yet thinking about welfare has traditionally been the response of the liberally minded social reformer in the face of conflict, poverty and disease. It has been the response of governments to problems of war and violence, both to deal with the problems of unemployment after wars and to deal with socio-economic issues (or root causes) present in transitional environments. Peacebuilding, mediation, and peace work in general has always been torn between social reformism (or transformation) and human needs on the one hand, and the capacity of governments to socially engineer certain forms of behaviour on the other. In this sense, welfarism was a form of the romanticisation of the local, drawing on the idealist argument that if social conditions were appropriate then individuals would enter into peaceful and prosperous relations with each other. This also carries a governmental and biopolitical aspect, in that by providing appropriate conditions via state institutions, polities and social relations would be reshaped to comply with the liberal state framework. Liberal, progressive thinking on peace in these terms rests on democracy, human rights, the rule of law, welfare and mixed economies rather than development and free markets, in this formulation. Until the end of the Cold War at least, received wisdom had been that a welfare system was an integral part of the liberal state and its peace, both internal and external, and was integral to the social contract and to an emancipatory form of liberal peace. Later this was transformed into an apparent consensus on neoliberalism, as welfarist approaches appeared to collapse often on the basis of citizens' rejection of intrusive governance, its cost and dynamics of dependency creation.

The need for welfare strategies in a stable polity was identified by Thomas Paine in his Rights of Man (1791–2). He argued that welfare was needed to provide both justice and stability. Welfare was not necessarily about empowering the individual, as Bismarck's workers' reforms which were designed to prevent them from rebelling indicated, but in their post-Beveridge form, this was a key assumption. Asa Briggs made the case in more modernist terms: the welfare state emerged to moderate the market by guaranteeing a minimum wage, dealing with economic insecurity and vulnerability, and providing universal access to key services.[18] As Lipset argued, economic development – education, prosperity, growth of voluntary associations, and a reduction in the social and economic costs of redistribution – was a requisite for stable democracy especially in the post-war context.[19] The questions this raised included how entitlement is calculated, according to legal, contractual or contributory, financial, discretionary, or professional criteria: who is entitled and why; and what methods are used to determine the above, allocate, and make payments?[20] The task of the welfare state, as Barr has argued, is to redistribute or compensate, and provide for social justice and economic stability and efficiency.[21]

In this context the welfare state has been described as the '... major peace formula of advanced capitalist democracies for the period following the Second World War.'[22] This obliged the state to provide welfare where the market cannot oblige in order to overcome societal contradictions between capital and labour. Such systems often emerged as a result of conflict or crisis (as Roosevelt's welfare plan illustrates).[23] They may offer universal or minimalist solutions to welfare issues. Welfare in the Keynesian environment was seen as an economic method to stabilise the political system. Indeed, the Marshall Plan, which was an early experience of the sorts of reconstruction that this indicated has been widely lauded since. Yet it was a Keynesian and social welfarist project that ran counter to the neoliberal strategies of the contemporary system of global governance or today's World Bank, IMF, or donor policies.[24] Some saw the Marshall Plan as indicative of a US superiority, of a totalitarian form of liberalism.[25] Others have abstracted from this experience the need to make the development of social capital a key part of peacebuilding/statebuilding, which would have the effect of making reconstruction as local as possible so that local participants own, define, control, and develop their own social capital. This would lead, so the argument goes, to much greater sustainability.[26] This was at least partly recognised in the US approach in Japan after WW2, where some limited attempts at understanding Japanese society were engaged in before reconstruction by the US, though of course the US team that led the reconstruction project had little knowledge of Japanese language, and no close links with Japanese partners.[27]

However, it is normally argued against the Marshall Plan as an exemplar for peacebuilding that both Germany and Japan were highly developed in terms of infrastructure before the war, had highly levels of social capital, and still had great potential capacity after the war. Even so, proponents of such arguments have claimed that indigenous institutions must align with international reconstruction paradigms (meaning the liberal peace), rather than the other way around. This means that the indigenous or local is secondary, a rubber stamp, for the reconstruction effort, which was also probably the experience of the reconstruction of Western Europe and Japan after World War II.[28] Legitimacy for international development and peacebuilding was thus to be found in international norms, and institutional and liberal knowledge systems.

During the early and mid-twentieth century, it was generally acknowledged among liberal circles and beyond, that welfare and needs formed a crucial part of the social contract needed to have political stability within and between states. The economic management of resources was seen as a key tool of governments in preventing economic crises from undermining social and political stability. The work of Keynes on the post-World War I global economy, Mitrany on 'functionalism', Polanyi on the failures of economic liberalism, Deutsch and others on integration in a European context, Burton on human needs and conflict, and many others attested to how far this had been widely accepted.[29] Yet, as peacebuilding approaches become more all-encompassing they turned away from this consensus after the end of the Cold War, and from its stipulated connections with a sustainable peace in favour of what are, in early post-conflict settings at least, untested approaches derived from marketisation and neoliberalism.

The key flaw in this move has been that without an engagement with needs and welfare, peacebuilding will not lead to a sustainable outcome because there are few peace incentives for citizens or elites. As Przeworski *et al.* have indicated, poor democracies are extremely fragile. When society is poor, the state is less likely to be stable or able to develop.[30] In response, Giddens has argued for what he calls 'positive welfare' which goes beyond wealth creation and also includes psychological welfare, avoiding creating situations of moral hazard in which individual behaviour follows a dependent pattern, and focusing on the development of civil society.[31] Bonoli argues that welfare systems have been crucial parts of modern democracies in sustaining successful political mobilisation through the creation of labour movements and social democratic parties, which lead to the adoption of market regulations, social insurance and welfare services.[32]

Despite the experience of the liberal states during their several centuries of development, that stability is easily undermined by economic difficulties of a direct kind for individuals (i.e. from the Weimar Republic to Timor in 2006), this kind of support is institutionally absent in most conflict zones. It is often only supplied in a patchy manner by a smattering of development agencies, donors, and NGOs, rather by than the market. A securitised development discourse derived from neoliberalism has instead displaced welfare and needs.[33] Because this involves a displacement of needs by rights, which includes protection for private property and ownership, this has displaced dynamics such as customary or social land tenure, which have often been thought of as a social insurance system in developing countries (especially where land is worked on a small scale by peasant farmers). In many developing countries, even where individuals have jobs they may also continue to work their small pieces of land as insurance.

Yet, it is generally accepted that development is necessary for and parallel to democratisation, and that a strong economy will lead to a representative politics undercutting and replacing both violence and unrepresentative political processes. Both are conditions for each other in that democratisation allows for a fairer distribution of both political and economic resources, and development provides resources to distribute as well as coordinating their distribution.[34] This provides navigation points for policy makers who become involved in peace-building processes in post-conflict environments, and whose role is to establish a sustainable and self-sustaining peace. It avoids the profligacy of welfare states, as well as their centralisation, but so far development strategies have often failed to provide the resources to make rights meaningful to its subjects. Local partners amongst the elites and civil society are expected to accept this framework, and the relationship this develops is structured around political and economic condition-alities, as can be seen with the World Bank and IMF, and the many organisations, and actors they cooperate with.

The neoliberal development model that is articulated in post-conflict zones by these conditional relationships does not meet the expectations of many, and particularly those concerned with social justice and opportunity (i.e. the vast bulk of the populations in these areas, and many commentators on development issues). Though HDI (Human Development Index) data shows a general increase over time since data nearest the end of the conflict and the present time in most cases (eighteen out of twenty-three cases) the Gini data shows a more problematic picture.[35] Inequality has increased or is marginally worse in fifteen out of twenty-three cases (see Appendix 1), especially where inequality was relatively low pre-war. This shows that increased wealth circulates mainly amongst the few, meaning a general peace dividend is marginal for most of the population, at least in material terms. This is partly a result of the nature of the liberal peace, especially given the NGO, business, and political elites it creates. Indeed, the data on these cases suggests that inequality tends to be worse in relation to HDI in UN backed cases of peacebuilding. This might be because it has tighter control over reform and allows IFIs (International Financial Institutions) more access. More stability often associated with UN involvement allows more foreign direct investment, which enables a very rich class to emerge. This exacerbates inequality and also indicates that the often claimed trickle-down effect is minimal.

Yet neoliberal strategies have not emerged from past experiences in pre-1990 post-conflict situations or amongst the donors, which often had both closed economies and welfare systems during their own development eras.[36] Neoliberal models do not represent international experience given that past reconstruction efforts, whether after the American Civil War or after World War II, involved a massive redistribution of resources. Development is now generally articulated at an international level: welfare is hardly ever referred to at all and contemporary neoliberal development debates have replaced discussions about social welfare. This shift rests on an international, institutional, epistemic legitimacy, not on local legitimacy and representation. One might point to calls in Iraq for a mixed economy, which were ignored by the US occupiers, or the shift in focus in Timor when a national poverty reduction strategy was formed in 2008 from World Bank and IMF (International Monetary Fund) priorities to local needs (as discussed in Chapter 3). It is now well known that neoliberal strategies have a number of contradictory consequences when development is a high priority: they increase inequality, hollow out democracy, and induce political and social unrest and instability.[37]

Social forms of democracy, which offer a compromise between welfare and neoliberalism, have been in a number of recent cases an antidote to such deficiencies by being more inclusive and helping in redistribution of resources, inducing social justice and cohesion, allowing for more progressive taxation, job creation and land reform, aiding labour regulation, social insurance, healthcare, education, and welfare provision.[38] The practices of social welfare systems it is often argued have reduced poverty and consolidated democracy by enabling strong civil societies in post-conflict societies.[39] The neoliberal state on the other hand favours elites and their often predatory behaviour, and reverts to condition-ality or coercion to quell social unrest. Indeed, Chang argues that neoliberalism undermines democracy by concentrating power in the hands of those with property, despite voting rights, and also reflects a managerial attempt to make politics irrelevant.[40]

A range of literatures touch upon issues these phenomena raise. Przeworski has argued that development requires structural transformation and ethical change, increases in growth, income, productivity, consumption, investment, education, life expectancy, employment, childbirth survival and other factors related to the qualitative experience of life by civilian populations in a liberal state setting.[41] These everyday dynamics have significant implications for thinking on development, and for the cultural assumptions prevalent in the liberal peace-building project about the prioritisation of political rights over the needs of 'others'. As a result, Carothers argues that many transitional states become stuck in a 'grey zone' between authoritarianism and democracy.[42] The fact that most peacebuilding now takes place in a low development context also means that civil society, and local communities and cultures are often defined as subsistence oriented, patronage-based, corrupt and nepotistic in contrast to the liberal/ neoliberal ideal. It should also be noted that the neoliberal version of the state represents a conservative rather than liberal vision of peace, even though it is commonly thought that neoliberalism is merely another version of liberalism. This elision has the indirect effect of absolving international actors of needs and welfare responsibility and indicates that local actors are incapable of developing without external direction. This is also a classic colonial-style move from the perspective of many local actors.

Such apparently negative strategies entailed in subsistence and patronage, however, are often substitution and coping strategies. Neoliberal development debates disguise the lack of welfare substitution, and imply local culture is deemed unsuited for development without intervention and transformation, rather than neoliberal strategies being deemed unsuited to the local environment. So by targeting these deficiencies on the ground the liberal peace, influenced by neoliberalism, fails to provide for needs or welfare, it undermines what little substitution strategies there are, and infantilises local culture. It endeavours to build a limited liberal capacity where it is suspicious of the tendencies of local agency, while remaining unaware of, or even worse unconcerned with, its own cultural assumptions and deficiencies. What is more, as Przeworski *et al.* argue, economic growth may not be linked to democracy in poor states, especially where sufficient income replacement is unlikely or absent. In their view egalitarian income distribution is a necessary condition for the development of democracy. Stability is therefore dependent to a large degree on income replacement.[43] This raises the question of why the liberal peace has been influenced by neoliberalism and has disconnected needs and welfare in the context of statebuilding, when so much evidence points to the symbiotic relationship between democracy, civil society, the rule of law, and needs?

There now arises an important question as to why income provision or replacement is generally not taken to be part of the short-term peacebuilding attempt to consolidate transitions from war. After all, given such strong evidence that democratisation requires individuals to be able to count on economic survival, that neoliberal strategies are too long-term to provide this immediately, and that aid agencies and NGOs struggle even to provide emergency assistance on the scale that is often needed, it would seem to be obvious that an international agency tasked with the provision of income replacement in association with local bodies, could take on this role in post-violence situations. This would give substance to rights frameworks offered by liberal peacebuilding, and allow the expression of cultural agency, and for the development of a vibrant civil society which provides legitimacy for the state. Furthermore, because peace processes often take place in developing countries where incomes are low or absent, the costs of such a process would not necessarily be exorbitant at least in the short to medium term. In most cases, a few thousand US$ per annum would suffice to provide individuals, families, and indeed communities, with transitional support where needed and undercut incentives for, or temptations towards, violence. The obvious benefit – beyond its humanitarian contribution – of such a scheme would be to prevent further marginalisation of individuals, their radicalisation, and their co-option into grey or black markets or into militias.

Of course, there is also a danger that the actors who managed such a scheme would also see it as an opportunity for their own interests to be inserted into the project, reverting to a form of governmentality. Similarly, some have argued that welfare activities on the part of governments provide them with opportunities to claim rights and exercise powers over individuals and communities that they would not otherwise be able to do.[44] This has always been the danger of welfare schemes. They often depend upon an external actor's definition of welfare, which in turn rests upon their own cultural and social assumptions in the context of politics and the economy. Welfare developed in the context of the stabilisation of states during industrialisation and after major systemic wars. Neoliberalism developed at a later stage in more stable circumstances – despite the Cold War – within the already relatively wealthy Western bloc. Indeed the brief attempt of the US government to impose neoliberal strategies between 1945 and 1947 after World War II almost proved catastrophic for Britain, Europe, and later for Japan on several occasions. The reversion to a mixed economic mode with the Marshall Plan, and the turn to welfare states in Europe laid the basis for political stabilisation (and, ironically, for a later neoliberal turn). Of course, what emerged were hybrid forms of state and economy where the state provided redistribution and public services where necessary, but also protection of free markets where needed.[45]

Given this potential, and despite its shortcomings, ironically a more needs and welfare oriented form of peacebuilding and statebuilding (even in transitional guise) has generally been ignored by those working in mainstream IR, peace and conflict studies, development, and also by policymakers and practitioners, in recent times. This may be because of the hegemonic power that neoliberalism has been imbued with as an ideological outcome of the triumph of liberalism at the end of the Cold War. It has been widely accepted that socialist oriented economic strategies have failed, somewhat tautologically because the prevalence of neoliberalism (even after the credit crisis in 2008–9). Furthermore, welfare states do produce under-classes and new forms of poverty and dependency.[46] Neoliberals in general argue that welfare is a disincentive to investment and work and creates dependence.[47]

Yet, in the specialised context of liberal peacebuilding and statebuilding, welfare policies might, if supported through outside means in the short term, support the creation of a stable liberal polity, a relatively contextualised rather than externalised civil society, and a social contract. Individuals and communities, knowing that peacebuilding entails needs and welfare provision, might be more predisposed towards the development of a long-term liberal peace process in which their rights and the institutions of state, plus the security it provides, become more meaningful. This would necessitate the engagement of an approach or even a new international institution capable of communicating directly with local actors about their everyday needs, relatively free from external or neoliberal prescriptions and with a sophisticated understanding of local contexts.

Engaging with needs in a more sensitive way on the part of internationals in this fashion would also require a much more detailed knowledge of local contexts to prevent the resources being offered from being diverted for predatory reasons. This would enable an open discussion about what requirements might enable the construction of a social contract and prevent a reversion to violence. It would require that international actors and donors had linguistic and culture competency, and could engage with the local context. On this basis it might engender a locally led discussion about what policies would be necessary to stabilise everyday life and lead to democratic politics. These might include pensions, child benefit, unemployment benefit, food subsidies, free schooling, free health care, other public services and infrastructure, as well as an international discussion about how these services can be funded or supported – with some urgency. They may also include less developmental notions of subsistence, resilience, or approaches to land use, food production, and resource distribution.

This is not to say that such welfare oriented strategies would be irreproachable. Clearly they also represent a one-size-fits-all and expensive intervention in post-violence societies, and still require the institutions of state and international organisations and donors. But as social democracies around the world illustrate, they offer a different economic model compatible with democracy and the liberal, but not neoliberal, state.[48] It is perplexing that liberal peacebuilding has not adopted such conceptual frameworks more in keeping with their emancipatory goals. Of course, cost and coordination are significant barriers. It would involve international actors defining and paying for such a system, running the risk of unsuitable conditionalities being inserted into what might be called welfare oriented peacebuilding approaches and subsequent transitions from war to peace, again lacking contextual legitimacy in local terms and resting mainly on international consensus.

In social democracies the labour movements, the poor, and social movements often see democracy and the state as their ally – and indeed, it is more able to deliver them the liberal social contract, and the 'good life' as a result. In neoliberal states, the opposite tends to hold true, and the tension between poor and elites undermines any social contract and leads to the securitisation of the state. This is hardly conducive to peacebuilding. Sandbrook *et al.* argue that social democracy allows the local, whether labour groups or cultural identity groups, to organise the state themselves, and therefore to claim ownership over it because resources are distributed democratically, not according only to the market (which might be manipulated in the favour of an elite otherwise).[49] Many of the roots of conflict often cited are more directly and urgently addressed by such frameworks than the neoliberal system (which may be more suited to already developed polities). Post-war experiences have generally shown this to be the case, rather than the neoliberal development models which often produce political, economic, and social stagnation in post-violence situations. Of course, in many recent state-building or liberal peacebuilding operations, the vast majority regard the state as potentially predatory, but a more welfare oriented version of peacebuilding might be able to create more grounded legitimacy.

It is important to note the paradox of a welfare oriented peacebuilding system: it also needs a state, and it is highly interventionary, which is why it has so often collapsed into an institutional social engineering process, and has been criticised for being expensive and inefficient, creating massive bureaucracies, and 'big states'. States have tended to use welfare strategies to varying degrees to pacify or placate their own poor, and to try to dampen down the abrasive effects of socio-economic classes systems. Thus, welfare strategies are also clearly compatible with liberal peacebuilding while also mirroring its shortcomings. However, in post-conflict transitions, such complaints are probably less significant and more consistent with emancipatory claims about the liberal peace. If liberal peacebuilding aims at a sustainable peace then ethically and politically it is probably better off with this more consistent approach. It is a better conceptual match with liberal peace-building and statebuilding, which are also both social and political engineering processes. Welfare systems also potentially provide more space, though still limited by state prescriptions for civil society and for cultural forms of expression and representation. Both welfare and neoliberalism are compatible with the state, but in very different ways. Welfare redistributes (in this case internationally as well as nationally), equalises, and reduces the power of elites (if they are accountable and do not use welfare systems as a basis for patronage) so enhancing a social contract; neoliberalism does the opposite unless capacity and resources are already high and widely available. In this sense, social democracy might be a better blue print for post-conflict peacebuilding than neoliberal states have proven to be. But this does not fully solve the question of culture in peacebuilding, given that either welfare or neoliberal prescriptions rest on the reconstruction of liberal states via a universal model for peace. Indeed the sorts of local knowledge and capacity that international actors would require to adopt such an approach raises a new set of contradictions for peacebuilding approaches.

Conclusion

On balance a more welfarist, needs oriented, and social democracy aimed version of liberal peacebuilding might be plausible, or indeed more successful on binding citizens together within a post-conflict state. The redressal of needs issues might make the state seem worthwhile and legitimate, subject to a meaningful social contract. To be internally consistent, the liberal peace should probably engage with needs more directly than at present, as this is normally a significant concern of any democratic process in a fragile, post-conflict polity. Such limitations are all the more perplexing because of the well-known links between inequality, under-development, and lack of social welfare, and the related fragility of democracy. The assumption that democratic rights are more significant, rather than equal to, than economic opportunities is not widely supported in many local contexts, even in the very sensitive and nuanced situations of transitions out of violence – as in Northern Ireland, which has been subject since the peace agreement to massive British and European investment in public services, infrastructure and facilities.

The practice in the West is to develop both in an intimate relationship with elites in order to provide for both political rights and economic opportunities for the local. For example, social democracies provide an economic safety net for low earners and the unemployed as well as public services, which make everyday life more secure and meaningful for its participants. This enables rather than reduces cultural agency upon which legitimacy for any state might be built through the emergence of a national consensus. Neoliberal economies provide opportunities for all to buy such services and to have choice, but only when a large proportion of a population have reached a reasonable level of per capita income. The balance between social and neoliberal democracy represents the main difference amongst liberal states. Yet, in a post-conflict development context this balance is lacking, ignored or left to the [often non-existent] market. The lesson appears to be that the market does not provide for a stable civil society, or merely promotes an artifice unpopulated by local people. This undermines the social contract, given that this is the goal of the liberal state. A mixed economy and social democracy has far more chance of enabling a civil society at least while its costs are met externally. This raises the issue of what are the costs of such enablement as opposed to the costs of a collapse into violence or of dysfunctional societies, economies, and politics? It is probable that the latter outweigh the former significantly.[50]

Many post-conflict states which have been subject to liberal peacebuilding operate fairly authoritarian forms of democracy, as in Cambodia for example. This underlines yet another inconsistency within the liberal peacebuilding model, which consequently favours relatively undemocratic states, or the lack of self-government in the transitional period, or weak implementation of democratic reforms, in order to promote stronger growth. This is one way of addressing the problem that democratic transitions are often undermined by socio-economic problems, which avoids the externalised burden and costs of social welfare programmes. However, it also means that civil society, and a social form of peace may not come into being, meaning the state effectively represents an international imaginary of the liberal peace and an elite vehicle.

Neoliberal development strategies do not support the liberal peace, or at least its civil, emancipatory component. They supplant the local, negate cultural agency and the liberal social contract with the market, and drag liberal peacebuilding towards the conservative end of its spectrum. Indeed, often the post-conflict individual and community is abandoned in most respects in favour of institutions and markets. Liberal peacebuilding, and its neoliberalisation instead betrays a cultural blind spot on the part of peacebuilders and policy-makers, who do not see contradictions between replicating long stable liberal states in post-conflict settings, while treating context and the local as voiceless, unempowerable, and sacrificeable in the interim, while neoliberal trickle-down strategies emerge.

The proscription of welfare ties in very closely with the positivist emphasis of the state and system and its continuity with inherent order versus violence, and therefore with the subjugation of the individual and his/her subjective consti-tution through emotional, cultural, material resources and connections. The error of institutionalised liberal peacebuilding today has been its willingness to be co-opted within positivist, problem-solving methods and epistemology, which have effectively led to its failure as a practice in many varied parts of the world today. Neoliberalism in particular has been regarded as a science as opposed to an ideology. As a result, an unintended consequence is that the local and context is romanticised in a way which ensures that a social contract between it and the emerging state will not emerge, partly because welfare needs are not addressed by the state or internationals directly during the transition from violence to a form of peace. The delegitimation of transitional welfare has undermined engagement with the local, and is indicative of the hegemonic and non-pluralist culture of liberal peacebuilding – and of the absolutism of liberalism. This, as Duffield has argued, has led to the phenomena of 'surplus' and 'uninsurable' life, especially in conflict and post-conflict development settings, even amongst more progressive thinkers and policymakers[51] who effectively deploy governmental versions of peacebuilding. This represents a culture–welfare paradox, discussed further in the next chapter.[52] It undermines the very 'civil society' and civil peace that liberal peacebuilding claims to emphasise.

A welfarist or needs oriented, and social democratic version of peacebuilding is not without its problems of course. It may either maintain liberal governmentality, or rescue the liberal peace, but it does not address its broader problems in the context of a post-colonial world. Of course, both welfare oriented and neoliberal approaches romanticise the local in different ways. The welfare approach requires social engineering to be carried out by enlightened officials and politicians, and a strong social contract between them and society, institutionalised within the state. Needs may be guaranteed, but uninsurable life becomes so heavily insured that it may also be depoliticised and so the support welfare provides for civil society and a social contract may ultimately also become undermined. The capacity of the welfare system to 'save' people is romanticised, and needs are constructed in universal modes with little regard to cultural or social patterns or dynamics unless purely at the national level. On the other hand, market oriented approaches over-value political rights as the main priority of peacebuilding along with security, and then undermine them with market freedoms that induce inequality, particularly in fragile post-conflict environments. They allow the state to be hijacked by allied political and economic elites, and romanticise their capacity to mobilise on a large scale to enable society to 'help itself'. Add to this the pressures of the global market, and the liberal fiction that the local is helpless and without capacity, becomes a self-fulfilling prophecy that confirms its political, economic, social, and indeed cultural 'inadequacy'. This is why rights frameworks and the market have been able to supplant local agency in liberal peace oriented strategies.

Given the tendencies of both neoliberal and social democratic or welfarist approaches, it is more likely that a welfarist approach to peacebuilding in the early transitional stage would be more consistent with the liberal goal of a peace that contributed to regional stability. This would remove some of the costs of peacebuilding that neoliberalism has placed on the shoulders of the post-conflict individual and allow for them connect with the state – to enable civil society and the social contract. Costs would be shifted to external actors but probably not in the fragmented way that the current aid and development system often operates. In the longer term, the market might also play a role in this development strategy, but only if a clearer understanding of the economic strategies most suited to each context could be developed. This would be preferable to the current strategy of using the West's 'local' version of the interaction of politics, society, and the economy to dominate those in very different contexts. If liberal peacebuilding is to be rescued, a more welfare and needs oriented strategy might enable a more three-dimensional state, social contract, civil society, and everyday experience of peacebuilding to emerge for its subjects. However, as the next chapter discusses, this assumes that local cultural dynamics are not a significant modifying force for the liberal peacebuilding project or that cultural 'dysfunctionality' can be 'overcome' by its universalism. Such distancing strategies associated with the institutions and mechanisms of the liberal peace and its neoliberal dynamics maintain inequality and indicate a lack of understanding of the significance of cultural agency in peacebuilding.

2 The culture of liberal peacebuilding

Introduction

This chapter develops further the argument that 'governmental distance', partly through liberal and neoliberal design and partly through contextual ignorance, has hindered liberal peacebuilding and statebuilding processes. This enables governance without external actors becoming fully responsible for needs or welfare, or for understanding context or culture, as well as allowing them to introduce possibly painful reform. Its goal is the liberal transformation of the post-conflict political subject in the context of the necessary state and institutions. This reifies Westphalian notions of sovereignty, as well as modernist international institutions, a cosmopolitan international community of states and architecture of international peacebuilding. There are inevitable tensions in this architecture for international peacebuilding. It indicates that international actors also do not consider liberal peacebuilding as a product of a specific culture itself. The connection of peacebuilding and statebuilding with liberal institutions, neoliberalism and individualism, rather than context, culture, or needs and welfare, ignores the experience of post-war reconstruction and the development of the Western liberal state. The type of security which is produced by this approach tends to be of an international, regional and state nature, rather than grounded in local experiences or needs. It bypasses issues such as reconciliation and has a rather ambiguous relationship with transitional justice. This is particularly important in the context of the now common assertion that a stable and dynamic civil society (at least as it is understood in the eyes of the liberal peacebuilding community) is required, and that local cultural dynamics should be respected by external interveners whose aim is to build a state from the outside and a civil society to cement its legitimacy. But more significant is the oversight of culture as a site of peacebuilding agency. It is culture, custom and modes of organisation that are derived from these dynamics in specific contexts, that often substitute for the failures of liberal peacebuilding, ensuring survival and more. As a result there have been increasing attempts to bring custom and culture into liberal peacebuilding and statebuilding processes (as discussed in Chapter 6).

This chapter investigates the culture of liberal peacebuilding, which it argues has been unbalanced by neoliberalism and has tended to essentialise local cultures while ignoring the dominance of its own. Even more crucially this ignores the role of culture in constructing collective agency for peacebuilding, at a community level or in terms of institutions.[1] It examines these dynamics in the light of the last chapter's discussion of the way liberal peacebuilding and statebuilding has treated needs and welfare issues, supplanting them with rights discourses and the market by governmental strategies designed to distance the local. It illustrates how culture is treated by liberal peacebuilding, but also how its various forms and expressions have had an impact on external intervention itself. Culture is a site of peacebuilding agency, often ignored, which has modified the practices of liberal peacebuilding, especially in the latter's concepts of civil society and its cultural and economic formulations, as well as its modes of political representation. Neoliberal forms of peacebuilding are disruptive to these forms of capacity. It would thus be more appropriate for international actors to engage with them, as well as with the possibilities and problems of needs and welfare in peacebuilding. This would further accentuate a commitment to local ownership in contextual terms, as well as local capacity and resilience. This points to the need to develop a form of peacebuilding of a post-colonial nature, as well as the importance of its everyday and hybrid aspects. Rather than peacebuilding being representative of liberal subjects and their institutions and history, it would then represent a negotiation between the 'local' and the 'international' in simple terms.

Implications of culture for peacebuilding

Culture, as a concept, is derived from agriculture and cultivation and the notion of self-sufficiency as well as custom, identity, intellectual distinction and refinement.[2] It is notable that the more ancient etymological root of the word indicates distinctive expressions of cultural identity which may also be related to the word 'acre', indicating land measurement, use, and ownership.[3] This is crucial because it also connects to liberal understandings of individuality, and to property rights as the basis for the neoliberal economy and indirectly for political representation (as property gives everyone a stake in institutions and before the law in liberal thinking). It is linked to notions of self-expression, memory, self-government and self-determination, and a very broad engagement with politics, society, history and the economy. It implies difference and autonomy rather than homogeneity, universalism and dependence. This is contrary to the problem-solving and institutionalised reductions of most modernist theories associated with the state, conflict management, peacebuilding, neoliberal economic approaches and development.

As a 'web of meaning'[4] from which politics and peace emerge, culture is often regarded as a critical site of agency, often in hidden or marginal ways. This is one of the reasons why progressive projects of modernity often ignore it, because its agencies may conflict with modernisation or claimed universal or cosmopolitan norms. Culture highlights meaning rather than scientific law. Such a view contrasts instrumental understandings of culture against interpretative understandings,[5] which are far more able to comprehend the complex politics of peacebuilding. It precludes a 'view from above/outside' (even though most social science writing, including my own, often aims at this) and any analysis will inevitably be incomplete and slightly ambiguous because of its subtleties. Despite this, such semiotic analysis – and its implications for peace – offers more than merely intuition about peacebuilding but excavates the complexity of both agency and structure especially in areas IR has rarely been concerned with: beneath the state and beyond civil society.

Culture has often been associated with positions that resist modernity, or with resistance more generally: hence 'hearts and minds' strategies against insurgencies and repeated attempts to include cultural sites of influence as common opposite numbers in peace processes, while simultaneously denying the legitimacy of their cultural agency.[6] It has been supplanted in the liberal peacebuilding literature by the concept of civil society. This has the effect of negating its connotations relating to identity, alterity, or resistance as well as maintaining a division between 'liberal internationals' and 'illiberal' or 'non-liberal' local actors. As a result important stakeholders are ignored, partly because of the fear of not being able to deal with local knowledge or expectations. Such problems arise also because international actors, like the UN, have relatively little capacity at the local level though attention to such issues is now increasing though field missions and 'outreach' practices. Even so, local languages and culture remain widely acknowledged weaknesses of international actors.[7] The UN Peacebuilding Commission was partly established to provide complementary legitimacy to that of the liberal peace, and of course, field missions in general develop local contacts where they can. Even so, the local remains elusive for international actors.[8]

Culture implies a diversity of identities, custom, and practices, many of which are 'modern', transnational, and transversal in their expression of the 'local' even if not secular, explicitly rational, progressive or universal. Clearly it should not be essentialised, homogenised, and instrumentalised. Indeed, as a site of agency, it is unlikely that strategies designed for the latter will produce anything but more tension. It can be used to imply relativist and eternal divisions, though this possibility should not be used to censor culture from consideration of liberal peacebuilding's engagement with the local.[9] Yet, because of these dynamics, local cultures, institutions, actors, and practices are often perceived to be the liberal peace's other, and an obstacle to the project of liberal, rational governmentalism. Local culture is perceived from this perspective to be in opposition to the liberal peace and democratic government or development. It is from here that the disconnect that allows liberal peacebuilding to ignore needs, local agency and institutions begins and the local is made invisible or romanticised.

Yet local cultures often engender social and economic systems that are expressions of responsibility to each other, despite their limited resources and lack of market infrastructure, and in contradistinction to the elite, predatory state or class systems that attempt to concentrate power in the hands of one particular identity group. Liberal peacebuilding often interferes with this positive aspect of the local, while restraining but also supporting elites.

Twentieth century states were, in more classical and orthodox terms, to represent culture and identity in the context of the modernising nation (hence the term 'nation-building'). Modern statebuilding, which has swept along much thinking about peacebuilding especially amongst mainstream Western theorists, has in contrast focused on technical and institutional forms of state governance, but retains a sense of nation-building as a future outcome. Legitimacy according to this latter view lies in institutional coordination and efficiency of the state while often vaguely appealing for the creation of a national identity in the longer term. Along with this should be some discussion of citizenship, and what citizens require, though this rarely happens in practice, given the exigencies and stresses of liberal peacebuilding's crisis or donor-driven priorities from an international perspective.

The return of culture in post-violence liberal peacebuilding experimental states (ironically often in states such as in the Balkans where in the 1990s, ethnic and other identity conflicts raged), has shown this move to be flawed. Legitimacy also lies in cultural forms of representation, which are denied if the state merely provides 'bare life'[10] due to its neoliberal character or its reliance on the construction of empty institutions – a virtual peace. Such cultural forms of expression are often tied to land, memory, identity, religion, and history, but not necessarily to nation-states. Of course the modernist obsession with the nation state, and moves to enable universal self-determination have meant that independence is seen by most political groups as the only guarantee of peace and security. As Anderson has famously shown, these simulations of nationhood are imagined and often resist the impulse contained in statehood to objectify them.[11] But they are crucial to the liberal peace because they engender legitimacy, even though the liberal peacebuilding process has tended to avoid modifying pre-existing boundaries (often stemming from decolonisation processes) where possible, and relies on forms of legitimacy emanating from international norms, law, and institutions.

As with the difficulty in defining the concept of peace, it is also important to note the difficulty in understanding what culture actually means in different contexts. As Clifford has written, '[c]ulture is a deeply compromised idea that I cannot yet do without'.[12] The same might be said of liberal peacebuilding strategies' treatment of culture. Paradoxically, while welfare strategies might create more cultural space for peacemaking and legitimacy for the state, they also invite the state to take up interventionary positions vis-à-vis its citizens and provide an opportunity to manipulate the cultural and identity forms of society following the patterns established before or during a conflict. In other words, and in different ways, both neoliberalism and welfare oriented liberal states potentially make subjects of their citizens, in different but equally governmentalising ways. Neoliberal approaches to peacebuilding tend to disregard the importance of culture as a site of peacebuilding agencies. Welfare strategies might offer material capacities through which needs might be realised, but they may also contradict or deny cultural agencies in favour of state agendas and interests. However, in post-conflict zones welfare itself is a very basic need for much of the population from long after overt violence has faded. In this sense, it complements but transcends concepts of human security and provides the capacity for cultural and social engagement to democratically shape its environment, polity, or state, and when sufficient political and economic energy has been amassed perhaps to move into a more sophisticated form of polity. In the transitional, post-violence moment, however, neoliberalism represents a failure of liberal thought in peacebuilding terms, which creates subjects rather than citizens. It places too much reliance on the universality of the liberal peace, ignoring context.

Liberal peacebuilding is unable to take local culture seriously in this sense, either seeing it at one or other extreme and not reflecting on its own position. For example, locally organised projects – even if recognised as crucial – rarely receive donor or UN funding because of language and bureaucratic barriers. This has been a long-standing problem in the UN system, which has still not been resolved.[13] The local response to these dynamics is therefore predictable from a cultural perspective – resistance, rejection, or co-option of peacebuilding. These dynamics are exacerbated because little or no attention is paid to the inconsistency of building a liberal state that lacks the essential administrative and productive capacities provided by a welfare system designed for such a transitionary state, which would extend the social contract beyond potentially predatory or at least biased elites. This oversight or confusion has a very significant implication: the local is seen as not significant in terms of peacebuilding agency. This is very contradictory in the light of the liberal assertions of civil society and a social contract.

This leads to a self-fulfilling spiral: local culture is seen to be inherently flawed or violent, making external intervention and investment risky. Effectively, this means that international faith in democratisation, the rule of law, human rights, and neoliberal development is relatively insecure, meaning minimalist versions of these are adopted. The focus is consequently on neutral and imported institutions rather than local agency. It is indicative of the valuing of political institutions over everyday life, of neoliberalism over needs and welfare, and so of Western models over non-Western human life. This has a whole series of implications, not least the blind faith placed in neoliberal strategies (for attracting FDI, which hardly ever materialises unless it is for high profit enterprises, such as with resource extraction). Of course, there are also indigenous responses that ameliorate such problems. Crime, corruption, and violence are obvious possibilities, which are often locally described in less inflammatory ways. There are also localised socio-economic responses – informal economies and political systems based upon cultural and historical institutions and processes. These often run parallel to the empty liberal states formed by external intervention. Often they depend on customary governance and law, or communal land held by communities as welfare guarantees.

On first sight, this is obviously not a cultural critique of liberal peacebuilding, though in many ways it follows a similar path, extending it into institutions used to determine governance in peacebuilding and its focus on political rights rather than social welfare. On closer examination however, what becomes clear are the hegemonic, political, social, economic, and cultural assertions inherent in neoliberal patterns of statehood and global governance, with little regard for the everyday pressures of completely different, perhaps non-liberal and undeveloped contexts. Thus, liberal peacebuilding as a praxis has a very uncomfortable relationship with local communities and individuals, ranging from domination or co-option, to transformation, emancipation and liberation. Civil society from this perspective is actually empty of individuals and communities who do not accept this agenda – they are deemed uncivil, illiberal, or non-liberal. But this means a significant number of people are excluded from liberal peacebuilding. If it is the case that culture and welfare are ignored, then liberal peacebuilding and state-building can be generally seen as mechanisms of exclusion rather than inclusion. They benefit certain epistemic communities and their elite partners, but not the general population which is engaged in everyday life in a supposed social contract with their representatives, and with peacebuilders.

This blind spot on the part of internationals to culture (and needs) in local contexts reflects how the various intellectual and practical peacebuilding projects which were initially individual and community based and bottom-up processes, have been transmuted into contemporary statebuilding of a liberal, institutional, and neoliberal character. This instrumentally exploits, co-opts, or rejects local culture, all of which reflects the liberal and neoliberal culture of peacebuilding itself. This is by design so that individuals may be provided with conditions suited to the good life, that restrictions need to be put in place to prevent 'uncivil' (or non-liberal) behaviour, and that suitable conditions are created so individuals can fend for themselves. This blend of liberal and neoliberal thinking results in an instrumental romanticisation of the local and a dismantling of the really-existing local and its agencies. It is predicated upon the predominant thrust of liberal and neoliberal thinking that freedom is found through the creation of *a priori* governance institutions and self-help in a state context. Thus, needs and welfare are marginalised, and culture is seen to lie in quaint or unacceptable local traditions or patterns of behaviour, the enactments of which are not vital for the emergence of a sustainable state, or a grounded legitimacy. Nor is this culture–welfare nexus necessary for the creation of a liberal state and sustainable peace. At best, it offers a route through which top-down institution peacebuilding can co-opt the local. It is top-down and driven by international norms and institutions where the liberal peace process faces an absence of local agency in liberal terms.

Much hope has been placed upon the assumed 'natural' desire of civil society for peace, as a collective will. Some have seen this, as a product of a new cosmo-politan order, which allows for cultural difference, and may rest upon global governance. This is aimed at emancipation but reproduces the local as the following:

> The local is in these circumstances the exotic, the private, the traditional, the parochial, the non-democratic, the non-political. Culture ... [constitutes] that which is associated with the other of the modern, the progressive, the universal.[14]

What is rarely acknowledged is that this is endorsed by the construction of the liberal peace in post-conflict peacebuilding environments. It is also the cause and target of resistance, often from the local for identity and cultural reasons.[15] The local is often connected transnationally within the context of broader movements endeavouring to articulate their own emancipatory project. It is fully aware of the conditions of both domestic and international contexts. It is these connections that might later become significant for moving the polity beyond the instrumentalisation of culture and welfare.

This connection between the local and international (even though this division is somewhat artificial) often reifies a particular notion of local and international activism and the associated civil society, concerned with the main pillars of the liberal peace. This leads to individualism rather than a politics located within historical, social and cultural networks. Thus, the way that liberal peacebuilding projects the concept of civil society reflects the marketised and neoliberal ideology of developed states where political and social rights take precedence over all over human capacity. As Foucault argued, civil society is the product of governmentality in its neoliberal state form.[16] Yet, this is often contrary to local expectations and praxes. It is complicit with the state in the liberal view, rather than resistant to it or even riven by tensions which produce political debate and hence the nature of the state.[17] This ignores the role of emotion, identity, and custom in negative and positive forms in civil society.[18] Such dynamics are obscured by positivist problem-solving assumptions, so that when local recipients of this peacebuilding practice react negatively, it looks as if they are dysfunctional to the 'neutral' eye of the peacebuilder. Modernisation and liberalisation often leads to the reassertion of local identities as a reaction.[19] As Said has shown, cultural pluralism and an underlying shared humanity do not need to be contradictory.[20] Thus, such resistance is often discursive, political, social, cultural, or customary, rather than violent. It is often hidden, disguised by its perpetrators or blocked by external actor's biases.

From this perspective culture has to be an important theme in any discussion of peace, which should recognise both its fluidity and dynamism, and its connection with tradition and social cohesion derived from this.[21] The agency associated with culture becomes apparent from this perspective rather than the dsyfunctionality that internationals often perceive. Following on from this, the culture of liberal peacebuilding needs also to be recognised, if only to recognise its neoliberal characteristics and the consequences of this ideology in fragile polities. (Perhaps the best place to look for this is in post-colonial theory, as I endeavour to show in Chapter 5.)

Culture is often seen as a generic 'other' by internationals, which, where visible, should be incorporated into problem-solving universal institutional and discursive forms of the liberal peace, often in its most conservative of forms. It is not seen as a site of agency, but rather often as an obstacle to peacebuilding, barring a few references to traditional forms of mediation by internationals. As Escobar suggests, however, a form of institutional ethnography can uncover how biases and interests, often themselves of a cultural nature, are exported through peacebuilding.[22] This can be used to both unpack and critique the omissions and biases of the contemporary and mainstream praxis of peacebuilding, but also to begin to understand the needs and practices of everyday life in post-conflict peacebuilding situations: '... to train ourselves to see what culturally we have been taught to overlook ...'[23]

Contemporary practices of peacebuilding and statebuilding may be institutionally attuned, but not culturally attuned. In doing so they undermine their own claim to rest upon a vibrant civil society and blind themselves to the cultures of peace that may already exist. It is because these are interventionary activities that they – along with any social welfare system – require a recognition of the cultural bias of liberal peacebuilding. Furthermore, they require the recognition of local patterns of politics, of resilience, custom, alterity and identity especially in non-Western settings, where the vast majority of peacebuilding and statebuilding operations are located. The consequences of not engaging with culture for a civil peace, for civil society and for the local-local, have been enormous. Civil society itself has become representative not of the local, or of an authentic, organic or indigenous context and their many and fluid dynamics, but of an external veneer masking attempts at social engineering. Ironically, even this goal is undermined by its association with marketisation and alien institutions and associated conditionalities. Peacebuilding without a cultural engagement represents a romanticisation of the local. Effectively, the combination of liberalism and neoliberalism has blocked an open and empowering conversation between the local and the international, failed to build a social contract, and has undermined the liberal peace project and peacebuilding more generally. The praxis of romanticisation has infected peacebuilding, seemingly exposing local dynamics but actually disguising them, and often making them appear to be more suited to liberal peacebuilding than they actually are. The romanticisation of liberalism's own local, not to say its mythologisation, says more about the West's interests and attitudes, and is at least partially the result of an age-old failing of disciplinary liberalism.

The implications of neoliberalism

It is through such dynamics that both liberalism and neoliberalism appear to be plausible approaches to include in post-conflict peacebuilding. The claims of 'pacific' qualities through institutionalisation, freedom, law and markets, and the subsequent regulation of the person, state and international relations,[24] reflect a cultural bias and specific ideologies, which themselves reflect dominant interests. Clearly, the three main traditions of liberalism, which include liberal pacifism, liberal imperialism and liberal internationalism, all propose democracy as an essential component of peace, but make underlying normative assumptions about liberalism's universality that, when confronted, lead to tension between its supporters and those that reject its internal value system. Thus, according to Doyle, liberal states that are prone to war with non-liberal states, may make a separate peace amongst themselves, and have 'discovered liberal reasons for aggression'.[25] This logic can be extended to offer liberal reasons for hegemony and domination, for the focus on security and institutions, for the denial of culture, agency, and of course for the importance of needs for peace. It explains the need to distance the supposed non-liberal subject, predefined as such by Western elites, politicians, peacebuilders and administrators, in order to govern it in ways to which it may not automatically consent. However, this is difficult to sustain in a rights context, which is why the liberal peace system rarely compromises on democracy, rights, or law. In a needs setting though, if one accepts the separation of rights from needs, it is easy to argue that a peace with rights is superior to a peace with needs. Thus, peacebuilding is infused with a neoliberal culture in which rights cannot be compromised. Yet, ironically, the materiality of rights can be denied, or at least left mainly in the hands of post-conflict subjects. This seems to contradict strong evidence that needs, jobs, inequality, and welfare have always been key in conflict situations, which after all often revolve around the distribution of resources. Here the liberal peace displays its hegemony as it merges into a neoliberal peace which fails to address needs. This is ultimately a denial of cultural agency for rights bearing subjects.

What this indicates is that the liberal peace argument is strongly focused on political rights and their associated institutions in an international context and at a national level. This has produced an uncomfortable modern form of liberal peace, which is a hybrid of liberal rights and neoliberalism. These undermine each other because the materiality of rights and the importance of cultural agency is denied. An international peace between states is its overriding concern according to international standards, rather than local versions of culture or economic welfare. As a result it provides little space for the subjects of the liberal social contract (i.e. citizens and agents, not merely subjects). In a liberal context the civil peace is viewed from above, from the perspective of national and international elites, who are often trained to speak the same language (literally and metaphorically), who see the liberal peace as a superior knowledge system, and are strongly influenced by neoliberalism. The civil peace is rarely considered from the perspective of the actual subject so civil society is constructed according to individualism, property rights and the market. The idea that the subject might be an agent in other ways is a distant leap. Needs responses are essential for the post-conflict subject. Incorporating neoliberalism into peacebuilding may therefore be profoundly disempowering because of the failure to engage with needs, welfare, and context.

This represents a liberal-realist[26] discourse in IR in which power modified by liberal norms, status, and institutions are its main interests. This has a tendency towards emphatic reductionism with particular effects on human life and culture, through its neoliberal bias and its prioritisation of security and state institutions. Most critiques of liberalism fail to uncover this completely, and instead confirm the absence of everyday needs and cultures in their discussion of war and peace. Liberal-realism has the advantage of maintaining sovereign control, through a liberal biopolitics of 'peace as governance'[27] but only through the marginalisation of culture and welfare, the local, and everyday life amongst those deemed conflict prone and underdeveloped. Even an acceptance of local culture by international actors often merely represents a disguise for their refusal to engage with the basic welfare requirements and identities of the post-conflict other. It is not the state that is underdeveloped by implication, but the people. Yet they are denied the very material resources and recognition required to organise politically. The social contract is not recast as an ethical construct, nor can it engage with cultural difference and welfare needs, but instead is an institution of governance at the elite level which binds citizens in the context of political rights (and security needs) as a priority over all else, regardless of their social and economic conditions, history and culture.

There is an obvious inconsistency, or at least an obvious assumption, here, relating to the relative value ascribed to political, social, and cultural practices, and the need for normalisation within the liberal model, and a relative devaluing of the identity, culture, economic and welfares rights of individuals in post-conflict zones. This represents an institutional framework that implicitly argues that top-down political, economic and social structures need to be created, but accepts that they make an impact on post-conflict societies at different speeds. Democratisation is experienced as soon as elections are held, and in the interim period beforehand it provides an expectation of political rights soon to be established. Socio-economic intervention by agencies is longer term, generally accepted as not being effective for years or even generations. Votes and social change effectively represent abstract reforms in the context of the post-conflict individual and community in this interim period. Yet, after security, the most basic attribute of a liberal society is the ability to be productive and therefore autonomous, offering individuals the capacity to support themselves and their families as political and social reform develops. For all the trumpeting of aid and development, the role of the World Bank and the IMF, or the many NGOs donor funds, this aspect often lags far behind, meaning that individuals are left to fend for themselves. This apparent double standard has done much to undermine the legitimacy of the liberal peace, especially beneath 'civil society', which is the most disadvantaged by these strategies.

There is of course a long genealogy critiquing such strategies. For example, Schumpeter argued that the success of capitalism would lead to a counter-response; democracy would lead to the election of social democratic parties in order to introduce welfare states. Capitalism would collapse as democratic majorities demanded the creation a welfare system and civil society voiced grass-roots concerns about their access to resources in a capitalist system.[28] From this perspective neoliberal ideologies and systems are merely the extension of elite interests which perpetuate their political, economic, and cultural hegemony. Indeed, it might be said that neoliberal prescriptions place many areas of life and society outside of the democratic process.[29] That this is problematic is clear, but it is far more so in a post-conflict situation where international actors are attempting to introduce democracy or to enhance the space it covers. Neoliberal orienta-tions for peacebuilding do not respond to societal needs, but instead promote a top-down culture of neoliberal wealth creation that reiterates class, feudal, tribal, or patriarchal system of governance but without their various counterbalancing responsibilities, whether to preserve a tradition, an identity or an environment, or to provide welfare. Thus, set free from the responsibilities of their pre-existing institutions, however disrupted they may have been by conflict, liberal institutions are likely to be co-opted by the very elites that conducted the conflict in the first place. This form of peacebuilding ultimately benefits (or buys off) the elites. If the conflict was grass-roots led, then clearly the basic roots that caused the deployment of violence cannot fully be dealt with by liberal or neoliberal peacebuilding, which exacerbates marginalisation via its own top-down culture.

This critique extends into a development and modernisation context. Development studies have aimed to improve living standards and prosperity in the developing world using Western knowledge and technology rather than indigenous approaches, and encouraging self-help rather than dependency. Its focus explicitly prioritises the economic over the political, social and cultural. Orthodox development work often has little connection with local culture but rather focuses on material gain as it is conceptualised by modern forms of governance and political economy. This has been heavily criticised not just from the point of view of being counter-productive, but also for being inherently violent and a way of monopolising the 'developing' body and mind in order to homogenise polities within the broader liberal community of states.[30] This neocolonial critique requires that local knowledge and culture be reconfigured within a democratic, neoliberal statebuilding process entirely controlled by liberal peacebuilders. This has generally created 'bare life' for those who are being 'developed',[31] whereby their inter-subjective existence or their needs are not valued until they 'become liberal' – or more specifically, neoliberal. As Agamben writes, bare life comes about because of the Western political habit of exclusion that simultaneously claims to be inclusive.[32] Thus, bodies are managed and governed, and local agency or even resistance is not tolerated, even if it is an expression of agency and the contestation of politics. Even if society aspires to the liberal project, however, neoliberalism means bare life for many who suffer from poverty despite their aspirations for a liberal state. Even so, bare life engenders some forms of agency – and even resistance – to such practices.

For some post-conflict subjects this means death through conflict, or ironically through humanitarian intervention, preventive war, torture, genocide, human rights abuses, or poverty, with little direct concern from the liberal international community. Ultimately, the political culture of liberal peacebuilding has allowed a form of poverty-with-rights to emerge in post-conflict zones, or worse, insecurity-with-rights, in which rights are guaranteed by institutions, but local agencies are denied until they are expressed in liberal ways. If sustainable forms of peace must be locally grounded upon local agency, needs, and culture, then this effectively means a denial of alternative visions of peace by the hegemony of liberal peacebuilding. This often rather unrepentant culture may emerge unconsciously as a result of weak, exclusively positivist methodologies which enable exclusive metanarratives to be widely adopted before thorough contextual testing, and it may be more strategically prescriptive on the part of its main international supporters. Most plausible is that the culture of liberal peacebuilding has arisen through both: as a hegemonic expression of a mode of political thought about intervention (and a generally supportive academy mainly based in the West), and derived from a singular set of historical circumstances through which the West experienced war and peacebuilding in the twentieth century.

For post-conflict individuals and communities around the world, this represents long-term insecurity despite having political rights (some of which may be alien). Such subjects may be politically enabled but they are economically and socially vulnerable: the cultural assumption is that the two fundamental components of liberalism – rights and needs – previously connected in the West by a long agreement on a set of welfare oriented policies in most polities, can be disconnected in the developing, post-conflict world, because these are underdeveloped polities, in which 'civil society' is minimal.

The Western and liberal focus on political rights as separate and superior to economic rights betrays a certain Orientalism towards the inhabitants of developing states, which of course value political rights but might well place economic rights or needs as well as opportunities at a higher level of priority. Yet the liberal assumption is that political rights are always primary. Interestingly, the recent failures in Iraq have now led to more concrete policies being put in place for job creation there.[33] In both Iraq and Afghanistan, dealing with poverty through small-scale welfare schemes and larger scale job creation programmes, has increasingly emerged as a response to socio-economic and political dynamics of violence. This also represents an attempt to prevent the cycles of escalation that may have been the unintended result of a very high prioritisation of security and securitised discourses in both environments. But parallel development of these strategies, both from a theoretical and institutional perspective has not caught up with the growingly obvious needs on the ground in developing, post-violence contexts, nor with the notion that such a reorientation would necessitate a broader engagement with local cultural norms, and with the highly interventionary aspects of liberal peacebuilding. After all, it is probable that such a realisation necessitates either a change in focus for the UN, World Bank[34] and IMF, or new international architecture to take on this role. This would mean an engagement with liberal and neoliberal cultural assumptions which feed rational and technical approaches for creating the conditions for peaceful politics. It may also then indicate the possibility of a move beyond the negative assumptions of non-liberal incapacity.

Is there an economic reason for this lack of direct engagement with the everyday welfare and cultural aspects of post-conflict societies? As noted in the previous chapter, it is generally regarded within the neoliberal consensus that welfare is too interventionary, creates dependency, and is too expensive. It is well known that adding resources to a conflict situation, however well intended, might provoke that conflict. But does this mean that humanitarian assistance should not be extended into welfare during a transitional period, and that local cultural agency is therefore insignificant in the resolution and transformation of conflict? Alternatively, is there a cultural reason for this deficiency, that is rooted in the international perspective of locals and their situation and lack of understanding of the market, corruption, and good practice? International actors simply do not consider welfare, or the establishment of a 'Marshall Fund' type of approach in this neoliberal, ideological era, partly because of the common rejection of welfare processes for others, potentially non-liberal, non-citizens, but also because of a cultural relativism whereby a lack of concern for others' welfare is assuaged by a concern for their political and human rights. Again this anachronism represents the thinking of an elite Western culture, and the degrading of local cultures and actors. It reproduces the vicious spiral that is a fundamental flaw of liberal peace-making – that poverty may lead to violence regardless of whether a democratic system exists or not. It is crucial that political, social and economic justice is achieved if a state is to be stable. Democracy, rights, or prosperity alone are not enough for either the liberal peace to achieve its own emancipatory position or for self-legitimation.

This was recognised in a 2006 UNCTAD report on Africa, which to some degree reflected on the lessons of the Marshall Plan in Europe after World War II, in the context of contemporary liberal peacebuilding.[35] This called for generous, predictable long-term aid, without outside conditionalities or resorting to shock treatment. Furthermore, it is increasingly recognised that 'social peace' (or civil peace in my own terminology) depends partly upon social welfare programmes. Small but similar moves in this direction have recently been made in the context of Iraq and Timor Leste.[36] It is only through such provision that social justice, growth,and economic stability can be achieved in a balanced manner. It would be sensible to remember that the task of the welfare state, as Barr has argued, redistributes or compensates but in both senses provides for social justice and economic stability and efficiency.[37] These are crucial aspects of peace. What is more, this is not simply a choice to be made by peacebuilders, but is built in to the very standards that are held to be binding in international agreements, such as the *UN Covenant on Economic, Social, and Cultural Rights*.[38]

The liberal modernisation project clashes with the local where identity and cultural concerns appear to defy rational progress towards liberal governance. Indeed, some have argued, following Polanyi, that capitalism and its inculcation into multilateral development institutions is indicative of a disciplinary approach in which social relations are dismembered if they impede neoliberalism.[39] Polanyi argued that fascism was the outcome of neoliberalism's failure,[40] whereby civil society and indigenous resistance was disciplined by the capitalist state. On a larger scale, this sort of disciplining has become part of global governance whereby international institutions impose strategies that lead to bare life, and cause resistance, civil or otherwise, that require states to take on a more disciplinary role. This has provoked a fascinating and subtle range of responses from its supposedly powerless subjects.

The culture–welfare paradox

As a result, current strategies of liberal peacebuilding are subject to a culture–welfare paradox. This betrays something of the culture of both (despite their claims to represent science, universality, or timeless and eternal laws). In attempting to establish a liberal state and liberal peace, the focus on security, rights, institutions, and markets disempowers the very civil society and social contract they hope to create. The liberal focus removes culture and context and the neoliberal focus removes needs. Both are supplanted with rights and markets. The romanticisation of the local removes (or attempts to remove) cultural agency in order to distance it for harsh, externally driven, reform-oriented governmentalism, while neoliberalism vetoes the welfare model necessary to materially empower post-conflict citizens to take up their new rights. Without cultural and material agency, peace remains virtual, as does the state, which is controlled by predatory elites in collusion with international actors who cannot 'see' what is happening on the ground.

Addressing the culture–welfare paradox offers opportunities for the rescue of liberal peacebuilding, but with some significant caveats. Engaging with cultural dynamics may well push the peace that emerges from such processes 'beyond liberalism'. Indeed, as I argue later in this study, despite this culture–welfare paradox, and its detrimental impacts on the legitimacy of the state and the social contract, cultural agencies remain, provide material support, and often modify the liberal project *in situ*.

What has actually arisen as a result of the prioritisation of security, rights, and institutions over culture and needs, has been a romanticisation of the local.[41] This has emerged as a possibly unintended consequence of liberal peacebuilding. It is possible that the liberal bias or blind spot for the local is entirely conscious and plausible in its own local environment, but less so for those post-conflict environments in development and non-Western settings. This romanticisation represents a process by which the local is mapped and defined from an external perspective for the purposes of locating it in a rational 'liberal' state. This has become a cultural project of the liberal international community and its agencies, organisations, institutions and NGOs. It offers the view of the local as a zone of incivility in which 'new wars' occur and corruption, a lack of capacity, and 'primitive' political, social, and cultural practices are present. This perspective stems from the implications of a lack of a social welfare and local cultural engagement in contemporary peacebuilding practices. This has been dehumanising and marginalising, and maintains a distance between the international and the local akin to the 'ironic distance' that Connolly argues that liberalism induces.[42] This separation is essential for the maintenance of the technocratic, normative and cultural superiority of the international liberal project. It has been abstracted from Northern and Western 'locals' but it also paradoxically represents an attempt at positive engagement with the local: a co-option as well as a blindness to its many attributes.

This illustrates the culture of peacebuilding and statebuilding and its negation of local culture, voices and welfare – indeed the everyday-[43] via 'superior technologies'. At the same time it imagines common and universal norms, law, and system for the protection of human rights, civil society, democracy and prosperity. This might imply that liberal peacebuilding could be rescued from the failings that have emerged over the last twenty or so years if needs, welfare and culture (and so difference) could be engaged with. However, it may well be that liberalism itself precludes any equitable engagement with these issues in the specific contexts of post-war environments.

The solution to such difficulties is not to merely try to remap or redefine the local by building in an understanding of culture and needs for external appropriation, but to find ways of enabling local actors collectively (in terms of community, society, custom and individuals, and their own engagement with peacebuilding, liberal or otherwise), and the many internal or external actors who are involved in this project. In the light of the hegemonic weight of the liberal peace project, this raises the question of whether an engagement with the local and an enabling of its diverse voices can occur in the context of the acute resource asymmetries present in the international community's engagement with post-conflict situations, and whether liberal peacebuilding can ever achieve anything better than its current romanticisation of the local?

These failings of the liberal peace may be partly because the key feature of the dominant liberal approach to peacebuilding represents an *a priori* state form and a neoliberal marketisation of peace, rather than engagement with the agents and subjects of this peace. In contrast, what is needed, is an exploration of culture, needs and welfare-based approaches to peacebuilding that are context sensitive. Objectives of reconciliation, emancipation and empowerment, as well as the crucial terrain of civil society for the legitimacy of the state, require a redressal of needs in the context of rights, and an engagement with culture[s] as the site of agency from which politics and the state emerge. This is as opposed to the top-down export of a one-size-fits-all (neo)liberal state, which tends merely to produce the empty shell of the state when transposed onto a post-conflict environment.

As Escobar points out in the context of development, peacebuilding is also a contestation of culture and of otherness.[44] Contemporary peacebuilding has rested to some degree on an infantilisation of its recipients rather than a recognition of this contestation via local agency, administered by an increasingly professionalised elite and external institutions. These cannot 'comprehend' cultural needs or welfare issues as priorities in the context of security or institutional issues, or worse are blinded to such issues by the prescriptions of the liberal or neoliberal project.[45] This has become a political and developmental 'science' which has been heavily securitised since neo-Keynesianism gave way to neoliberalism[46] and liberal institutionalism displaced notions of emancipation and social justice. Liberal peacebuilding and statebuilding have become projects in which coordination, implementation and compliance are key issues, rather than peace, legitimacy, identity and needs.

This approach to peacebuilding is a particularly modern Western and Enlightenment derived discourse and praxis. It is far from culturally and socially appropriate or sensitive, and has little chance of establishing a locally self-sustaining peace as a result. A vibrant civil society, local ownership, and social contract are unlikely to emerge from such strategies. In this context, difference is only acceptable when it operates within the liberal framework, and cultures and needs are contradictorily denied. This represents a romanticisation of the local which consists of four key types:

1 Orientalism in which local grass-roots actors, custom, society, and their needs and institutions are seen as exotic (or indeed quixotic) and unknowable, thus justifying blueprint top-down and illiberal approaches rather than local engagement;
2 an assertion of a lack of agency and capacity in which local actors and institutions are seen as unable to play a role because they are incapable of liberal civility and helpless, again justifying top-down illiberalism;
3 an assertion of local deviousness and incivility, justifying external conditionality and coercion (often aimed at elites, but also affecting grass roots);
4 an assertion through which the local is seen to be a repository of indigenous capacities that internationals might co-opt where they foreshadow the liberal project, justifying external conditionality.

In none of these strategies is the agency of the local accepted, except in relatively negative forms. These strategies appear to construct the local in a positive sense as supporting the liberal peacebuilding framework, but in actual fact they distance the local from international peacebuilding for governmental purposes relating to security, rights, and institutions, with needs, justice, culture and identity often ignored. This reflects the liberal culture of peacebuilding and its hegemonic engagement with the local, which has been particularly problematic in its liberal UN and or more social democratically oriented EU driven contexts in 'late modernity'. What has emerged so far through this merging of the liberal democratic peace and neoliberal frameworks is a conservative form of the liberal peace.[47] This neither builds a social contract on the ground or between internationals and local actors, nor does it develop its own grounded, contextual and local legitimacy, reconciliation, a social contract, local resonance or sustainability.

A post-colonial turn

The reliance on neoliberalism to deal with modernisation, development and needs, and a lack of contextual and cultural capacity on the part of external actors have, as a result, led to a post-colonial turn for peacebuilding. What is emerging, follows similar lines to the critique that Fanon adopted of the post-colonial state in his first generation form of post-colonialism, particularly of Algeria. He argued such states were economically defunct, could not support social relations, and resorted to coercion to control unfulfilled citizens. They responded in a range of different ways (including through violence) in order to propagate their own anti-colonial agendas.[48] Similarly, liberal peacebuilders create capacity-less virtually-liberal post-conflict states and governments, in the expectation that society will respond positively and follow. Inadvertently, instead of helping the post-conflict individual recover, they may be indirectly benefiting those who drove the conflict in the first place.

Liberal peacebuilding may also be encouraging the appearance of its own hybrids, whether contributing or donor states moderating their own expectations consciously, or being forced by local politics to do so.[49] But as Fanon indicated, economic, social and cultural life are interlinked, and cannot be divorced in the way that [neo] liberal versions of peacebuilding assume. As a result the social and cultural glue that forms the key to the creation of a social contract between citizens, state and government that represents them in a liberal polity is lost. This is problematic enough in a developed context and in stable liberal states, but in a developing or cultural environment in which the group's social, community, customary, historical and spiritual relations may be valued more than political or economic institutions or resources (especially where the latter are equated with corrupt, predatory, or feudal practices), this is unlikely to work. It may also be that a different ideological position is preferred. Either way, a post-colonial critique follows closely behind (as I discuss in Chapter 5). By implication liberal and neoliberal peacebuilding identifies local politics in post-conflict situations as deviant, and constructs democratic and market processes to replace these as soon as possible. The subtext of this prioritisation is that there is no local culture or need worth intervening for, and the focus of any intervention and assistance should be on security, institutions, and marketisation. This means liberal peacebuilding's importation of resources (material, status-related, and intellectual) is directed towards elites, who are better able to engage at this level.

This relates to debates emanating from first generation post-colonial theory, which juxtaposes Western liberalism against others who are identified as 'barbaric' against the liberal norm.[50] Those who are not engaged in violent acts of resistance or terrorism are essentially the pupils of liberalism; this means they are invisible[51] until they have graduated into the school of mature liberal societies and states. Of course, this mainly benefits pliable elites. For Said, in his later iteration of post-colonial thought, the cultural implications of this, denoted 'Orientalism' in which liberals discursively dominate and dehumanise the 'non-liberal', non-Western subject.[52] It has become a key assertion of later versions of post-colonial theory that such dynamics have implications for the coloniser, and have a very significant effect on them – from their dehumanisation and their preference for problem-solving knowledge systems, to their realisation of hubris and their own relative incapacity and naivety. Ultimately, their own political cultures were significantly modified by colonialism.[53]

Some of these issues are now being investigated in the context of emerging literature on culture, conflict resolution and peacebuilding, or on local ownership, custodianship, and participation in peacebuilding, and on the question of indigenous methodologies and ontologies of peace.[54] There is very little extant work on the question of how peacebuilders perceive the indigenous by focusing on rights and political representation or identity, which is constituted according to the interveners' own cultural and normative frameworks and their social or political expectations. This omission biases peacemaking efforts towards the replication of political life via top-down governance in post-conflicts zones as a parallel to that in developed liberal states. The problems this formula for peace brings about relate in particular to a general belief that culture, identity and peace are universally constituted and understood by liberal peacebuilding actors; that civil society equates to the indigenous (as least its positive liberal qualities and aspirations); and most perplexingly, that social welfare need not be institutionalised even in fragile transitional phases. This latter point is indicative of a significant inconsistency, wherein the immediacy of an individual's need for a productive life is unquestioned, but that in a post-conflict setting individuals need to rely on their own strategies for survival in the interim, sheltered only by rights and institutions before neoliberal marketisation and development strategies make their mark. This, of course, means they may revert to subsistence strategies, grey or black markets, or even join militias, in order to develop a productive life. This is something which would not normally be tolerated in a liberal state context, not least because these dynamics are not conducive to peace, order, and stability. Yet the immediacy of human and political rights is a given in any peacebuilding context. This raises the question of whether this denotes a relative devaluing of productive life in post-conflict development contexts? Indeed, without a civil component, what exactly is the liberal peace?

Where there is a concern with local culture and a so-called 'indigenous peace' this is also associated with identifying local cultural psychoses, ethnic entrepreneurs and their motivations, tribal warlords or recalcitrant chiefs, or with romantic views of indigenous peacemaking. This is rather than the provision of resources necessary for individuals to survive at a sufficient level to be able to contribute significant capacity to their polity or exercise their new right. One could see this as a form of cultural oppression aimed at reinforcing traditional power and resource hierarchies. (Indeed, some thinkers have made the connection between modern discourses on knowledge, identity and culture propagated by mainstream thinkers and policy-makers, with older and discredited discourses on race.[55]) Civil society, in this context, represents an imported and romanticised version of the good liberal in a vibrant, democratic, prosperous social context. It is an idealised version of civil society imported from outside (where it also probably does not even exist in this form).

What emerges from all this, is the massive emphasis on top-down institution building, external trusteeship and administration, and the importation of liberal values (political, social and economic) and development models, by an epistemic community of peacebuilders, statebuilders, peacekeepers, development specialists,and other international planners of local and regional order, who focus on blueprint institutions over individual needs, culture, and identity. These actors profess to 'do no harm', and often turn to local cultural practices in order to assimilate them into the top-down construction of the liberal peace, and to give the project a sheen of legitimacy and grass-roots consent. But this normally does not occur until after a top-down institutionalist approach has been tried and has begun to show signs of failure. From an internal, local-local perspective (as opposed to the more artificial concept of civil society) and from that of scholars versed in the analysis of colonial structures, class, power and domination, there is little wonder that the result looks very much like a colonial or imperial system, subject to class, cultural, or racist double-standards.

From this perspective, liberal peace interventions depend upon the local acceptance of imported hegemonic normative and cultural systems. Where this does not occur, limited attempts at a mutual negotiation between international peacebuilding norms and local normative frameworks may emerge, but normally in an assimilative sense. This approach often appeals to a rather romantic ideal of local culture, while at the same time blaming it for being subject to practices that led to the conflict in the first place, and also underlie any spoiling violence while a peace process is underway. Perhaps even worse is that this same critical analysis could be directed at the liberal peacebuilding and statebuilding actors, theories, and methods. This reflects the mindset of liberal modernity and neoliberalism exactly, in that a blueprint based upon a set of assumptions about institutions and economic development establishes a situation where privileged or wealthy actors are enabled in order to drag along the rest of society. Culture and welfare are again secondary, and not seen as significant in the short term. The implication is that a different kind of 'romanticisation' is taking over the liberal peacebuilding process – or at least its mythologisation. This is deemed to be normatively universal and beyond reproach, if technically and methodologically experimental. The local becomes a laboratory, with all of its attendant methodological and ethical issues, and in particular its impact on human life.

An indigenous, civil peace emanating from civil society actually represents a dichotomy much-noted by pluralist thinkers, and also by indigenous actors in post-conflict zones, who often point to the gulf between them and the socially engineered and artificially promoted civil society imagined by international actors. Though there may be little or no material capacity, however, this does not mean there is no local agency (as I shall attempt to illustrate in Chapter 7). Historical, cultural, social, religious, and often ideological forms of everyday agency, exist. This often represents critical – or resistant – agency vis-à-vis elite and external interventions in such areas, and represents forms of agency that internationals rarely acknowledged.

Taking a broad view of statebuilding interventions since the end of Cold War it is clear that these have generally have led to increasing levels of local resistance, in terms of political discourse and even in terms of violence targeting international peacebuilders, humanitarian workers and soldiers. This can clearly be seen in the policy evolution that has occurred from Somalia to East Timor, and extends into Afghanistan and Iraq. Consideration of local cultural knowledge, ontologies, reactions and requirements has been extremely limited, if it has occurred at all in these locations. Where it has occurred it has tended to be instrumentalist. Instead, an escalation of interventions has occurred, each driving the next, deeper, as well as more governmental intervention, which together indicate that international actors do not think local actors are capable of running their own affairs. As Chandler has long argued this is contrary to self-determination and self-government despite its stated aim of being supportive.[56] It is politically disabling and represents an assumption that cultures of violence and poverty are too deeply in place to allow local actors to act freely along the lines of the liberal peace framework without international tutelage. Internationals therefore assert their own identity by virtue of having access to superior knowledge systems.

Locals, by contrast are culturally primitive, and economically and institutionally corrupt. Yet what internationals fail to see is that they are offering frameworks that do not provide for needs, and often actively intervene to prevent indigenous welfare institutions from supporting populations –this further disables cultural agency, giving rise to a post-colonial critique.

Conclusion

Thus far the liberal and neoliberal approaches to peacebuilding are derived from specifically Western and Enlightenment derived discourses. Their exclusivity makes them appear to be guilty of the range of the romanticisation flaws I have identified, leading to a culture–welfare paradox. They appear to be far from culturally and socially appropriate or sensitive, are unable to comprehend the 'non-liberal' other or its difference, and deny the role that culture plays in producing agency, and collective political projects. The local is seen as distant, exotic and unknowable: there is no local useful capacity; there is only local deviousness and self-interest, and even amidst such contradictions about local agency and autonomy, there are very limited local capacities for conflict resolution. This allows for and justifies the classic liberal move of relying on coercion and blueprint top-down and illiberal approaches, especially pertinent to the introduction of neoliberalism into peacebuilding. This rests on the legitimacy of Western liberal knowledge, even though this is also 'local' (and so alien) in specifically contextual terms. At best it represents a weak cosmopolitanism.

It is poignant that such criticism also appears in post-colonial discussions of British rule in India, echoes of which are precursors to modern peacebuilding, aid, development and statebuilding practices, in very disturbing ways. For example, Mehta charts how the great liberal thinkers of the nineteenth century wrote about progress, liberty, and government, and asserted their viability in an alien context while also denying unfamiliar and local versions of these by responding to resistance via power, whether of ideas or in its more material forms. All this occurred without having any experience of what they prescribed or denied, for reasons of classification or comparison (i.e. organisation and problem-solving). It appeared cold and unfeeling, lacking understanding or empathy, and designed with interests, race, strategy, and profit in mind. Theirs was a gaze designed to dominate the world through the connection of its improvement with British interests.[57] For Mehta, liberalism has been impoverished in its capacity to comprehend the local from its very beginnings (with the exception of Burke's approach which he argues was based on 'colonial subjectivity' and some sense of a 'shared order on the ground').[58] Thus, the colonial encounter of subjects and imperial power, as with liberal peacebuilding and statebuilding with its subjects today, was an encounter of strangers intent on domination or resistance for the benefit and detriment of others:

> They literally do not know each other, do not speak each other's language (in the various senses of the term), and do not share values, cosmologies, or the quotidian norms and rituals of everyday life.[59]

Worse, there was then as there is today an assumption that there are few significant and viable political structures, organisations, or groups at the 'native' level.[60] Most of the administrators of the British Empire were young, idealistic and inexperienced, while also regarding local actors as children.[61] This is what made imperialism acceptable to its proponents in the same way the connection between conflict and apparently non-liberal forms of politics, social organisation or non-neoliberal economic systems appear to make liberal peacebuilding and statebuilding in neoliberal form possible today. This results in the separation of local actors from any capacity, and ultimately in the denial of their sovereignty. At the same time it also endorses the connection, inverse or otherwise, between liberalism and the territorial state, while maintaining the fiction that needs are not related to conflict.

Even more notable is that this parallel can be extended. What occurred next, according to the post-colonial critique of British rule in India was that its incapacity, normative inconsistency, naivety, discrimination and racism, was exposed for locals and internationals to see. This happened in small and often hidden ways, or through violent confrontation, necessitating British military reinforcements over time. It also occurred on a grander scale via the political organisation and non-violent resistance to Empire organised by Gandhi, which projected a new political order on a platform that colonial rule could not occupy, and which moved the struggle for political autonomy and agency, denied by imperial rule, into a sphere which rendered it both visible and insurmountable. Limited versions of these dynamics also now apply to liberal peacebuilding, in the same way that it represents some of the dynamics of colonial rule, even if it is based on a responsibility for others modified by its core interests, history, and culture (as liberal imperialists also claimed). Emulating even limited forms of colonial praxis,[62] whether through methods, objectives or ideals, is consequently self-defeating if peace is its objective; it also paradoxically stimulates local agencies to reassert local forms and cultures of politics.

Given the capacity of the local implied by this analysis, despite assertions of incapacity by international peacebuilders, the latter often revert to what increasingly looks like the default setting of interventionary liberalism – even where it is deployed for peacebuilding purposes. Thus, the common response to difficulties emerging in the liberal peacebuilding process is to identify the local as deviant and to make recourse to conditional and coercive strategies of intervention, whereupon liberal statebuilding can commence. This is in line with the linear and rational progressive streak of liberalism which follows a conservative line in order to prove its own legitimacy complete with rhetorical allusions to future emancipation. But what is being emancipated if needs and culture are rejected? This sort of move can be seen clearly in the development of peacebuilding from *Agenda for Peace* in 1992 to the *Responsibility to Protect* and *High Level Panel Report*. This is not to negate their humanitarian purpose, but is to point to the dangers of their equation solely with liberal ideologies of statebuilding. From this perspective, the assumption of neoliberal strategies, the rejection of the institutionalisation of needs, and an engagement with the local (whether cultural or identity based, or in terms of everyday needs or even with its modes of resistance) represent the West's export of its own local, its own biases and interests. It undermines the liberal social contract and the rejection of any possible alternative, including voices now perceived as 'uncivil' even though they may represent a significant part or even a majority in a specific population. This effectively undermines a culture of peace and replaces it with cultural, economic, and political hegemony, redefined as liberal and civil.

Grand institutional solutions to local conflicts fail to address the dynamics of the local, or the problems of such institutional designs (which are probably no more sophisticated than the operatives who control them and implement their mechanistic approaches, and certainly are not able to comprehend the local, the diverse or the different). These represent metanarratives of governance, not peace nor peacebuilding. Moreover, they are not even wholly consistent with political liberalism except in its most conservative of forms. It raises the question of whether, if liberal peacebuilding could adopt a more sensitised approach to cultural forms of local agency, this would rescue the liberal peace? As I will argue in following chapters, this may be a good start, but it is more likely that cultural agency will modify the liberal peace model.

3 Critical perspectives of liberal peacebuilding: Cambodia, Bosnia Herzegovina, Kosovo and Timor Leste

Introduction

As the previous chapters have illustrated, the inherent biases of liberal peace-building have meant that little attention has been paid to the issues of culture, identity, needs and social welfare during the interim phases of peacebuilding, or to how a range of local actors respond to the liberal peace project or even develop their own politics of peace.[1] This has the intellectual result of inducing and legiti-mating discriminatory patterns of thought and policy between existing liberal states and those that are being built, indicating that a lack of cultural sensitivities at the grass-roots level amongst international actors masks their relative lack of interest in the lives of individuals (beyond their political and human rights). Yet it is also widely accepted that economic expectations and rights need to be resolved early if the state itself is to be protected from political and social instability. Thus peacebuilding is practiced via rights, institutions, and states, even though it is well known that there is more to peace than rights and institutions.

The preceding chapters have underlined how liberalism (and neoliberalism) acts to negate the local, culture, and their existing institutional, social, political, and material capacities. This makes them dependent on the liberal peace in theory, but in practice it also evokes alternative understandings of peace and local capacity, especially where culture is seen as a site of agency (rather than merely dysfunctional). This has undermined the capacity of so-called non-liberal others to be heard or to act on the international stage as well as in their own post-conflict polities, and so has undermined liberal peacebuilding. Indeed, such intended and unintended strategies represent the infrapolitics of peacebuilding amongst donors and agencies, especially state backed or ideologically motivated, such as the UN with its inherently liberal stance, or the World Bank, with its more neoliberal approach. Similarly, the local 'infrapolitics' of peacebuilding, often aimed at needs and derived from cultural frameworks interact, if only to block, international approaches. More importantly the international approach to liberal peacebuilding has both resisted and spurred on the development of hybridity, and a new consensus on peace processes in each different context. Such externalised approaches are not without contextual responses of course. In the following chapter I examine what this has meant in a number of country cases studies in peacebuilding and statebuilding contexts, specifically during the apogee of post-Cold War peacebuilding and statebuilding.

Cambodia: absent citizens and the simulation of a liberal state[2]

In this early peacekeeping/peacebuilding/statebuilding operation, it soon became clear that the distinctions between traditional peacekeeping, a peace process, and peacebuilding, had now collapsed into the project of building a liberal state in the period around the end of the Cold War. The focus was initially on a regional peace agreement at the diplomatic and elite level expressed via the negotiations leading to the Paris Peace Accords from 1989 to 1991. These were thought then to form a basis for what was essentially an early statebuilding process run by the UN, which focused mainly on democratisation and subsequent elections. It was generally accepted that regional and international considerations of *Realpolitik* provided the framework in which limited opportunities for a liberal state might arise in a difficult regional and local environment, one that was not Western, modern, nor development-oriented, and had little pre-existing capacity also because of the violence inflicted on society by the Khmer Rouge. It is little wonder that a hybrid liberal and authoritarian state was to emerge in the years after 1991, with an almost invisible civil society and a subsistence-oriented population beyond the capital, where aspects of modern liberal and authoritarian politics co-existed with more immediate customary processes of governance. Yet in this context the peace agreement and the subsequent implementation process were seen to be generic and based on the now mythical capacity of the liberal peace during these early years after the end of the Cold War.

Much criticism has been levelled at the subsequent peacebuilding operation for failing to engage with the more localised realities of Cambodian society, or to distribute a peace dividend more widely. Indeed, while the Human Development Index has risen since the agreement, inequality remains at a very high level (see Appendix 1). This probably means that much of the new wealth is concentrated in the hands of elites. Yet, from the perspective of top-down formal peace-keeping, peacebuilding and more recently statebuilding endeavours, this case is often represented as a great success.[3] This is despite the fact that the attempt to construct a liberal state and neoliberal economy has had little impact on Cambodia's predominantly subsistence economy. This represents a neoliberal blind spot for the internationals present, particularly the World Bank which has, at least until recently, refused to evaluate the local informal economy by Western standards, in particular with statistics on unemployment which is deemed to be hard to measure given the high levels of subsistence activity present. Indeed, the predominantly subsistence economy (involving perhaps as much as 85 per cent of the population)[4] is at once seen to be an indigenous response to poverty, and by implication a way out of international responsibility for welfare, and so as a number of little consequence for internationals. It is also, from this perspective, a sign of inability of local political culture and the state itself to mobilise on a large scale. Yet, in practice, in everyday terms, substistence strategies are sign of mobilisation, however fragmented, and to some degree make the current state form viable. They effectively subsidise the state and its 'weak' capacity. Similarly, it indicates the weakness of internationally backed growth and investment oriented strategies so far. But the blame for this is placed not on the strategies of international actors such as the World Bank, but on its local recipients, from corrupt or authoritarian political elites to 'traditional' rural subsistence farmers and their cultures of corruption, patrimonialism, and nepotism. From an international perspective there has been little interest in local needs beyond urgent humanitarian assistance, or in local forms of politics, society, and economy, which has instead been seen as pathological in the eyes of international actors.

In general, the focus has been on stabilising the state, institutions, the police, military, democracy, markets, and civil society. The emphasis has been on high level politics, supporting economic growth, and attempting to prevent corruption. The latter is often claimed by international actors to represent a significant 'tax' on donor inflows every year. This has supported a predatory elite and off the record is sometimes described as an informal bribe to prevent conflict from returning. By comparison, the vast bulk of the population are hidden from the liberal gaze because they are seen as unproductive. Because they are often subsistence farmers or operate in an informal economy and related political sphere they are not included in the main statistical indicators produced to illustrate the state of the economy.[5] In these terms a subsistence farmer is not 'unemployed' in much the same way that the grey market or corruption are not deemed to be part of the legitimate economy or acceptable means of income substitution by a pragmatic, if very poor population.

This effectively means that a virtual peace has been built within a virtual state, which is now less often seen as a success for liberal peacebuilding. This is partly because of the internationals myopic perspective of the local, now configured around an increasingly authoritarian government, absent a strong civil society or social contract. This has had the uninintended consequence of allowing the state to be hijacked by predatory elites determined to protect their privileges and vision for the state. It has become a vehicle for authoritarianism and corruption – effectively a hijacked state.[6] The normal service and accountability functions of the liberal state have been blocked. The fact that a very large proportion of the local population is not involved in the state's formal economy means that the neoliberal aspects of statebuilding have been a hindrance to peacebuilding, with an extremely detrimental effect on democracy, civil society, and the local-local below it. Similar dynamics can be observed in the context of democratisation, which many critics agree has also been diverted towards autocratic and authoritarian modes of politics.[7]

Corruption, authoritarianism, subsistence and the lack of democracy should not be explained via an inherency or culturalist argument, of course, which is what the rendering of Cambodian politics from the international perspective tends to do. The assumption that an indigenous political, social, or economic system is absent or deviant and itself is responsible for such dynamics is an oversimplification that has been used to legitimate the installation of the liberal peace framework upon a *terra nullius*, or indeed a *res nullius*. This has occurred with little regard for actually existing practices and institutions, which are automatically delegitimised even if they were not part of the dysfunctional politics that led to conflict in the first place. Instead it has focused on preventing deviation from the ideal form of liberal or more accurately neoliberal state associated with liberal peacebuilding. This reflects a bias of liberal peacebuilders, who established the liberal peace via the installation and reform of governance in all sectors of the state as a way of filling the vacuum perceived in the local context. Yet, what they see may not tally with what is actually there, and represents a blindness rather than an absence, a bias rather than a benevolence. This has substituted the institutionalisation of a semi-authoritarian system for reconciliation. This vacuum may actually be a result of liberal and neoliberal prescriptions, ideals, assumptions, and methods, rather than an accurate depiction of the reality of local politics. At best it represents a caricature of the local, supported by the determination of donors and internationals to focus on transforming the state in the hope that this will trickle down to civil society.

It might be thought that the local NGO community, supported by international donors, provides many of the resources or capacities that the liberal state should, and has become the *de facto* state from the perspective of civil society. Civil society is excluded from the state and elite level politics, and from the formal economy, partly because of the authoritarian nature of the state because of the effects of neoliberalism, and partly because of the negation of local culture. It is a widely held belief that if the internationals withdrew even the conservative, elite level virtual peace would disintegrate.[8] International donors, frustrated with the endemic corruption and the weakness of state governance, tended for a while to circumvent the bureaucratic inefficiency of government and instead fund NGOs directly. Although this had obvious short-term gains it also reaffirms the creation of a forum shopping mentality amongst NGOs – of which their representatives are very aware – and the adoption of goals for reasons of funding rather than because they are directly relevant to the issues people face in their everyday lives. Indeed, as a result, and as in many other locations, a new NGO class has emerged which is distinct from local civil society (i.e. the local-local) and the grassroots, which floats above it and represents an artificial, external imaginary of civil society. This has formed a small, new and often transnational middle class framed by the liberal peace but disconnected from their own state. Yet, this type of civil society is also often critical of the internationals' rendering of them, who often work on their own projects in disguise.

If the liberal goal was 'capacity building', then little indigenous capacity has developed other than in opposition to the state or government, or to international approaches to peacebuilding, as a way of subverting the role of internationals and the resources they offer. This form of 'capacity destruction'[9] creates a dilemma: peacebuilders and donors need to remain closely involved to support democratisation and capacity-building in other areas of the liberal peace framework, but by doing so may undermine local capacity or divert it into open or hidden confrontation with the liberal project, which is locally perceived not to meet the needs or respect the identities of local actors. Indeed, it benefits elites far more, even if they are relatively authoritarian. If local actors do not remain closely involved with peacebuilding however, local elites may return to their competition over the monopoly of violence, authoritarian politics, and reject the progressive values of the liberal peace. Elites effectively use this to ensnare donors. They may hijack the material aspects of the liberal peace project and construct their own forms of politics. These unintended consequences have the greatest impact on the already marginalised civil society especially in local-local form, preventing a peace dividend and maintaining their marginalisation in the Cambodia state. Paradoxically, and also perhaps more hopefully, it also indicates local-local resilience, levels of agency and autonomy, and unexpected capacities to reframe the peace project.

This is made problematic, however, by the continued hegemonic domination of political power that underwrites the patronage system in Cambodia and allows networks to be constructed from the top down, based on loyalty and rewards. Incidentally, to some local eyes this also seems to parallel the role of international peacebuilders, shorn of their masking rhetoric. Such dynamics can be seen in many liberal states of course, but political defeat and the possibility of marginalisation from power are of relatively more consequence in a society where resources are particularly scarce. The Cambodian polity is overlaid by a network comprised of a multi-dimensional clientelism and patronage that links individuals to centres of political, social, economic and customary forms of governance. International actors have become complicit in a form of state which does not engage with diverse local agencies, and indeed avoids them, preferring to attempt to transform authoritarian elite level politics in the absence of a vibrant civil society and a neoliberal market structure.

From the perspective of international peacebuilders this explains why local social, political, and cultural dynamics are responsible for a lack of progress, rather than inadequacies in the liberal peacebuilding framework itself. It is unsurprising in the light of this that it is widely argued that civil society does not exist in Cambodia (though many local activists beg to differ). From this perspective civil society only emerged during and as a result of the UNTAC era, facilitated by donor funding.[10] Because of the institutions of clientelism and patronage, doubts plague the constitution, membership, and effectiveness of this new civil society with regard to the access and political influence that NGOs and other groups have, and their dependency upon external funding.[11] This civil society is quite possibly an illusionary 'virtual' or 'parallel' society, matching the virtual state created by the presence and funding of the internationals, and mainly visible to international eyes, perhaps even performing a therapeutic role for them. It does not represent the local-local but allows the state, elites, and donors alike to ignore the immediacy of the plight of the poor, inequality, and human needs more generally in favour of their structural and institutional reform processes. Far from aiding the development and sustainability of an indigenous civil society, or a local-local in its transnational and transversal as well as rural or localised contexts, it is representative of conditionality and dependency rather than local autonomous agency. It is driven by unreflexive, internationally controlled processes, informed by muscular approaches to problem-solving, heavily mediated by elite level co-option. They are underpinned by a romanticisation of the local which places context beyond the reach of liberal peacebuilding. Even worse (from the perspective of an immanent critique) for any attempt to resuscitate liberal peacebuilding, context is placed beyond the reach of the very social contract that underpins the liberal state.

What has emerged in Cambodia is a virtual liberal state and a virtual peace in which authoritarian elites profit from their control of the shell of the state and the donor resources it attracts, and from an international inability to comprehend the nature of local politics. Thus, the local is disempowered, distant, and all but invisible to the liberal and especially neoliberal gaze of elites and the international community. This represents all the aspects of this type of romanticisation that I have identified previously. It rests upon an Orientalist support of the superior technologies of governance. It makes the local populations distant or invisible because of their lack of capacity in both political and economic terms. It facilitates their governance by internationals and state elites without high levels of local consent or legitimacy. Genocide, conflict, poverty and other local pathologies are deployed to explain these dynamics as a cover for the inadequacies of liberal peacebuilding and statebuilding.

A de-romanticisation of the local in Cambodia's case might enable the development of an understanding of historical, social, economic and political dynamics to reshape peacebuilding in a way which makes its contextual relevance far more significant, not simply to justify liberal peacebuilding/statebuilding approaches. It would mean a far more culturally sensitised and needs-based assistance process to empower civil society, as well as a reluctance to allow statebuilding to mainly benefit the state's elites, as it has done so far.

Bosnia Herzegovina and Herzegovina: whose stalemate?

The development of a sustainable civil society is taken by most international actors as a good indicator of the progress of peacebuilding from a conservative to a more orthodox or even emancipatory version of the liberal peace. Yet, if international actors' policies and analyses rest on the types of romanticisation of the local I have outlined, this does not indicate the incapacity of local actors to adjust to the liberal peace model. Instead it points to the inflexibility of the liberal peace model itself and its incapacity in recognising the uniqueness of context, culture, or (somewhat paradoxically) to the importance of needs in building peace. Thus, statebuilding projects, focused on security and the political level, almost inevitably have floundered at the level of the individual and the community – and this case is no exception.[12] Indeed, the focus on building civil society from the grass roots emerged as a strategy to circumvent international, elite level and institutional political stagnation in Bosnia Herzegovina Herzegovina.[13] Yet, over the last fifteen or so years it has been commonplace for international actors, from the OHR to the EU, to argue that the stalemate emanates from contextual political disfunctionality, accounting for the fragility of the state, rather than engaging with the shortcomings of their own polities, attitudes and prescriptions. Nor have they seen fit to empower citizens materially in order to give some substance to the rights their state is supposed to protect, or to enable their political agency to transcend the now long-standing political stalemate.

Though civil society is presumed to represent an indigenous socio-political space, engagement with it is driven by political and social agendas derived from bounded perspectives and more importantly, by interests and the material restrictions of international actors. Thus, 'civil society building has been conceived as an externally driven process that is dependent upon external resources …'[14] with little connection to local indigenous and cultural practices, despite the overarching forms of ethnic identity present. As a result, NGOs in this area are increasingly regarded as builders of a 'new elite' or 'new sector'[15] that draw funding from the internationals by speaking their language and playing their game in classic donor-driven rather than locally driven style. This has made civil society elitist and distant to the local-local. NGOs concerned with local conceptions of needs and culture tend not to be funded. Civil society, even in an environment of apparent cultural and educational similarity to the West has little connection with the local, and far more with the international or transnational. Indeed, it represents the internationals' romanticisation of their own local (i.e. normally from Western donor capitals) and projecting this as an exemplar for the local to adopt. It represents by implication very negative perspectives of the actual local – a romanticisation familiar from the colonial era.[16] It is used to catalogue, explain, govern and organise, but not to understand.

Even so, international actors have acknowledged that the existing institutional framework has stunted rather than supported the growth of civil society. The result has been in many local eyes the consolidation of a problematic peace treaty (Dayton in 1995) and a widespread international and local view that little progress can be made towards a self-sustaining peace which would be stable without the presence of international institutions and actors such as the UN, NATO, the OCSE, World Bank, and EU. Yet, now there are significant political voices arguing that the internationals themselves have become part of the problem.[17] Some argue that the development of Bosnia Herzegovina's civil society and in particular institutions such as the electoral process, political parties, and the media have been unable to move beyond political exclusion caused by the Dayton Agreement's vision of the state. This has been accused of ethnicising politics in a way that was not common before the war and of failing to understand the legacy of socialism or deal with local needs.[18] This suggests civil society could be developed by discussion and consensus between interest groups, greater independence in the media, and cultural and institutional reform of the formal political process.[19] These are familiar problems affecting all the components of the liberal peace, along with the difficulty of overcoming the reluctance of elite actors to engage and extricate themselves from the ethnic political agenda in which Dayton has continued to embed them. But even these positions assume the sacrosanct nature of the liberal peace rather than engaging with the sort of issues its romanticisation of the local have raised. In Bosnia Herzegovina these imply a misidentification of civil society and of the essentialising role of identity, and an underestimation of local political agency at both the elite and local levels. This has removed from view a range of ideologies, identities and cultures, from religious to socialist, while focusing on ethnic identity as being the major problem. It perhaps also involves an overestimation of international agency. Perhaps most importantly it leads to a diagnosis of a lack of local compliance with the liberal peace as being the result of ethnonationalism rather than being related to a more complex set of contextual matters – institutional, material and identity related – or the weakness of international capacity for statebuilding. It also overlooks the fact that since 1995 the HDI index for the country has not significantly improved for all, while inequality has increased (see Appendix 1).

Responsibility for the limited development of civil society in Bosnia Herzegovina is due, at least in part, to the non-cooperation of political elites across ethnic lines and the focus on constitutional reform of the Dayton Annex, which laid out a complex post-war framework for governance. One would expect that civil society approaches to peacebuilding would have, through design, avoided this trap, and would have opened up areas of cooperation and reform outside the stranglehold of ethnic politics groups and elite politics. Yet, the difficulties of developing a sustainable civil society at the grass-roots level suggests that derailing the liberal peace is not just the preserve of the political elites: individuals too, have opted out of the process in very self-conscious terms because it has little resonance with their own political, cultural, and historical identities, needs, and objectives. This is doubly interesting because from a Western perspective it is generally assumed that the Balkans are not subject to the kinds of alterity that other, non-Western conflict zones might be, and so should be more suited to liberal peacebuilding. This failure has arisen partly because the political process has not responded to its own weaknesses and ethnic relations remain very tense, but mainly because the peace dividend in terms of prosperity, employment, representation and recognition has been very limited. In short, a social contract has not developed, and all the entities see their identities as separate and under threat from the others at the multiple levels of government in the state, entities, and federation – which has also filtered down into civil society. Many civil society groups see the peace that the internationals are offering, as ambiguous and less sophisticated in terms of social justice – a major aspiration of many – than the socialist model of politics that existed before the war.[20]

If civil society groups or NGOs, some of them brought into being by donor funds, are critical of the peacebuilding agenda that has been exported into Bosnia Herzegovina, this should be a source of significant concern for internationals. Instead, the latter tend to adopt positions critical of civil society actors and elites rather than reflecting on the compatibility of their own agendas with those of civil society, or the local-local beneath. Thus, this discourse on peacebuilding has been framed by an unwillingness of internationals to move beyond their elite level partners who have vested interests in representing politics in ethnonational ways. This unwillingness is caused by the difficulty of moving beyond the liberal and Western conceptions of civil society at play. Yet it is here human rights and social justice come into being. Civil society requires, above all, participation.[21] This requires the injection of material resources and a sophisticated cultural understanding if international actors are to engage with and support another's civil society. The former without the latter would leave such engagement open to hegemonic discourses and to domination, which are naturally going to arouse opposition (as indeed they have in the Bosnian context),[22] whether in terms of direct or hidden forms of obstructiveness and resistance.

Very similar problems have emerged when compared to states like Cambodia or Timor Leste in the disjuncture between the international and local, especially in terms of needs and culture. Indeed, it seems that the dynamic introduced by the interaction between them rests on international assumptions of only very small levels of responsibility directly for the post-conflict individual, or that any responsibility can best be met at an institutional level. Internationals from this perspective have a duty of tutelage and training rather than empathy, care and understanding, the former being the marked characteristic of liberal peace-building in Bosnia Herzegovina, where these deficiencies are very apparent and widely commented upon.

Of course, this is not to say that all peacebuilding, statebuilding, or activities of all peacebuilders and officials betray such difficulties. It is also apparent that some donors and internationals are realising the limitations of their actions and increasingly thinking in terms of more engagement in Bosnia Herzegovina with local culture as a way of understanding the roots of the conflict and the sites of power or peaceful social practices that might be supported. 'Local ownership' has become a key phrase. However, the period of experimentation that occurred before this realisation indicates that the internationals' starting point was their own experience, culture, and ideology, and its penetration of the local. Moderating this only occurs when these strategies have failed, and the costs of such experiments are generally ignored. Those more sensitive internationals who are aware of such problems tend to be ignored.[23]

The donors are at fault here, as whilst they might unconsciously or consciously employ the rhetoric of liberal peace and statebuilding, their emphasis is often focused on tangible and prompt returns on their 'investments'. This generates competition for resources and creates a highly exclusive and specialised environment that probably excludes exactly the individuals and groups that it was designed to include, whilst erecting even more barriers to social inclusion. It also creates a short-term NGO community that lurches between fashionable projects, where donors, not the actors on the ground set the agenda.[24] This undermines longer term projects, based upon the complexities of the local (as opposed to the reductive forms of Western governance and management techniques). Ultimately, as many analysts even within the orthodoxy now agree, this degrades the local self-sustainability of civil society, inducing a difficult mix of disillusionment and dependence, and maintaining poverty which prevents the actualisation of rights. The economic project of liberalisation in Bosnia

Herzegovina has negatively affected pensions, social welfare and healthcare, compared to before the war, and the insertion of neoliberalism into the peace process (much as in Iraq) has caused opposition to the overall liberal peace agenda.[25] This also has a wider effect on the accountability of peace and the structure of peacebuilding than even the presence of the OHR might have suggested, in that actors and agendas are centrally uncoordinated, often unaware of each other's programmes or indeed where they fit into the 'big picture' of liberal peacebuilding.[26]

A realisation of these problems has emerged in certain quarters at least: in 2008 SIDA (Swedish International Development Cooperation Agency), for example, funded three Swedish NGOs that worked in the field in Bosnia Herzegovina. They were not project funded and were in long-term partnerships with local NGOs, often deploying ethnographic methods and expertise rather than solely managers, administrators, and officials.[27]

Nevertheless, the international community has been quick to blame the NGO community and some local actors for civil society problems by suggesting that the availability of funding streams promotes 'forum shopping' which demonstrate 'the mentality of the NGOs as self-serving.'[28] This may well be the case, but this is also caused by donor strategies, and even though such organisations may give lip-service to their expectations, they often carry on regardless with their own projects – in disguised form perhaps. Where organisations are not able to compromise, feeling that this may undermine their integrity, or indeed their own understandings of what peacebuilding may mean, they are often forced 'underground' where they continue their work in a subsistence mode.[29] The fact that they are even able to do this is very significant, as Chapters 5 and 6 will illustrate.

Even so this suggests that internationals and donors in Bosnia Herzegovina regard the local as merely a site for their social engineering projects associated with the liberal peace, though some, such as SIDA may now have begun to try to understand the local rather than manipulate it. At the same time, they have failed to recognise the important of basic human needs at the local level, and see the local through a lens which aspires to freedom, self-government, and self-determination but also fails to allow a divergence between local and international institutional aspirations. Where this divergence produces tensions with democratisation processes, with the attempt to construct a rule of law, human rights, and free markets, internationals tend to revert to ignoring or romanticising the local rather than engaging with it. Thus, coercion and conditionality appears to be an international default – the unbecoming face – of liberal peacebuilding, where the local's complexities are partially exposed but not understood and at best seen as a site for biopolitical[30] forms of governmentality to be applied. Where the local's 'simplicities' are the object of international valourisation, their romanticisation ensues – as with their common assertion of the fixity of ethnic identity in the Balkans. Where their complexities are avoided, a demonisation through rationalisation and simplification occurs, which follows similar patterns. Where international shortcomings in terms of dealing with needs, welfare and identity or cultural matters are exposed, the liberal peace retreats into such positions in order to enable its more coercive side to be deployed rather than to admit its own inadequacies. This might be better known as conditionality ('negative' of 'positive') or even 'transformation'.

In the context of Bosnia Herzegovina, this displays the inherent confusion in liberal peace as it began to take the form of statebuilding as well as the divergence between the agendas of the internationals partnered even with pliable political actors and NGOs. It is illustrative of the stalemate liberal peacebuilding and statebuilding finds itself in because of its low levels of local legitimacy. While the state is assumed to have been built for the benefit of its citizens and for a vibrant civil society to emerge, the state has become the beginning and the end of the peace, owned by internationals in an ever shifting alliance with locally entrenched elites in a political contest over the nature of peace and the state, rather than with its citizens. The failure of civil society is not just a failure of local communities and citizens to avoid conflict, but also of the international project of a distinct but partially integrated patchwork of communities with differing levels of sovereignty linked to their state and to each other for Bosnia Herzegovina. This latter perspective replicates governmentality rather than peacebuilding, and indeed governmentality requires a romanticisation of the local to occur in order to maintain its legitimacy amongst its external constituencies.[31] As a consequence, local actors, beyond or beneath 'civil society' remain marginalised from the state and from each other, partly because of the reductionist, simplified, instrumentalised and essentialised focus on the state and on ethnicity (perhaps as opposed to the complexities of everyday life in a pluralist polity). The focus on civil society is heavily constrained by the problem-solving, institutionalist, and neoliberal myopia of internationals, undermining the liberal project itself. The culture of liberal peace/statebuilding that has emerged has undermined its own claims of an emancipatory potential, partly because of its development as a vehicle of conditionality. It was telling that Ashdown, after years spent as the OHR's Special Representative with far-reaching powers, was warning by 2008 that Bosnia Herzegovina was in danger of collapse after more than a decade of liberal peacebuilding and statebuilding.[32] The local has become a laboratory for international peacebuilding and statebuilding with all of its biases, rather than a site of politics and everyday life, constituting a local and contextual form of peace.

That civil society in Bosnia Herzegovina has been slow to develop is only part of the picture, however. A pluralist version of civil society certainly exists in a few adventurous NGOs (e.g. the Nansen Dialogue Centre for one). Mono-ethnic civil society, on the other hand is far more visible partly because of the focus of international rhetoric. This is what internationals mean when they claim that 'civil society in Bosnia Herzegovina does not work.'[33] In response, internationals initially endeavoured to increase their influence in Bosnia Herzegovina by effectively denying self-government via interventionary practices – until recently. Though this has been in order to increase the stability and reach of the liberal state, effectively this undermined civil society because the space for independent development was reduced by the intrusion of political elites, local and international.[34] Later, the same mistake was made by the EU Commission and the Special Representative in an attempt to promote the independent local implementation of the SAPs. Add to this the lack of cultural engagement, and perhaps most importantly, the difficult economic situation and the lack of welfare provision, and there has been little space for civil society and the all-important liberal social contract to emerge.

One could argue, as many mainstream commentators have, that this is due to elite stagnation and local disinterest, or that international statebuilding processes are inefficient and ill-coordinated, but on the right track. But the inherently distant relationship between statebuilding in Bosnia Herzegovina and the everyday lives of its citizens indicate deeper problems. Although the rhetoric of the internationals is occasionally positive about the development of civil society,[35] it is clear that it is subject to a lack of committed participation from both the political elites and individuals and their subversion of international assistance to create new local elites.[36]

Such blind spots are perhaps most evident in international assessments of Bosnia Herzegovina's economic progress, another crucial aspect of the attempt to build a liberal state and a 'viable' civil society in which rights are meaningful. According to the World Bank and UNDP, since the end of the conflict Bosnia Herzegovina has returned to pre-war levels of development (a claim which is an anathema to local actors who remember the safety nets available under the old socialist system).[37] This represents a neoliberal focus as opposed to a social democratic framework of analysis. Economic growth is fragile and key reforms have been blocked mainly at the political level. Pugh suggests that this economic change is '... adversely affecting economically vulnerable sectors of society':[38] it represents international social engineering in which the liberal peace has become an end in itself. Predictably, the economic space provided by the introduction of capitalism and the levels of individual empowerment provided by neoliberalism has led to the hijack and monopoly of economic resources by war elites and ethnically defined political elites to the detriment of the economic development of society. Perhaps worse has been the undermining of the previous systems of social welfare, for pensions and for healthcare, which in a post-conflict setting would have played a valuable role in stabilising social relations. Generally speaking, internationals have seen it as too costly to invest in these areas even though this forces people into the grey market, which also undermines attempts to develop a viable economy in neoliberal terms at least.

As a result there has been throughout the peacebuilding/statebuilding process a growing gap between rich and poor. The estimated unemployment rate varies: in 2006 was estimated at 30 per cent,[39] and according to the World Bank 40 per cent of the economy is unregulated.[40] Others argued that unemployment was about 42 per cent (though World Bank personnel were quick to point out that this was only 18 per cent if one took into account the grey economy). This raises questions regarding the suitability of this model. Indeed, it has been asked if such a model '... would work in Texas.'[41] Half the population have also been living on a minimum wage in order to avoid a 68 per cent income tax, effectively opting out of economic development.[42] Local economic advisors suggest that international investment has opened economic competition but without protecting local economy and business.[43] Instead, it has created a false economy which not only expects poor or unemployed individuals to survive on their own but also to make extensive contributions to the growth of the economy without their having a real a stake in it, and even more implausibly to compete in global markets. This disconnection between the development of pluralism and the lack of social justice and a safety net underlines the ambivalence of the liberal peacebuilding project in Bosnia Herzegovina, derived in part from its use as a vehicle for neoliberalism and from its governmental distancing of needs, local society, and cultural dynamics.

Such discussions are not just a product of 'distant' academic or policy analysis, but are present in local critiques of the peacebuilding practices which are now emerging.[44] As the OSCE has pointed out, there are major issues with the gap between domestic and international standards, the criteria for granting assistance, and the identification of which groups are vulnerable in Bosnia Herzegovina.[45] This is so even after fifteen years of international engagement. Yet, even these claims are based upon the idea that standards are set internationally and that those standards provide adequate cultural and welfare resources, which is clearly not the case. A consideration of the local which is actually multi-dimensional rather than merely reductionist, would provide valuable insights through which a more sophisticated civil peace might emerge. This would, perhaps in the context of the embedding of the region in the EU, allow for a more hybridised form of state, more conducive to a local understanding of the patterns of identity, of culture and of historical resonances, and of needs as well as rights. From this perspective it is the international romanticisation of Bosnia Herzegovina and Herzegovina as a space of conflict and violence, of acute ethnonationalism, as lacking the capacities and qualities needed for compromise and for liberal politics, which has prevented local actors from being able to engage sufficiently with each other, with donors, the EU, and with their political apparatus to bring about a sustainable peace. Liberal peacebuilding or statebuilding has ultimately been disabling, rather than enabling, and from a local perspective represents an international ignorance of local politics, history, experiences, and embedded methods and dynamics, as well as needs issues which provide conflict and division with much of its traction (See Appendix 2 for an elaboration of local versus international views). Thus, when international actors talk of local pathologies and an incapacity to reform, or to make the necessary decisions to do so, they are encountering the political dimensions of peacebuilding. Instead of rejecting these, romanticising or demonising the local, and mythologizing the liberal peace, it might be better to engage with these dynamics, and to be more open to the modified forms of peace emerging, as well as to engage with the complex issue of how such hybridity may also maintain the claimed integrity of the liberal peace model.

Kosovo: from standards before status to a unilateral declaration of independence

In Kosovo international actors (including the EU, OSCE, UN, and NATO) took control of government, security, the economy, and a broad range of policy areas in order to facilitate pluralism and also to create a liberal framework to empower that pluralism. To some degree they replicated the liberal peacebuilding and statebuilding process that had developed in Bosnia Herzegovina after Dayton. This most difficult of tasks was made far more complex by the fact that Kosovo's status was heavily disputed by Kosovo Albanians and Serbs, and that a parallel underground system had long been in existence, before and after the arrival of UNMIK in 1999 and its partners. Though the new mission adopted the guise of statebuilding with the possibility of EU accession in mind, the very concept of statehood was one of the sources of the conflict.

Even so, when the SSRG arrived for one of the first meetings with the representatives of the new provisional institutions for self-government, it was clear that self-appointed elites had taken charge, that civil society was not really represented, that internationals were naïve about the local political situation, and the local elites were intent on taking advantage of their naivety.[46] The internationals assumed that Kosovo could not become a state without international support, or without international consensus, and to some degree that local compliance would be forthcoming, even if not completely necessary. The development of the 'standards before status' argument meant to both hold back and to encourage Kosovan desire to form a liberal state, was indicative of this paradox. Yet, the hidden registers of local politics – which might be called the infrapolitics of peacebuilding – ultimately led not merely to stalemate or obstacles in the liberal peacebuilding process, but to statehood and independence. This was based mainly on a nationalist framework derived from a specific set of cultural assumptions though it also represented an infrapolitical (read local and informal) capacity to deal with pressing needs issues in the absence of a state able to provide public services, and an international community focus on rights and institutions. Independence came about unilaterally, despite significant local problems and some international opposition, and the internationally prescribed liberal standards not having been unequivocally met.[47]

After more than a decade of international engagement, ethnic divisions between Serbs and Kosovans are still deep, there has been limited progress on the economic front, and regular complaints about the historical and cultural ignorance and lack of respect of internationals. The apparatus of the modern state is now present, even if it is mainly controlled by one or other ethnic group, depending on the area. Even the issue of statehood has not been resolved, in that the unilateral declaration of independence (UDI) from the Kosova dominated government in early 2008 has been accepted by various states, including the US and many EU states, and has equally been rejected by others, notably Serbia and Russia. As a result there has been a further strengthening of ethnic division and the 'enclavisation' of various communities in Kosovo contrary to the liberal and pluralist project of Western actors and international institutions. Many local actors have also long argued for a pluralisation of politics. Yet, the entire process of statebuilding has been contradictorily predicated upon ethnic division at the same time as respect for pluralism. These foci have outweighed any concern for the interplay of cultural identities, or for welfare and needs, which might have been used to avoid a form of nationalist statebuilding. This has undermined attempts to overcome the significant ethnic divides, and encouraged the continuing ethnicisation of politics and institutions. In the light of the skill with which the peacebuilding process in Kosovo was captured by the Kosovan Albanian ethnonationalist agenda, the state which emerged reflects a very compromised version of the liberal peace and in which ethnic reconciliation is unlikely to occur.

Internationals have perceived the roots of the Kosovo conflict to lie in the struggle for power between ethnicities (Albanian and Serb), represented by elites and states.[48] This is fuelled by conflicting structures and historical narratives, national discourses and opposing identities,[49] territorialised and historicised in order to maintain implacable enmity between the Serb and Albanian communities. These are compounded by familiar socio-economic issues, discrimination and marginalisation of minorities, underdevelopment, poverty and crime.[50] It is no wonder that UNDP was soon complaining that a 'democratic deficit' was undermining the very institutions that the internationals were trying to build,[51] that voter turnout was declining and that individuals felt they could not influence decision-making.[52] This was particularly important for Kosovo Serbs, who boycotted elections and refused to present candidates or take up their constitutionally allotted political posts in the Assembly. This confirmed the international view of an ethnically driven conflict and their efforts to invoke liberal standards before status issues could be settled.

Unwittingly in some aspects, and in others with complicity, the peacebuilding mission rapidly slid into a statebuilding mission in which the political withdrawal (or lack of consent) of Serb actors enabled the Kosovo Albanian monopoly of political power and the maintenance of their nationalist project.[53] Local claims for autonomy and international understandings of local ownership facilitated this process, given that they also resonated to a large degree with international expectations for an independent state to emerge as a result of statebuilding processes in place. As a result, in acting to develop democratic principles and accountability UNMIK effectively reinforced the claim of the Kosovo Albanians for a separate state. Liberal peacebuilding became statebuilding and national liberation, even if in exclusive form. This affected the democratic institutions, prejudiced the outcome of status talks, and implicitly supported the unilateral declaration of independence in 2008, even with so many issues still unresolved. Statehood was achieved via an ethnonationalist project, deploying the expertise and resources of the very internationals which were supposed to be guiding the development of the new liberal peace. Instead the tables were turned because the internationals were not able to engage or even understand local political debates and processes, or see how they were being maintained with international complicity.

Local co-option of peacebuilding by the majority group which had the best access to the international community of peacebuilding was the dominant local response. This harnessed the experience of the Kosovo Albanian pre-war parallel institutions and 'civil' society, which had developed as exclusively ethnic organisations in order to provide governance, services, and autonomy to the Kosovo Albanian community under Serbian rule. Some have argued this led to the LDK resistance movement taking over civil society and the emerging government.[54] This was compounded by the post-communist culture of distrust of central government, which also bred a tradition of non-communication and non-cooperation with central government structures, today particularly relevant for the Serb communities.[55] UDI now maintains the mono-ethnic nature of the Kosovo Albanian project in the new state (although many of its supporters argue that it is indeed pluralist and that the onus is on the Serb communities to cooperate), to some degree irritates regional stability (having a knock-on impact in the region for other secessionist impulses), and it has reiterated the division of local communities.

Even so, a form of civil society has burgeoned due to the influx of international funding and NGOs, though this has been affected by the fickle nature of donor priorities.[56] This means, as in other cases, that most NGOs run short-term projects without strong constituencies, and these have tended to dissolve or become inactive after donor funds have been spent.[57] Thus civil society is represented by a range of artificial and ever-changing actors, which are temporary and do not, overtly at least, represent the range of views amongst the different communities, but rather the agendas of internationals. This casts doubt on the plausibility of a pluralist civil society especially as donor funds have tended to go to one community, and anyway were reduced due to the problems caused by local and international positions on final status, and after the international community began 'drawing down'.[58]

A common view amongst internationals has been that there is no real civil society present – a classic international formulation of incapable local agency. Thus, it was internationals themselves who constituted civil society, and perhaps were somewhat careless about, or naïve towards, the issues of who would constitute it, whether local people were actually involved, and to what degree (as senior UNMIK and donor officials later admitted). The development of civil society was thus monopolised by foreign internationals and exploited by local, often ethnic, entrepreneurs. The post-conflict individual and community was largely ignored or included only notionally. Civil society emerged either according to a mixture of international prescriptions about who and what should be involved, or local ethnic divisions and agencies. Because internationals failed to recognise the existence of a Kosovo Albanian parallel society they instead concentrated on creating new NGOs and institutions in their desire to create a liberal civil society rather than working with what already existed. This initially led to a flood of foreign relief workers and the marginalisation of local staff and indigenous NGOs. The UN argued that this was necessary because of the ethnicised and politicised nature of the parallel society, though Holohan argues it was more to do with the 'old' UN attitude of colonial superiority.[59]

As local communities reacted to this and a 'Kosovanisation' campaign began to emerge (reflecting many such campaigns to localise the work of international donors and agencies elsewhere) internationals began to respond by employing more local employees in order to train them. Because of this a new dynamic began to emerge. As international actors sought to enable rather than disable local agency in response to this critique (most violently expressed in the Kosovo Albanian riots of 2004, 2006, and 2008), their strategies inadvertently supported the parallel project for a Kosovan state. Internationals' knowledge of the local, its dynamics, agencies, identities and politics was so limited by the blind spots created by the liberal/neoliberal discourses of peace that they practically handed the state to the majority community, risking its integrity as well as that of the peace that they had spent years trying to make.

Predictably, a pluralist civil society has not emerged as a result, and this has been exacerbated by the internationals' often repeated belief that many NGOs running multi-ethnic projects are actually exploiting funding streams and are only involved 'just to get funding',[60] as well as the imbalance between Serb and Albanian NGOs, and the de facto division. As Kosovo Albanian actors have effectively dominated political institutions and access to internationals, they came to represent their own civil society, while the Serbs were portrayed as representing the 'uncivil' for reasons of recent historical events and bias. The Serb communities' agendas became far more distant from the internationals than the Albanian agenda. Those civil society actors who were compliant in following donor preferences also often supported the broader move towards independence dominated by Kosovo Albanians, and most see little contradiction in this. Here local agencies were expressed and played out in complex and hidden ways, playing on Western sympathy for the Kosovo Albanian cause, as well as the normative expectations of liberal peacebuilding. The latter community, with its experience of parallel politics and institutions under the shadow of the Milosevic regime used this to maintain their nationalist agenda. The infrapolitics of peacebuilding in Kosovo have consequently led to the contemporary situation where a state came into being despite significant local and international divisions, in a startling display of local, but hidden agency. Yet it was a state which reflected a deep ambivalence about liberal rights, norms, and institutions. Such dynamics have had a significant impact on the development of human rights, despite the extensive programmes and political rhetoric (both international and local), and was the central focus for international and local criticisms of both the UNMIK and PISG leadership early on. UNMIK admitted that their involvement unintentionally affected the attempt to create a human rights equilibrium in favour of the Kosovo Albanian majority.[61] Again, this was useful in building their case for statehood.

Perhaps as importantly, in terms of everyday living standards, the lack of engagement with welfare and needs meant that, with the economy remaining dependant on external support and remittances,[62] 37 per cent of the population under the poverty line,[63] and more than 40 per cent unemployment,[64] ordinary individuals could not take full advantage of the democratic process or the market in order to shape the outcome of the peacebuilding process in a pluralist sense.

Yet, the need to be aligned with the emerging state meant that what resources there were to be redistributed tend not to reach Serb communities. Instead the majority mobilised according to a nationalist agenda, excluding the relatively weak minority communities while claiming that there was space for their political representation. The prevalent informal economy became an important basis for the support of the Kosovo Albanian project of statehood.

The attempt to develop a rule of law also presented an array of difficult technical problems because of the existence of parallel structures and multiple versions stemming from local custom, from each community, and from the former Belgrade model,[65] and the parallel societies this represented.[66] This is partly because cultural and historical barriers in Kosovo preclude human rights from being understood as individual rights, but instead as collective or group rights.[67] International actors have been unable to convince local communities that mono-ethnic units are less safe than human rights or minority rights regimes in a multi-ethnic unit.[68] Such local perspectives are buttressed by view amongst the local human rights community that the internationals have violated human rights simply because of their continuing presence, by holding reserved powers, by being unaccountable,[69] and until the declaration of UDI by denying the majority community control of a sovereign state. This played into the hands of those who controlled the infrapolitical aspects of peacebuilding and confirmed the Kosovo Albanian state project. The various forms of the liberal peace's inability to engage with the culture or welfare supported this.

As a result, neither civil society nor a civil peace has developed in a pluralist or sustainable manner. The unilaterally declared state represents the paradox of infrapolitical agency, resistance, and peacebuilding, as well as the role of international actors in liberal peacebuilding. The latter's blindspots for local agency, needs, culture, and politics in lieu of the prescriptive version of the liberal peace have spurred the evolution of statehood in the very contexts where the state and its territory are contested. This has been rights based, alluding to the way in which liberal rights might be read as majoritarian and indicate self-determination. This imbalance illustrates how liberal peacebuilding, even on the scale and depth employed in Kosovo, is susceptible to local co-option, and how local agencies exploit its weaknesses in order to make space for political agendas which may not be commensurate with its praxis, reproducing exclusion (even if they do not necessarily intend to do as some Kosovan Albanian politicians certainly did not). They achieved this by deploying the language of the liberal peace while maintaining their own interests – in this case an ethnonationalist agenda – in a discourse which they claim is universal and open to all citizens equally. In doing so, they have exploited both the contextual naïvety of international actors, and their unwillingness to use the embroynic institutions of state to redistribute resources. Thus, international ignorance and local inequality provided the conditions in which nationalist rhetoric remained both convincing and effective, mirroring similar dynamics in Bosnia Herzegovina.

This raises serious questions about international rhetoric about local 'ownership' of or 'participation' in the peacebuilding process, again present in Kosovo, especially after the emergence of the Kosovanisation campaign. The role of international actors in not engaging with local needs, welfare, or culture, enabled local comparisons with colonial practice amongst the Kosovo Albanian community.[70] This created space for and enabled a range of local political agencies to maintain the ethnic divide and simultaneously contest ownership over the soon-to-emerge state, as well as over the territory it controlled. Local responses thus indicate more capacity than internationals supposed. Kosovo Albanians were soon infiltrating the peacebuilding process in far greater numbers than Serbs or other minorities, and its so-called 'Albanianisation' became indicative of both local desire for custodianship and international disquiet about their own role. Replacing international capacity with local meant hoping both Albanian and Serb agree on power sharing, and trusting local actors to take on such roles in good faith. But Kosovo Albanians were rapidly replacing internationals in positions from where they could influence the peace process. This subverted the liberal peace agenda by solidifying two parallel societies, which is often a consequence of majority rule,[71] supported by donor governments.

This illustrates another paradoxical outcome of the liberal peace project and its negation of the local: while the ideals of local ownership and agency are thought to lead to a more sustainable peace, they also entail compromises on the liberal peace model and its norms, and a loss of control of peacebuilding, which is taken over by the multiple dynamics of local political agencies. They may replicate local power relations rather than a transformative project for emancipation, or they may do both. Ultimately the Kosovo Albanian approach before the war of developing parallel institutions cast a long shadow over the peacebuilding process and became the basis for their response to international prescriptions, as well as an expression of the infrapolitics of peacebuilding. Eventually, it might be said that these parallel institutions became those of the self-declared state by 2008, developing from the subtle and extremely effective Kosovo Albanian co-option of liberal peacebuilding. It soon became the Serbs' turn to develop their own parallel institutions after UDI, starting a new cycle of ethnic competition and sovereignty claims, which may spread across the Balkans if not resolved.[72] So far, the prospects for a self-sustaining peace emerging from these hybrid dynamics appear limited.

Timor Leste: international sovereignty and the failure of the social contract

The history of the Timor conflict is well rehearsed, but suffice it to say that Indonesian withdrawal and the conflict that ensued between pro-independence and pro-Indonesian supports, provided the platform for a standard liberal state-building programme. This focussed on establishing a neoliberal state in one of the world's remotest and poorest, territories. The internationals, and the World Bank in particular, focused on nation-building. In the period from the Indonesian military withdrawal in 1999 to its independence in May 2002, when 'draw down' began, the focus was on institutional development and on establishing liberal governance from the top down, ignoring the very politicised and active citizens of the new state, who were increasingly aware of how the new context represented their needs and rights, and how their new state and international patronage did not measure well against such standards. Indeed, with a large proportion of the country's population being very young, unemployed, unsettled or dislocated, pressure to make the peace dividend meaningful for them was immense, yet more or less ignored. Only around a third of donor funds for Timor remain in the county.[73]

This mission was focussed on statebuilding rather than the implementation of a peace agreement, one that is much further along the continuum that developed in the 1990s – from elite compromise and democratic institutions to the broader approaches required to develop a fully liberal state. The process saw the UN act as a sovereign government, and then, with a Timorese government in place, international actors tutored the new state while under the illusion that a sustainable peace had already been created which had been widely accepted at both the grass-roots and elite levels. The liberal peace's local recipients were romanticised and it is unsurprising that there was also a disregard for local welfare. In Timor Leste's case, independence and progress in political governance was deemed sufficient to withdraw much of the UN mission from 2002 to 2006. The key problems of poverty and unemployment had not been addressed, despite the internationals' withdrawal, indicating that IOs, NGOs, Agencies, and IFIs did not see these problems as a major threat to political stability. They were soon to be proved wrong: their implicit consigning of the poor and unemployed to poverty, albeit peaceful, soon proved to have major implications for democratisation and for stability. The cultural assumption that political rights come before economic and social rights proved to be dangerously flawed, if not disingenuous. This indicates a romanticisation of the local and indigenous in order to take away agency and insert another. Yet, the signs of a breakdown were present soon after the UN initially left in 2002, and the near collapse of the state for political and socio-economic reasons in 2006 should not have been a surprise. Indeed, the HDI index has only marginally improved since 1999 (see Appendix 1).

It is widely thought that the UN left too soon, but of course it was under great pressure to do so, locally, from elites anxious to exercise sovereignty, and internationally for financial reasons. From the liberal peace perspective, however, the local signs of this were invisible. Yet, socio-economic factors in particular were clearly recognised in the UN Secretary General's report soon after the 2006 collapse. This report focused in particular on poverty and deprivation, unemployment and a lack of opportunity.[74] In other words, an understanding was belatedly beginning to emerge at the international level that the state was meaningless if it did not mean something in material terms to its citizens. Often, alien notions of rights, and promises of future prosperity were simply not enough, and indeed betrayed a simplistic attitude to the capacity and agency of local actors even when faced with the (relative) material, normative, and technological might of international actors. This is partly why local actors, from government to grass roots took on an increasing role in negotiating new 'country poverty reduction' strategies over time.

A familiar international complaint has been that locals could not contribute to the statebuilding exercise meaningfully because of a lack of capacity. A counter-complaint has been that internationals tend to ignore what local capacity there is.[75] However, there was an awareness that there needed to be support for indigenous peace processes by international actors, particularly because there had been little effort to deal with social justice and welfare issues.[76] Yet, internationals and the UN assumed that the wide array of local actors from the local-local, from civil society, and from the elites, could not participate in governance or development fully because they did not have the skills, experience, or language to cooperate over the implementation of this myth.

This meant that Timor became a *terra nullius* where cultural considerations or local consent – the content of everyday life itself – was less significant than results in building the institutional, security, political and economic architecture of a liberal peace. To paraphrase a well-known dictum of an earlier era in IR (International Relations), form and function had become disconnected by a narrow set of prescriptions about peace, and in the functions of the state. This somewhat Orientalist mindset came about not because a directly colonial intent, but because of a reliance on assumptions of the universality and superiority of the 'liberal' in all contexts. This was effectively a colonial approach to the liberal peace as a form of hegemony. It allowed the UN and other internationals to claim and establish a sovereign authority, while searching out, manufacturing, and forming alliances with local political elites. UN governance was developed to replace lost or non-existent political capacity. But it is questionable whether this improved upon 'bare life' for Timor's citizens.

Indeed, the 'lack of local capacity' became a mantra that internationals deployed to legitimate their control of governance, as elsewhere. Local actors, who pointed instead to the many internationals' lack of local language skills, cultural understanding and empathy, and understanding of society, as well as inter-organisational competition and conflict, dispute this absence of course.[77] Translating these opposed views indicates the gap between the liberal and the local (in simple terms) and an inability to engage with the existing capacities of each. Given the relative resources available for liberal peacebuilding it is surprising that such antipathy towards it from supposedly powerless local actors on such grounds was able to block its prescriptions.

During the UN-led operation, political, cultural and economic problems culminated in a 'Timorisation campaign' in which local actors called for more control of their affairs (reminiscent of a Kosovonisation campaign for similar reasons). But this (as in Kosovo) was essentially a movement aimed at reclaiming the powers that the internationals had taken on relating to governance for local elites. It was translated by most internationals into a claim for more local ownership. Indeed, some international personnel, famously Jarat Chopra, left the UN operation in disgust at its inability to encounter and negotiate with the local on its own terms. He then published a series of critiques of the role of internationals calling for the transfer of more responsibility to local actors.[78] Instead of the liberal state accruing legitimacy in the eyes of the local population (or 'Timorisation')[79] the reverse had occurred. The implication of this adds weight to critiques of the ideological faith of that epoch in neoliberalism and liberal institutions even in such highly specialised transitional situations.

This connects with the accusations that have been levelled at statebuilding as neo-colonial, deferring self-government and self-determination until international actors are sure the liberal project will be taken up, as well as being economically predatory in that the costs of statebuilding are placed on the shoulders of those least able to bear them (while elites often profit from deregulation and corruption). Ultimately, it implies the construction of illiberal forms of state, absent the very social contract upon which legitimacy is taken to rest. In such circumstances, local reactions are inevitable, especially if the social contract is not replaced to some extent at least by a local contract with international actors. It was partly from this experience that the call for more local participation in, and ownership of peace-building, emerged. In Timor's case, as in Kosovo, it was ably led by some of the political elites.

Even so, what became statebuilding in Timor emphasised top-down peace-building and governance at the expense of bottom-up peacebuilding, social justice, and welfare. This imbalance was rationally constructed upon the edifice of Western experiences of statebuilding. It allowed the lessons of liberalism in the West to be ignored and an idealised form of the liberal/neoliberal state to be exported as if it were an uncontested formula for peace. Ultimately, in Timor, this marginalised the political experience, history, culture, and needs of its subjects. Its focus on secular, public spaces for politics, on marketisation, on rights over needs, and on various institutions and programmes, effectively disenfranchised the vast bulk of the population, often through strategies of romanticisation.

The violent events of May 2006 underlined the weakness of the process of statebuilding and its associated knowledge systems, which severed or blocked their connection with its subjects and their politics, ignored the cultural priorities of local communities and failed to address their socio-economic concerns directly. It has been blind to the obvious point that politically free peoples cannot enjoy their freedom without material and cultural spaces and resources. Where these are not distributed, a more predatory market, grey, black, or violent develops, which also provides opportunities for political elites to mobilise in ways which reify their own exclusive power rather than that of the state's citizenry, via representative processes. Elites may actually lose out because of democratisation, so they may be inclined to create tension and consolidate their positions. Indeed, a struggle for self-determination at multiple political levels does not automatically end because liberal statebuilding has begun and claims it offers peace and prosperity. Thus, in Timor it became apparent that international actors not only romanticised local counterparts and communities in ways designed to downplay their material needs and politics, but also romanticised their own capacity. The myth of the capacity of the liberal peace was gathering momentum even as it limitations were being made apparent.

The then president, Xanana Gusmao, was aware of the problems that had emerged with the liberal peace and many of the dynamics mentioned above. In one of the most explicit documents in existence from the policy world on the nature of peace he argued that the experiences of peacebuilding in Timor Leste indicated that peace was not just a normative aim but a basic human right that involved preventing not just international and civil violence, but an engagement with socio-economic deprivation, a lack of development, and an engagement with the experience of recipient communities on the part of internationals.[80] This argument neatly underlined the latter's myopic vision of the liberal statebuilding project with regard to local needs, identity and culture, and local responses to such narrowness, which also maintains a liberal-local division of inequality in rights and needs.

As in Cambodia, it might be thought that the NGO and humanitarian sector should be able to engage with such issues as they are more closely involved in issues related to everyday life. In particular, local NGOs in Timor, many of which have worked in parallel with the UN, UNDP, and World Bank, have long tended to confirm criticism of the agencies and IFIs as not being concerned (until recently at least) with short and medium term needs and welfare issues, and also of ignoring local cultural norms and expectations in their endeavours to import the liberal peace.[81] Some quite radical NGOs have found themselves marginalised from the mainstream humanitarian space because they resisted such mantras, and argued that international actors tended to ignore ordinary people and their political positions as well as everyday needs. Such marginalisation has significant financial costs for those organisations that opt out of donor streams.[82] Indeed, even if international NGO staff working in Timor position themselves (as some have done) within a more anthropological version of peacebuilding, working in local-local organisations and adopting local perceptions of what should be done, they then find it hard to draw on funding. Some have adopted this more localised position over many years of work and have retained access to international funding, of course.[83]

But the main dynamic is one of a lack of consultation between international and locals, except in certain specific elite or national level venues. Even locally based international actors tend to focus on the sheer scale of the development problem NGOs are attempting to ameliorate, and accuse the agencies and IFIs of doing too little, generally too late, of being wasteful and excessively bureaucratic, and of erecting barriers to local participation through the latter. This indicates a romanticisation of the Timor context (in its diversity) in international analyses, which betrays a perception that local issues, whether needs, culture, custom or identity, are secondary to the institutional framework of the state and the market. Although this is partly understandable, given that resources are stretched and coordination is difficult for internationals in an environment in which they understand little, it is not conducive to the liberal state they are supposed to be building. From a local perspective it has proven far from acceptable.

In 2007, UNDP reiterated the argument that the ongoing crisis was a result of poverty and unemployment (despite Timor's significant oil and gas resources).[84] Yet, the key to dealing with poverty was again placed at the door of the private sector while it was simultaneously acknowledged as unlikely to be resolved in the near future.[85] The focus of internationals has been on political and institutional reform, while the primary problem has been the lack of social welfare and the very culturalist rendering of poverty and politics in liberal form. This placed security, politics and institutions above all, and relegated poverty and needs to an insignificant position, because 'the Timorese people have always been poor' until such time as self-help strategies became plausible and the state was able to compete in the global market place.

After the near collapse of the state in 2006 the need to address poverty and even for a basic form of welfare was acknowledged. This included payments for veterans, OAPs, and job schemes. UNDP, for example, tried to address the issues raised by welfare in the context of the local 'cooperative culture', which pre-existed the new state, as well as the need for welfare institutions (which by 2008 the World Bank appeared to support). This continued to be tempered by the usual neoliberal prescriptions, however, though the financial collapse in the West in 2008 also coincided with the introduction of new welfare strategies to deal with social justice issues and to try to prevent youth and the unemployed from seeking alternative modes of engagement (often conflictual in form).[86] These strategies might be taken to represent a renewed attempt at social engineering in liberal form by international donors, but they also have widespread support at the grassroots level.[87]

Local attempts to make the economic aspect of peacebuilding more suitable were visible before 2006, with the drafting of the PRSP (Poverty Reduction Strategy Paper). This was drafted internally and included many Timorese voices. Indeed, in Gusmao's introduction to the plan, he claimed that thousands were consulted, '… from school children to elderly people …'. It focused on current needs and future generations, and highlighted his equation of peace with '… security, freedom, tolerance, equity, improved health, education, access to jobs and food security.'[88] Alkatari noted that 120 officials, representatives of the Church, civil society, NGOs and private and public sector groups, were involved.[89] Importantly, this document equated democracy with a 'vibrant traditional culture' and a sustainable environment, prosperity, equality, national unity, broad representation and decentralization, though it also repeated the usual concerns with efficiency and transparency, and focused on markets and the rule of law (without querying their in-built bias).[90] However, it also noted that development should be context, not donor driven; that both the market and the state had an important role to play; and that decentralisation and participation were crucial. It even proposed an Ombudsperson.[91] Even in the context of IMF and World Bank involvement, resistance was mounting against some of the externally driven dynamics of peacebuilding.

Timor has thus been caught between a tense representational relationship between internationals, and the government and its constituencies. If the latter are unable to form or operate in the context of a social contract there is in effect no liberal state, and politics mainly becomes of a predatory and competitive nature amongst elites, mollified only partly by international presence. This applies to both international and national actors. The experience in Timor illustrates that internationals are correct to see civil society as the key to a legitimate liberal state, but wrong to see it as existing mainly in a range of externally funded NGOs (even though they often discriminate against local NGOs). As a consequence, the statebuilding operation in Timor has been based on an attempt to construct an artificial and compliant civil society rather than on the actual local context in which communities and constituencies, and their needs, rights, and opportunities are present. Given that a social contract is the apparent goal of liberal statebuilders there was little choice after the violence and collapse of 2006 which brought the UN back to Timor, than to start the entire project from a reconstituted view of civil society and its needs and rights, rather than from the empty state and its institutions.

Yet this has occurred only partially, illustrating something of the inflexible culture of liberal peacebuilding itself, which has focused on the very conservative end of the liberal spectrum rather than the more emancipatory graduation of liberalism. This has occurred because security and risk tend to drive peacebuilding and statebuilding, using apparatus that has been designed with war rather than peace in mind. In addition, the very presence of internationals operating according to their own preconceptions about a peaceful state leads to a set of interactions that reconstitute an elite and class oriented political system, with internationals at the top followed by local elites, and then those who cooperate with the liberal peacebuilding mantra. As a result the virtual state of Timor Leste was dislocated from its actual everyday, historical and culture realities on the ground, needs and power asymmetries. The local was absent and civil society was seen as flimsy and dependent upon international benevolence. Yet, as I will argue in Chapter 6, it is becoming clear that there is far more peacebuilding capacity at the local level than international actors believed or could see.

Conclusion

This chapter's examination of four recent cases of liberal peacebuilding and the treatment of needs and culture therein is indicative of some of the key failings of liberal peacebuilding. All these cases illustrate the deficiencies of liberal peacebuilding and how needs and cultural issues both undermine and modify it. Six main points can be drawn out.

First, there is an absence of an international debate about culture, needs, welfare and the related agencies which might give meaning to the social contract, the liberal state and the rights frameworks which are deemed to be so essential to peace in an everyday setting. Secondly, it illustrates the bias and self-interest that has percolated through liberal peacebuilding via its negation of cultural agency, its construction of non-contextual notions of civil society, and its focus on neoliberal versions of peacebuilding as opposed even to probably more suitable social welfare oriented approaches. Thirdly, liberal peacebuilding romanticises the local rather than genuinely engaging with its potential for peacebuilding. Fourthly, the culture–welfare paradox removes agency at the same time as liberal peacebuilding claims to facilitate it. Fifthly, what is also clear is the degree to which making peace is a political activity in which supposedly weak local actors exercise their own peacebuilding agencies against what appear to be insurmountable odds. Sixthly and finally, the peace that has emerged in each case is in hybrid form, part liberal, part local, and represents only a mediated part of what internationals and a range of local actors aim for.

4 De-romanticising the local: implications for post-liberal peacebuilding

> ... a series of governmental rationalities overlap, lean on each other, and struggle with each other: art of government according to truth, art of government according to the rationality of the sovereign state, and art of government according to the rationality of economic agents, and more generally, according to the rationality of the governed themselves .... What is politics, in the end, if not both the interplay of these different arts of government with their different reference points and the debate to which these different arts of government give rise. It seems to me that it is here that politics is born.[1]

Introduction

In the examples referred to in the previous chapter the same mix of international certainty about the peace format to be applied and turning a blind eye to needs, welfare, cultural agency, and local agency, indicates a romanticisation of the local. Thus, a dominant political view of international actors, including within the UN, is to start from what internationals can achieve without requiring local engagement. Then internationally agreed strategies are passed down to field offices – but even these are focused on the national level as being representative of the local.[2] Accountability is to the internationals who define benchmarks and success, rather more indirectly to local actors – elites, civil society or local-local.[3] Sometimes this has been very disempowering for post-conflict citizens (as in Timor and Cambodia), or it has enabled political elites to continue their conflict-inducing activities (as in both Cambodia and Bosnia Herzegovina). Or it has mobilised both citizens and elites for a national project (regardless of whether it was fully inclusive) as in Kosovo. While security and rights provisions may improve, however, inequalities have remained or worsened. Liberal peacebuilding has been used to construct institutions and states rather than to engage with the core issues of the conflict and the everyday lives of the territory's inhabitants. This has failed to produce grounded legitimacy though it may have improved basic security. Even so, as in many parts of Latin America where indigenous movements have resisted the oppressive state more directly, the state is actually virtually absent and has not produced the outcomes external actors claimed and indeed on which much of the legitimacy of liberal peacebuilding rests.[4] Indeed, liberal peacebuilding is a direct challenge to the customary, community, and social rights that many people in post-conflict environments associate with political institutions.[5]

A hybrid form of politics and state has tended to emerge reflecting the power relations of internationals and local elites and some aspects of the liberal peace. It depends on international support, and on the re-establishment of sovereign boundaries – at best a very conservative or negative form of the liberal peace.

Yet, some local actors can only maintain their legitimacy by not having contact with internationals, who are beginning to realise that the reality of liberal peace-building is somewhat hubristic from their perspective and more a process of local negotiation or cooptation.[6] There have also been signs of more transformative and localised agencies emerging at the local-local level, sometimes in cooperation with certain national or elite actors or specific international actors or individuals working within them. These critical agencies for peacebuilding emerge in civil society, sometimes beneath it at the local-local level, sometimes via international support or sometimes autonomously, as hidden forms of resistance or forms of 'subsistence peacebuilding'. They represent the 'rationality of the governed' to some degree. This is discussed further in Chapters 5 and 6. This chapter begins to outline the dynamics which have made the local and context visible in peace-building and statebuilding endeavours, despite their predominant bias against this.

Implications of the liberal peace critique

Because of the instrumental certainties of the liberal peace model and the rejection of needs and cultural issues as key to peace, there has been only a limited realisation of the continuing depth of the conflict throughout the peace process in these cases. In the case of Kosovo this allowed the local co-option of the peace project and the continuing dispute over the state. In Bosnia, it can be seen in the weariness with national and international strategies that have prevented progress with especially problematic implications for social justice when citizens compare these with the old socialist system. In Cambodia it has allowed the continuation of elite and authoritarian predatory politics and state co-option, and in Timor it allowed the collapse of the new state (and its later rebirth). Many of the key values and institutions of the liberal peace have been overturned and diverted in these cases, ironically with international acquiescence. Their complicity was brought about by their avoidance of needs and culture and reliance on romanticisation to distance and govern without grounded legitimacy, even to create liberal political subjectivity, but with little engagement with deep-rooted problems or causal factors.

This raises the issue of what and whom this peace was for? Was it aimed at a regional order, or at the individuals and communities who comprised the state? Or is it more a matter of an imbalance between the two, that can be corrected by intervention and institutional conditionalities? Either way, the net result has been to support the power of nationalist, authoritarian, and inflexible elites, and to confirm rather Orientalist views of the local while confirming liberal stereotypes of the other – in this case directed at religious, cultural, ethnic, or post-socialist identities, while rejecting their political salience – rather than to address the socio-economic difficulties that were prevalent and might have been crucial in creating a social contract predicated upon liberal ideals. This has also rested on an attempt to confirm the international legitimacy and universality of the liberal peace model.

In both Cambodia and Timor Leste, the focus on institutions, rights, and neoliberal strategies have relegated the individual and community to a local that was far from congruent with everyday life, or indeed relevant to its local context. Governmental distancing of needs and culture is necessary for such strategies to maintain themselves. A locally self-sustaining peace seems far away given such strategies. Orientalism is rife in the assertion of no local capacity, and deviousness. There has been little recognition of any indigenous capacities for peace, at least until recently, and only then in more pluralist methodological circles. This represents the classic *res nullius / terra nullius* view that political and economic institutions are needed to save what there is of civil society from its incapacity, from its own elites and proclivities for poor governance. So far a liberal social contract and the local legitimacy of the state are limited, even if international support via agencies, international organisations, and NGOs appear to provide these externally.

Thus, in Kosovo the Albanian identity group became dominant not just because of its numerical advantage within the reconstituted territorial area, but because internationals deemed them more able to operate within liberal peace-building frameworks and their dominant conception of the local. This particular local, however, in return defined itself as a state, illustrating the depth of the conflict issues remaining in which the state is paradoxically used as a vehicle for resolving conflicts over sovereignty. Both the international and the local are romanticised in these cases, normally at the expense of non-state actors, the local-local below civil society, and especially the poor and already discriminated against. Local agency is accepted by internationals for geopolitical and expedient reasons, rather than for a genuine and pluralist engagement with post-conflict communities. Conversely they mythologise their own capacities. It is little wonder that 'Timorisation' or 'Kosovanisation' campaigns emerged amongst the so-called capacity-less local actors (or that an 'Afghanisation' campaign is also now being discussed amongst local counterparts of the statebuilding project in Afghanistan).

In these cases, the flaws and limitations of the capacity of internationals to reflect on their agendas beyond the parameters of the liberal state project itself, means that the statebuilding project has focused on the liberal institutions of a state as *simulacra*,[7] saving resources for prioritised security matters and institutional reforms that focus on rights over needs, on liberal blueprints over the local. It hopes that these would then play a role in inducing local political stability, and economic growth. This can be criticised as a blind and somewhat ideological faith in the capacity of liberal institutions and neoliberal market forces to achieve this, or a subtle rejection of ethical responsibilities towards the welfare of others in post-conflict environments. It is particularly apparent that the focus of the UN agencies, the World Bank, and international donors on good governance and free market reforms ignores, for the most part, the very complex local political dynamics and conditions. There has been little attempt to develop an understanding of indigenous peace capacities, other than via a number of very small NGOs. Effectively the lack of agency at the local level has been seen as a result of indigenous inability, not a lack of resources, exclusion, poverty, or the dominance of liberal or neoliberal assumptions. There are double standards, here, and very strong shades of discrimination. This means conveniently that capacity, not resources needed to be supplied, fitting in with the technocratic character of liberal statebuilding.

The liberal approach to peacebuilding often leads to empty states, a virtual peace, and a focus on institutions over the variations of everyday life. The neoliberal approach denies the post-conflict individual and community the resources needed to engage in the liberal social contract, and to express the locality of peace. The rationalist and institutional focus of liberal peacebuilding denies cultural agency. These strategies have little chance of establishing a locally self-sustaining peace in which difference is recognised but not institutionalised, and conflict resolution and peacebuilding can move beyond their liberal guises into direct relevance for the local. These force international peacebuilders into a position of coercion over the local; they distance the local and block out external understandings of its agency, culture and needs. They locate an episteme of peace at the international and state level at the very moment when its local expression is most needed. Under the guise of engaging with civil society, these strategies are counterproductive both for the liberal peace and for broader forms of peacebuilding that may emerge as a result of a more genuine engagement with the local. They also significantly hinder the capacity of the liberal peacebuilding project to learn from its exposure to conflict and to other political systems, or from alterity.[8]

This is similar to Duffield's 'biopolitics of life',[9] resting on 'peace-as-governance' with its propensity to reproduce bare life, empty states and a virtual peace, rather than a liberal social contract. Thus, as Escobar argues in the context of development, the liberal West might have to confront the problem that peacebuilding *unmakes* peace as much as creates it, partly or mainly because of such problems.[10] As Chandler has argued this means a 'peace without politics'; that self-government and self-determination are undermined;[11] and the empty shell of the state is more important than the people who live in it and are supposed to bring it into being. This double standard in the harsher graduations of liberal peace for 'others' hints at racism.[12]

Peacebuilding-as-statebuilding, implying nation-building, follows peace-as-governance and represents a contestation of culture and otherness, infantilising its recipients, seeing all politics as about securitisation, institutionalism, production, discipline, and normalisation in the creation of a new state to replace conflict. It is produced by a muscular version of social science and a belief that 'power' can transform, rather than is generally subverted. Peacebuilders, the professional elites, and international civil service, which operate these programmes are often complicit in what is ultimately pacification or 'riot control'[13] rather than the construction of a self-sustaining peace, while reifying the universal priorities of liberalism.

What this means is that the original, emancipatory agenda of peacebuilding aimed at producing a positive peace needs to be kept separate from liberal peacebuilding and statebuilding agendas, in order to make such dynamics visible and to be able to respond to them. This fourth generation approach to peacebuilding represents normative agendas and processes of emancipatory and other positive forms of peace. Its goal is a peace which represents and enables responses to issues relating needs, rights and identities, in a political, social, economic and cultural context, determined by its subjects and mediated by those who are in a position to assist at the international level. It is not a quasi-colonial, ideological project. Liberal peacebuilding represents an ideological, narrowly ethical (according to the liberal metanarrative), institutional agenda: and statebuilding represents its technological processes. To connect these different agendas may be a plausible task, and there are limited signs that this is slowly evolving, as argued by many who are supportive of the UN's institutional project and some of the 'recessive'[14] dynamics of liberal peacebuilding (whereby even the liberal peace carries some resonance with its range of post-conflict subjects).

But equally, without culture, human security, social and welfare considerations, institutional and methodological pluralism, and the more standard 'check list', it is unlikely that this connection will be equitable. The liberal peace reproduces global inequality along with the liberal state. The UN has been powerless to address such concerns comprehensively because of the restrictions of its sovereign construction and methodological and ontological 'problem-solving' nature. It is subject to deep divisions between its 'distant' political and bureaucratic machinery and its humanitarianism. This is indicative in the small scale and capacity of the relatively new UN Peacebuilding Commission, which one would have expected to become a major institution given the scale of post-conflict contexts around the world, but instead remains only a relatively minor actor in the UN system and the broader architecture of international peacebuilding.

The liberal peace is believed to be locally self-sustainable, but as a worst-case scenario it is solely sustained by international actors and bypassed by local-local actors, while elites prosper. This stems from the assumption that governance, development and indeed conflict resolution are 'before' culture. Uncivil society is the implication if it is left unregulated. This logic justified peacebuilding in Timor Leste that was explicitly acultural, and in turn led to, for example, the attempt to sideline the local language, Tetum, in favour of Portuguese.[15] It also justified the anti-democratic, anti-self-determination, anti-self-government, liberal but illiberal behaviour of internationals like the OHR (Office of the High Representative) in Bosnia Herzegovina and its tendency to overrule local political processes; UNMIK (United Nations Mission in Kosovo) in Kosovo and its 'standards before status' approach; and of the World Bank in Cambodia with its marginalisation of the already marginal poor. As documented in the previous chapter all these 'post-conflict' sites remain very tense despite a decade or more of international engagement. The same logic permits the reification of the liberal subject, not the citizen, and of course of the Westphalian liberal state and its territoriality, rational institutionalism, and hierarchy over needs, context and culture.

The current liberal/neoliberal model of peacebuilding leads to the building of an empty shell of the state as opposed to the creation of a social/political contract between citizen and state. This might be rectified by incorporating a social welfare system as envisaged by Held into statebuilding,[16] or making peacebuilding in its liberal forms far more focused on social justice and its everyday context, as opposed to materially efficient and rational institutionalism. Considering social democratic alternatives in this context rather than the neoliberal state model might also be necessary given the powerful critiques that have emerged against the latter and the empirical evidence in support of the former in transitional and post-conflict contexts.[17] Local ownership and local participation requires a material stake in the state, its politics, identities, economics, and society at a minimum if the liberal peace is to be rescued. This requires a recognition of local, social, cultural, historical, economic and political systems even where they deviate from liberal norms.

Yet the romanticisation of the local often means that these aspects are ignored – people are poor because they have always been poor and need educating out of their primitive/romantic torpor; conflict subjects are perceived to be unable to engage in peaceful politics throughout society, regardless of its causal factors or key actors. Local actors either resist liberal peacebuilding for negative or barbaric reasons, or fail to comply with the elevated pinnacle of liberal/neoliberal state institutions because of a lack of capacity. Local and international actors attempt to influence and co-opt each other for their own agendas and so fail to address such issues, even if they claim to be doing so. Meanwhile, the failure of economic reform and development (at least in short to medium term) leads to grey and black markets, and alternative forms of social, economic, or political action, and a reliance on customary systems, which represent both positive and negative challenges to international agendas for peace.[18]

The failure to provide security evenly across all communities has a greater impact on civil society than internationally sponsored elites. Likewise, the version of civil society sponsored by internationals is an artifice, not normally reflecting the indigenous civil society, which includes modes of politics, society, and culture, that influence ownership, production, exchange and pricing that enables a more locally acceptable mode of order and sustenance. In practice, neoliberal aspects of the current peacebuilding model reduce individuals to rational automatons bereft of any cultural life, just as internationals assume locals to be. At least, any cultural life, diversity and mechanisms are assumed to be alien or dangerous. Thus, the core components of the liberal have become little more than corporate brands in the context of the mainly international economy of peacebuilding/statebuilding deployed to remake collapsed or fragile states with little regard for the history or identity of the people who inhabit them. Because this sort of peacebuilding is constructed upon the edifice of Enlightenment thinking there is little room for cultural agency or needs, and instead a technocratic focus on rights, reason and rationality, producing bare life for its subjects rather than liberal forms of citizenship. Institutions rather than discourses are what shapes the liberal peace strategy, denoting a formal rationality that values political rights as prior to social and economic rights, and therefore culture.

Indeed, as Hughes has recently shown, the post-colonial maintenance of such approaches via international liberal peacebuilding is essential to the reordering of post-conflict political subjects envisaged by international peacebuilding approaches. This tactic justifies moral and material inequity and the attempt to deploy the liberal framework as universal exemplar, as well as the perceived barbarianism or incapacity of the local. Such difference becomes the basis of top down institutionalism rather than cultural or welfare and needs engagement – making such strategies appear completely natural.[19] Even where such issues are starting to be noticed, as in Bosnia or Timor, assertions of social assistance as a core human right tend to fall back on the market solution, or fail to deal with the problem of who amongst the peacebuilding actors should change their behaviour or indeed pay for welfare projects. This is merely an expression of the failure of the very specific culture of contemporary peacebuilding, which blocks out, romanticises or blames the indigenous. If individuals' direct physical needs are not dealt with, any expression of interest in culture and its implications for peacebuilding and international intervention in post-conflict zones, is merely an example of the instrumentalist approach of neoliberalism – and internationals who value their own interests more than the local identities and dignity of the recipients of liberal peacebuilding.

This unmasks the darker side of the Western liberal peacebuilding project. It relies on the distancing and depoliticisation of the local, to ignore responsibility for its needs and to validate itself as the only plausible local that can be universally constructed. In essence liberal peacebuilding romanticises the West's own local, and legitimates the international asymmetries as they currently exist rather than encouraging their investigation and redressal.

However, even the bare life this induces contains local agency in the context of peace processes. This is supported by the recessive traditions of liberal peacebuilding whereby some of its planners, officials, administrators, and practices become more sensitive and more sympathetic to both such critiques, and to local agency as an implicit response to the shortcomings they perceive in the very model they themselves are implementing. It is also enabled in an unintended way by liberalism's blind spots, which provide space for such activities and expressions of politics, political organisation and mobilisation in alternative form, and of peace. If liberal peacebuilding is to lead to a self-sustaining peace then the first step would be to open up a process of communication between internationals and the recipients of peacebuilding, and it is here that the welfare/culture link would become very obvious, and where a mutual de-romanticisation might occur. This might, however, push peacebuilding beyond liberalism and its current welfare/culture paradox.

A de-romanticisation of the local would mean a far more sensitised and needs based assistance process of peacebuilding, in addition to the wide and necessary institutionalisation of rights. It would also require the recognition of cultural agency for peacebuilding. Dealing with neither leads to 'empty' states and virtual forms of peace; dealing with one or other but not both undermines the sustainability of the peace. Engaging with needs and cultural agency, as well as rights and institutions, looks far more promising. This would lead to a more finely tuned and balanced outcome, more representative of negotiating and of consensus between the international and the local. It would mean a more diverse and pluralist international architecture of peacebuilding, and would provide more representation for the post-conflict individual. It also indicates the need for a contract between peacebuilders and subjects, especially in the absence of a firm peace. Liberal peacebuilding and statebuilding would then be merely one of many priorities, albeit a nexus around which polities would be organised, which would begin with a very serious institutional and donor engagement with the nature of everyday life and the sort of resources that were required to stabilise it.

What emerges from this analysis is indicative of the need for a new discourse of peacebuilding amongst internationals, which is driven not by their own interests or world views, but those of the local, and a local-local which is as 'authentic' as possible as opposed to civil society (i.e. recognises the fluidity of local identities at grass-roots levels, and engages with local needs as well as internationally constituted rights). This authenticity should not provide an excuse for another authoritarian or ethnonational metanarrative to reproduce new elite and local struggles for power and resources via territorially sovereign states. Transcending this may open up the possibility for a hybrid form of peacebuilding to emerge that is relevant to the rights, needs, institutions, and cultures of others in varying contexts. Indeed, it may well be that the politics of peacebuilding on the ground mean that this is already occurring to some degree at least, as later chapters attest.

To unpack this peacebuilding needs to be intellectually separated from *liberal* peacebuilding and statebuilding. Local and contextual processes of *peace formation* need to be investigated, in particular in the way they constitute legitimacy.[20] Furthermore, a *via media* needs to be developed between any peacebuilding agenda and its recipients, which will not be resisted for either party for reasons of expediency, efficiency, cost or interest, nor which compromises the integrity of mutual conflict resolution and peacebuilding agendas. This *via media* might be the basis for a mutual acceptance or resistance – or a liberation from conflict – but transnational, transversal, liberal and local channels of communication must be open and connect the most marginal to the most powerful in a transparent and accountable manner. This might seem to be a major task – but this is what is required if peace projects are to become self-sustaining and materially and culturally relevant to the lives of its 'subjects', especially for the most marginalised (often women and children, which also incorporates an everyday and a generational aspect to peacebuilding and conflict). This means treating the post-conflict individual's dignity and quality of life in each context as significant, and not just treating them as prospective, but often unlikely, rights bearers, voters, producers and consumers. It should not be assumed that the post-conflict individual is constituted within a social Darwinist politics, moderated as an afterthought by liberal rights and institutions, as often seems to be the case. Such discourses and praxis often inadvertently create a new class system in which internationals and local elites (often with dirty hands) benefit. The evidence so far shows that non-elite forms of post- conflict politics are not complicit in such processes, nor legitimate them.

It has become clear that peacebuilding needs more immediacy. This requires a rethink on the part of relevant international institutions, or perhaps a discussion about the creation of a new institutional approach (or even a new institution itself) focused on providing a platform for local discussions and engagement with such issues. The form of cultural engagement and the level by which welfare issues are mandated should be treated as matters of mutual dignity and integral to the localised social contract in its emergent polity.[21] Perhaps after basic security and aid, these should be seen as the next key priorities, and, even before institution building, worthy of donor and international attention. Overall, a new language for understanding conflict and for making peace, is implied, perhaps as a hybrid expression of both international and local versions of causes of conflict and appropriate responses, without undermining difference. As Duffield has argued in a different context, the social insurance of the 'uninsurable' surplus population now needs to be addressed.[22] This requires a relative privileging of contextual voices and sources of legitimacy to prevent a local perception that peacebuilding and statebuilding represent forms of occidental governance.

This echoes the voices of Iraqi and Afghani scholars who have, for example, called for peace and statebuilding processes that engaged more with local experiences; that are open to tradition and religion; that focus on communities and collectivism; that meet everyday needs; that resonate with democratic practices and mixed economies; that engage with the extra needs inherent in very slow transitions out of violence: and prioritise jobs, welfare, education and social justice as well as security.[23] Yet, 'becoming liberal' has also often become the international aspiration for the local, which both denies the experiences of many post-conflict subjects around the world today of their own peace dynamics and needs, and what role internationals might play. In doing so it represents the 'unbecoming' side of liberalism. Critical forms of local agency, resistance, and aspirations for liberation are probable outcomes.

The liberal peace's culture–welfare paradox lies in the common assertion that peacebuilding can occur without an engagement in either of these areas of concern. In fact the reverse is true, as the last two decades of practice has shown. To engage with welfare and culture is to empower peacebuilding, and the recessive aspects of the liberal peacebuilding project enable the reinsertion of local political agency into the production of peace, ironically taking advantage of liberal peacebuilding's blind spots. This raises the question of what is necessary to achieve an everyday state where the local is de-romanticised, rather than merely a liberal state or even a 'no war, no peace' situation?[24] This is where the local politics of peacebuilding at the local level actually lie- i.e. its infrapolitics. Here the meeting of local and internationals that peacebuilding implies – the interface between the liberal and the local – would not be depoliticising or evade key discussions of needs, welfare, or culture, or of the normative systems of its various constituencies, but instead would see in them and any subsequent negotiation process the basis for a meditated form of peacebuilding. The local would become visible in its own right, and issues of identity, welfare, needs, culture, and context would immediately become evidentially part of the broader institutional aspects of hybridised forms of peacebuilding and of hybrid forms of peace which might then emerge. Understanding how this might occur is the next step that needs to be made to move beyond institutional versions of the liberal peace and to allow a local-liberal, hybridised version of peace to emerge. Local, civil and 'uncivil' society will be crucial to this hybridity, and to its legitimacy.

The civil peace that peacebuilders often imagine for others is social democratic rather than neoliberal, and in practice engages with needs directly rather than waiting for rights, institutions and markets to do so. Indeed, the costs of transitional welfare are probably far less than the costs of political collapse, particularly given the heightened cultural engagement this would facilitate[25] (see Appendix 3). This raises the questions of which institution would carry out such work, and with what type of safeguards, as well as who would pay for it? The question of who should pay for traditional security has long been settled by most states. It is now time to work out how needs might be met by institutions at the state and international level, in order to induce a more comprehensive local, state, and international form of representation through peacebuilding, which ensures its legitimacy at those levels. It would of course also be necessary to determine how this should be funded. This should take place in the context of a better understanding of the local, of context, and of how cultural engagements can be facilitated by new and interdisciplinary peacebuilding methodologies, in post-conflict polities. A basic transitional welfare system in situations such as in Bosnia, Cambodia Kosovo or Timor Leste where populations are small and costs are relatively low[26] would be enormously offset by the costs of a relapse into violence and might provide a basis for a more stable state and a social contract. They may even provide a basis for a more developed form of market to emerge more quickly, but they would at least provide more material substance to the trans-posed norms, rights, and institutions of the liberal state. This would, of course, also need to navigate risk of legitimising social engineering and biopolitical forms of governance. The benefits of attracting citizens into the state and into sustainable and peaceful activities via such a system make it relatively attractive nonetheless from the liberal perspective, especially if it enables political debate about reconciliation.

These are important issues if a civil and emancipatory peace (even if it still represents a form of liberalism) that is rather more nuanced than the current conservative form of the liberal peace, is to be attained.[27] This might represent an emancipatory form of the liberal peace, but it would also respect and integrate local cultural practices conducive to representative, free and fair local politics, in which the individual's identity, culture and needs were prioritised in a hybridised rights and institutional context, perhaps as a route to a social contract and a legitimate and viable state. Collapsing the distance between the 'local' and 'inter-national' should be a conceptual priority, first. But through local knowledge and engaging with the emerging local-liberal forms of peace, one should not recreate new 'native administrations' to govern and rule 'more humanely', or divide humanity into the peaceful and the non-peaceful, as Duffield has pointed out.[28] Beyond the liberal peace, it might be necessary to think about non-territorial, regional and hybrid forms of polity (such as hinted at by the contemporary situation in Northern Ireland) in which the liberal aspirations for universal partici-pation, representation, in a formalised, constitutional and international structure, are integrated with a far more localised and culturally appropriate form of politics which allows, in an empathetic manner, a politics of everyday emancipation to emerge; one that is far more broadly resonant in local contexts.

Local actors are, if not materially, then discursively able to resist the implications of liberal peacebuilding and statebuilding strategies through vocal and physical resistance (sometimes violent as during the various riots in Kosovo or in a different sense via direct attacks on the UN in Iraq and Afghanistan); discursive deconstruction of institutional frameworks for their governance; and through a process of negotiation over the nature of the liberal peace that is being laid down. It might be said that they resist the narrow culture of liberal peacebuilding using strategies available to them, rather than meeting the liberal project on its own terms. However, local actors also call for liberal peacebuilding to live up to its own version of emancipatory standards.

Such critical agency and resistance often results in a subtle co-option of the liberal peacebuilding process by local actors which are assumed to be its subjects, as has occurred most obviously in the Kosovo case.[29] But clearly, the existence of liberal peacebuilding's blind spots has created a space in which local agencies, often in a minor register or completely hidden from view, indicate the infrapolitics of peacebuilding – perhaps even expressive of bare life – and enable hybrid forms of governance to also emerge. To some degree, this represents a reclaiming of local political space (these dynamics are the focus of Chapter 5). In this sense the new social contract that is emerging as a reaction to neoliberal versions of peacebuilding represents a reassertion of the local and a reaction against the political culture of peacebuilding itself.

Many international actors and individuals, not to mention some organisations and NGOs (such as International Alert)[30] agree that such a process is necessary, whether through policy or in private. They recognise the recessive aspect of liberal peacebuilding that Nandy notes in relation to the relationship with colonisers during the era of liberal imperialism.[31] This recessive aspect of peacebuilding allows international personnel, officials and administrators from agencies, international institutions and organisations, as well as NGOs, to recognise the limits of their policies, and capacities and dynamics at the local level – effectively the meeting of liberal and local. This provides a space in which the local and international may attempt to find creative ways of enabling both, drawing on aspects of their identity which extend beyond liberal/neoliberal institutional and market settings, individualism with regard to property, economic and social life, secularity, and rationalism, or from the local perspective, context. My field notes are full of such characters, who feel constrained and concerned by their professionalised roles in peacebuilding, statebuilding, aid and development, and their various programmatic aspects. They find creative ways of maintaining their integrity in a far more contextualised manner than liberal peacebuilding expects of itself or of local actors. Recessive dynamics facilitate this but they are also partly caused by such local agencies becoming apparent as international actors move away from their nested situation in the liberal peace paradigm and begin to encounter contextuality for themselves.

Towards a post-liberal peace

Engaging with the local, context, the everyday, and crucial agencies implies a radical critique and an attempt to understand hidden, subaltern perspectives on peace, as well as a subsequent repositioning of peacebuilding. Recognising its politics, context, culture and needs, requires an engagement with the everyday, with methodologies that are contextually ethical, as well as the agencies that arise in such contexts. Ultimately this indicates that a transformation of the liberal peace is underway, producing a local-liberal hybrid form. The following section offers some thoughts on the implications of this for the emergence of a post-liberal peace. These set the scene for the rest of this study.

This more radical post-liberal peace lies 'beyond Westphalia'[32] and in a new moment of inclusion and its related ethical practices. It reflects and extends the historical expansion of the concept of peace that has occurred, from the medieval 'Christian peace', the Renaissance humanist and 'non-infidel' peace, to the utilitarian peace, the peace based on reason, and then later concerns with disarmament, international organisation, civil society, labour movements and social transformation.[33] The interdisciplinary agenda implied by a contextualised and ethical critique of the liberal peace probably cannot develop while clinging to notions of a territorially bounded, sovereign and state-centric international space. The everyday, society, culture, needs and community are distant to such discussions.

A post-liberal form of peace would not foreground a search for a new metan-arrative of peace. Plant warns that most critical and 'revolutionary' thinking displays a concern with meta-narratives based upon a '… nostalgia for truth, meaning, immediacy, and liberation'.[34] These are often depoliticising, as with the contemporary praxis of the liberal peace. Instead, this approach highlights the importance of local voices and narratives (not just local elites), and enables self-government, self-determination, empathy, care, an understanding of cultural dynamics, and the everyday. In these senses, developing a more sophisticated understanding of peace connected either to the liberal universal project or with multiples and hybrid forms of peace, can be connected to an excavation of the model self and the states of exception that might impact upon it, rather than merely a focus on the state as its organising principle.[35] This is not to say that the regulation of boundaries, the construction of viable states, and the modern state system's location of the self is not significant, but to offer other, significant locations of forms of peace.

More radically, it raises the question of where modifications or alternatives to the liberal peace agenda may be derived from, and what they may entail. In this respect, areas such as gender can be read as requiring a radical restructuring of representation across political, social, professional and economic spheres, and within the public-private/agency-structure and care debates. Similarly, environmental debates generally point to the unsustainability of many political, economic and social practices that lead to the consumption of non-renewable resources and irreversible environmental harm, and additionally reflect an unequal demography of consumption. Focusing on marginalised or subaltern actors raises the question of their agency within the broader structures of IR, and whether and how they can be represented. The problem of poverty has long been linked to a tendency for violence. It also refreshes the debates about whether relative economic equality is a component of peace; whether welfare should be centrally or socially organised, or whether needs should be left to markets and individual capacity to remedy. Behind all this is the lurking question of whether liberal paradigms are able to engage with, and equitably represent 'non-liberal' others and the rights conceptions they, rather than international personnel, may aspire to – those for which it infers a lesser status.

The incorporation and study of such inter-subjective issues has necessitated methodologies that facilitate research that examines how individuals, societies and communities operate within this context. For example, the adoption of discourse analysis and ethnography allows for greater, and culturally appropriate, access to everyday life, and to facilitate a clearer understanding of how institutions and their creation or development affect the individual, communities and society. Yet, ethnographic methodologies in IR are generally taken to have achieved little more than providing an overview of civil society actors, or how war, conflict and violence affects individuals and groups. Often research is heavily oriented towards official statistics and reports which themselves tend to be compiled via mainstream statistical approaches (often based on very limited local data).[36] Where ethnography is applied it is often marginal, though the sort of 'institutional ethnography' that Escobar has called for is now slightly more common.[37] Such research may open up contextual and subjective knowledge – even about security, rights, and institutions – as opposed to universal claims about objective forces and laws. It offers socially and culturally sensitised understandings of peace and conflict issues. It may lead to a clearer understanding of what motivates individuals and social groups to enter into conflict, criminality and grey/black markets, or to develop a more harmonious existence with their neighbours. It requires that local academies and policymakers beyond the already liberal international community are enabled to develop theoretical approaches to understanding their own predicaments and situations, without these being tainted by Western, liberal, and developed-world orthodoxies and interests. In other words, to gain an understanding of the indigenous and everyday factors for the overall project of building peace, liberal or otherwise, a *via media* needs to be developed between emergent local knowledge and the orthodoxy of international prescriptions and assumptions about peace.

Using the notion of the everyday might enable a response to the constraints of the liberal peace, but it also represents an alternative site of knowledge for peacebuilding. One related contribution can be found in the work of de Certeau and is developed further in Chapter 5. For de Certeau, the everyday represents how individuals navigate their way around and try to create space for their own activities while taking into consideration institutions of power.[38] People are able to adapt and take ownership over structures and institutions so that they begin to reflect their own everyday lives rather than reflecting structural attempts at assimilation. This reappropriation through the everyday then becomes a site of politics and represents a move from subjects to active citizens, from depoliticisation to self-government and self-determination. The everyday often represents an often hidden, diffuse form of politics, not institutionalized but able to shape, resist and choose institutions and strategies.[39]

A post-liberal agenda therefore entails an everyday praxis that would enable political, social and economic organisations and institutions to represent and respect the communities with which they are effectively in a contractual relationship. As a consequence, international forms of peacebuilding would be more likely to be participatory, empathetic, locally owned and self-sustaining, socially, politically, economically and environmentally speaking. They would be enabled to provide a *via media* between different identities and interests. They would also be adaptable to changing circumstances and needs. As far as possible, these interlocking and interrelated versions of peace would also provide justice and equity, and avoid violence both direct and structural. This would either counter-balance or supplant the liberal peace's obsession with hard security, territorial sovereignty and statehood, and institution-building over the everyday. This might, in liberal terms, lead to a modification of current global statebuilding agendas and a refocusing on needs at the civil level, rather than mainly on rights. More likely it would entail an everyday tactic of engagement between liberal states and non-liberal alternatives, or locally imagined polities that provided for political, economic, and social requirements in their immediate context, whereby the strategy approximates the tactic, the institution responds to the characteristics of the local via an ethic of care. It is difficult, from a liberal and critical position, to image this being achieved without some conception of democracy, law, human rights, and development or welfare support. A deeper contextualisation of peace may allow for hybridised, localised and internationalised praxes of peacebuilding to emerge that are more locally sustainable, resilient and legitimate than what has been the result of the recently evolved liberal peacebuilding/statebuilding praxis. In a very preliminary sense, this points again to need to understand contextual processes of peace formation as opposed to externalised processes of peacebuilding and statebuilding. This is not to supplant the already existing research agendas dealing with everyday issues such as neo-patrimonialism, rent seeking, spoilers, criminality, militias, or corruption, but to provide a balance to the general tendency to essentialise mainly contractual or institutionalised rights-based responses to these, which then spill over into the core everyday life in its 'civil' rather than 'uncivil' senses.

The hybrid outlined above necessitates the development of a system that protects difference and allows for exchange and cooperation in a way in which all its participants believe is beneficial for their needs, to define themselves and cooperate with others.[40] This is a difficult problem as it involves mediating relations between differently bounded and comprised units subscribing to different forms of peace. It signifies that it is unlikely that a universal form of peace will persuade everyone.

It also connects to the more common research agenda on a just peace.[41] Such research generally argues that justice through peace is preferable to justice through war and the most marginalised provide guidance to the powerful in understanding what peace means. A just peace is normally taken to require respect for free speech and human rights, and that individuals have primacy over states in terms of their rights, freedoms, and participation. It acknowledges that recognition is a central part of peace, as are the ways in which categorizations are made to include or exclude others.[42] Of course, recognition implies reconciliation, but the latter cannot occur before the former.[43] The language of Western liberal institutionalism or of sovereignty alone, are a limited basis for a just peace, because these offer obstacles to the recognition of certain others, favour liberals, and continue the process of marginalization. Reconciliation cannot stem from this (hence the inability of states to recognise even their own native peoples). Again this points to a need to engage with the everyday. Allan also adds a requirement for a global concern with care to the concept of the just peace.[44] This care ethic supersedes a positive peace in liberal terms, drawing on the eponymous feminist concept.[45] This, he argues, can be seen in the liberal discourses relating to the needs for recognition, a culture of non-violence and respect for life, solidarity, economic justice, tolerance and equality, and common empathy between human beings.[46] Tolerance and solidarity coalesce within care in that difference and uniqueness are accepted, and sympathy for the difficulties of others and a willingness to assist are present.[47] This also connects with pre-existing debates on human security, particularly its emancipatory aspects.[48] It reflects the agenda in recent international documents such as the Responsibility to Protect.[49] The question is: who will provide this care and who will define its reach, terms and definition? International institutions, policymakers, states, NGOs, agencies and scholars are currently part of an embryonic version of this process, though with differing approaches. Focusing on what this means in everyday life might prevent this from becoming another hegemonic agenda.

The notion of care has a number of facets, invoking both a moral association and solidarity. The Hegelian notion of a struggle for recognition is certainly significant, in that it leads to equality, mutual understanding and respect.[50] As Dallmayr argues, it is possible to draw out an intellectual connection between the Stoic notion of 'self-care' in relation to freedom.[51] As Foucault argued in his last works, freedom can be taken to be the ontological condition of humanity in everyday terms relating to self-care and care for others. He argued that this was an Enlightenment replacement for the cultivation of the soul (lost in modernity) and is analogous in particular with self-government.[52] Indeed, Foucault's entire project was to show how, from Socrates onwards, European thinking has been aimed at '… wak[ing] others up from the slumber in which they conduct their everyday existence …'. This is aimed at the transformation of the self, echoing Walker's comments about a post-liberal peace's connection with the excavation of the modern self.[53]

Both would require radical methodological change for peacebuilding. They indicate, as Bauman has argued, that '… the moral is what resists codification, formalisation, socialisation, and universalisation'.[54] Translated into peace, this has far reaching ethical consequences. The ethics of peace are not found in exporting institutional governance as technology, or 'branding' exercises (for democracy, neoliberalism, human rights and rule of law). They reside instead in the empathy and care of human relations, in 'unscripted conversations'[55] about self-government, needs, identity, culture, rights, institutions and security: and are reflected in the informal relations of individuals and communities in the official framework of the polity and its own relations with other polities. This fluidity resists formal institutions and boundaries unless mutual care and empathy provides their everyday ethic. Thus, rather than merely being a contest over rights and rules, an ethical version of peace would be heavily influenced by specific contexts in balance with responsive international institutions and norms.[56] This would, of course, need a constant process of negotiation, and would have to include a broad range of voices from the local to the global. This would perhaps involve global elites, officials, and states taking responsibility for the reframing of their interests and activity by the poor, powerless and marginalised, and their everyday concerns.[57]

What the everyday, a just peace, and the 'care of the self' expose in the context of the juxtaposed liberal peace project is its general tendency to harvest power and resources for politicians, officials, experts and institutions. This forms a liberal discourse that removes individual and societal agency and autonomy at the expense of empathy and care, and therefore of a sustainable peace. This is a side-effect rather than the goal of liberal governance in the specialised circumstances of its export to post-conflict environments, but the net effect is the displacing of community, culture, identity and welfare in favour of external discourses of expert knowledge. These are tinged by their own ideology, culture and interests. The everyday, empathy and care unsettle liberal institutions rather than merely confirming them, adding additional dimensions and sensitivities and the ontological dimension that they imply. It is important to remember that Foucault saw care in the context of self-governance as a way of escaping or moderating the hegemonic tendencies of liberal social and political governance. Power and resistance are entangled within liberal polities but empathy and an aspiration towards self-government, especially within a 'deep civil society' (the local-local) derived from a more empathetic engagement, offers a conceptual way forward without delving into a new grand narrative of ethics, and with an eye on the everyday as a contested site of identities, care and empathy, as well as interests.

One common criticism of arguments concerned with prioritising the local and the everyday is that such inclusivity and openness in peacebuilding environments may be relatively inefficient compared to the sort of progress that can be made via more limited and reductionist prioritisations (such as those encouraged by the orthodoxy of liberal peacebuilding). Slow progress or constant political in-fighting is taken to undermine progress towards a centralised unity, as can be seen in the context of the tribal networks and the deliberations of the loya jirga in Afghanistan[58] or in Iraq where tribal leaders have also had some involvement after early criticism that government, whether by the coalition or by 'local' actors, was extremely limited in its representation of the range of Iraqi groupings.[59] Stalemate rather than progress is the result according to this view of the dangers of the local, undermining reform and institution building, and the development of liberal governmentalism. The examples of Bosnia, Kosovo and Timor Leste show that both a deferment of and to the local, and a retention of powers amongst the internationals can be very problematic, as shown in Chapter 3.[60] In these cases local tensions retarded or blocked reform, or co-opted the state project for ethnonationalist or predatory agendas. International direction of peacebuilding did little better, however: either empty institutions were built which were not then taken up at the local level, and/or resources were deployed in ways that often depoliticised the local (as Chandler has shown in the context of Bosnia),[61] or they had little impact on the local. In all these cases attempts have been made to involve the local, while simultaneously depoliticising it by failing to deal with everyday issues. Local actors in these cases have, while acknowledging the benefits of peacebuilding and statebuilding in some areas, also tended to see this as undermining the legitimacy of their peace process; as depoliticising, undermining their right of self-determination and human rights; as portraying a lack of respect for their cultural norms; or as examples of either hegemonic or ideological Western conditionalities. These indicate serious dilemmas which the post-liberal peace might avoid via its concern for the everyday.

When internationals engage in conflict zones, they might ask of disputants at the many different levels of the polity there might be, what type of peace could be envisaged, what and how care might be provided, and what is needed to understand, engage and support everyday life? Security, institutional building, democratisation, the rule of law, human rights, marketisation and development might be constructed from these informed perspectives. This would have to occur in the explicit context of responses to the root causes of the conflict, meaning that peacebuilding occurs at two starting points. Rather than mainly stopping overt violence from threatening regional stability, it would concurrently establish an understanding of a local and everyday peace. This would require a conversation between disputants and internationals, avoiding exclusionary practices, to undercover a consensual discourse ethic and praxis by which a post-liberal peace might be achieved. This appropriateness would be negotiated from the perspective of the internationals, custodians and other interventionary actors, and most importantly, local actors, and not necessarily to pre-existing models, agendas or scripts.

Rather than producing bare life[62] such critical research agendas for peacebuilding[63] offer an eirenist reading of the connected areas required for the consideration of the possibilities inherent in post-liberal forms of peace, as in the local-liberal hybrid and its interface. These aim to reflect and become embedded within everyday life and the societies it affects. This may seem naïve to many working within a more orthodox tradition, but to others who are working around these traditions, resistance to these ambitions seems naïve – destined to repeat the traumas of realist or liberal 'history'. As Jabri has shown, this version of peace engenders a capacity to resist violence and to struggle for a just social order that goes far beyond the endeavours of a liberal 'international civil service'. It represents the everyday issues and solidarity of individuals, communities and social movements. For Jabri, it is this solidarity that produces a more sophisticated form of peace.[64] Indeed, this indicates that individuals and communities have primacy over states in terms of their rights, freedoms and participation.[65] Thus, recognition is a central part of the way in which categorisations are made to include or exclude others[66] (think of the way non-state groups such as the Turkish Cypriots, the Kurds, the Palestinians, and many others have often been excluded from peace processes on such grounds, to the detriment of peace). Recognition implies empathy, care, and thus, reconciliation, but the latter cannot occur before the former, and little can be achieved without a contextual understanding of the everyday.[67] The limitations of liberal and neoliberal versions of peace mean that the state is empowered to interrupt this ethic of care, solidarity and empathy at its borders, and tends to focus on risks rather than opportunities.[68]

Two possibilities are to be gleaned from this: the rescue of the liberal peace by incorporating the everyday, and the production of hybrid forms of peace, neither liberal nor local, but made up of both. Local agency, autonomy and many efforts to develop these in the everyday space of peacebuilding (left vacant by liberal peacebuilding/statebuilding's many blind spots and omissions) leads to 'peacebuilding as resistance'. This agenda indicates the potential for a *via media* between different polities and their forms of peace, as well as creative responses to the inadequacies of the liberal peace, particularly in terms of its shortcomings in the areas of cultural pluralism, indigenousness and transitional welfare provision. These areas allow the identification of the components of the everyday peace, from bottom up grass-roots areas to local, state and regional institutions, or international architecture. The priority here is how the local, everyday requires, draws on, creates, modifies and resists the higher levels. What are the exact qualities of the everyday and the local? Clearly they are elusive and multiple in nature: fleeting, transversal and not amenable to easy and distant conceptualisation. For this reason, the types of agency that emerge are critical – or radical – but often hidden in everyday experience not amenable to institutions but also significant for their legitimacy.

In this area, perhaps, lies the salvation of the liberal peace, through a reflection of its original conceptual mechanism for the attainment of the good life via a social contract. Many of these mechanisms already exist: notions of basic human needs and human security, first and second generation human rights, in the context of physical and material and spiritual stability and security, preservation of culture, identity and institutional stability. However, a post-liberal peace, resting on context, the everyday, empathy and care, does not need to follow the liberal peace: indeed, it might be that in a certain context, society and local peace is structured in a very different way, reflecting local culture, tradition, custom, religion, tribalism, feudalism and different modernities of political, economic, social or cultural dynamics. Clearly, there are very specialised circumstances outside the West where polities exist that are non-liberal, though they are not post-liberal in the sense that they are very much still based on Westphalian norms of sovereignty, rather than a post-Westphalian sensibility.[69] There are also many non-state communities, often tribal and indigenous, that do not conform to the liberal state or liberal organisation, but do offer some hints of the post-Westphalian, post-liberal hybridity and sensibilities.

With this in mind critical policies for a post-liberal peace might engage with the following:[70]

1   Building any form of peace relies on an detailed understanding (rather than co-option or 'tolerance') of local culture, traditions and ontology as well as needs; and acceptance of peacebuilding as an empathetic, emancipatory process, focused on everyday care, human security and a social contract between society and the polity, as well as internationals, the latter two which act as providers of care rather than merely security:

2   An economic framework, focusing on needs, welfare and empowerment of the most marginalised, should be determined locally, but assisted internationally. Internationals may assist in free market reform and marketisation/privatisation not on the basis of external expert knowledge but on local consensus, but they should also consider a socio-economic safety net to bind citizens and labour to a peaceful polity (rather than to warmaking, a grey/black economy, or transnational criminal activities). Otherwise, neoliberalism clearly undermines any social contract and leads to a counterproductive class system;

3   Any peacebuilding process must cumulatively engage with everyday life, care and empathy, custom and culture, as well as institutions;

4   Any such peace will tend to be constructed in relation to the liberal peace model as this is the preponderant outlook of the international range of actors engaged in peacekeeping, peacebuilding, statebuilding, development, etc;

5   This indicates a hybrid form of peace, which respects alterity, alternative processes, positions, norms, interests and goals, while also recognising that they modify each other;

6   This requires a peacebuilding contract between internationals and local actors which reflects the social contract within the polity;

7   It also requires thinking about peace beyond the liberal state mechanism and Westphalian sovereignty (rather than using peace to propagate liberal states), and moving beyond territorial forms of sovereignty and democracy;

8   Local-local ownership and joint ownership of contextual, regional and global processes of peacemaking;

9   Local decision making processes should determine the basic political, economic, and social processes and norms to be institutionalised in context; peace should be an expression as far as possible of local autonomous agency, meaning that of its subjects, constituted by their own needs, identity, cultures and customs, as well as the liberal peace model;

10   International support for these processes, guidance on technical aspects of governance and institution building without introducing or endorsing hegemony, inequality, conditionality or dependency;

11   1–10 should result in a process whereby a post-liberal peace is installed that includes a version of security, human rights, rule of law, a representative political process that reflects the local groupings and their ability to create

consensus and legitimacy, as well as broader international expectations for peace (but not alien 'national' interests);

12 Overall, these points imply the development of a local-liberal hybrid and a commensurate interface in each context.

To some extent, these points reflect the potential of the liberal peace, but they also emphasise the need to construct local consensus before blueprint thinking or policies are developed or applied. Peacebuilding actors themselves must be subject to a set of requirements to prevent them from treating every case as the same, and to actualise a social contract between internationals and local populations of post-conflict areas. This requires the following from peacebuilding actors:

1 That care, empathy, welfare and a consideration of everyday life, especially in its cultural and needs terms, are the basis of a social contract required between societies, emerging post-conflict polities and international actors:

2 Recognising that peace may not come about without forms of international intervention, peacebuilding actors must not work from blueprints but should develop strategies based upon multilevel and contextual consultation in each case. They should quickly develop relations with local partners which reach as far as possible, enabling grass-roots representation. They should endeavour to see themselves as mediatory agents whereby their role is to mediate the global norm or institution with the local norm and institution. This requires that international analysts, whether academic or policymakers, develop a new set of methodological capacities in order to enable agency, politics and local versions of peace rather than to prescribe the liberal peace;

3 Peacebuilding actors also operate on the basis of the norms and systems they are trying to instil, such as democracy, equality, social justice, etc. Theorists and policymakers cannot ever be beyond methodological ethics, and must acknowledge peacebuilding's reflexive and reciprocal qualities, which requires an engagement with context and the local-local as the key sites of peacebuilding from which a form of state arises as a result of political debates;

4 Theorists and peacebuilding actors need to move from an institutional peace-as-governance agenda to an alternative or at least additional everyday agenda for producing a hybrid form of peace. Putting communities first entails a rethink of the priorities of peace. In terms of peacebuilding this would place human needs, particularly economic and security needs before free market reform, and in parallel to local custom, context, institutions, democracy, second generation human rights – and a rule of law that protects the citizen in context, and not just their prospective rights and property. This would probably require the parallel creation of social welfare oriented and customary peacebuilding institutions, funded by donors and other international actors in whose interests a self-sustaining peace ultimately lies;

5 Finally, peacebuilding should not be used as a covert mechanism to export ideologies of peace, but instead should seek open and free communication

between post-conflict individuals and peacebuilders about the nature of peace in each context.

Conclusion

Post-conflict communities and individuals for the most part want to lead meaningful and prosperous lives, but many do not solely aspire to Western developed forms of liberalism.[71] Instead, what are crucial are their own needs: identity, representation, autonomy and agency. Where these are weak they expect external assistance; where they are ignored they may become involved in the dynamics of resistance. In the longer term, the notion that powerful states or even international organisations can independently create order, or even peace, without an intimate contract with the peoples who are part of that order and peace has proven to be a blind alley.

The resurgence of the everyday as a concern for peacebuilding and IR more generally entails several avenues for investigation, including the local experience of peace, tradition and religion, communities and collectivism, everyday needs, democratic practices and mixed economies, the extra needs inherent in very slow transitions out of violence, jobs, welfare, education, and social justice as well as security.[72] The consideration of such issues requires opening up 'unscripted conversations'[73] untainted by hierarchy, hegemony, and problem-solving. This is crucial if empathy is to be carried through communication, policy and institutions, via critical policies for peacebuilding towards an everyday peace. Pugh, Turner, and Cooper have argued that this requires 'permanent critique'[74] and a wariness of grand narratives, even in the guise of responses to crises.[75] At a broader level an eirenism needs to be placed at the heart of the various disciplines and sub disciplines used to develop peace after war.

In order to de-romanticise the local, peacebuilding needs to escape its current methodological biases and find ways of engaging with needs, culture and everyday conditions, as well as with critical agencies for peacebuilding, and even resistance to dominant narratives about norms, rights and institutions. After basic security has been stabilised, this is how its legitimacy will be evaluated and interpreted by its recipients. This means reflexivity on the part of the liberal peace project, and focus on the local in its many dimensions, provision for material assistance, on income generation and poverty reduction and so distributive justice, as well as understanding the need for cultural engagement and space, avoiding treating these in a neo-colonial, biopolitical fashion. Peacebuilding approaches need to establish meaningful forms of participation for local actors and civil society.[76] Local agencies and recessive liberal peace dynamics constitute the infrapolitics of peacebuilding in which more productive strategies might emerge.

More productive would be an engagement with, via an excavation of the genealogies of, local and transnational cultures of peace, and the production of hybridised approaches to peacebuilding by the international actors currently investing in liberal peacebuilding. This would see the inclusion of the kinds of agencies indicated in needs and cultural contexts which liberal peacebuilding has found convenient to ignore in its prioritisation of security, rights and institutions. Indeed, what emerges from the above discussion is the eventual realisation not of a liberal peace, but that even a liberal peace is effectively representative of a transitional moment from which a hybridised praxis of peace may emerge. This will be part representative of the international liberal peacebuilding consensus, but also part local. This is local-local, transnational and transversal, as well as everyday. It involves international peacebuilders having to cross international/local divides, and to cross liberal boundaries into order to engage with the local: to understand, to value it, and to connect its everyday potential and compatibilities with a broader peacebuilding project, which ultimately will have to transcend the liberal peace even in its emancipatory form.

This would allow for a more nuanced understanding of what constitutes the 'success' of peacebuilding. Success would not merely be the completion of a short-term and limited mandate focused on hard security matters or political institutions, but would have a contextually specific focus on longer term processes. These would entail the gathering of an understanding of local contexts, politics and society, and therefore on the realisation of hybridised versions of peace. This would no longer necessarily be conditioned by liberal notions of rights over basic needs (and their differentiation), institutions, sovereignty or statehood. Instead, these would be placed in a conversation with, and conditioned by, the local, as it constituted itself in relation to these elements of liberal peacebuilding, and would form part of a broader praxis of peace no longer conditioned by a search for its universal form.

Ironically, it might well be, to paraphrase the quotation taken from Foucault's famous lectures on the birth of biopolitics at the start of this chapter, that the liberal peace and the shift towards liberal peacebuilding and statebuilding has inadvertently caused a rebirth of politics. In trying to produce freedom through the delineation of the nature of politics it has enabled local voices to elucidate their own terms in the face of the international misdiagnosis of the dynamics of the conflicts they face.[77] The blinds spots of the liberal peace project, emanating from its methods, epistemology, ontological claims, ideological orientations (especially away from direct engagements with culture and welfare), its focus on state sovereignty and territorial arrangements, mean that its various ways of romanticising the local, have also left space in various areas.[78] In these hidden registers, which collapse the public and private distinctions of Western modes of politics and uncover political agency even in those actors it deems marginal, it might be possible to find new insights for a revitalised, perhaps fourth generation approach to peacebuilding. Local agencies, autonomy, resistance, and recessive spaces thus constitute the infrapolitics of peacebuilding, in which hybrid forms of peace may emerge. Of course, such arguments must be careful not to overstate the capacity of such hidden registers, nor underestimate the hegemony of the liberal peace or the interests inherent in global inequality. Yet, despite this preponderance, such agency has had a significant impact on the liberal peace and heralds the recognition of the significance of grass roots forms of legitimacy for peacebuilding. The next chapter investigates in more detail how these dynamics may enable a post-liberal debate about peacebuilding.

Part II

Hybridity and the infrapolitics of peacebuilding

5 Everyday critical agency and resistance in peacebuilding

The will of the people shall be the basis of authority in government.[1]
The colonised refuse to accept membership in the civil society of subjects ...[2]
... the intellectual is complicit in the persistent constitution of Other as the Self's shadow ...[3]

Introduction

Part II of this study illustrates how the distancing process by which liberal peacebuilding has enacted governmentality and its own priorities while marginalising local needs, culture and agency – ultimately reconciliation – in favour of institution-building. Yet, it has inadvertently become the stage upon which local agencies re-emerge. This is whether they are politically organised, identity, community or family organised. Through such a post-colonial turn, they have begun to reclaim peacebuilding, through what might be termed 'critical agency' often expressing non-violent forms of resistance, in unanticipated and sometimes controversial ways. This partly explains the emergence of hybrid forms of peace, which respond to the culture–welfare paradox, re-inject politics into peacebuilding and lead to local-liberal forms of peace: the post-liberal peace. This chapter attempts to provide some theoretical substance to such concepts, which emerged in the first part of this study as a result of the ongoing critique of the liberal peace.

Such efforts based on everyday issues and capacities had much in common with a fourth generation[4] of peacebuilding activity recognising identity, difference, structural constraints and inequality. Liberal peacebuilding has instead reaffirmed territorial sovereignty and hierarchical epistemologies of modernity. In Duffield's words, liberal peacebuilding determines the sovereign limits of modernisation.[5] This type of peacebuilding has become subservient to statebuilding, rather than statebuilding being one among many peacebuilding tools. It romanticises both the non-liberal and liberal self and operates in unanticipated ways at many levels of violence, cultural, structural, economic and physical.[6] This is an unintended consequence of the third generation approach which has merged peacebuilding with statebuilding. It has given rise to its own 'auto-immunity' in which its own limits have been reached and ignored, thus undermining its local legitimacy.[7] The liberal peace has become a brand of atomised liberal civility which diverts the state project away from its liberal functions of democratic self-determination, rights and needs, law, and agency in post-conflict situations via a rational choice approach and neoclassical economic assumptions. It is notable how documents like 'Responsibility to Protect' or doctrines such as 'do no harm' are internationalised rather than localised and fail to engage with everyday life other than in basic emergency and narrow security terms.

This liberal (and neoliberal) branding of peace has diverted attention away from local contexts, communities and individuals. Much academic and policy work has become complicit with this tendency. This is also true of the older projects of internationalism, peacebuilding and conflict resolution, which have been diverted away from individual and community conditions of peace in the context of the international, to sovereign 'peaces' organised around states and their territories, following on from a hegemonic liberal peace directed from a Western core of states and international organisations.[8] The general derivation of internationalism from social advocacy and action, from the citizen, the informal sector, and the most marginalised, has been deferred in favour of the state, elite bureaucratic, political and business classes. Statebuilding has become the focus even as critical contributions to IR theory has problematised the state, sovereignty, embedded liberalism and the international system. The most marginalised, the individual, community, kinship, agency, needs, culture and context have been subsumed while only rhetorically being recognised.

Complex responses and reactions have emerged in an interdisciplinary and transnational context, as opposed to one which is disciplinary and national. The liberal peace failed to negotiate with entrenched practices, commonly thought of in terms of custom and communalism in a classically colonial intellectual move designed to distance the everyday lives of post-conflict individuals (and those in 'development' settings) so that inequality can be effectively justified by alterity. Unsurprisingly, the age-old dynamic of colonial anxiety and local resistance has re-emerged in liberal modernity. At the same time the common requisition of post-structural insights in order to understand emerging agencies and resistance to liberal modernity and its emancipatory claims undermines, it is often claimed, the latter's stable, rational agencies, and so 'reduce [s] politics to critique and "resistance"'.[9]

In this struggle a possibility of a post-liberal politics emerges, in which everyday local agencies,[10] perhaps a technology of the self in Foucauldian terms,[11] rights, needs, class, culture, custom and kinship are recognised as 'webs of meaning' in opposition to territorial notions of sovereignty.[12] This move away from 'imperious IR'[13] and a willingness to emphasise local context and contingency[14] lays bare those paradoxes and tensions derived from territorial sovereignty, the overbearing state, cold institutionalism, a focus on rights over needs, distant trustee style governance, and a hierarchical international system in which material power matters more than everyday life. From the struggle over such deficiencies a hybrid local-liberal peace emerges in which agencies are expressed that contaminate, transgress and modify both the local and the liberal. They do not defer self-determination of power, they expose it.

Of course, the difficulties of escaping to the hegemonic discourse must be borne in mind.[15] An emerging local-liberal form of hybridity should not simply represent the acceptance of a priori liberal blue prints and their marginalisation of local agencies, which is why foregrounding the 'everyday' is so significant. Nor should it romanticise the capacity, resistance, and agency of the local. At the same time, it should be recognised that 'metropolitan time' (meaning Western modernity) – or the liberal peace – may not set suitable standards for the evaluation of non-Western time[16] (meaning context, custom, tradition and difference in its everyday setting), and often essentialises it.

This is a partial response to the recent claims about a 'critical impasse' between orthodox liberal debates and the critics of statebuilding or liberal interventionism. Indeed, these claims are premature: the mainstream has not moved to address any of the issues that have been raised by critics in any concrete way (other than via rhetoric about 'local participation' or 'ownership' or ideological defences of liberal universalism, internationalism and cosmopolitanism). Indeed, it might be asked if the mainstream is capable of addressing the criticisms.

A peacebuilding praxis located around the everyday, as compared to the 'incomplete modernity'[17] of state, territory, security, development or the market, needs to avoid the trap inherent in critique, of removing individual agency in favour of general claims of cosmopolitan or critical virtue or acting as an apologist for the failures of the liberal peace.[18] Focussing on the everyday allows us to escape the essentialisation or romanticisation of the now very diverse and often translocal local, the marginal, the subaltern, the customary and hybridity, not to mention northern epistemologies. It is the enervation of agency and the repoliticisation of peacebuilding that is the objective here, either by reforming the liberal social contract and so salvaging liberalism and the state, or more likely, by opening up a discussion of an individual agency beyond territorial sovereignty and the cosmopolitan or communitarian liberal state. Given the influential critique of statebuilding praxis that has been directed at its parallels with colonial praxis and epistemologies, this could be seen as an inevitable post-colonial response to the failings of political liberalism and its use as a global template.[19] This move also offers an avenue through which democracy and human security might be re-situated via the everyday, context, needs, difference, empathy and emancipation therein. This is not just aimed at situating peacebuilding as a bottom-up process, or introducing the everyday to the liberal peace, but providing an avenue through which both can listen and comprehend the discourses and spaces of the everyday.[20] This is the eirenist challenge for peacebuilding and the connected enterprise of statebuilding. This may also uncover more localised processes of peace formation.

Drawing on civil resistance

Resistance has a long pedigree in political thought in everyday settings. It has been widely linked with democracy, democratisation and social justice, the creation of civil society and fairer institutions and laws, and with self-government and self-determination, throughout its history.[21] This includes the Roman Plebeians who withdrew from politics until their grievances were attended to, establishing a strategy of open non-compliance, various religious obligations to disobey laws or commands regarded as sinful (as argued by Aquinas disobedience may be necessary against certain rulers and tyrants), and radical movements such as the Levellers, Diggers, and the Quakers (variously interested in campaigning for universal suffrage and equality often through civil disobedience).[22] Machiavelli noted the vulnerability of rulers to defiance from their subjects, an observation borne out by the French and American revolutions. Locke too thought that rulers may need to be opposed by their subjects, through passive resistance, dissent and agitation towards colonial rule (probably predating the American War of Independence). The writings of Thoreau and Tolstoy, and later Shelley, developed concepts of passive resistance, as could be observed in the gradual organisation of such resistance in coherent social, political and economic movements from the eighteenth century onwards in particular. Godwin, Paine and Wollstonecraft began to sketch out in more substantial terms the capacity of subjects to resist power in a range of issue areas influential in growing labour and social movements, such as the Chartists and others. These were often spurred by dispossession, a lack of representation, poverty and identity issues. Sometimes such resistance was organised to protect and enhance workers' rights, for social justice, for national liberation (more problematic in terms of avoiding actual violence), for the vote or for ideological reasons.

Later Gandhi's success in his non-violent resistance to British rule in India and in laying the basis for civil rights movements later on in the twentieth century (in the USA in particular), as well as a wide range of peace movements drew together the various strands of such movements and practices.[23] This is exactly what his famous 1930 'Salt March' drew on, meeting the material and epistemic power of the British Empire in a manner which undermined its legitimacy and its punitive power (at least if legitimacy was to be maintained). Gandhi did not just draw in colonial subjects to his campaigns, but also appealed to the British public. Even though his campaigns were very public they were also very hard to suppress while maintaining any legitimacy. This was because his 'disobedience' was civil, based on personal integrity and dialogue, and aimed at producing a compromise. Disobedience or resistance in this sense was based on a moral right.[24] According to Parekh this was because the British had fought unnecessary wars and maintained civil and military infrastructure at India's expense; destroyed local industry and agriculture; caused unemployment and famine; undermined national identity, religion, culture and heritage; and foisted external values on India's peoples.[25] Less public forms of agency, suppression and legitimacy are no less significant in this sense, and Gandhi was certainly aware of their significance in terms of networks, agency and impact.

Passive and non-violent forms of resistance became a tool of movements for political, social and economic reform, for the defence of hard won rights aimed against oppression, for self-determination, or for the realisation of idealistic political ideologies. They could be seen in movements for civil rights, for disarmament and against nuclear weapons, for democracy in the Philippines, Haiti, Korea, Chile, and across Latin America, against Israeli occupation in the West Bank and Gaza, and against Apartheid in South Africa.[26] They were also crucial in the collapse of the Soviet Union and the democratic movements in Eastern Europe which then emerged. Historically, civil resistance represents the agency of the supposedly weak and powerless, mobilising and organising on a scale thought by elites to be implausible. They also represent the capacity of even small-scale forms of resistance to have an impact on politics without taking the form of major public campaigns, strikes or demonstrations. Smaller scale expressions of agency through resistance are generally designed not to be public and to avoid retaliation. Either way, such forms of resistance have had impressive outcomes. Sometimes, as in Latin America, resistance is expressed as sporadic rebellion or through popular cultural activities, including narrative, dance, rituals and indigenous forms of debate and consensus building.[27] It often focuses on the preservation of land rights, responding to need and poverty, or resisting elite predation. It often forms hidden or visible networks which span the local and the international. As Tilly has argued, such movements have had competitive, reactive and proactive dynamics through which groups compete with each other, react against the state's centralisation of power, or make new claims for social justice, separate to or under the auspices of a state.[28] These become the basis for various responses and relations, based on rejection, suppression and oppression, conditionality and assimilation, cooperation and accommodation. Generally speaking, non-violent forms of resistance, or more generally of local, critical agency, try to avoid any retaliation from their targets, whether other groups or states, and attempt to influence the shape of cooperation, accommodation, inclusion and even assimilation. They may often quickly accrue transnational and transversal dynamics, even if they maintain a low-key relationship with power. Success is measured often not in direct confrontation and 'victory' over power, but via its gradual de-legitimation and reform.[29]

The literature on civil resistance also offers some insights into the types of strategy that may be used publicly, from protest, persuasion, noncooperation, and non-violent actions directed often towards political, economic, and social matters.[30] Actions range across the spectrum of public and organised activities, from social movements, strikes, demonstrations, marches, sit ins, boycotts, ostracisation, noncooperation, go-slows, sanctions and defiance of laws, institutions or organisations. These can be seen as having symbolic impacts, rejecting or denying their targets, of undermining their legitimacy.[31] They draw attention, polarise and express solidarity, perhaps even forming a community, moral, civil, identity, political, social or ideological. Social, customary, religious, political and civil organisations, groups, media, NGOs and other actors become involved in this political process, sometimes publicly, or behind the scenes. Rejection or repression of such dynamics have significant costs in material and normative terms for the actors being resisted. It underlines the inconsistencies and contradictions in hegemony or dominant theories or policy designed from afar. Such approaches illustrate the awkward but effective everyday agencies that exist beyond the more formal centres of power. Some are directly relevant to peacebuilding, but it is the more hidden or disguised version of such agencies that have had the most impact in modifying the current liberal peace system, precisely because it is supposed to be rights and consent oriented, and requires broad legitimacy. This is a notable capacity given the epistemic and material weight of the contemporary liberal peace project. This represents the other aspect of the narrative presented in Part

I of this study: it is not just the internal contradictions of the liberal peace but also the agency of its subjects that shape its outcomes.

The state vs the everyday

The rejection of the state – the de-centring of power – is not enough to justify the now well-known critique of the liberal peace, without the development of alternative or modified understandings of political agency which most importantly, do not dilute the capacity of the political subject. While Chandler appears to argue that some solid form of state is required in order to provide political rights, and so agency for all, this ignores the difficulties raised by the paradox that state, sovereignty and territory and their associations with the grand project of international order since the nineteenth century have generally displaced the subject through war and securitisation, elite institutions and the market, and often counteracted the gains they may have made through peace, democracy, human rights, enfranchisement and welfare.[32]

The everyday offers a small way out of this problem, but of course it does not confirm the state in its formal positivist, territorial form. Some form of state and of institutions which represents the interests of political subjects is necessary. This should include rather than exclude the everyday, however, because it is a site of critical agency, resistance and politicisation, solidarity, local agency and hybridity. It indicates the potential of the everyday for repoliticisation of a 'state' shaped around the everyday.

What would the purpose of the state be in a non-sovereign, non-territorial, non-institutionalised, non-securitised mode? As a provider of human security, starting from the most marginalised, without restarting any universal, paternalistic patterns of power, status, or inequalities? This implies peacebuilding should begin from the local, the everyday, from the bottom up, and wary of any problem-solving metanarratives relating to power, security, sovereignty, status, or territory, or even emancipation, which involve the claims to know on behalf of others, to govern on behalf of others, to secure others, or to defer agency and self-determination, without an acknowledgement of the acute sensitivities of such claims. This is so even if the latter stem from international norms and institutions, because they are not yet fully representative of many local actors. If there is to be a universal, it may only be that the contextual everyday delineates the various sites of knowledge for peacebuilding, relatively unmediated by concepts that allow the hijacking of rights and resources within liberal modernity. Thus, the post-liberal peace is not to be constructed only at the global level (the ambition of liberal internationalism and its cosmopolitan progeny) but at the local, where citizenship, needs, rights and duties, have everyday meaning.[33]

This is part of a move towards the local, context, and related questions of representation, defined as alternative spaces. There has been a growing interest in the local, the everyday and the customary. This raises the issue of considering the ethical implications of 'taking part' (even if we do not actually do so) in the everyday lives of the societies, regions, states and systems studied, not merely contributing to policy. Such research is contextual and emancipatory, not merely managerial and status quo oriented, aligned with dominant policy interests. What is more, there is also the issue of whether and what the local and everyday should gain from research, and which and how local voices are selected? This is so that not only the sites of the state, the international, or the transnational, benefit from scholarship.[34] In this context the latters' relations with the everyday, local, custom and culture, need to be understood in the context of material inequalities and imbalances, gate keepers need to be uncovered, and assumptions and stereotypes need to be interrogated.[35] The dynamics of 'studying down', from privileged positions towards those of the marginalised, poor, oppressed and conflict ridden (as opposed to the normal habit of 'studying up' towards states and institutions) need to be more widely understood, falling as they may somewhere between 'going native' or co-option and complicity, and the tendency to move towards ethical or universalising, responses.[36] This is especially so in the context of research on peacebuilding where context differs, and needs and rights have often been denied, where institutions and states have often been regarded as predatory and uncaring, and so different methodologies and sophisticated contextual ethics are required to make peace, as opposed to merely ensuring compliance with dominant norms and interests.

This should not establish another set of binary oppositions, this time between the everyday and local and the international/state, the non-liberal other with the liberal, but instead to see the everyday as a site where these meet and are negotiated, leading variously to repulsion, modification, or acceptance, and thus hybrid forms of peace in political terms. It should be noted that the concept of hybridity is taken by Bhabha (one of its leading exponents) to include the way in which even in domination the colonialiser invokes hybridity. In other words, producing hybrid forms of peace may represent an exercise in power, reproducing a colonial relationship.[37] To understand this, what Butler has called a 'labour of translation' needs to be undertaken.[38] Otherwise any engagement with the everyday will be skewed towards the currently predominant 'liberal' mode with its attendant contradictions, masquerading as hybridity. It would be limited by the '… grid of the nation state system …',[39] vis-à-vis the authoritarian production of liberal spaces, as well as the Millian improvement of peoples for the benefit of supposedly autonomous others.

This represents a stepping stone from the critiques of the liberal peace towards a discussion of how peacebuilding might be reformulated, rather than reproducing patterns of liberal contradiction and so resistance. It avoids merely inducing subjects to 'become liberal'.[40] This has the paradoxical effect from the perspective of a contextual empathetic, and everyday form of peacebuilding, of leading to an unbecoming liberalism, whereby subjects engage in almost inevitable resistance because this may not reflect their context or needs, even though it may offer more sophisticated rights.[41] Indeed, they may already consider themselves liberal. As with previous and more directly colonial experiences, this is also unsettling for its agents, who were in the past colonial administrators, and today may well be UN, UNDP, World Bank, EU, OSCE, donor, agency, NGO, or state officials or employees.[42] Often they may be concerned that the policies and approaches they follow do not even live up to liberal standards – a kind of 'colonial anxiety'.[43]

The concept and space of the everyday illustrates how the liberal and the local may avoid such anxieties and engage in a mutual remediation of political space and both overcome and maintain boundaries between them, where necessary. Indeed, in the context of a *longue durée* perspective of debates on peace and in its positive and ambitious forms, the everyday has always been crucial. It has been common for critical, post-colonial and post-structuralist thought to invoke the everyday. Indeed, most of the major developments in peace praxis through liberalism have connected closely with everyday issues. Certainly, democracy connects the everyday to an institutional setting and to organised and public political debates. Human security was a way of reconnecting security to the everyday, implying a social contract and the provision of public services, as well as redistribution of wealth, after the state-centricity of Cold War politics. Much of this debate has indicated that peace needs to be institutionalised and/or 'localised',[44] whether through 'hearts and minds' operations, human security, international norms, local ownership or capacity building approaches, or through intimate conversations between the local and the international in full acknowledgement of implicated power relations.[45]

Inherency arguments, on which political realism is based, have now been widely discredited in most other disciplines/sciences.[46] It has remained dominant in some quarters mainly because a small but influential academic/policy nexus which seeks to maintain its epistemic role for its own advantage, necessitating the use of violence in some cases, and so the justification of realism. Outside of these small but influential groups, often sustained by problem-solving and formal modelling, realism has little intellectual currency. Furthermore, such approaches are intellectually maintained by research methods that do not directly engage with individuals or communities involved in conflict and peacebuilding; they remain distant subjects, not critical agents. Their everyday is distanced and made irrelevant. It privileges the information provided by intellectual and policy elites remote from ordinary people and conflict environments, rather than people directly involved, to maintain the formers' intellectual hegemony, neutrality, or conversely, bias.

All the major advances in the study of order and peace creation have come from a positive epistemology of peace,[47] often from those schooled in liberal norms and aspiring to cosmopolitan values and approaches (e.g. for democracy/enfranchisement, human rights, anti-slavery, gender, disarmament, international organisation and government and the UN, Congresses, Leagues, decolonisation, development, and welfare, and the market). Many claim that a focus on positive peace counterbalances material and discursively created violence and allows space for civil society to develop fully democratic and productive human relations.[48] This opens up the dynamics of local agency and resistance, and in particular in local resistance or local elite co-option of neoliberal states that emerge from current international statebuilding practice. It is in this resistance that an older Marxist critique of liberalism can be seen, though this is not in the context of limiting the solidarity of the working classes over their claims to the means of production, but in liberal terms of a political contract with government and state that provides both rights and resources to citizens. Of course, most liberal philosophers associated with developing concepts such as internationalism, democracy, the social contract, human rights, and rule of law saw this in the context of liberal peoples who used land 'productively' (i.e. were capitalist).[49] The indigenous, local, nature, and 'other', has been excluded and systematically 'cleansed' from their homelands, masked by a discussion of interests, norms, and rights. This has laid the theoretical basis for imperialism, racism and even genocide – and certainly for a very powerful critique.[50] Yet arguably, even Kant understood the need for the liberal to engage equitably with the non-liberal other to avoid such pitfalls.[51]

Conservative, liberal, and radical politics of peace rest on the distribution of material, political, and social resources, on recognition and representation, and the establishment of order and agency in the face of competition for scarce resources via a range of institutions. The emphasis on each may differ, but in practice the core of political debate is supposed, in liberal states and in those emerging from conflict zones, to mediate interests, norms, identity, and resources in a representative and consensual fashion, with the help of governmentalising institutions which offer both regulations and freedom, and perhaps even aspire to a level of equality. For the majority of people conflict and war means the fight for everyday survival in the face of extreme conditions – whether fleeing or hiding from violence, searching for food, or attempting to preserve political, social, economic, or family relationships.[52] Peace, in turn, represents the attempted restoration of normality and agency to everyday life, as its inhabitants would see it, not necessarily as liberals might conceive of it. Pragmatism prevents responses to others' distress. States, officials and peoples, regularly use such arguments to avoid engaging with the everyday of others. Indeed, most discussions of IR, or of peace, have tended to focus primarily on the territorial state as the locus of power and order. Some idealists focus on world government and systems and as internationalists see this as a more plausible site of a sophisticated form of peace.[53] Others focus on constructing liberal world order. More radical thinkers have often come to rest on identity, culture, representation, context and the local as a more suitable site for an emancipatory or ethical form of peace or order.[54] Even this has limitations in understanding contemporary problems of peace without including the everyday.

Implications of the everyday

Casting a brief eye around the contemporary inter-discipline surrounding IR and peacebuilding one might find: Boege and Brown (*et. al.*)'s 'everyday social reality';[55] Escobar's encounters with development, particularly in South America;[56] De Certeau's approach to the everyday;[57] Foucault's work on self-care and self-government in the everyday;[58] feminist theory on the everyday and on care via Gilligan and others;[59] Habermas' work on rational, 'everyday practices of communication';[60] Linklater's anthropological understanding of the dynamics of everyday life for universal communication communities;[61] Bhabha's work on culture – and in particular on everyday encounters where agency emerges that challenges and shapes that of the elites;[62] Spivak on the subaltern;[63] the range of post-colonial theory; Bleiker's work on emotion and aesthetics;[64] work on identity and on indigeneity such as that of MacGinty;[65] Jabri's references to 'everyday security';[66] Sylvester's everyday realm of international relations where 'empathetic cooperation' has potential;[67] Mosse's work on the ethnography of development;[68] Pouligny's 'tricky everyday' in the context of peacebuilding;[69] Smirl's everyday practices of aid workers;[70] Luckham's deployment of human security as an engagement with insecure peoples' lived experiences;[71] Spencer's everyday struggles in the context of politics in Sri Lanka;[72] Scott's 'everyday peasant resistance';[73] Mark Mazower's historical work on the everyday in and after WWII in Greece;[74] Melucci's 'democracy of everyday life' and converse colonisation of the everyday;[75] and many more.[76]

Even so, where the everyday does receive attention it is often seen as banal, taken for granted, repetitive, and constrained by biopolitics.[77] However, this perspective is not one which chimes with peacebuilding's local everyday, where life, well-being, human security, politics, culture, identity and community are at stake in contrast to the local's understanding of everyday life in the West (where it may well be one of banal consumption). Much of the literature on the everyday does focus on the West, rather than on the more acute forms of everyday life in conflict, post-conflict and developing polities. Whether there is disagreement on the mundanity and banality of everyday life, it is clear that in both Western and non-Western contexts it is a site of perceived subaltern agencies or lack of them, of resistance to depoliticisation, of activism, agonism and alterity – of both radical passivity and activity as well as passive and active radicality.[78]

Much liberal, cosmopolitan and constructivist theory, recently actualised through documents such as 'Agenda for Peace' or 'Responsibility to Protect' or the 'High Level Panel Report', reaches implicitly for both the legitimacy of the everyday, but also to emancipate and facilitate the everyday.[79] Such work differs not on whether the everyday is significant at all but whether it is uniform across the world in its most basic sense of needs and rights, and whether it should and can be facilitated, guided, and protected from above, via an *a priori* rights-based approach or should emerge as a result of individual and local agency and self-government. Couched in this way, problem-solving debates inscribe their progenitors' attitudes about whether the local can act for itself from below and according to its own agency, or whether it is full of helpless or devious subjects who need to be saved from themselves and each other, or whether the local is an empty slate on which governors should write for the good of a 'local' that cannot 'know' for itself.

The politics of the everyday have generally been seen in juxtaposition to the conservative politics that preserves existing power relations between classes, social economic groups and identity groups, or the liberal politics which focusses on the institutional structures of governance that preserve state frameworks (large or small) for the benefit of communities and in particular individual rights. They may be associated with solidarity, revolution even, and the notion that society (not individuals or institutions) is pre-eminent in politics. Such positions are also often consistent with attempts to oppose metanarratives which essentialise the everyday, politics and identity.[80] Some have seen this as approaching anarchism, while others have seen it as a more accurate and holistic attempt to represent in political terms the requirements, interests, cultures and identities of everyday life, rather than those of elites or institutions. Indeed, in this context, this latter version of the everyday is often perceived in the context of resistance to institutionalism and elitism where they have in the eyes of society lost touch with a social contract or the context of the majority.

De Certeau, perhaps one of the most famous thinkers to develop this concept, argued that the practices of everyday life are distinctive, repetitive and unconscious. He focused on productive and consumptive activities, rather than culture or resistance – two other interpretations of everyday life particularly relevant to post-liberal debates. For De Certeau, the everyday represents how individuals unconsciously navigate their way around and try to create space for their own activities while taking into consideration institutions of power.[81] People are able to adapt and take ownership over structures and institutions so that they begin to reflect their own everyday lives rather than structural attempts at assimilation. This re-appropriation through the everyday then becomes a crucial part of politics and represents a move from subjects to active citizens. These institutions of power do not determine individual everyday responses, but instead represent obstacles that individuals find ways of overcoming. They are influential, but not deterministic. De Certeau was concerned about the everyday in the context of the developed state and society, and in their Western context, what he perceived as growing alienation and atomisation. Yet, this approach offers opportunities to develop theoretical and methodological approaches to connect peacebuilding praxis with everyday life, which do not automatically concur with power and its distancing praxis, but instead shape power and institutions, and IR.

De Certeau outlined strategic and tactical forms of behaviour vis-à-vis the everyday. Institutions operate in a strategic manner to which people adopt tactical responses.[82] A strategy offers a relatively inflexible dominant order which is physically manifest and controls significant material resources. It is thus embedded in a dominant order. However, because the goal of a strategy is maintain itself, this creates the need for individuals to find ways of 'domesticating' the strategy, while it causes the strategic actor to need individuals to become predictable, homogenous and malleable. Thus, both become engaged in mediating institutionalisation. De Certeau also illustrates how strategy and tactic (i.e. institution and individual) only have very indirect contact with each other. Effectively, the tactic becomes distant and engaged in resistance against biopolitics, even through scattered and hidden transcripts which challenge the ruling elites[83] and their conception of 'success' (in this case often that of the internationals). This binary represents politics in this subsequently fragmented terrain. Individuals in particular are separated from each other by the strategy inherent in such institutions which undermines social trust (though they also resist this). Tactics (representing the everyday) are unencumbered by hegemonic institutions; they are unencumbered by their material weight, and indeed are often too transient to even acquire labels. They represent a methodology which is ultimately more flexible and able to adapt more quickly than centralised methodologies. De Certeau argues that they are makeshift, resourceful, and can bide their time. Thus, they are more personal and invisible to eyes that are attuned to orthodoxies of state and power. The tactical in the everyday is a diffuse form of politics that is not institutionalised but is able to shape, resist and choose institutions and strategies – an everyday agency.

Post-colonial uses of the everyday have become common.[84] Here it is deployed as a terrain in which an everyday life exists that is both commensurate with, in opposition to, and modifying of colonial practices of government. In this terrain a hybridity emerges which reflects cultural, customary and social patterns, material inequalities, patterns of colonial power, disguise, time-lag, and blind-spots – as Bhabha has so eloquently illustrated.[85] It is a site of resistance, assimilation and adaption, and of hidden agencies. It is also the site where power is often experienced in its most negative forms.

Crucially, this approach captures a 'place of hybridity' resting on such critiques and translations, leading through dissensus, alterity and otherness, to an agonistic process of negotiation.[86] Hybridity is produced by colonialism but is also a sign of resistance rather than mere mimicry (though it may be more mimicry than resistance).[87] It is not aimed at reproducing 'civility' in its liberal and heterogeneous sense. Neither does it reproduce an indigenous golden era. Its locality is complex and multifaceted, focused on the '... contest for political and social authority within the modern world order' – meaning, over liberal standards for political culture, order and peace.[88] This move rests partly on the reconstruction of peacebuilding using the discursive critique of post-colonialism, and the material critique of dependency theory.[89] If a sovereignty is to be found that reconstructs the state in terms of an emancipatory peace, it is one emerging through de-territorialised democracy, cognisant of class, inequality, culture and custom, of alterity, liminality, and of time lag vis-a-vis modernisation based theories.[90] The agonistic politics of representation, of needs and rights, and of identities, opens up a bridge between difference, based upon empathy, in an everyday context in spite of its agonism. Indeed, it is agonism itself that presents the possibility of empathy, and requires an engagement with the everyday.[91] What Bhaba refers to as the 'in-between space' represents the emergence of hybrid forms of peace, and the translation from and to an interface between the everyday and the international, even despite its liberal tendency towards claims of the universal, timeless, hegemonic fixity of a dominant Western, customary praxis. In the latter lie the telltale signs of governmentality[92] as opposed to the *vox populi* of an everyday context.

Post-colonial approaches reveal the subtleties of hegemony (or the liberal peace) in subverting alterity, the everyday, and making them appear abnormal or insignificant. Its response is, of course, sometimes ambivalent about local agency, and much of the debate circulates in Western contexts.[93] From this perspective, local agency is best recognised as limited and ambivalent about its derivation in colonial or hegemonic power as opposed to the local.[94] As can be seen in many contexts, not least in the subversion of the liberal peace, and in contradiction to the common metanarratives of state sovereignty, local agency is widely ignored because of the absence of contextual everydayness. Even post-colonial approaches see the local as often to be found in the 'language of the master', which also itself becomes hybrid via the local.[95] These agencies may be more than mimicry, but they offer a politics less than local self-determination, and may reconfirm hegemonic power. Here lie subversive, subverted and hegemonic practices of authorship and claims to authenticity. Ultimately, the languages of both the 'master' and the 'local' become hybrid.[96]

Ethnographic approaches have also been widely seen (after their early and colonial roles) as enabling a crucial critical move which would allow a clearer engagement with the other, with alterity, and with the everyday in the name of emancipation).[97] Ignoring the colonial antecedents of such approaches is probably a sign of how much deeper the methodological crisis has been by comparison, even if a large wing of anthropology has become involved in empirical mimeticism, Orientalism, and worse habits. The ethnographic turn has the everyday at its heart and is responsible towards those it studies, if only in comparison to the failure of IR to enable the very rights it often assumes in its liberal guise, along with democracy, security, a rule of law, and development. This should be wary of tendencies to 'bearing witness' and 'truth telling' without due consideration of bias and reflexivities, of course as this would replicate the worst missionary tendencies of peacebuilding and statebuilding, as well as the tendencies of mainstream social sciences. As Eckl has noted, applied anthropology has focused on uncovering the subaltern while critical anthropology has been more wary of such claims to emancipation and more concerned with the dilemmas that arise from the uncovering of the subaltern.[98] Thus, Eckl argues that anthropological works aimed at the everyday, such as that of De Certeau (and others, including Bourdieu and Scott)[99] are limited by their own incapacity to understand their own effects on their subjects (or 'cultural contamination'). This is a valid point, but this problem is of a significantly lesser scale compared to those of formal social science which acknowledges no space or relevance for the everyday at all. An engagement with the everyday would entail a reflexive acknowledgement, especially as such research aims at 'social action' and should be cognisant of the dangers of using knowledge for purposes related to the preservation of disciplinary or political authority[100] or even of emancipatory representations of alterity beyond the usual modern/premodern binaries of orthodox, sovereign IR. Engaging with the everyday requires the relinquishing of absolute sovereignties and of the myths of territorial statehood, and a non-essentialising incorporation of cultural engagements beyond the usual stereotypes of the premodern, the barbarous, or the authentic.

The concept of human security also developed at the end of the Cold War in part as a way of allowing such a move.[101] Broadening security to include a range of political, social and economic factors allowed for the consideration of security in the context of everyday life. This was soon attacked and labelled as implausible and unable to be operationalised, of course.[102] As it was adopted in by various states and international organisations it developed into a liberal institutionalist form, rather than the emancipatory form that was often envisaged.[103] Everyday forms of peacebuilding would also draw the concept of human security towards an emancipatory and post-liberal focus, as a response to the failings of the liberal peace.[104]

Democracy is crucial in this respect, but not merely in the institutional form that is encapsulated by a state (and often has been regarded procedurally as drained of substance)[105] or necessarily in cosmopolitan form,[106] but as a '… broader attitude towards governance, political community, and life in general.'[107] This might be of the communicative turn that Aradau and Huysmans have outlined,[108] or it might be in terms of the 'democracy to come' outlined by Derrida, Newman, and Connolly.[109] In other words, the aspiration to democracy and self-determination cannot be satisfied purely by state institutions, but also by an everyday form of democracy, one that also operates transnationally, informed by independent and radical agencies beyond mere rationalism and sovereignty.[110] Democracy reaches for self-government on everyday, contingent terms, rather than institutionalism and a 'tyranny of the majority'.[111] This is reminiscent of the deterritorialised democracy, agonistic respect, and critical responsiveness, especially for the most marginalised that Connolly has proposed, or the agonistic democracy of Mouffe, or to a lesser degree the deliberative version of Habermas.[112] It also requires a conception of human rights, a framework for wealth redistribution or social welfare, and a rule of law in a constitutional setting in order to guarantee the political agency of the individual. In these terms, this would represent a post-liberal development for both democracy and human security, through its connection with the everyday, as well as its strong connections with the liberal peace model. This also has implications for the democratisation of international institutions. Implicitly, democracy is also about resistance in a variety of forms, implying a tension with the liberal peace project as it has become, as technocratic, institutional and bureaucratic.[113]

Social movement theories have also been widely ignored, despite the rhetorical focus of liberal IR on the role of the social contract, legitimacy and individual agency. These, as made clear by the work of Melucci, tend to see the everyday as a site of resistance, struggling against colonialism through materialism, power or institutions.[114] Thus, the stereotype ascribed to the everyday by pre-existing elites and the influential processes and institutions of which they are part tends to follow suit: radical or revolutionary actors seeking state power (a very imminent liberal critique of its other). This may partly explain the reason for antipathy towards the everyday, but may also rest on such tendencies as a defence of class structures, privileges, and fear of revolution, authoritarian or paternalistic. Melucci's argument is instructive here: social movements and agency arises not just because of opposition to hegemony or state power, but also as an expression of the cognitive, affective and creative, relationships between people, which then translate into social action.[115] Situating peacebuilding in an everyday context thus sheds serious doubt on instrumentalist tendencies and discussions about 'success' and 'failure', because the key outcome of the everyday has to be a focus on contextual processes, which may not end at convenient, epochal moments.

From such developments it has also become relatively acceptable to discuss contextual, local, customary forms of politics and authority in a positive manner without romanticising them, as they offer approaches to conflict resolution, to social support, or legitimate politics.[116] This has traditionally stemmed from and allowed for a focus on everyday politics and the cultural and collective agencies therein, and quite often on resistance even in the face of disastrous conditions.[117] Local claims for autonomy and expressions of agency take multiple forms, connecting agency with resistance, with liberation (even in national terms), with emancipation and ultimately with hybridity. It might even be that it represents an attempt to 'escape' the state, subject status and statehood in general, and their propensity for predatory behaviour (even if only conscription, taxation and centralisation).[118] Local agency may attempt to replace these with a more localised understanding of peace formation, requiring political resistance and even cultural refusal.[119] It may lead to the emergence of parallel administrations, often decentralised, or significant state reform.[120]

The problem of agency in the everyday

This raises the generally ignored question of agency and autonomy of the subject in the context of peacebuilding. This question has dogged attempts to emancipate, critique and reconstruct new forms of politics contra the liberal-realist anti-politics that seem to emerge from various dominant strands of Enlightenment thought. In the above discussion of the everyday there features the assumption that agency exists *a priori*, or at least in the very existence of the individual, culture, and the community, which enable agencies that are also autonomous. The problem of autonomy is the first issue here: can local, everyday agency be autonomous in a post-conflict environment? Can there be agency in the everyday without autonomy? Can there be autonomy at all, even for international actors, and if not, is there any real everyday that might be distinct from the praxis and discourses of such power?[121] For Foucault, at least in his earlier work, emancipatory agency on the part of individuals was severely and discursively restrained. Later, he saw power as almost automatically giving rise to resistance, and so to graduations of autonomous agency, to the extent that he was accused of supporting very individualist (or neoliberal) forms of agency.[122] These issues are particularly problematic when it is remembered that the concept of agency is connected to rights, property and the market, and those individuals without either in liberal thought (and liberal imperialism) were considered primitive and part of a *res nullius*. Thus, rights are not enough to denote agency. This is a crucial problem peacebuilding should address.

As Foucault said, the autonomous subject is something of a myth.[123] Agency is, of course, an Enlightenment concept, ascribed from a scientific, rational and progressive position whereby once freed and simultaneously constrained within mutually agreed cosmopolitan regulatory frameworks, it will be exercised autonomously for the good life, circumscribed and facilitated by institutions. Agencies that are not restricted and removed, raise the questions of which are legitimate? and who should decide? Generally speaking, peacebuilding and state-building debates all assume that international actors have significant agency, even if constrained significantly by structures or lack of access to property and markets. It is this agency that enables policy which follows security, interests or norms, which allows for a praxis of empowering others to overcome their conflicts, enables mediation or peacekeeping, or local ownership of peacebuilding. The assumption of agency underpins all statebuilding approaches, though it is normally couched as good international agency versus problematic local agencies or the passive local.

What is interesting about the question of agency in these contexts is not whether it exists – as most academics and policymakers, as well as local community actors assume it does in limited forms though they may see it very different ways – but how it relates to autonomy and self-determination. Indeed, agency is the basis of all liberal politics. Thus, increasingly common local calls to engage with local ownership or the everyday are indicative of an attempt to relocate politics away from international actors, be they states, donors or the UN, in favour of local actors exercising their own agency, realising their freedom, and exercising their basic right of self-determination. Thus, the aspiration is for agency to emerge at the local level, and implying that so far it does not. Local expressions of such agency can be termed 'critical agency' and are often couched as hidden resistance to the models that elites or internationals offer, in an attempt to modify them.

Here peacebuilding and statebuilding encounter a significant problem. What if agency does not concur with their liberal agendas? What if, in their search for freedom and self-determination, localised forms of peacebuilding become expressions of resistance? Both Heidegger and Foucault in their later work concluded that agency meant freedom, and the capacity to change oneself and ones' own society or milieu, even if agency could not be autonomous.[124] In other words, agency is related to freedom, self-determination and self-government in everyday contexts. Everyday practices give meaning to life and community, and thus form the basis of peace,[125] before institutions. Subsequent institutions should reflect this. Peacebuilding should therefore be led by local agency rather than international agency if emancipation is to occur in a way that is resonant at the everyday level.

Calls to describe an alternative paradigm of 'peace', or to enable its operationali-sation, miss the point that such agencies are already developing though they may not fit closely with liberal prescriptions. This is not to essentialise and categorise: contextually reconstructing peacebuilding or statebuilding enterprises cannot be achieved in general theory alone. Contextual peacebuilding theory needs to be written obliquely, cognisant of time-lag, of aporias, of catechrisms, of alterity. It should be sensitive to the many subalterns, without whom legitimacy cannot be achieved, especially in its localised, transversal sense. It must engage with local agencies rather than denying them.

Reconstructing peacebuilding must start from the problem of contextual legitimacy and how it may emerge amongst the many subalterns who do not enjoy the privileges that those in the West view as a minimum. Here the task of politics is to undercover and enable local, everyday agencies, and the infrapolitics of peacebuilding, and to make each capable of translating, engaging, recognising, assisting and negotiating, without reverting to the old colonial/racist patterns of domination. It is necessary to understand how the infrapolitics of peacebuilding emerge through the expression of local agency in spite of international tendencies towards governmentalism and romanticisation. The track record of liberalism has in this task been one of offering the bare minimum to maintain legitimacy amongst both the subaltern dependents and liberals. Effectively, reversing this reclaims an everyday essence of peacebuilding.

This 'modernisation' of politics that has undermined the sphere of the everyday in favour of territorial sovereignty and institutionalism. As a consequence the space of the local, everyday, and its attendant actors are often seen as sites of violence, poverty, illiberalism and resistance, sometimes along Fanonian lines, rather than varied and dynamic sites of politics in their own right. The everyday is where formal explanatory capacity loses its abilities, and where inductive and critical approaches gain traction; it is also where the 'vague' and 'fuzzy' concepts associated with everyday life are most apparent. Yet, for the critical thinker, the everyday is real, clear, sharp, and precise, and is where its ethnographic, democratic, and political form often begins.

Ultimately the everyday is unmapable and disinclined to accept metanarratives of universal praxis, despite the inclination of liberalism, rationalism and positivist approaches to delineate intellectual, social, material and physical terrains according to numbers, hierarchies, resources and territory. They attempt to govern the everyday while denying its agencies. Yet, the literature invites a consideration of the qualitative dynamics of political, cultures, and societies as they form and act upon politic agendas for constructing peace. Its focus is on developing an empathetic understanding of such dynamics, even if they lead to resistance, rather than a dispassionate explanation. The former would argue that biopolitical approaches eventually defeat themselves by overlooking the everyday and its resilience and the lived experiences of communities and peoples as essential to order, stability and the formation of peace. This provides space for localised agency to operate. The latter approach by contrast appeals to an innate, universal, liberal civility, and where this is absent it reverts to conditionality and coercion where material and normative interests are sufficient, and dispassionate and neutral observation from above where interests are absent. Where the former appeals to human societies as the key units of politics and international relations, the latter reifies the state, its institutions and functions.

Thus, the everyday represents an unsettling capacity for the rebalancing and re-occupation of peacebuilding by real and lived experiences and agendas rather than merely as an empty and virtual space where only powerful states and elites reside. It offers an opportunity for empathetic relations to emerge between the international and the everyday. It offers a balancing framework for say, Habermasian discourse ethics where its impulse might be to valourise liberal values, a field site for post-structuralist scholars, and of course, uncovers a conveniently forgotten level of analysis for more orthodox approaches ranging from realism to constructivism. A sociology and ethnography is required to balance the securitised and institutionalized responses of realist and liberal approaches. But, this would not, as with constructivism or critical theory, begin with the core assumptions of realism and liberalism, but instead with those conceptual, theoretical, methodological and ontological puzzles offered by the everyday in its local, transnational and international contexts. For the everyday, the issues of formerly marginal actors and dynamics in a formal asymmetrical situation would be exposed. These would be represented in a proper perspective and balance, as opposed to the marginalisation of populations in poor or conflict prone, or non-Western, contexts that arises via most mainstream theories. Rather than such actors fulfilling their needs while appearing to conform to the strategic institutions of biopolitical governance, a more honest and realistic political landscape might emerge.[126]

What is clear is that the current understanding of the everyday in peacebuilding is very limited, despite the fact that it represents really existing lives in liberal democracies and beyond, or that many are aware and may empathise with those whose everyday experiences are marred by war, violence, and poverty. Yet, with the exception of work on gender and its focus on the 'private' arena, empathy and care, or peace and conflict studies, IR has tended to focus on the structures of state and global governance and international architectures, systems, and processes in liberal terms at the expense of the everyday.[127] Social contracts with states or with world governments have been the terrain of discussions about peace, and political theory has developed by cycling between these two dimensions. Peace is generally constructed in either a state context or an international context. This relates to the old argument about state government versus world government. Recently it has been focused on social contracts between populations and states, partly as a result of the 'war on terror', which displaced the earlier global, post-Westphalian turn of the early post-Cold War period.[128] In either case the focus has been on the contract itself, rather than on the 'social'. The everyday has been lost in all of this.

Ironically, one of the key effects of this failing has been that the emergence of a hybridity affecting liberalism in contexts where the liberal state model has come into close contact with its others. From within the 'West' liberal states have important nuances and differences. From the Balkans to Timor Leste and the Solomon Islands, from Cambodia to Sierra Leone, the engagement between the liberal conditionalities attached to a discussion of foreign policy, of global governance, and of peacebuilding and statebuilding, has led to subtle modifications of both the really existing liberalism that has arisen in such contexts and the local political, social, cultural and economic dynamics which have started to modify it. More broadly, this can also be seen in the development of more alternative or traditional state polities, such as in China, Russia, South Africa, India, Brazil and so forth. Liberalism is modified by its contacts with its others:

non-liberal, non-Western polities are modified by their contact with liberal polities and conditionalities. There is a meeting, mediation, negotiation, and clash, of different 'locals' and their political cultures, and its processes (not to say outcomes) are determined by the resources and hegemonic standing as well as discursive capacities of the 'actors', societies, practices and cultures which connect or repel each other in this process. But this is as much in a context of ideas as it is of materialities, and in both, the respective everydays' of populations are crucial in the discursive formulation of such connections and of course, of their legitimacy. This is not an argument that the alternatives to the liberal peace, or the hybrids that currently exist are more legitimate amongst their subjects than those they may aspire to. The point is more how forms of peace are negotiated from the dynamics, especially between contexts and institutions, states and internationals, and how such hybrid forms of peace might measure up to any emancipatory claims.

This is also observable in more formal moves made by international state-builders in response to the problems that have emerged in the liberal peacebuilding efforts of the last twenty years.[129] One of the key liberal responses has been to incorporate local actors and dimensions more closely into their attempts to deal with security, to establish liberal institutions, to promote development, human rights, and a rule of law. Concepts such as human security, civil society, local participation and ownership have been influential in the work of the UN, World Bank, and major donors. Local movements for more self-determination in the peace processes emerged in Kosovo and Timor Leste, among many others. In Afghanistan, the Tribal Liaison Office was aimed at bridging the local and inter-national. In Iraq, tribal politics were soon understood to be both the cause and solution to the violence during US and UK attempts at liberal statebuilding. In sub-Saharan Africa, there has been a serious attempt to incorporate indigenous forms of law and governance.[130] These reactions – spanning an incorporation of custom and traditional structures and the elevation of local voices and agencies – can be read both as examples of the reinsertion of local agency into technocratic forms of statebuilding which were leading to empty states and virtual forms of peace, and as a liberal realisation of its own failings. Here the interstitial interface between the liberal and the local is producing hybridity, but often in ways which represent the international more than the local. Yet, in response to such diffi-culties, the international 'model' for peace has been significantly modified by such dynamics. It might be that conflict resolution and peacebuilding are emerging more effectively through local approaches, and with greater legitimacy. It may also be a reconciliation between political liberalism and its others. This might be the basis for the reconstruction of more contextual and legitimate forms of peace, more able to emancipate and more self-sustainable.

In effect, local agencies have emerged around the praxis of peacebuilding which has required them to conform to its own dominant thrust. They have become more post-colonial, democratic and rights-oriented beyond the confines of liberal sovereign borders. But the reverse has also happened in that the infrapolitics of peace have modified the liberal peace in an attempt increase its content. These critical agencies are in the process of establishing a form of social contract and new accountabilities, beyond the Westphalian state, revolving around often liminal everydays. Local-liberal hybridity is an ongoing process that has emerged with both stabilising and 'malevolent' effects, as in many of the examples mentioned above.

For some liberal thinkers it has led to uncomfortable normative compromises (say over Shariah law in the Afghanistan 'liberal' state) or weak states (in all recent statebuilding examples). For local communities and actors, similar problems emerge, but this time in relation to how to reconcile liberalism with their own versions of norms, law or political institutions; how their material capacities are overshadowed by the developed world; and how rights have been diluted by the international. So far this process has been fraught, and the divorcing of liberal capitals from their rural hinterland in post-conflict sites has often been the case. Indeed, in Guatemala, many indigenous communities, constituting perhaps 60 per cent of the population of the state, do not regard the capital city as part of their country. They see it as a concentration of power and resources favouring a minority, who have historically controlled power, wealth, institutions and land, permanently biased against their own institutions, norms, values and interests – a problem which some local organisations have set about responding to.[131]

Everyday peacebuilding

The tendency to focus on the state in its Westphalian context as the main 'singularity'[132] of peacebuilding and statebuilding is a moment of exclusion. It undermines the capacity to understand the local in its everyday context. The everyday raises the question of what is necessary to achieve an *everyday state* (of peace formation) rather than merely a liberal *state*.[133] The broader politics of the everyday represent a local-liberal interface which produces hybridity in the forms of peace that might emerge.[134] This move towards hybridity and the questions it raises, are also representative of a very critical stance towards the conservative and liberal thinking that has tended to dominate political theory, philosophy and international relations in the past. It is also here that we see the 'unbecoming' face of liberalism, where it reverts or diverts to coercive strategies in order to prove that the Enlightenment equation of peace with 'becoming liberal' is not challenged. The interface between the local everyday and liberalism has all too often diverted the local to liberalism, which is after all the West's local, not necessarily a universal model for peace. The liberal is not the sole site of knowledge for peacebuilding (but then neither is the local). This does not mean that there is widespread rejection in post-war or post-conflict zones of the liberal peace, but it does mean that there is an expectation that the liberal state will actually achieve what it offers. There is often also a clear local aspiration for a liberal (Western) everyday at play, though coloured by local nuance but there is also an aspiration to preserve local 'authenticity'.

This raises the following questions – is a global liberal everyday form achievable? Will it provide what it offers? So far the experience has been that this form does not achieve the sophisticated forms of peace and order that were expected by its supporters. Can it offer pluralism and hybridity, or will it merely drown out calls for recognition of material and non-material rights and needs? A key assumption is that everyday life should be, and ultimately is, shaped by contextual agency. Thus, everyday politics represent agency even in the face of seemingly insurmountable resources, rhetoric, consensus, institutions, condition-alities or coercion, especially where these practices fail to recognise the agency inherent in the everyday.

Utilising a parsimonious, Enlightenment oriented and problem-solving approach, the politics of the everyday in post-violence situations might be thought of as the following in approximate order:

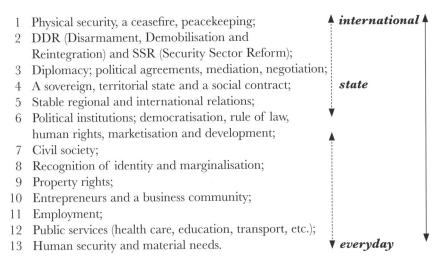

1 Physical security, a ceasefire, peacekeeping;
2 DDR (Disarmament, Demobilisation and
   Reintegration) and SSR (Security Sector Reform);
3 Diplomacy; political agreements, mediation, negotiation;
4 A sovereign, territorial state and a social contract;
5 Stable regional and international relations;
6 Political institutions; democratisation, rule of law,
   human rights, marketisation and development;
7 Civil society;
8 Recognition of identity and marginalisation;
9 Property rights;
10 Entrepreneurs and a business community;
11 Employment;
12 Public services (health care, education, transport, etc.);
13 Human security and material needs.

Figure 1 The Everyday in Liberal Peacebuilding

This is an approximate list and the ordering of its elements shows their distance and impact on everyday life from the perspective of citizens in a community and state setting, thought of in liberal and cosmopolitan terms. It favours a state security and institutional perspective. To some degree it counterbalances the liberal hierarchy of priorities which has emerged in the recent praxis of state-building. Liberalism is also supposed to focus on individual freedom; the liberal state on a social contract; and cosmopolitanism on at least a thin universality. According to the traditional orthodoxy, the everyday is relatively less visible than that of power, states and interests. From the perspective of everyday life, political agency is constructed through security, human security, material needs and public services, culture, custom and identity. In liberal terms this creates a hierarchical and progressive teleology, leading to the construction of a state which guarantees everyday life, regional peace, cemented by international institutions.

A more critical or emancipatory agenda might include the following:

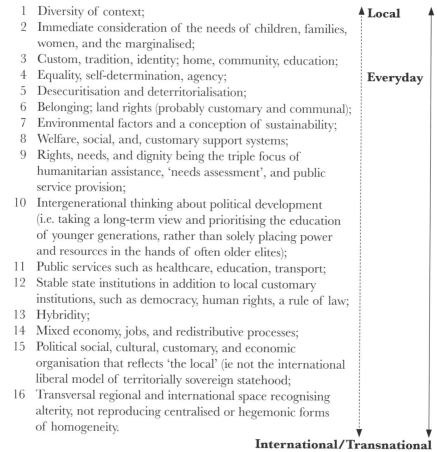

1 Diversity of context;
2 Immediate consideration of the needs of children, families, women, and the marginalised;
3 Custom, tradition, identity; home, community, education;
4 Equality, self-determination, agency;
5 Desecuritisation and deterritorialisation;
6 Belonging; land rights (probably customary and communal);
7 Environmental factors and a conception of sustainability;
8 Welfare, social, and, customary support systems;
9 Rights, needs, and dignity being the triple focus of humanitarian assistance, 'needs assessment', and public service provision;
10 Intergenerational thinking about political development (i.e. taking a long-term view and prioritising the education of younger generations, rather than solely placing power and resources in the hands of often older elites);
11 Public services such as healthcare, education, transport;
12 Stable state institutions in addition to local customary institutions, such as democracy, human rights, a rule of law;
13 Hybridity;
14 Mixed economy, jobs, and redistributive processes;
15 Political social, cultural, customary, and economic organisation that reflects 'the local' (ie not the international liberal model of territorially sovereign statehood;
16 Transversal regional and international space recognising alterity, not reproducing centralised or hegemonic forms of homogeneity.

Local

Everyday

International/Transnational

Figure 2 The Everyday in Post-liberal Peacebuilding

What is notable about this list is that it partially represents a merging of the liberal peace framework with local, everyday contexts and their critical agencies. The mediation between the local and the liberal makes it very difficult to place the emphasis of statebuilding, peacebuilding and the organisation of a polity on a territorial and sovereign state. Thus, agency provides a conceptual location for this mediation process, but is not defined in material ways by its territory or its boundaries, institutions or state, at least in conventional terms. This connects with a discussion of the nature of the post-Westphalian polity:[135] Connolly has called for a post-territorial form of democracy,[136] Linklater has called for a post-conventional morality,[137] Held has called for a global covenant,[138] and authors such as Bhabha and Spivak have opened up discussion about the need to recognise culture and the subaltern on their own terms, and of the nature of hybridity.[139] A deterritorialised, non-sovereign polity would be the outcome of incorporating the everyday as a key priority of peacebuilding in desecuritised form, maximising critical agency rather than the national interest of the state or interests of donors.[140] It is here that a viable local-liberal hybridity emerges representing a self-sustaining consensus on which a new peace might be built.

What this also indicates is the degree of the organic nature of an everyday peace, with implications for the institutions and state that should reflect it. A peaceful everyday is the key indicator of conflict resolution, yet is often displaced in favour of security reform, DDR, and institutional and state development. This reflects the interests and identity of external actors. The everyday polity, democracy and human security are experienced organically from below, and from these conditions being met, rather than from external intervention in a statebuilding guise. Peace cannot be successfully imported without first or simultaneously dealing with these issues. Otherwise it will rest on a state without a social contract, failing to meet the everyday needs of its population, and so indicating merely international not local legitimacy. In such contexts, the state will have an inbuilt propensity towards elite led co-option and predation.

The list offered above could be taken to imply a new essentialisation of post-conflict polities and institutions to be offered as a blueprint to peacebuilders, donors and statebuilders alike. This is not the aim: a new meta-narrative would rapidly move the focus from the everyday to the interests of elites, national interest, statebuilding and the donor community – as has already occurred within the liberal paradigm. Methodological positivism has endorsed this problematic move because of its probably unintentional, inherent bias towards northern epistemologies of peace. Context specificity for the everyday is required to prevent this slippage and its resultant elisions of peace and war, and the unthinking validation of alien norms and self-interest.

The methodology of the Everyday

To reverse this, supporting the ongoing shift in theoretical and methodological frameworks for peacebuilding, from problem-solving rationalism to those implied by an everyday frame is an obvious but difficult move. The everyday is fluid, and can be viewed materially, semiotically and inductively, as a deep and hidden set of interwoven meanings, symbols, signs, cultures and practices.[141] The key is to prevent the slippage from the everyday back to the institution or to security from constantly recurring on the grounds that the everyday defies easy understanding, or indeed is obviously recursive. Indeed, a comparison of the everyday and the liberal orthodoxy offers some core similarities: but the liberal orthodoxy retains its blind spots towards the local. Thus, without a contextual understanding of the everyday, the differences between the liberal and the local/everyday appear insignificant. If methodological approaches are used to expose the everyday, the gulf between the two suddenly becomes enormous and decisive. This gulf should be exposed with great methodological and ethical care, not hidden away, otherwise the post-colonial critique of Western epistemologies and resultant politics becomes all too relevant.[142]

The starting point here is that the everyday is far more visible in reflexive and recursive terms, and as such a priority, not merely secondary. The recent work of Amitav, Buzan, Shani, and Bilgin,[143] offers an opening in which alternative everydays, the indigenous, the non-Western, as well as the authenticity of what is often claimed as Western and liberal can be scrutinised. This means that there also has to be a methodological shift in order to enable us to see and account for the everyday. It should not be the only aspect and should not necessarily be to the detriment of more traditional approaches, but that this area and related methodologies needs to be more obviously part of any balanced discussion or analytical stance. This reconstitutes old theoretical and methodological battles (with a hint of ideology attached) as struggles over context, where it is far more profitable to accept the multiplicity of contexts, and therefore the need for a range of voices, theories and methods to match. The everyday should be ever-present in any theoretical discussion to prevent reductionism and problem-solving parsimony from unbalancing any discussion and undermining the agency of the often non-Western subject. New ways of knowing, in theory now need to enter the praxis of political reconstruction and peacebuilding.

So what sort of methodology uncovers the everyday? There are already diverse geographical, philosophical, sociological and ethnographic contributions to the discipline and to its increasing interdisciplinarity,[144] as well as widely echoed calls for interdisciplinary research, beyond rationalism, and selective sensory capacities. Other disciplines have long been developing methodologies through they are able to engage with the other and alterity, and to develop a conception of everyday lives, and social, customary, political, and economic systems. Of course, such disciplines – including anthropology – have long been in crisis partly because of this attempt, in terms of representation, of power, and colonial praxis. Anthropology, sociology, and other disciplines offer ready-made conceptual and theoretical debates through which the everyday can be integrated into the understanding of the politics of peace and war. Via such strategies, the colonial echoes of a mainstream elitist and liberal value system and political biases, and the resistance that this causes might be avoided or mitigated. The everyday should not be mapped by explorers wielding traditional Western methodological tools, as the early colonial anthropologists once did,[145] but should be allowed to speak for itself in a discipline that turns its attention to providing a diverse and representative everyday through which to voice conceptions of the local and international, rather than providing a platform for the liberal to speak for itself on behalf of absent others. Such research and contributions inevitably lead to a modification of theories and methods and the emergence of new. In this case, the everyday has already been touched upon in sociology and cultural studies, and in post-colonial, anthropological and ethnographic work. So there is a clear basis to proceed given the widening call for a more representative peacebuilding, rather than merely a liberal-colonial form. Using an understanding of the everyday is a natural outcome of adopting an eirenist approach.

But there are also ethical issues here, in that if the print-capitalism[146] of the new orthodoxy allows such knowledge to be deployed biopolitically then this undermines the very intent of bringing in the everyday. Strategies of social engineering have long been discounted yet this could be the outcome of strategic applications of the everyday according to the latest dogmatic method, theory or institutional positivism. Yet, the representation of the deeper dynamics and causal factors inherent in the discipline is also pragmatic – more so than reductionism, which has now been conclusively proved to have dangerous and costly unintended consequences, not to mention producing ethical vacuums, and even sowing the seeds of its own collapse. So incorporating the everyday is more pragmatic than the self-proclaimed 'pragmatic'. But, this is so because of its richness and complexity, not because of its simplicity. Even the shift towards statebuilding as one of the core agendas of international relations is in itself a complex endeavour, and in its liberal guise must engage with a social contract. This also requires an engagement with the everyday, which entails a rethinking of the classical liberal notion of the social contract between state and society to include international and transnational engagements with communities and individuals undergoing peacebuilding or statebuilding.[147] Beyond the Western and European self, Enlightenment and the everyday might be reclaimed and self-government become practical. It is in these terms that Mosse *et. al.* have argued, that the local is transversal, translocal and transnational as well as contextual.[148]

Peace Formation and the Everyday

This body of theory, and related methodologies, results in a need to begin to theorise from the everyday context and those most affected. There are two main possibilities, the first offering a mere modification of the liberal state system, and the second far more radical in its sense of a move away from territorial sovereignty. The former might lead to an 'everyday' social contract rather than one that represents a fine balance between a population or constituency and the government. Or it might produce a form of hybridity more biased towards the local context than the liberal state. This, in line with a requirement to move beyond the strategic nature of mainstream conceptions of peace, needs to represent everyday life in all of its dimensions and local contexts. Given that the expectation in today's politics of liberalism is that all citizens, whether government or governed, act democratically and respect each other's rights (if not dignity),[149] a social contract is constituted not between rulers and ruled over their respective powers, but between citizens, individuals and communities, and their varied forms of representation over the nature of everyday life that is acceptable to each other in a local and global context. This may also mean however, that the modification of the liberal state system enters a more radical phase.

It is now possible to attempt a preliminary summary of the impact of the adoption of the everyday. The politics of the everyday seeks to incorporate social and community contexts into peacebuilding methodology, epistemology, theory and policy. These become a basis for the construction of an everyday peace, in part international and institutional, democratic, observing rights and needs, with a rule of law, and in part representative of local identity, custom, culture, institutions and expectations. It reflects the local-local, and its transnational, transversal connections, including with the many agencies of the liberal peace, but also increasingly with those actors who are outside this consensus. This implies a facilitation of localised processes of peace formation. This would probably require an elevation of debates about equity and acceptable levels of living standards, security, identity, culture, custom, gender, rights, and needs in context. This would require a reconstitution of the focal point of politics around the state, territorial sovereignty, security, constitution, elites, modernisation and development as they currently stand to one that focuses on the agency of the population and community, and their everyday lives in a customary and intergenerational, transnational context in conjunction with a focus on political representation and private property rights within the shell of a state. The state may merely be the vehicle for the everyday, not the end in itself. This would become the focus of hybridity, modifying sovereignty and the liberal state in favour of an aggregation of local voices as opposed mainly to international or elite voices. From here an everyday form of peace may arise as through local agency, resistance, as agonistic relations between the liberal and the local.

A consideration of the everyday would offer a repopulation of essentially 'empty states' and the virtual forms of peace that have arisen. In practice such states tend to be social democracies, whether developed or developing.[150] This means that polities emerging from conflict do have a choice about the nature of their polity, whether neoliberal as in the UK or US, or social democratic as in Scandinavian states, Germany, Costa Rica or Chile, or influenced by other ideological formulations, custom, culture, religion and other forms of identity, as in many emerging hybrids in the developing world. These choices are, however, never allowed for conflict polities undergoing 'statebuilding', even though there is much evidence to show that citizens in Iraq, for example, would have had such a preference.[151] This is not a radical version of the politics of the everyday, but through the everyday, presents a modification to the processes of liberal peace-building that would be relatively easy to engage with. Another aspect of this moderate debate is the standard move made towards formulating a states-system based on universal norms or law, as with the work of Rawls and critical theorists such as Habermas, or with the earlier work of idealists and liberal internationalists.[152] Those working on world government, regimes, international law, and globalisation also represent this move away from state monopoly in an effort to reinforce peace within and between them, but the focus is on legalistic and constitutional structures, and international regimes and mechanisms, or markets that are even more distant from society, though of course also have an impact on it.

A more radical version would need to engage with the way such everyday dynamics produces forms of peace less obvious to the liberal gaze. This raises the following issues. The state is traditionally taken in liberal thinking to provide a set of institutions through which peace can emerge. The lessons of roughly one third of the states in existence today concur to a large degree with this lesson. The legitimacy of most developed states does rest on a social contract, and everyday life to a large degree does offer enough resources and legitimacy to provide stability, an acceptance of state and government. But this leaves a large number of states where authoritarianism, poverty and violence displace the everyday, even where the liberal-institutionalist framework has been constructed (often imported through liberal peacebuilding and statebuilding). There are two questions here: why does this occur in some states and not others, and why is the everyday context relatively low on the agendas of those more 'successful' polities which are currently engaged in the peacebuilding/statebuilding project where elites benefit most? There is one final issue, which centres on why the territorialised state is taken to be the fulcrum upon which all of these debates rest, given that territory and statehood often form the focus of a conflict. To escape this tautology, an engagement more directly with the everyday, one that is not conditioned by the restraints of statehood and territory might be more productive. Thus sovereignty is not the issue to be contested, but the everyday life, or situation, of communities and how these might be ameliorated. Sovereignty, if it is to be brought into being, should start from this discussion, not from an a priori, externally supported state.

This more radical shift suggests that local ownership, democracy, self-government, self-determination and participation, as well as a vibrant civil society are key to a social and civil peace, not just to a 'trading society',[153] as well to peaceful statehood. But this must be redefined and broadened to include the local-local in its breadth, and not represent a top down process of governance, but a bottom-up process of self-government in the parameters of government and state are locally established rather than externally imported. Here, the distance from the international or state is reduced. A conceptualisation of the everyday is able to navigate between the local, state, market, and the impulses to centralisation and internationalism, while remaining connected to them in ways that do not compromise self-government or self-determination, international norms, law, order, or custom, culture, identity and needs. Difficult compromises may be necessary of all parties, but their everyday legitimacy, if broadly present and representative, will not be compromised. The everyday is the essential zone of the political, so often missed or treated as exceptions subject to the exceptional.[154]

It is thinking about the everyday that actually reduces the distance between those who discursively construct the international and the local as broad categories. Without the everyday, politics reverts to elitism or neo-colonialism: democracy and human rights are subverted; and culture, needs and critical agency can be easily ignored. This undermines the legitimacy of peacebuilding and statebuilding. The everyday offers an alternative site of knowledge for the international, and one that without which, the international cannot succeed in peace but only in a messy conglomeration of fragile truces.

Conclusion

Peacebuilding may now be seen as partially a site of international assistance, and partially as local acquiescence, or local co-option: of critical agency often expressed as multiple and often hidden forms of resistance – and of peace formation. There are international and local public and hidden transcripts at play which expose the tensions and openings between them.[155] Both local and international offer a public transcript framed in mutually understandable language about how each may help each other, but there is a hidden transcript which betrays a lack of understanding, care, or agreement, and antagonistic relations of domination and resistance.[156] Both accept, co-opt, resist, or reject each other as the 'natural order of things' but also attempt to naturalise themselves, which also has the effect of spurring internal and external critiques of international and local practices where they are deemed to interfere with autonomy and agency.[157] This may be termed peacebuilding-as-resistance from the perspective of context which determines the politics, legitimacy and success of external approaches locally.

This is predicated on the ability to engage with the politics of peacebuilding, to resist overwhelming technical superiority, and to modify it marginally, or only to mimic it. This occurs locally through a range of 'minute, individual, autonomous tactics and strategies …',[158] the constant everyday forms of resistance through which local agency may be expressed despite overwhelming authority. This is a resistance to some of the central claims of liberal peacebuilding and statebuilding; its celebrations of pluralism-as-liberalism; its claimed rights to adjudicate and manipulate material resources, to legitimate; its underlying celebration of individualism and deference to the market (if imposed by states and international institutions); its underlying claims that only certain forms of agency are always present even for the most marginalised; and its validation of national identities, sovereignty, institutions, rights and justice in prior forms. It may involve becoming 'modern' or becoming 'liberal', or remaining 'local', but in heavily or subtly modified ways, rather than merely rejecting fully the liberal peace model and romanticising either local resistance or international authority.

Local forms of peacebuilding are reconstituting themselves as resistance to the relatively empty signification of doctrine of liberal peacebuilding itself and its assumption of liberal state creation. Resistance at the local level provides a site from which a new peace begins to be imagined in contextual and everyday terms, politically reconstituting a social contract and a state, or even moving beyond Westphalia. Local actors engaging in the project are thus producing a more sustainable form of peace in local terms, but are also engaged in the political reform of the liberal peace project. Hopefully, such dynamics will lead not to mutual resistance but the emergence of more viable contextual forms of peace, as well as a better understanding of civil, state and institutional or international peacebuilding discourses.

Peacebuilding-as-resistance represents a form of agonism between the liberal and the local, experienced mainly at the level of the everyday, rather than via revolutionary alterity.[159] It is often through resistance that a civil society and a social contract comes into being in agonistic terms, overcoming the distancing that liberal peacebuilding tends to bring about. Thus, peacebuilding-as-resistance may lead to emancipation. This can be seen in two ways: either peacebuilding-as-resistance revitalises the liberal social contract and gives these externally constructed states substance, or more radically it enables a more proactive encounter between the liberal peace and its others, in which the hegemonic weight of the liberal peace project is countermanded and hybridised, producing new global and local norms and institutional reform.

This allows for a complete rethink of the role of the everyday, alterity and resistance, in peacebuilding terms. It also enables an understanding of local legitimacy, even though local actors, intentions and processes silence themselves in the interests of maintaining their remaining space,[160] or as Spivak said, are simply muted by international dominance and a liberal aversion to non-liberal symbolic productions. Yet, engaging the local with peacebuilding requires engaging with local understandings of peacebuilding which may well entail resistance to modernity, to modernisation, to centralised state power, sovereignties outside of limited communities, liberal norms and institutions, the market, and conceptions of rights over needs. Peacebuilding-as-resistance prioritises self-determination, community, agency, autonomy, often democracy, rights, dignity, custom, and a sense of nation, and sometimes the materiality of liberal states.

Thus, there are parallels with liberal peace frameworks and cosmopolitan or internationalist aspirations, but there are also acute tensions, some of which play out agonistically, but others lead to blockages in the negotiating process between the local and the liberal. Until recently, the tendency has been for the international to take priority in such situations, but this has disenfranchised the very populations for which it sought to govern. Peacebuilding needs to incorporate local discourse founders[161] as well as received international wisdom, which act together to produce new political subjects in post-conflict environments with a complex mixture of agency, autonomy, resistance and acceptance,[162] and which create their own status as subjects to a large degree.

Consequently, the modern liberal peace and statebuilding project has already become hybrid; it has been modified by its contact with various local spaces (even if it has not recognised this). A form of localised peacebuilding has modified the modern liberal peace project by resisting or co-opting it, often in unlikely places by unlikely actors. Post-Cold War liberalism has not had the flexibility to recognise this, and even the emancipatory graduation of the liberal peace still requires its subjects to convert to liberalism, following Rawls (or even Habermas). Yet this hybridity may in future prove to be the liberal peace's greatest strength.

Liberal peace will remain in an agonistic relationship with its others, probably until this hybridity allows both to change while maintaining their differences and localities. Thus, hybridity represents a coexistence of difference, rather than assimilation and internationalisation. Liberalism tolerates or co-opts while contextualism resists, modifies and adopts. Liberalism territorialises whereas hybridity deterritorialises. Peacebuilding has to negotiate these terrains, negotiating the liberal statebuilding project and particularistic communitarianism via agonistic hybridity. Peacebuilding thus constituted recognises difference, supports agency, enables autonomy, and stays clear of state or social engineering. Of course, statebuilders may argue that the state is needed to house this project and promote regional order. But what if post-liberal peacebuilding implies a polity that does not conform with the modern liberal state?

Peacebuilding cannot just be reduced to romanticised notions of localised resistance of course: indeed it is notable how today many members of the 'international civil service' of peacebuilders privately both accept and resist aspects of liberal peacebuilding themselves.[163] Of course the programmes introduced by liberal peacebuilding generally remove or constrain local agency as resistance in various sensible but some often often unintended ways. DDR and SSR removes weapons and concentrates them in the hands of national security services requiring massive restructuring of a major institution. Marketisation removes protectionism but makes competition and so livelihoods very difficult for new post-conflict entrants in the market system, often adversely affecting most poor citizens. Democratisation focuses politics on the party system and their general and often conflicting nationalist agendas. Human rights supplant human needs or local conceptions of custom and dignity. The rule of law endorses all of this and protects private property and may even subtly entrench socio-economic inequality and a class system. International support, loans, grants, advice, companies, peacekeepers, agencies and NGOs are supposed to compensate for any loss of agency in these areas, and to focus on empowering civil society, citizens and the state to operate in their confines. This sleight of hand is what makes the everyday so important, and is what leads to the paradox of civil society and localised forms of peacebuilding becoming platforms for deep, local-local resistance, however marginal, and for the development of an agonism between the liberal and the local, which forms the basis of a new potential social contract and for state formation and a politics of peace beyond the state.[164] Hybridity emerges in different ways and at different times in these polarised relations via local resistance, co-option and domination, or compliance and accommodation, between local and liberal forms of peacebuilding.[165]

Considering the everyday in peacebuilding praxis requires that rather than being policy driven, elite driven, externally driven and donor driven, it is 'context driven'. Here, the repoliticisation and enabling of relatively autonomous agency necessary for democracy, rights, needs, justice, and culture and identity that does more than produce bare life, may occur. Context driven approaches require an empathetic response between 'liberals' and 'locals' over their mutual and separate everyday norms, interests and lives. It requires a detailed and ethnographic, not just securitised, or institutional, or statistical or trend-based understanding of each other's positions and contexts. It opens up the world of the local to peacebuilding approaches, also perhaps re-enervating an emancipatory notion of both peace and human security. It requires at the very most a thin version of the liberal, cosmopolitan project,[166] but preferably an engagement with less easily essentialisable approaches to deterritoriali-sation, the avoidance of othering and emphasising narcissistic difference, or on the reconstruction and pluralisation of exclusive communities.[167] As Chabal and Daloz have argued in another context, we should '... stop operating on the assumption that observable diversity is but a veil over fundamentally similar processes'[168] where the state, peace and agency, might be easily uncovered. The site of the everyday is probably not a place to reconstruct a single cosmopolitan everyday or to aspire to communitarian boundaries, but instead represents pluralities which meet, interact, integrate, react, resist, mediate and negotiate.

The liberal peace has evolved into a new frontier of international politics. The claim that there is no real alternative is a liberal fantasy derived from neo-colonial, if well-meaning, dreams of cosmopolitan universalism. In fact there are alternatives and significant modifications to the liberal agenda which, though not unproblematic, are already intellectually available and empirically observable (as the next chapter will begin to illustrate).

Thus, an agenda for a post-liberal form of peacebuilding might include the following:

1   Avoiding metanarratives for peace, development, humanitarian, and stabilisation projects;
2   A move beyond Westphalia – deterritorialisation and a recognition of alterity especially;
3   Engaging, listening to, and translating dynamics of resistance and peace formation, not mapping and instrumentalising the local;
4   Recognition of multiple and overlapping, transversal contexts, whether local or international;
5   Dynamics of inclusion/exclusion to be replaced by agonism;
6   Inequalities, class, socio-economic needs to form navigation points for policy;
7   ethnographic and reflexive research to counterbalance problem-solving approaches;
8   Use of institutional ethnography;
9   Recognition of the everyday and of empathy to underpin the above;
10 Self-care/self-governance, and self-determination to be the focus of peacebuilding, not removing politics through an institutional/market/securitised focus;
11 Hybridity, and a recognition of the local-liberal agonistic relations therein;
12 Recognition that local forms of peacebuilding can also legitimately take the form of resistance to international discourses of liberal peace/statebuilding;
13 Production of rights and needs based institutions at local, state, regional, and international levels on this contextual basis, rather than following external liberal blue prints.

One of the most interesting aspects of the emerging post-liberal peace is that it rescues and reunites both the liberal and the local. It does not aim to depoliticise the local or to remove politics from the international, but to highlight the evolving relations between them. Of course, liberalism is actually a form of customary political community, derived from the Western experience (i.e. the West's own 'local'). But most non- or partially liberal environments have emerged from their own authentic customary experiences, which have survived colonialism, war and poverty, often because they represent social support and resilience or specific identities despite such experiences, and have remained more relevant to peoples' everyday lives than their often predatory or failing, virtual states.

The liberal-local hybrid can represent either a combination of very negative political practices (for example, rigorously determined liberal institutionalism and market development solutions with patriarchal, feudal, communal, or sexist, practices) or it can be more positive in that it connects complementary practices related to self-determination and agency, democracy, human rights and needs, and a rule of law, with customary social support networks, and customary forms of governance and political order; or it can connect both negative and positive practices (meaning both the liberal and the local develop elements of attraction and rejection). Though the problem posed here might be that liberalism and customary forms of governance block each other and deny each other's existence, this is not always the case. Liberalism, more specifically, is less likely to recognise the local, the contextual, customary order, and to actively marginalise it than the local is to marginalise the liberal. This is partly due to the power relations between liberalism and the local which inevitably favours liberal political orders and lead to them appearing to have colonial characteristics. However, there is a mutual attraction between the liberal and the local, which in many conflict and post-conflict zones, is in the process of producing a hybrid, perhaps because they share liberal aspirations or their values, aspirations, and interests display mutual goals. In fact, this represents the growing development of alternative political communities, forming and reforming themselves, sometimes assisted by the interface between the liberal and the local offered by mainly liberal international actors, into political communities that represent both the liberal and the local.

This hybrid represents a post-liberal peace emerging in diverse locations, from El Salvador, Guatemala, Namibia, Cambodia, to Bosnia, Kosovo, Sierra Leone, Liberia, Uganda, Timor Leste, Solomon Islands, Afghanistan and Iraq. This is not necessarily an emancipatory form of peace (as theorised in my earlier work).[169] But this hybrid offers greater potential for a more locally resonant form of peace to emerge than simply transplanting the liberal peace into post-colonial, post-conflict, development settings, as has been the recent approach, and 'muddling through'. It does not abandon the Enlightenment–humanist project, but neither does it represent it as universal.[170] The emergence of hybridity is the result of the clash and connection of fundamentally different forms of political organisation and community. It should not be taken that either liberalism or a malevolent hybridity will emerge, as difficult compromises on values and norms, as well as institutions need to be negotiated by both the liberal and the local, separately and together. It should be noted that hybridity in practice still often preserves the 'master discourse', whether liberal or of a nationalist state, so the preliminary post-liberal move is only part of a longer intellectual process of reflection and theory development.

The liberal-local hybrid might be taken as a 'post-conventional contextualism'.[171] This everyday is not a benign space, but an tense episteme requiring understanding and translation (not mapping, explaining or essentialising) via which other voices can attain agency and represent themselves – so that the subaltern may speak, even if only to try to explain their predicament.[172] This is where the 'infrapolitics' of peacebuilding lie, and a relatively hidden realm where culture, identity, agency and structure *from beneath* has a significant effect on its more visible mainstream dynamics such as the development of institutions and states.[173] Consequently, the infrapolitics of peacebuilding have given birth to a post-liberal peace in many contexts.

The post-liberal peace is not an alternative to the liberal peace, but instead offers a hybrid of both liberal and local processes and institutions which differs according to each context. It would see the coexistence and re-negotiation of liberal versions of democracy, the rule of law, human rights, development and the market, all contained by the modern state along with local or customary forms of governance. It would include the recognition of the dynamics of the everyday, from the needs of communities and citizens in subsistence and customary settings, of tradition, history, and non-liberal identities, of customary law, hereditary and tribal institutions, different notions about the use and ownership of land and property, of the role of the state, market or community/collective in providing services, and so forth. This is not to re-establish a juxtaposition between the liberal and the non-liberal, the modern and the traditional, but instead to see how the modern liberal peacebuilding project is modified by its subjects, whether they are liberal and modern or not, towards a more resonant and localised form of politics. The next question would be how this form of peace would be organised in each context.

These post-liberal processes, and expressions of critical agency, whether through resistance or acceptance of the liberal peace project, lead to forms of emancipation not necessarily envisaged by liberal modernity. They may also be indicative of a desire on the part of local stakeholders for international peacebuilding to play a facilitative rather than directive role, to allow the post-liberal peace to emerge in a range of spaces that internationals may not fully understand because of their lack of contextual knowledge. It may require them to respond more urgently to material deficiencies that destabilise everyday life for citizens, rather than their current focus on elites, governance, politicians and a business class housed within a formal state. Institutions, and potentially states, designed in this more sensitive manner by local actors and facilitated by external actors would make a much better job of shaping participation and rights, of democracy and inclusion, and be much more empowering than at present. They might also escape elite predation and corruption to a greater degree, and facilitate political mobilisation without power struggles, a nationalist state project or gross inequality emerging as an unintended consequence.

Thus, peacebuilding-as-resistance (effectively to governance and governmentality in liberal guise) represents a complex mix of international hegemony, local resistance, mimicry, agency, and subversion.[174] Beyond governmentality and biopower/politics, beyond essentialised notions of culture and identity, lies a range of hybrid processes – the often marginal modification of hegemonic praxis by hitherto hidden local agencies. The everyday captures these dynamics and spaces where a new politics may emerge.

Everyday peacebuilding and the local-liberal peace, where local agencies, radical, passive, active, subaltern, moulded by both local everyday dynamics and liberal international aspirations, meet the liberal international, makes post-liberalism already a reality. In each context it may differ and in each it must negotiate the contradictions that arise in the often abrasive relationship between international understandings of the liberal peace, institutions and the liberal state, and local processes of politics. With further contextual research, deploying methodologies designed to enable and empower the local and the everyday, it may well transpire that a post-liberal peace might more fully recognise the common and differing capacities of both the liberal and the local. Here local-local and critical agencies, liberal and post-conflict, appear transnationally and share common aspirations for peace and respect mutual difference. They entail the realistic acknowledgement that the 'power' of liberal peacebuilding is inevitably fragmented. The infrapolitics of peacebuilding represent and protect the weak and the hidden to a degree. For peacebuilding's reinvention, and as Fanon argued in another context, a critical consciousness is required that is '… freed from colonialism and forewarned of all attempts at mystification, inoculated against all national anthems.'[175]

6 De-romanticising the local, de-mystifying the international: aspects of the local-liberal hybrid

The progressive principle is [...] antagonistic to the sway of Custom. The greater part of the world has, properly speaking, no history because the despotism of Custom is complete. This is the case over the whole of the East ....[1]

Introduction

A 'liberal-local hybrid' form of peace determines peacebuilding and state-building operations of the current era, and partially resolves the liberal paradox of freedom versus governmentality or (neo) colonialism. Hybridity in this sense represents a transmutation of both the liberal and the local discourses of peace, even in view of their relatively unequal material relations and of course, their differences and similarities. It also allows for the putative 'line' between the liberal and the local to instead be seen as a blurred margin marked by transnational, transversal, complex relations.[2]

This is also where the international tendency to romanticise the local in very Orientalist ways as well as romanticising its own superior capacities becomes visible. Even the move towards 'mapping' the local contexts and actors, underway in a number of international fora including in UN agencies, continues such dynamics,[3] ignoring the lessons of a previous era of colonial anthropology. Likewise, the local tends to mystify the international liberal model in terms of its power, capacities, and technologies. Conversely it also applies a post-colonial critique to its supposed will to power and domination over the local. It is notable that the international in particular sees itself unreflexively as Western, muscular, masculine, and capitalist; efficient, normatively and governmentally superior, rights oriented, and able to supplant 'non-liberal', everyday forms of politics, society, government and economy.[4] The local tends to imbue itself with deep and hidden Geertzian meanings, especially via its cultural milieu and the tension between tradition, custom, community and Western modernity, and defines itself and its agencies in relation to a wide variety of networks and others.[5]

Many actors involved in peacebuilding, humanitarianism, and statebuilding are acutely aware of the different roles of the local, often in negative terms: its participation, stakeholders and ownership, its legitimising effect, resilience of civil society and needs and of social mobilisation. Increasingly, this, via inductive and semiotic techniques,[6] has opened up the realm of critical agency, informal, customary forms of politics and social structure, along with the more defined areas of inequality, social class, and neopatrimonialism. Many agencies have developed an interest in 'bottom-up' or grass-root and indigenous approaches to peacebuilding and 'community resilience'.[7] This is derived from an assumption that there is a pre-existing or imagined social, political and economic community structure to draw upon (also as with UN's recognition of traditional forms of knowledge).[8] This recognition has broad implications for the way in which liberal peacebuilding and statebuilding engages with the local, which have not yet been fully explored. It also requires recognition that the international community has tended to avoid discussions about local cultural patterns and norms because it fears they are often contradictory agencies. There has, of course, been an increasing employment of local staff (though international and local personnel partnering and 'opposite number' schemes) in more significant roles in peace-building projects in some organisations, and some notable attempts to avoid conditionality in favour of building trust, respecting autonomy and strengthening civil society.[9] The latter, of course, does imply some sense of a normative conditionality but it is also a response to local critiques.

To understand these dynamics which represent the infrapolitics of peace-building[10] this chapter illustrates some of the arguments of the previous chapter and outlines the interaction between liberal and local process of politics and peacebuilding found in both Timor Leste and the Solomon Islands. A discursive hegemony and contest at different political levels is at play at the 'interface' between the liberal and the local. Recognising this is necessary for the de-roman-ticisation of both the liberal and the local, which must occur if a post-liberal peace is to emerge (from cultural, post-colonial, and more traditional state-centric/institutional perspectives). This concurs with the post-colonial argument that the liberal-local hybrid – even in the guise of liberal peacebuilding and state-building – in Timor and the Solomons is partly the result of a colonial encounter and often mainly on the colonist's terms.[11]

Some aspects of local-liberal hybridity

So far a dynamic of opposition has occurred between the local and the liberal in peacebuilding and statebuilding operations. This process often focuses on urbanised notions of marketised 'civil society' in order to redress human needs issues, provide for human rights, and endorse democracy and debate. But this civil society, often described as mythical by anthropologists,[12] is a Western normative veneer, meant to supplant the local-local and to undo what are often seen as anti-democratic, patronage-based, neopatrimonial, corrupt, inefficient, and often patriarchal, non-secular practices. At the same time, scholars often point to the need for 'local capacity', 'local ownership', 'local participation', custom and tradition. Yet, where the local is not equated with violence, it is normally defined as 'national' and ownership is thought of within the liberal framework, rather than being understood contextually. Strong arguments are made against the local and context, often by referring to rights and gender issues where the local resists international norms (recent discussions over negotiating with the Taliban, or Afghanistan's marriage laws, effectively allowing marital rape, or genital mutilation, are examples). Sometimes it is associated with direct violence rather than with the parallel activities to redress needs, provide services, and mitigate violence (as was the case during the first Palestinian *intifada*). Sometimes it is associated with hidden responses: with the suspension of cooperation with authorities or occupiers, including in bureaucratic terms, withholding taxes, boycotts, or noncooperation, all of which undermine centralised power, as also occurred in the *intifada* and since.[13] Thus, the local is appealed to, but the local that is part of the Western civil society imaginary while the rest is deemed violent and intolerable. To some degree concepts such as neopatrimonialism, clientelism, and patronage represent a discursive usurpation of local forms of politics and agency.[14] Such processes are very open to a post-colonial form of critique. They are also open to local strategies which nullify or moderate hegemony, as Thoreau illustrated long ago.[15]

There are three key dimensions here, often overlooked. The first relates to the local attempts to develop their own, distinctive processes of reconstruction, politics, legal, economic, and social frameworks after conflict, assisted by internationals rather than led by them. The second relates to the really-existing form of externalised governance that comes to represent 'peace' on the ground, even if liberal international actors do not recognise it as such. Drawing from this, the third represents the emergence of hybrid forms of institutions, law, economic and social organisation, and so a post-liberal form of peace, whereby the liberal and the local meet each other on the ground, react, modify, co-opt, resist, or accept. Even in spite of the hegemony of the liberal peace model, the local shows itself to have significant levels of agency in modifying the liberal model. It has also shown itself to have significant fluidity, and perhaps to be much more flexible than managerial and technocratic liberal governmentality that has arisen.[16]

The local can be thought of in terms of everyday social reality.[17] 'Of particular interest are processes of peace formation therein.' This includes customary processes and institutions, as well as indigenous forms of knowledge, traditional authorities, elders, chiefs, communities, tribes, and religious groups. Of course, it also includes the life of modernity, and the impact of liberal state institutions and markets. As Boege *et al.* have argued, this accounts for a large proportion of post-conflict and development populations: and such informal institutions and approaches are in tension with, complement, and substitute for the modern liberal state.[18] Thus, the local, everyday, and the customary, have an ambiguous position in the eyes of the West: they are premodern, undeveloped, clientelistic, patriarchal, patrimonial, corrupt, romantic, but they are also able to support the modern state. They permeate the modern liberal project, and perhaps subvert it.[19] They may modify the liberal state, they may resist it, or they may be co-opted by it.

What has in fact occurred has often been a resurgence of traditional systems and customary or locally resonant forms of governance within the liberal state, perhaps reducing dislocation, redressing the local agency gap somewhat in the liberal peacebuilding context, and certainly also significantly modifying the liberal state. The customary or contextual should not be seen as fixed, primitive, indolent, or barbarous. Instead they offer resilience: socio-economic systems of support, political institutions and stability, law and even security, and identity oriented processes of situation. The local is also able to engage with (or permeate) liberal state and international mechanisms.[20] This is not to romanticise the local, but to uncover its positive attributes as well as the more normally perceived negative attributes.

Such dynamics, positive and negative, have been observed in a range of peace-building and statebuilding examples. It has long been known, for example in Bosnia, that democratisation can be hijacked by nationalists. In much of sub-Saharan Africa it has been observed that development models based on attracting FDI do not succeed quickly (unless elite predation is termed a success). In Cambodia it has been observed that human rights may be culturally alien in societies used to communal living and social, patronage-based networks. In sub-Saharan Africa, the Middle East, Central America, and parts of Asia it has become clear that the customary law and governance may be more efficient than alien attempts to introduce modern practices and institutions. Hybrids have emerged as in Rwanda, even if they are complex mediations of inconsistent practices.[21] A significant scattering of articles published on peacebuilding in Central America, across Africa, parts of Asia and the Pacific, since the early 1990s, now chart the emergence of hybridity, and the role of local actors in shaping peace (these texts perhaps represent the academic infrapolitics of peacebuilding and statebuilding).

For example, the cases of Guatemala, Namibia and Mozambique have long been taken as relative successes for the liberal peacebuilding project. Liberia is also increasingly seen as on the 'correct' path by donors. Indeed some commentators argue that its peace process started locally, in civil society, and particularly amongst women's groups (who are normally excluded from peace processes).[22] Yet, in part this 'success' has brought about a modified liberal peace,[23] sometimes politi-cally authoritarian, resting on a liberation consensus, and marginalising political opposition, not to mention needs and everyday life. In various ways, different groups are marginalised by the liberal peace, such as in Guatemala with its majority indigenous population.[24] Key needs and cultural dynamics such as acute inequality are also marginalised by the liberal peace. These particular cases have seen the emergence of localised, *subsistence peacebuilding*: often sympathetic with the marginal political opposition, having lost international donor support because of this, yet working on human rights, cultural, indigenous, or rule of law issues, but also bringing in local cultural and historical resonance to such liberal institutions.[25] This process of peace formation is often carried out with minimal resources and little external help as donors follow neoliberal policies and shift away from rights and civil society, but also carries local resonance and legitimacy.[26]

As one interviewee in Mozambique argued, in a discussion of the key role of the Electoral Observatory which monitors elections and represents an alliance of local actors within civil society and beyond, local actors have the capacity to develop their own variant models of peace: and they have the capacity but lack the resources because international actors have turned peace into a 'business' in which they expect to use their own expertise and resources rather than engage with context. Their context is international not local, thus they cannot understand that peace without material means has little impact at the grass-roots level. As a result, most local peacebuilding in Mozambique has come to rest on a subsistence mode, mainly invisible to international eyes.[27] In Namibia, widely thought of by donors as a successful case, a 'Namibian Way' has emerged which has allowed the dominant political party to maintain its relations with Western donors, following the liberal peace model, but also to make space for local, traditional actors and customary law. This allowed significant local ownership, if only for those who were compliant with SWAPO's party's structures and goals.[28]

Generally speaking, in these cases, individualistic versions of society and prefabricated models are regarded with suspicion, on customary and religious grounds, but also because the negative experience of state predation and of socialism in the past. It has an impact on the sort of agendas political parties contest, and has been important in raising issues related to inequality, customary forms of law and institutions, in the context of the modern state.

One of the big issues in Mozambique is land ownership. Most people in civil society support the government's ownership of the land, as this was partly what the liberation struggle was fought for. Yet, the World Bank is pushing hard for privatisation, partly to reduce the power of the government. Civil society has been instrumental in preventing this, and making sure that people retain their current access under the existing approach to state land. The government in turn see privatisation as passing ownership to elites and banks.[29] Many fear that if the World Bank has its way, conflict will return, so they maintain many levels of resistance to such inappropriate strategies, from government to civil society. This has been one of the reasons why local actors took over the drafting of the PRSP (Poverty Reduction Strategy Paper) in 2004, rather than allowing the World Bank to do so. This has been seen as a process of reclaiming local ownership over development and peacebuilding.[30]

Similar dynamics can be observed in Somalia, long seen by internationals as a hopeless case. Here, it has become clear despite almost two decades of 'collapsed statehood' that everyday life has continued, and in various ways has maintained itself including via the provision of security, law and order in their socio-historical, cultural and customary, contexts, but also in terms of the types of public service the modern state is supposed to provide.[31] These are of course, heavily disrupted by violence, but it illustrates the potential that exists. In the absence of a state, local organisation, governance,and law have developed based on localised peace agreements. Many have been very successful. The international preoccupation with statebuilding has provided space for this, ironically. Statebuilding has tried to consolidate and centralise authority, whereas local peacebuilding has created resonant processes of compromise and moderation, for security and for service provision.[32] According to Johnson, Somali-led peacemaking has rested upon consultation, respected leadership and mediation, inclusiveness, legitimacy and credibility; incrementalism, broad consensus about security matters and investment, and localised and resonant forms of dissemination of agreements. Of course, it is also acknowledged that imbalances of power and discrimination have been harder to deal with in this context.[33] Yet, the customary law has retained its resonance both in highlighting such issues, the impact of the civil war, and in guiding localised responses to peacemaking especially vis-à-vis reconciliation and reparation in collective ways. At the same time, customary and localised processes have demonstrated a practical legal pluralism with both religious and liberal systems: such capacity has been far less obvious at the national level or in the UN sponsored process. It is clear that external expertise and capacity is essential in terms of rights and needs, and to end the cultures of violence and impunity, but with reference to the local context (which in Johnson's words '... trumps everything'). They should support not drive peacebuilding processes.[34] These are important insights, repeated often across the post-conflict world.

In such cases the state is, to varying degrees, absent from the rural areas, where high unemployment and/subsistence predominates. This maintains power relations and poverty but it also enables autonomy, allows the continuation of customary institutions, for all their varying qualities, and in the longer terms creates a mediation of the liberal state, dominated by donors and elites, by its citizens. Where there is an absence of state there is resistance and some space for contestation,[35] and there is little alternative but for the development of tactics to lead to some form of cooptation or hybrid in this manner. For this reason, international actors, such as with the UNDP in Liberia, see a hinterland of slightly resistant or passive politics, where local legitimacy lies. Yet, this response represents a critical agency for peacebuilding, if not forms of hidden resistance designed to maintain and improve the conditions of everyday life. This has even arisen in Liberia, which has long been regarded as one of the most problematic of cases. Such actors survive and impact upon the peace process in unintended, hidden, yet very significant ways. They offer the problematic potential of stabilising a distant and uncaring liberal peace which benefits their elites more, but they also make everyday life bearable for themselves. They need few resources to do so as they operate in subsistence mode.

In the recent statebuilding attempts in Afghanistan and in Iraq efforts have been made to liaise with and integrate tribal practices and institutions into peacebuilding. In Iraq, widespread social, economic and political discontent, and violence forced even the US military to seek local, social, and customary knowledge and support, even if this was instrumentally applied and often ignored. As Ucko has shown, the US occupation of Iraq was eventually forced into an uncomfortable relationship with sectarian leaders in an attempt to engage with local actors and so acquire legitimacy.[36] Ironically, this led to a relationship with actors which were neither fully representative nor legitimate even in their own contexts.[37] This is a common dynamic in the liberal-local relationships that emerge in such contexts. Even so, the swift location by international actors of 'indigenous authorities' has increasingly been seen to be vital, requiring local knowledge.[38] Inevitably, this has uncovered critical agencies which have also enabled new forms of peacebuilding.

In Afghanistan, the Tribal Liaison Office aimed to integrate traditional community structures, networks, and approaches into the international attempt to build a modern liberal state.[39] Initially, international actors rejected this approach, but recently have embraced it (even including the former High Representative of Bosnia Herzegovina who was well known for his heavy handedness).[40] Of course, this embrace has perhaps been rather too uncritical and more related to expediency in the face of mounting costs and casualities, rather than for peace-building. The emphasis on the speedy construction of a pre-packaged peace, rather than a deliberative, participatory, and nuanced evolution of peace via reconciliation rather than merely institutional design and perfection, has meant that the liberal state in Afghanistan barely reached across all of Kabul-[41] a pattern replicated in many other examples, as in Timor or Liberia, for example. An international *volte face* occurred as this became apparent, and engagements with 'indigenous peacemaking' became part of the international strategy. Yet, in both Afghanistan and Iraq, where engagements with the local became part of peacebuilding, criticisms were still widespread that internationals had failed to understand the importance of rural matters and communities, and the role of traditional structures for security and governance, despite the fact that often the majority of issues at the local level is dealt with through informal mechanisms.[42] What seems to have occurred in Afghanistan is an uneasy balance between rural warlords (and the order-inducing as well as conflict-inducing practices that emanate from them), and the weak state located mainly in Kabul. Both see each other as a threat, and both see a parallel civil society as undermining their role. Internationals fear validating either – and especially the Taliban but ultimately have to cooperate with both. Where customary elders have been invoked by international peacebuilders they have tended to be seen in instrumental ways, and manipulated to construct the Western imaginary of civil society, rather than to represent their own social networks, patterns, and issues.[43]

In the Balkans, internationals have been heavily criticised for being ambivalent about human life and needs, and for focusing on rights and institutions, as well as building neoliberal states.[44] Locals are externally viewed as burdened by conflict and socialism, and thus needed to be forced to accept democracy and the market.[45] In Bosnia and Kosovo, the imposed liberal states have failed to invoke a civil society or gain local legitimacy amongst all communities, as in many other places across the world, except in nationalist form. In the Balkans, a communal memory of social justice provision during the socialist period is often presented as being superior to the offerings of their newly imposed liberal states, with their virtual civil societies and focus on political and human rights over economic needs.[46]

In the South Pacific enough of these dynamics can be observed to generalise the argument that differences from the liberal state model and its universal claims about society, economies, politics, and customary governance in this region has had a significant impact on the export of the modern state. It is clear that customary and mixed governance might provide 'grounded legitimacy' for the state because of its organic cultural connections.[47] In such settings there are no clear boundaries between customary and modern practices, but there are distinct approaches, actors, venues, and issues that can be observed, as well as a connection with social order. Processes of assimilation, resistance, co-option, and adoption emerge in this order. In the South Pacific, custom is not just related to continuity, but also ownership, legitimacy and authenticity, for reasons of social welfare, justice, and order. In effect, the underlying aims are the same as with liberal peacebuilding even if the method and approach is very different. The hybridity that is emerging between the liberal and the local is also replicated across differing local contexts, though the hegemonic weight of the liberal political and economic model makes its influence more palpable in the development of local and national political identities and cultures.[48] On the other hand, the resilience of societies in the region – as in Timor – is often placed at the door of custom both as a historical reading of and contemporary approach to mobilisation and politicisation. Ignoring such factors weakens the liberal state, undermines local order and stability, and biases the local-liberal towards the liberal, thus locally delegitimating it. What mainly matters to international policymakers is peacebuilding's international legitimacy, rather than its localised effects.

Liberal statebuilding in Timor Leste and the Solomon Islands

Statebuilding in both cases has not been a happy experience for the international community, whether UN, IFI, or regional state led.[49] The liberal state was imported and the international community pushed both in the direction of a neoliberal version of the state. In Timor, as has already been discussed, a trusteeship situation emerged from which the liberal state was to be built after 1999 by the UN and the usual range of international organisations and donors. The UN drew down its operation after reaching the heights of its 'kingdom' in Timor after independence in 2002, but returned after the violence of 2006.[50] In the Solomons, the collapse of the prior Townsville peace agreement, the near collapse of the state and prevalence of political violence- due partly to unequal development- led to the establishment of a regional assistance mission by the Australian and New Zealand governments, plus the Pacific Island Forum in 2003. This was not meant, however, to replace the government but merely to assist it in areas of law and order and the 'proper' functioning of the state. RAMSI (Regional Assistance Mission in the Solomon Islands) intervened on the invitation of the Solomon Islands prime minister, for what was thought to be a 10-year term. But the peace process has become ensnared in constitutional reform debates for much of its life to date.

The very concept of the state, with its attendant territorial fixes, national interests and homogenous populations, and its uncontestable sovereignty, has been a source of tension, for entrenched political classes, dominant and often corrupt business classes, and for the customary leaders and their resources at the local level. In these cases, the state's formal institutions have been created but are not widely used other than by elites. Informal institutions are more locally resonant and swifter, even if they may not conform to liberal norms. Many local and international analysts perceive that the statebuilding processes had been captured by a self-fulfilling oligarchy in both states. Many are local elites, but some are also from international ranks, or are perceived as complicit with international institutions. Some local actors even complained that internationals are indirectly complicit in the breakdown of the state, and they are now 'shopping' for the least 'biased' internationals.[51] Democracy, security, development, the rule of law, and civil society have all been adopted as important agendas, but it has widely been regarded that the states that have been produced are empty states in which there is a virtual peace, having had little impact on the daily lives of the vast majority of the population. Liberal statebuilding has had limited impact outside the local capitals, and has been less than locally owned. People have limited understanding of the liberal state: what it does or what it is for. This has been the perception of groups competing over the state's material advantages, but there has also been a philosophical challenge about why a state and what should it be for? There has been a mixture of post-colonial, anti-capitalist or customary opposition. Finally, and most practically, such statebuilding practices are yet to provide security, both against violence or hardship. Thus, many local actors, critical of such practices have called for more grass-roots peacebuilding, and indeed have returned to their own older, perhaps imagined, traditions of peacebuilding, conflict resolution, of political life, and social support.

Vignettes of local peacebuilding in Timor Leste and the Solomon Islands

Peacebuilding in Timor Leste and the Solomon Islands has had a linked, but not necessarily parallel, evolution to that of the statebuilding process. The meeting of the liberal international aspiration for a liberal peace through statebuilding has had significant impacts on the ground, but it is emerging in heavily modified ways. Its encounter with its own others has led to a significant redevelopment of the liberal state in both contexts, in ways which were generally resisted by internationals, but many have now become more sanguine about this process of modification and adjustment – the development of a local-liberal hybrid.

Where peacebuilding has focused on long-term grass-roots relationships, projects, and processes, it has developed a discursive presence not revolving around inefficiency, corruption, and retraining in the context of liberal institutions, but around a connection with customary institutions, practices, and processes. There has been a recognition of their value and the resilience of local communities (as well as a countervailing fear of malevolent local practices become normalised). Rather than being viewed as without agency, local peacebuilding organisations have moved to develop processes that connect socially and culturally at the community level, either directly or through the modification of liberal-institutional, high-level and top-down agendas. This is inevitable as their perspective on the requirements of peace are locally grounded, but also internationally informed.

Timor Leste

For a person in need in Timor the first port of call would be the church, the family or the international agencies, but not the state. Many are not attracted to a subsistence lifestyle but have little choice.[52] About 80 per cent of the population still depend on the subsistence economy and between 40–56 per cent are unemployed despite the state and its oil wealth (apparently there have been revenues of up to $3b, yet, poverty is the norm amongst the country's small population).[53] A peace dividend has not emerged for most of the rural communities, where the government and its institutions have little reach. Indeed, there has been a 10 per cent increase in those under the poverty line since 2002.[54] UNDP has focused on veterans for example, rather than on the very poor. For these reasons, recent strategy has moved towards short term job creation on a large scale, using the recently available oil revenues from the Timor Gap[55] to create infrastructure and services (though there have been complaints of the imbalance this has created in the budget). This indicates there is a need to supplement the rural economy, rather than displace it, and to be supportive of local context.[56] These strategies show how international actors are adapting their strategies in response to both international crises vis-à-vis the liberal state, and to local pressures. The country director of the World Bank argued, for example, that there needed to be a mix of safety nets, oil revenue expenditure, and private sector development in order to support a more viable form of peace during the transitional period towards a more advanced liberal state where the private sector might eventually take over many of these functions.[57] However, human capital issues mean that this is a generational process because educational development was also needed to enable this to happen. Clearly, there has been a significant shift in World Bank strategy, and it was even intimated to me in a focus group discussion that there was some concern that 'Washington' was out of touch with the views of its local office on what and how development might now occur. Now it was believed that during the transition a Keynesian approach was needed until the private sector was able to step in, and hopefully before oil supplies ran out.

Symbolic of international distance from local contextual demands are the premises of many internationals, such as USAID (United States Agency for International Development) in Dili, which are heavily fortified[58] as is common now with international agencies the world over. This is despite professing to work in a range of community development areas which one would expect would be widely welcomed locally. Indeed, it is hard to understand how even local staff could see such fortification positively. However, one local employee argued that the Timorese could take the best of international praxis and remove the worst of their own, through such roles, referring specifically to women's rights.[59] Following this pattern, Dili itself is a liberal enclave and an enclave economy, though urban immigration has made its situation very tense. In an indication of the urban/rural divide, there are few banks at the sub-district level. Both the capital and the banking system are the site of epistemic knowledge and material resources, which local actors seek to engage with but which have little reach, nor it seems, little interest in the world beyond the capital.

Some international staff also referred to themselves as 'local' in the sense that they were in the field, whether in the field headquarters or the rural areas, and argued that they operated in a top-down managerial environment where orders and doctrines came from foreign offices with no local contact or knowledge rather than from the field staff (whose time was wasted with 'best practice' forms of bureaucracy).[60] Headquarters and their fads drive peacebuilding and security agendas, not field experience, and the former are confirmed by expensive visits by consultants who endorse centralised global agendas (as also in the case of the Solomon Islands).

Yet, by contrast, staff at a prominent local NGO expressed the view that internationals were just not interested in the local or needs, unless as a canvas for the projection of Western values and institutions.[61] Indeed this is what they meant by the local, or by describing themselves as local staff. People from villages also made the same arguments.[62] Conversely, international staff generally saw their position as internationally informed and transmitting via their local bases as positive: they wanted to see the formal sector take over the informal.[63] They were focused on inter-organisational deficits, inefficiencies and incoherence in relation to implementing reform and development projects. Yet, local staff often complained that some of these frameworks were sometimes self-defeating (such as free trade and anti-protection measures, and FDI), and indeed that liberal peacebuilding had become a vehicle for the power and enrichment of a small, new transnational elite. Economic reform and development has mainly enriched a business class that focuses on providing for international markets (plantations, etc) rather than local needs. Party politics has adopted oppositional positions on economic development models (ie the Singapore model (CNRT) versus social welfare (FRETILIN)). For this reason elite level political debates commands little authority with many communities.[64]

Local community life, as is often argued, is regularly referred to as revolving around interwoven levels of lifetime and intergenerational reciprocity and mutual support, though there were often references to its potentially negative aspects (the treatment of women and the 'bride-price' were often mentioned in particular by international actors). Indeed, local forms of democracy (for example at the *suco* level) are normally subverted by 'family voting' or community allegiances.[65] A seasoned international observer stated that even now the UN does not have an effective partnership with the Timorese people, arguing they were trapped in a cycle of ignorance between New York and field offices but not the local contexts themselves.[66] Clearly, donor funding cycles bear no relation to local community life, and donor driven strategies bore little relation to needs and context.

However, this has not meant that local actors are incapable of engaging in the life of international institutions. It is interesting to note, as with the evolution of local agency in connection with international agencies in Kosovo,[67] that Timorese staff are becoming prominent in international agencies as compared to the situation a few years ago before the Timorisation campaign. Of course, levels of education are reportedly low. There are very few PhDs on the island (twelve was a figure I was quoted) and there has been very little investment in education.[68] Local staff who were very critical of the liberal and neoliberal peace project, and were focused on rights, development *and* needs in a notably empathetic manner, were adopting a position of far less distance from the local than internationals commonly adopted. Examples of their intents to modify international praxis in Timor were often drawn with reference to a recent weekend spent 'at their village' with their extended families.[69] Examples were replete with discussions of local agency and how it might be organised and supported, by transversal task forces from the ministries to the villages, for better representation more consonant with context, for needs, even for mobile banking, and for better forms of communication between internationals, local individuals and communities. Instead, they argued, internationals talked amongst themselves, had little concern about continuing or emerging inequalities, while the government embarked on 'white elephant' projects often at the behest of the IFIs.

Consequently, there is a widespread dissatisfaction with the state and its alien praxes supported by international agencies, which have marginalised what it means to be Timorese for many people, and does not connect with their everyday life. As in many other instances of peacekeeping, even the peacekeepers and international police often express views that their role is marginal, that international organisations efforts are misdirected, that international personnel are arrogant, and that they do not respond to the pressing issues they see around them. Some international personnel translate the perceived nominality of their role into tourism, though they also acknowledge that their mere presence is stabilising, especially in remote areas. They also note that local people are unwilling to cooperate, felt a sense of entitlement, and are apathetic, or not interested in their state.[70] Almost no internationals speak Tetun, and though they preach local ownership and participation they are rarely able to discuss this in local languages. Accusations have been made that internationals on occasion go to great lengths not to have links with local people.[71] All of this perpetuates separate elite and local conversations which have little connection, fostering local and international approaches which neither negotiate nor mediate with each other, but instead distance and ignore each other. Yet, the state has also tried to reconnect with local practices. In 2004 the government began to engage with informal institutions, introduced local elections for customary leaders and councils.[72] Community leaders are widely perceived as the key authority in the country.

In one of the remoter districts where there are still significant local tensions, the District Commissioner was very clear in arguing that peace, and eventually a stable state, had to emerge from within such districts as his and via presence of the 'spiritual solidarity' of the Timorese people.[73] He spoke a modern vocabulary of peacebuilding (translated into Tetun and Portuguese), and was critical of the lack of a peace dividend and great confusion at the local level as to the type of peace internationals were trying to develop. He was suspicious of this peace – the liberal peace – and thought of it as somewhat oppressive. He was critical of 'top-down' approaches, of development, and even offered some doubts on democracy. He wanted grounded and bottom-up versions of these processes in order to avoid dependency, which offers an interesting twist on donor views on dependency. One might dismiss such arguments on the grounds of naïvety or interest (as a translator did) but in the wider perspective about what has been developing in Timor, this District Commissioner was not just voicing his own critique, but relating dynamics that were changing the praxis of peacebuilding in his region. He was clear that such positions are now re-negotiating the model the internationals assumed to be suitable for his region, the sum of a range of public and hidden local agencies.

Longstanding patterns of resistance to oppression and to hints of colonialism are soon invoked in such conversations. There are often complaints that democracy had led to elite competition in a form that had betrayed the whole point of resistance to Indonesian occupation. From such discontent rapidly emerged local campaigns for local ownership and accountability for the peacebuilding process. From here, traditional and customary socio-political traditions were retrieved in order to create order where the UN had failed.[74] Many people thought that the peace the UN had established was fragile and might not survive the UN's withdrawal in 2002: they proved to be right. The UN had proved security, monitored institution building, and acted as a donor. During and despite this, new fault-lines have emerged, between tradition and modernity, urban and rural, age groups, migrants and locals, but perhaps most importantly between the technical world of the liberal peace processes and the spiritual and ancestral worlds.[75] The former – in particular the UN system – had regarded the latter and local forms of politics as patriarchal, tribal, controlled by the church, and passive.[76] Yet, it was commonly argued that Timor's cultural and customary systems had 'saved' Timorese people during the occupation and during the economic difficulties since. Both had affected culture and custom negatively, but it had been a site of relative stability compared to the state and its politics.[77] Of course, it is also widely argued that there are very problematic practices associated with the customary resistance to individualism over collectivism (especially relating to property rights and ownership), modern health care, education, justice, and more specifically, its patriarchy, the bride-price system, and its endorsement of traditional authority. Certainly, some customary systems are egalitarian, matriarchal, and very consensual and can and are making a significant contribution to peacebuilding, contrary to the tendency of many international analysts and policymakers to ignore them. It is clear, then, in this case that the local agencies invoke a range of hybridity in the context of peacebuilding. Kinship and social networks are often crucial in the expression of such critical agency.

It has been the spiritual world, related authorities and agencies, and its connected kinship systems, and especially the 'sacred house' (*uma lulic*) and their related social and historical family networks, that have seemingly provided the impetus for peacebuilding where technical approaches have failed.[78] Citizenship in the new state or partnership in communal life cannot occur without membership in an *uma lulic*. Sacred houses are also connected to the churches, another key but often ignored aspect of Timorese everyday life. These dynamics produce notions of unity and solidarity (and more problematically, territory). From here alliances and thus communal relations have emerged.[79] An ancestral view of the land as sacred and a set of ancestral rules (*Bandu*) are widely observed (which if broken lead to war, starvation, or disease).[80] This gives rise to a social contract and to peace (*dame*) which is thought of as long-term stability.[81] This provides a set of localised, customary approaches for conflict resolution, with a practical aspect recognisable even within the statebuilding context, but which also offer a cultural, spiritual, social, and environmental dimension which may not be immediately apparent. It is here that 'local ownership' has been experienced, rather than in the formal liberal peacebuilding process, which is often associated with colonialism.[82] Indeed, it is widely thought that informal approaches to peacebuilding need to be applied before the formal approach is used.[83] It is also widely acknowledged that historic practices particularly relating to gender roles need to be modernised, and that individualistic notions of human rights may not be easily compatible with local, communal, patterns of politics.[84] These amount to sophisticated and self-aware critiques of the liberal peace model on the ground, which have arisen through the engagement of local and liberal discourses about peacebuilding.

However, incompatibility has been experienced in a number of ways. The usual failings of newly constructed liberal institutions and public services have been widely noted. There has also been a widely noted discord between local and international value systems, and custom and tradition especially in rural and peripheral contexts, even though these are referred to in the modern constitution.[85] Trindade has revealed that many of the respondents of his own research in these matters in Timor Leste stated that ignorance of traditional values and authority was the reason for much political instability, leading to a curse (*Malisan*).[86]

For such reasons it has recently become clear that the peoples of Timor Leste have intervened in unheralded ways in the statebuilding and peacebuilding process that they have been undergoing at the hands of the international community for over a decade (as has also occurred in Bougainville and Vanuatu). This has forced a mediation, partly though the renegotiation of community agreements about collective governance and social issues (*Tarabandus*) all over the country, of previously disconnected international and local perspectives on politics, society, culture, custom, economic issues, law and the justice system, language and education. Calls for local participation may be interpreted as a desire for community and customary forms of governance to be taken seriously in the new state and society.[87] Indeed, such calls may even provide a hint of pre-existing forms of democracy in Timor, now returning to visibility. As Palmer and de Carvalho have argued local actors and processes are remaking laws, revitalising customary practices, re-engaging with tradition, and relegitimising their own agency in the peacebuilding process.[88] A hybrid justice system, as with other 'public services' has come into existence.[89] They have integrated the liberal into the local by finding parallels between the two, but they have also begun to occupy the liberal state. Its constitution is being seen in a new light, as a sacred, customary object (*Sasan Lulik*).[90] This even reaches further than the modern state into areas such as resource use, harvests and land tenure, and both runs contrary to, and compliments at other times, the flow of modernisation and development.[91] Culture and history, even if imagined, is being put to very practical uses, as well as enjoyed as a social praxis and as a spectacle. This should not be unexpected, of course, given what we know from post-colonial theorists such as Bhabha about the politics of agency and resistance in such situations, and what this means for the production of hybridity (even if it is mainly on the external actors' terms). The Timorese people resisted Indonesian occupation on the grounds of their cultural uniqueness, and have continued to express their agency in and through the peacebuilding process since. They have been searching for their own legitimation and legibility in a context where the state is mostly absent or distant, and even regarded as better that way so its blind spots and absences can be exploited. The new authority associated with the liberal state has not displaced the customary authority and legitimacy, but in fact has highlighted its significance, especially because custom and tradition still holds the modern and traditional Timorese subject in its thrall.[92] Indeed, according to Trinidade, the 'essence of life' represents a balance between material and spiritual worlds, past and present, in Timor. Peace and reconciliation are seen in these terms, and increasingly influences the modern state.[93]

One of the more concerning dynamics of the situation has been, partly because of its very young population, a significant youth reaction to post-conflict conditions, to displacement, poverty, forms of dislocation (including of custom by the new state), their lack of prospects, and the seeming inability of political leaders or internationals to move beyond their interests or dogmas, respectively.[94] This partly led to the phenomena of youth martial arts gangs, which have formed themselves as a reaction to the perceived hopelessness of young men and boys, perhaps also in the vogue of a long tradition of resistance to oppression (colonial or otherwise). In some areas, as around Viqueque in early 2009 (which is a remote and depressed area) a significant number of families were displaced because of such fighting. There have also been many conflicts and tensions arising from the return of refugees and the displaced, relating to such incidents. Often these outbreaks of violence trace their roots back to the turmoil of 1974 and the pro-independence or pro-integration (with Indonesia) campaigns. With this recent violence, one of the responses from senior members of the government was to deploy a well-known and historic reconciliation ceremony, the *Nahe Biti Bo' ot* ceremony.

This public ceremony has associations with attempts to reach agreements in 1974 after the collapse of Portuguese colonialism, and again in 1999 after the withdrawal of Indonesian forces. This translates as 'the stretching of the big mat' (literally, bringing people together on a woven mat) and is a locally recognised process of dialogue for reconciliation within and between communities, families, elders, and disputants. Reconciliation should be attained in both material and spiritual terms, between the living and the ancestors. Compensation and voluntary acceptance of an agreement, by all parties present (i.e. not just the disputants, but also elders etc.), are its aims. Youth leaders from martial arts groups and local community leaders signed an agreement safe in the *adat* (customary) knowledge that reneging on a *Nahe Biti* ceremony would anger the spirits and lead to misfortune for them and their families. Government officials saw this as part of an emerging association between a new national and ancestral/traditional consciousness, between individuals, gangs, communities, and the state.[95]

Clearly, this resort to the pre-modern in support of the modern and modernising state project in Timor Leste, is partly imagined, artificial, perhaps superficial, and somewhat paradoxical, especially given that the underlying socio-economic issues that led the martial arts groups into violence have not been resolved. An accommodation was brought about at a customary and cultural level, one might say, rather than at a material level because of the structural difficulties inherent in any material advancement or development in Timor. Yet, while perhaps appearing discordant to the international liberal eye, at the local level it clearly resonates (as any outsider who has observed such ceremonies will probably attest, ruefully or otherwise).

One does not have to look far in contemporary Timor to see other and prominent examples of the re-establishment of traditional cartographies in support of the state and local communities. The phenomena of the rebuilding of the traditional ancestral homes (*uma*), and sacred houses (*uma lulic*) many of which were burnt down during the Indonesian period, or as the military withdrew, is evident in many villages around the country. These houses form an important part of family and community life, being used to house ancient relics, and for traditional and social meetings, for celebrations, politics, and conflict resolution. They form part of networks of affiliation, exchange and alliance, and both markers and institutions of social structure and stability.[96] They were often destroyed because they were perceived to be markers of resistance and local solidarity,[97] even though during the Indonesian occupation they were used in an attempt to create unity. Traditional houses are re-emerging as markers of social and ethnic identity, and cultural heritage,[98] in parallel to the attempted construction of a modern state. Indeed, the house in indigenous culture represents social relations amongst its members. It is a social as well as physical construction, and one that is common to all of Timor's diverse linguistic communities.[99] In many ways, it is far more pervasive than the new state itself. There is strong evidence to suggest, for example, that the occupying Indonesian military understood these dynamics clearly, and targeted or used them for their own purposes. Recently there has been use of the *uma lulic* in national political meetings, the creation of a national *Uma Lulic* and of including it in national iconography, such as the flag.[100]

Yet, it was only relatively late in the international peacebuilding engagement with Timor that many peacebuilding actors also recognised these dynamics were crucial for the stability that they sought, perhaps more so than the alien institutions of the liberal state itself, which had partly become sites of new elite political contestation. Indeed, local resistance to liberal statebuilding as with Indonesian rule has been both public, conducted through political structures, and family based, conducted in a more private setting around the house and the kinship affiliations it represents.[101] Until recently the peace process has mainly engaged those public aspects, and for a variety of reasons, it has failed at the private level because of an innate bias towards technocratic solutions and towards inventing a new state, against the grain of the local and customary. Yet, for the majority of the population, based in rural environments, the state and political manoeuvring means little in contrast to longstanding '… reciprocal obligations and house affiliations'.[102]

One of the characteristics identified by internationals, whether official or NGO about Timor Leste over many years, and turned into a cliché in its own right, is the so-called resilience or endurance of people and communities in the face of great hardship.[103] This is often argued to be the outcome of a tightly woven social and cultural structure and a long experience of subsistence in the face of poverty and hardship. But this resilience has also connected with the search for the key elements of the liberal peace – democracy, security, human rights, development, a rule of law and civil society, gender, equality, and so forth. By extension elites have framed these in the context of the state, with the assistance of internationals and have questioned traditional authority and processes as a result – especially where they may have collaborated with Indonesian rule previously.[104] Thus, the population has become aware of the state not just as a national symbol but as a provider of security, law, and services, meaning that they have begun to see their own famed resilience in a new light – *contra* poverty, underdevelopment, hardship, a lack of human rights, and a lack of public services. This highlights the failings of international models and of their own state. Equally, where this has invited comparison with the resilience the state facilitates, communities have been forced to fall back on the older, communal dynamics of resilience – hence the reclaiming of their customary symbols, traditions, and processes, now cleansed of colonial implications. But this occurs in the knowledge that the liberal state is supposed to do much more and in actual fact is undermining the old patterns of resilience. The liberal state has been held up to the standards of the customary processes that reproduce this resilience, and found to be lacking. This is not to say that the population wants a return to the mythical old systems of customary governance (such as they have been re-imagined post-independence). Elections have consistently shown support for modern forms of democracy, for example. But what has emerged is an interaction between aspects of the customary and of the modern secular democracy, so aspired to in the independence struggle, and by internationals alike.

Thus, the development of a stable Timor probably depends on the integration of the traditional and enduring house structure of society with the aspiration for a liberal state, which may both support rather than reject each other.[105] Whether a house oriented state borrowing aspects of the liberal state emerges, or whether the liberal state makes some room for the house system remains to be seen. But so far, in at least one district, representatives from respective houses are elected as opposed to representatives from administrative districts.[106] In this sense there is little contradiction between custom, culture, and democracy. Ironically, there are many contradictions between the preferred administrative approach to democratic processes, which marginalise such dynamics. Thus, the move to electing *suco* (village) heads, and others, seems to be a major modification of the liberal and local state frameworks, and offers the development of a hybrid form of polity as it evolves further.[107] Of course, this also connects to issues of land tenure and common property (such as the sacred houses), which has so far been fraught and complex but might be more easily managed in a customary context, rather than in the liberal and property oriented state.[108]

The interaction of house and state raises some interesting questions. Certainly, in Timor's context, the re-emergence of the customary has broad cultural resonance and popularity, is locally often seen as part of a crucial sophistication of self-determination and democracy itself, though of course it is also problematic for the modern rights focus of the liberal state. It is also seen locally as part of the search for both security and continuity.[109] The *uma lulic* may well be more influential in developing a sophisticated form of peace in Timor than the modern liberal state. The vision of connecting the liberal state project to local practices of politics and conflict resolution has been widely understood as leading to a better form of peace, more connected the local everyday context. This would require that the current political elites based in Dili break free of the current paradigm of the liberal peace, in which they benefit from control of power and their relations with international donors. This might lead to a national peace campaign, a national 'laying of the mat ceremony', a national blood oath to mark a peace agreement (between East and West), the construction of a national *Uma Lulik* and collection of national *Sasan Lulik*. While these may fall into the same trap of moving politics away from the everyday in the long term such moves certainly seem appropriate for the connection of the liberal state project to the Timor Leste context.[110] Furthermore, where the sacred house was a site of resistance during occupation, to some degree it has become one again in the process of trying to work out a way of making the house work with the state, where it might then return to being a site of political and socio-economic organisation rather than resistance.

One of the more apparent 'liberal' modes for the bridging of state and custom is the emerging welfare system. This occurred from about 2006 as a somewhat panicked response to growing unrest and violence,[111] even though the statebuilding process since 1999 had been firmly neoliberal.[112] Prime Minister Gusmao supported a move towards social justice, believing that now the country had been liberated the people should be freed.[113] Before 2006 the drafting of the PRSP was undertaken internally, and included many Timorese voices such as officials, representatives of the Church, civil society, NGOs, private and public sector groups.[114] It focused on current needs and future generations. Peace was now to be defined as '… security, freedom, tolerance, equity, improved health, education, access to jobs and food security.'[115] These were to relate to 'vibrant traditional culture' and a sustainable environment, prosperity, equality, national unity, broad representation and decentralisation.[116] Development was redefined as context, not donor driven, introducing some tension with neoliberal prescriptions and the conventions of the rule of law in liberal terms. Contextualism meant that both the market and the state had an important role to play, that decentralisation and participation were crucial.[117]

Such dynamics were, in a previous field trip of mine in 2004, rejected by the then Country Director of the World Bank. When I remarked upon this to the current Country Director he argued that a welfare system had now been recognised as necessary for the stability of the state, and is indeed coming into existence with the blessing of the international community (though funded by Timorese oil and gas revenues): "... we are all Keynesian now" he quipped.[118] In addition to the usual DDR and SSR type programmes, veteran pensions and payments have been set-up. Payments to mothers are made for school fees and to victims, the families of 'martyrs', as well as to people over 60. Old-age pensions are also being paid.[119] A health system is also being developed. There are 'food for work' and 'clean up' programmes, though many of the people in the rural areas see these as short term and fear that many of young people want to leave Timor for good (even though diasporas are a significant source of family support).[120] However, there has been a lot of international and local political resistance to such moves from those elites who support neoliberalism.[121] These developments depend on the flow of oil funds, of course. But amongst local commentators, there are significant questions about why such moves were left so late by the international community and by local political elites. In a telling comment made by one of my local interviewees who works for a major donor, the internationals arrived with a pre-packaged solution for Timor, which involved no requirement for local input; their mission would ultimately need to be ended if such input was made the focus of their projects. No local actor has yet been 'brave' enough to tell the internationals this.[122] Instead, internationals have been channelled towards more contextualised processes by a range of hidden and local agencies. In the context of development, the neoliberal approach led to tension over inequalities, which the nationally developed 2010 Strategic Development plan hoped to deal with via state organised forms of development and redistribution.[123]

The argument that custom should be connected to the projects of state formation and to peacebuilding in Timor is also very convincing, in that it opens up hidden agencies engaged in peace formation, which are otherwise ignored or even destroyed.[124] It connects the state to socio-political institutions, local justice systems, culture and custom. It represents the beginning of an evolution from both local and international forms of peacebuilding and politics towards a post-liberal synthesis of both. For example, a Council of Elders has been proposed and there are moves afoot to draft a customary law. This local-liberal form of hybridity appears to be producing a form of peace more locally resonant even if it does not closely fit the international ideal of a liberal peace or state. Many of the spiritual, identity, public, and material resources required for political stability already exist at this level, and are often expressed as resistances to aspects of the liberal peace programme or to its failure to live up to its own claims. Many of my interviewees, both local and international queried not just the bias against local custom, but also against the extensive network of widely respected churches on the island (while noting that that such bias was now finally breaking down). This is not to say that the customary forms of governance and the localisation of the state, or indeed the enabling of local political agency will lead directly to social justice or prosperity.[125] But without responding to Timorese voices, the state will either not survive, or will remain externalised and dependent on international support. Indeed, this is where important political tensions between the local and the international reside, and where a hybridity biased towards either liberal or local may emerge. It is in this debate that legitimacy will emerge, and where a mutual dialogue, perhaps national reconciliation, may contribute to the reconstruction of a more stable political culture.[126]

The Solomon Islands

Since its inception in 2003, the RAMSI has been seen by its leader – the Australian government – as a statebuilding mission designed to inculcate the ordering mechanisms inherent in the liberal peace (with its neoliberal connotations). It was, of course, immediately noticed by those working on or in the RAMSI mission that the Melanesian cultural context needed to be acknowledged as well. The mission was named in local pidgin '*Helpem Frem*'.

The conflict was seen as arising from a weak government and weak institutions run by a semi-feudal cabal,[127] rather than from identity issues, poverty, and internal migration. The longstanding tensions between indigenous Guadalcanalese people and Malaitan migrants over land tenure and inequity (in which neoliberal forms of ownership are strongly contested by customary rights),[128] and population pressures have been viewed through a security prism via RAMSI rather than a needs *and* rights prism during an international epoch where such approaches have become commonplace. Customary land tenure was overtaken by incomers who want to use the land for profit, trade, and resource extraction. Varying approaches to land use and ownership, from customary to neoliberal, has been one of the most controversial and conflict-inducing issues in this region. This made the whole of the archipelago appear to be a dysfunctional state when in reality it was mainly on Guadalcanal that violence occurred regularly (though coups and the interruptions to public service and governance affected all). The state was marginal to everyday life at least in positive terms.[129] The Townsville Agreement failed to resolve these core issues, partly since though it favoured traditional owners the High Court has favoured trade. Even though casualties and displacement were small in scale (around 200 people, and 30,000, people respectively) external perceptions of the Solomons as a modern state, despite its many sovereign irregularities, enabled a 'failed state' response. This was confirmed for regional policymakers by major riots in 2006.

RAMSI focused on multilevel and multidimensional statebuilding through the provision (often through a secondment system) of Australian expertise in government, security, development, and the rule of law. In this way it followed a capacity building approach, designed through technical assistance to develop and perfect local institutions. Yet, while other such missions around the world were under pressure for their apparent ideological bias rather than technical expertise, a conservative and securitised version of the liberal peace model was adopted wholesale in the Solomon Islands. As in Timor, local actors have been highly critical of the lack of local ownership of peacebuilding, and of its lack of local accountability. Many, however, though critical of RAMSI, believe that if it were to withdraw there would be a return to violence (RAMSI provides security, monitors reform, and acts as a donor). Paradoxically, RAMSI has also attempted to shift centralised patronage systems into the modern framework of liberal politics, simultaneously unsettling patterns of social support and of local politics. Notably, customary land tenure has been torn between the demands of neoliberal development (i.e. highly exploitative logging industries), growing RAMSI concern with local custom, and the dislocation of communities, social and economic life.

Though widely welcomed when it arrived, RAMSI rapidly became subject to what Bhabha has called 'time-lag'.[130] It followed the UN/global model for statebuilding, as the fragility of the state and its apparent trajectory towards collapse via repeated coups in the early 2000's were seen to be potentially destabilising for the region. Yet this global model was itself losing credibility because of the unintended consequences of the 'war on terror', failures of other missions, resistance to neoliberalism, and the apparent fragility of Western market economies. RAMSI has more recently turned to capacity building, following the logic in UN integrated missions.[131] It confronted a local romantic view that the 'old' Solomon Island system needed to be rediscovered with a modernity which itself was fragile. In contrast to the UN in Timor Leste, RAMSI has acted as a partner to the government (though local politicians and bureaucrats are somewhat scornful of its use of conditionality).[132] Its mandate focused on partnership, capacity building, comprehensive engagement, and a long-term commitment. As with the OHR in Bosnia it has met certain dilemmas because of the prolonged local political stalemate, and local practices not commensurate with its liberal statebuilding perspective. This involves developing or impeding local capacity, assisting or guiding the Solomon Islands Government –RAMSI Consultative Forum, and taking the lead in the context of the Pacific Islands Forum.[133] According to RAMSI's own mission design it sees itself as a mid-level facilitator of local and regional order, following the liberal model. It claims to have developed its role with relative sensitivity towards the specific context, allowing for significant local space through which the liberal model might be modified.[134] Of course, in some ways it is a de facto government.[135] That said, RAMSI has had some successes in providing order and policing, and many local people are concerned that if it left, such gains would be easily lost.[136] However, given that conflicting versions of the relationship with land is central to reconciliation and long-term conflict resolution, such successes are relatively superficial.[137]

As in Timor Leste, of course, the usual tropes about local dependency and cultural equivocation, as well as references to a 'hasty' post-colonial transition are present in RAMSI's discourses. RAMSI personnel argued that a key problem with their role was the limited ability they had to spread a material peace dividend around the general population.[138] Its chosen focus on the cash economy means that it is unable to engage with the wide array of social, customary, political, and economic dynamics that are not part of this sector, indeed, a significant part of the whole environment. Local commentators argue that RAMSI refuses to negotiate with them and that donors in general often withdraw rather than conduct local negotiations, and refuse to recognise the significance of customary processes, even though this might facilitate reconciliation.[139] Yet many want RAMSI to remain and to become more involved in cementing a social contract by supporting civil society as well as by building or modernising the state.[140]

There are several obvious areas in which RAMSI's approach produces contradictions. The social and economic dimensions of a liberal social contract are especially difficult in scattered island communities that are putatively tied to a centralised state, represented by a capital on a distant island. The attractions of urbanisation and the centralisation of development make it difficult to distribute what limited peace dividend there is, and a lack of welfare provision forces people to move to urban areas or the capital (the scene of much violence over land and space) or to fall back on customary processes and subsistence which separates them from the state.[141] Centralisation also produces pressures for decentralisation.

In my meetings with RAMSI personnel, I heard similar arguments about local capacity as in other situations, such as Timor, endlessly repeated: the people lack capacity and experience; they became independent too soon; they are trying to run their institutions in ways that defeat the institutions themselves; there is too much corruption, not enough investment; culture and tradition are both obstacles and present opportunities; people resist reform and expect handouts; there is no national identity; the state is weak.[142] From the international perspective these complaints make perfect sense. From a local perspective they appear superficial, sometimes insensitive and arrogant, hinting at colonialism. This dichotomy represents a romantic/mystic mismatch in that liberals and locals hold valid positions in separation to each other. When put together this shows how little they are able to understand each other – echoing mutual resistance and through these emerging agencies, the hints of hybridities to come.

It was the modern centralised governance and market system that failed in the Solomons, because of their own contextual deficiencies, not because of the inability of local actors to act politically, economically, or socially – or indeed culturally.[143] The elite political culture has been co-opted by an elite, male group with little ideology other than an interest in power, wealth and their own aggrandisement.[144] Among other things, this has concentrated power away from the people and the provinces. A very high turnover of political actors and officials has not helped matters.[145] The modern market system is not compatible with the customary system and exacerbates the crucial land issue, adding more levels to an already complex problem. Most people perceive the government and elites as profiting from statebuilding at the expense of the customary system with little sign of their sharing their 'peace dividend' or of a 'trickle down' occurring.[146] For older generations in particular, the tension between liberal state and custom is very pronounced, and in general it is customary systems, not modern, which are used by society, as in Timor Leste. The customary system is generally seen as faster and more reliable, though in another sign of hybridity, people expect the state to provide previously non-existent public services.[147] Many of my interviews expressed the view that customary systems of subsistence and welfare had to suffice as the state was not developed enough, being mainly focused on law and order as its first function. There was a limited sense that welfare and services were the prerogative of the state, or that only international donors could support such a system, in a mark of how far the neoliberal state has becoming embedded even in the Solomon Islands and how far its claim of national identity/unity is disassociated from mutual support.[148] This was not the case in Timor Leste, where people are beginning to recognise that oil and gas revenues mean the state should do more, and are beginning to use democratic pressure for these reasons.

As in Timor Leste, the failures of peacebuilding in everyday life is a familiar criticism repeated regularly, though some local and international actors recognise the need for both Western forms of peacebuilding and an interface with local customary practices as a response.[149] Indeed, it has been argued that they have the same goal – to end conflict – and if Western approaches could enhance what chiefs are already doing, for example, while improving their capacity and understanding in line with 'modern practices' this would be very useful.[150] Though this in itself is a romantic and essentialised characterisation of customary governance, it is probably true to say that meaningful reconciliation should be found with localised praxes,[151] assisted where possible by international actors rather than impeded or blocked by them. On paper this appears to be RAMSI's intention, though the practice has been rather different. In general, because the state has long been in crisis, people operate in the more 'authentic' customary system in everyday life and *in extremis*, often seeing the state as predatory. Informal political organisation is far less problematic from this perspective. Of course many politicians and elites have used the state to redistribute resources along the lines of more traditional forms of patronage, which is ironically facilitated by the international focus on political elites.[152] All this undermines a nascent social contract, as well as to some degree any pre-state contract. It emphasises the discrete interests of local, national, and international actors, rather than synthesising them. Again very similar patterns can be observed in Timor Leste.

Also similar to Timor, the collapse of the state was in reality a struggle between an externally introduced and an indigenous modernity, in which competition for resources caused the modern state to become the discredited vehicle through which they could be captured. For example, the attempt to introduce capitalism and a free market is not compatible with various customary land issues, and is one of the major destabilising factors.[153] Just the fact that local languages are widely used means that the salience of Western modernisation practices are difficult to translate, and more importantly, need to be translated if there is to be any local connection with them, beyond predatory state and market behaviours. Tensions between trade oriented land appropriation and customary land owners on Guadalcanal is one of the key problems over which there has been little agreement and much contradiction between local courts and international statebuilders.[154]

The state itself has little local authenticity in an even more pronounced way than in Timor where there is a national consensus of sorts. A focus group at the Ministry for National Unity, Peace and Reconciliation argued that liberalism represents a different political culture and modernity; human rights did not connect with tribal and communal approaches; that the market contradicts traditional land ownership and social support mechanisms; and that democracy itself contradicts community and tribal relations. Furthermore local communities connect peace to land use, rather than to statebuilding or to the institutions of a liberal state. Thus, so far reconciliation has not occurred particularly because of the role of multinational corporations in appropriating traditional land for logging, etc.[155] Some members of this team were of the view that it was unacceptable for state law to contradict customary law, particularly because this blocked traditional reconciliation practices and undermined the informal but significant position of chiefs on the islands. Indeed the current constitution hardly recognises customary practice and how far peoples' lives were embedded in it. (Despite such views, this ministry was also centralised in Honiara, the capital.)

Paradoxically, RAMSI came to the rescue of the failed state and attempted to deploy the modernisation processes associated with the liberal peace (starting with the police and justice systems)[156] rather than the indigenous modernity, where they may now be coming to realise their support might be better placed. Its confirmation of the legitimacy of modernisation confused local actors and communities who are embedded in more traditional approaches to political reconciliation.[157] Until the riots of 2006 there was little attempt on behalf of RAMSI to engage with the local, other than rhetorically or unless to reform it, personnel stayed only for a few months and were often professionally oriented and junior.[158] Devolution, decentralisation, and calls for the incorporation of customary forms of government to enhance the agency of the periphery are now common, however. Yet one of the most widely embedded actors on the islands, the various churches, has been ignored in this process even though they constitute 'civil society' for the most part.[159] This is because the churches are generally aligned in opposition to the modernisation strategies of statebuilding and of RAMSI, in favour of their own version of civil society (though they are divided over what this might mean). Even government ministers recognise the very limited reach of government and the significance of the church, while also noting that customary governance and the role of the church could be very useful in complimenting the role of Western peacebuilding actors.[160]

Yet the government has not been able to produce tangible results in guaranteeing law and order, welfare and jobs, human rights or a democratic politics. Many of my interviewees thought that despite RAMSI's intervention the next elections would probably be violent because there had not been a significant peace dividend. Many also defined peace as more than mere security, or beyond Western style institutions, and saw it in everyday and customary terms in the absence of state capacity. Many were also suspicious of what state capacity might be used for by predatory political and business elites, and how it might undermine local capacities.[161]

Perhaps the main dimension of local governance lies in the *wantok* system, which has traditionally offered a measure of social support. It is now under great strain (and some argue it has created dependency).[162] Customary social support, subsistence, and local governance structures have remained intact and mitigated the worst of the violence and political problems for many, however.[163] While the modernising state praxis barely reaches outside of the capital, justice, policing, access to land and its use, and social support are still mainly provided through customary, community, and village means.[164] Unemployment is estimated at about 60 per cent while subsistence farming and other activities account for about 80 per cent of the population.[165] It is the *wantok* system that binds these various dimensions of customary governance together in an intricate web of family and community relations and support, with a significant political dimension, perhaps mirroring the 'house' system of Timor Leste.

Though liberal peacebuilders and statebuilders have only reluctantly come around to custom and cultural issues, local leaders have long seen both significance and problems in the peacebuilding, development and statebuilding agendas. In a focus group of local chiefs I attended, many were concerned about security and public services, jobs or welfare, which they felt should be provided by the state. Otherwise, what was the point of the state other than to operate as a predator? Western rights-based institutions and development had little meaning in the face of the material issues they faced though that is not to say that they were not aware of democracy, human rights, rule of law, corruption, or gender issues – or the international discourse about these.[166] They also felt that the state and international statebuilders had ignored or undermined their own role in stabilising society through the customary means at their disposal, especially given that most people on the islands lived 'far from the state' and actually relied on local processes.[167]

Some of my interviewees saw peacebuilding as a Western practice, imbued with authority and legitimacy, but were explicit about the fact that it needed to be made more locally resonant, and that there were also lessons liberal peacebuilders could learn themselves from this process. Even in government ministries, I heard the view that the 'chiefly system' should be incorporated into the modern state (via a council of chiefs).[168] Though this sounds a romantic view it has already been experimented with in Vanuatu, and it is equally romantic to claim that the statebuilding can create capacity without local knowledge or contextual and critical agency. As a result of the latter discourse, order is not closely connected to the centralised institutions of the liberal state experiment. Rather, governance is very rural, lacking police, courts, focused on the *wantok*, chiefs and consultation, as well as informed by Christianity, over how resources could be distributed and sustained in such specific contexts.[169]

Of course, traditional forms of governance are themselves problematic. For example, women may not be able to become chiefs and nor are chiefs always elected (though chiefs do have a limited legal constitutional position within the state and also want a chiefly council to be formed in the context of the state).[170] They may well want to retain historical privileges and access to resources. Yet, many see the importance of democracy and often appear willing to embrace it, along with human rights, tempered by their communal approaches.[171] On the other hand, some chiefs believe that compromise with the state on such matters (for example, allowing women to take such roles, and being elected) clash with tradition (meaning with their own power and role). Partly as a result, the default option for the international community has been to avoid such difficult issues by focussing on modernising the state in its externally understood guise rather than engaging with its contextual potential. Yet, given that the state is mainly only relevant and visible in the capital, Honiara, this means that the vast bulk of the population is effectively excluded even if they want the public services a state might provide.[172] Notwithstanding, the customary and the state are in a complex and often hidden mediation of each other in ways which express their very different agencies.

Though both the failed state literatures and praxis, and neoliberal approaches to development have been heavily criticised they are in full flow in the Solomon Islands, and indeed, elite neoliberal practices are partly to blame for social disorder and for the weakness of the state itself, because of elite predatory practices and non-sustainable industries, such as logging.[173] These have undermined political legitimacy and state institutions, social and economic customary praxis, and also the authority of customary leaders who were supposed to offer welfare and guard sustainability across generations. In the Solomon Islands, as to some degree in Timor, concepts of private ownership of property are relatively alien. The land owns the people, rather than the people owning the land; social, political and economic formulations begin from this point.[174] Modernisation and (neo) liberalisation are thus destabilising: ultimately one might say the same of liberal peacebuilding and statebuilding if they are not able to connect with such alternative epistemologies.

In an influential report produced by no less than Francis Fukuyama for RAMSI (working for the World Bank and hosted by RAMSI), he detailed the difference between the Melanesian social and cultural context and the liberal political and economic context.[175] He argued that the *wantok* system of kinship, relationships and networks derived from this system. These he regards as pre-modern, as opposed to the atomised and individualist societies that make up the developed liberal community of states.[176] He argued that the fundamental weakness of this system is its inability to conceive or mobilise collective action, though he acknowledged that they are often very egalitarian, participatory, and flexible. He was also of the view that it has been *wantok* networks that have preserved some level of order, and that to remove them would be very dangerous because of their capacity for social support. The crucial issue from his statebuilding perspective, however, is their inability for large-scale political organisation, which can only be provided within the context of the liberal state. Of course, such large-scale mobilisation is also an anathema in such a context: it is feared as predatory and given the state has few resources to redistribute is seen as unnecessary for the most part. Of course, infrastructural reconstruction and development has occurred because of the state, but much has also arisen through local resilience and ingenuity.

What is apparent in Fukuyama's report is the tension between his recommendation for a stronger state to supplant these problems, complete with a simulated national identity, and the recognition of the importance of the customary level of governance (which he mischaracterises as an obstacle in any case because of its lack of capacity for sustained political organisation or mobilisation). There is a great tension in his Enlightenment repetition of the hierarchy of local versus international modes of political and economic organisation, despite his attempt to acknowledge the social and some aspects of alterity which arise with this move. There can be no state or sovereignty, or property rights as the basis for the liberal polity where the customary *wantok*, land, and chief system, exist. Property rights are crucial to modern liberal states and neoliberal means of economic development, meaning that land is seen as a commodity, and customary modes are to be removed (which is why so many classic liberal philosophers and thinkers, Locke and Bentham among them, saw imperialism and colonialism as necessary to wrest control of unproductive land from indigenous peoples, as opposed to Burke's more sensitive position that this did not justify colonial power and undermined local legitimacy).[177] Thus, the prevalence of *wantok* networks and customary land in the Solomons is an obstacle to the organisation of many aspects of the modern liberal polity, not least its economy. Yet, if culture is a site of political agency, as it clearly seems to be in the Solomon Islands, these also represent what resilience and social support there is. Fukuyama, as a result repeats tired colonial and neo-colonial anthropological tropes of categorisation and hierarchy, governance and modernisation, forcing customary practices to operate in opposition to, rather than in cooperation with them.[178] Because of this the *wantok* appears as the antithesis of good governance, prosperity, and civil society. Any capacity it may offer is placed in a difficult confrontation with the global political economy and norms of global governance. The latter succeeds in building an externalised and virtual peace, while one would expect the customary to disappear.

In fact, this has not happened. Customary processes of governance, social support, law and culture survive and indicate a dynamic of critical agency, if fragmented, often hidden or disguised – for peace formation. They enable resilience and resistance. Rather than being supplanted they have actually offered much towards the stabilisation of society. But they may well hinder the modern state's development or lead to an alternative form of polity, which internationals cannot imagine or engage with, preferring to believe instead that 'segmentary societies' are incapable of broad political organisation or consensus. Customary governance needs to be thought of as a localised process of politics, as yet far more inclusive than the modern state project, both of which are to be renegotiated and incorporated.[179]

This means that the chief system has also been misinterpreted. Chiefs are not (necessarily) feudal lords as often caricatured by Western commentators and policymakers. Their legitimacy rests on the fact that they work for the good of the community – of course understood in their own historical terms – for which they arbitrate, rather than via the exercise of arbitrary power (though this happens). This indicates that they may play a positive role within the state and constitution, representing a crucial crossover between the 'traditional' and the 'modern'. Thus, they should not, as is often thought, raise taxes or buy and sell customary land (particularly to extractive industries) which it is often assumed they can. They are guardians rather than executors. They are bound by *wantok* as well as being at its apex, and are custodians of the land and environment for future generations. They see the need for custom to be incorporated into the modern state and vice versa, and with good reason.[180]

Unfortunately, the extent of the recognition of such local custom was very limited in RAMSI's mainstream mission objectives. The usual problems associated with poverty, land and custom were ignored in practice. Asking Fukuyama to explore them in the context of the statebuilding agenda endorsed the fact that the local context was less relevant to World Bank planning than neoliberal reform.[181] Effectively, Fukuyama issued a call for the co-option of custom into the national agenda on the grounds that this would provide the state with legitimacy, while ignoring the agency that it also represented. He did this by assuming that the priorities of the liberal state and its norms reflect those of the inhabitants of the Solomon Islands, or if they did not, the liberal peace framework was automatically superior and legitimate by virtue of an international consensus.

In Timor the slow acknowledgement of local contextual matters was a last resort when statebuilding collapsed into a ruin of rhetoric and the internationals' failure had become widely evident. Context was mainly used to justify the transfer of political agency to RAMSI and a national agenda on the grounds of security – that of Australia and New Zealand rather that of the Solomon Islanders themselves, even so. Furthermore, the focus on neoliberal reform has meant that RAMSI could not address issues of poverty and property rights properly. Given that this is one of the key issues of the recent conflict, which prompted the flow of islanders to search for land and jobs (and so provoking the conflict), this is a fairly serious flaw in RAMSI's programme of alleviating insecurity. It was partly neoliberal strategies of resource extraction that sparked the conflict in the first place. Thus, for all of RAMSI rhetoric about an engagement with the customary, such issues are generally seen as an obstacle for liberal democracy and for the market, and more generally for the establishment of security.

Despite this, RAMSI has gradually been forced to acknowledge the prominent customary level to everyday life and politics, which indicate political, social and economic practices which differ to those of the liberal state, and yet are deeply embedded and respected. At the constitutional level, a small team of external experts have also been working on the reworking of the constitutional framework along liberal lines that goes with all such liberal peace interventions – but with a difference. It has been addressing how to build customary practices into the modern state, and as well as crucial issues such as customary land tenure and usage, and the status of chiefs within the modernising state.[182] This is aimed partly at producing a local-liberal hybrid polity rather than a classic liberal or modern neoliberal state. It is an embryonic recognition that alternative forms of statehood are necessary. But, given that since its independence, the state had been used to distribute patronage and manage conflict, the design of the new liberal state has inadvertently made the development of local political agency very difficult (because of elite capture of the state, inadvertently supported by internationals). In the attempt to build a liberal state and to engage with the local, some recognition of cultural practices has emerged. For example, in romantic vein, during reconciliation attempts bringing Guadalcanal and Malaitans together, government officials and customary practices have often engaged in traditional ceremonies designed for conflict resolution. RAMSI has also been represented in such processes.[183] This can be seen as a three-way dynamic around a fantasy of an imagined golden age for the Solomon Islands, progress towards a modern state which is more locally representative, and integration of the state into its local context.

Following this logic, Fukyama's report also called for the incorporation of some aspects of the customary system into the state. This, he argued, needed to rest on some sense of a shared public good and a national identity. This would overcome the *wantok* system and the contradictory and anti-democratic loyalties it produces. He saw a need for the deliberate manipulation of cultural symbols in order to produce an institutional hybrid biased towards the liberal normative system.[184] This may only be achieved, in the medium term at least, by the continued system of shared sovereignty (using Krasner's recent concept)[185] between RAMSI and the Solomons' government. It was only this sharing of sovereignty that prevented the hybrid form of governance slipping back into local rather than liberal forms. This analysis provided the basis for the attempt to meld the customary into the constitution. This has not yet formed a political community that resonates though there are signs that it may. While its focus lies on creating the state and a national identity, however, it may continually be blocked by predatory elites who see this area as their prerogative. This is a difficulty which may also arise in the similar approach emerging in Timor Leste.

Merging of the customary with the modern constitutional order is still problematic in the sense that it appears to be at least partially driven by external actors, but it is a start in finding a more resonant form of political representation. For the leader of the team working on this project, following the views expressed in the Ministry of National Unity, Peace and Reconciliation, political community should follow local praxes. Formal political institutions being built by RAMSI – and their hijack – are the source of the Island's problems, rather than their saviour. Cultural, geographic, post-colonial, and design factors have facilitated the use for material power for elites rather than the welfare of the people. Informal institutions that traditionally provided for the latter have been displaced by the Western-backed focus on formal liberal institutions. Thus, civil society has not emerged: alternatively, it cannot be found using the usual lens state planners and officials apply because it lies in the informal and customary politics of the islands. This has resulted in significant tension between communalism and liberalism, between *wantok* and rational individualism.[186] The *wantok* inspires loyalty far beyond the law, the state, democracy, or a national identity. Similarly, the role of churches is also significant. But these informal systems are not scripted nor obvious, and are particularly hard for liberal statebuilders and external actors to recognise. Thus, they operate in parallel to officialdom and compete with it.[187] According to Woods, and repeating the position offered by Fukuyama, they tend to be particularistic and localised, based on patronage, and unable to engage with the notion of a public good.[188] Even so, political systems with cultural resonance, and with some social and economic capacity, become paramount and prominent in re-negotiating governance, rather than merely rights and markets.

According to Woods, the local context offers a culture of conflict avoidance and if conflict does occur, of quick reconciliation. Indeed, local customary strategies for doing so are more effective than approaches brought in by Western conflict resolution experts. Even so, many local actors still view Western techniques as more advanced and have lost confidence in their own practices.[189] Woods argues this confidence needs restoring because most citizens operate in its everyday context, which enables their survival and resilience. At the same time, rational political institutions enable politicians to use patronage to corrupt the system, enrich themselves, and protect those who do so because it is based on an individualist set of assumptions.[190] Where this does not apply, clientelism infects the political process without bringing the benefits that may accrue at the local, customary level through its own systems which are designed to cope with such issues in various ways. Thus, liberal statebuilding interferes with conflict avoidance and quick resolution. A double movement has occurred. Democracy and a social contract have not been created as, instead, the state has been informalised to reflect client relations, and the traditional role of customary governance has lost its ability to provide the social cohesion and security it once did before the state encroached on its roles. The liberal state has been hollowed out, and the customary has been emasculated – the worst of both worlds. This has allowed corruption, patronage, and resource extraction to lead to a collapse of both state and society – and the emergence of a rentier, neopatrimonial rather than liberal, state. Rent provides for elite power and for basic local welfare in the form of patronage. Politicians seek rents from extractive industries to distribute the perpetuating the system. The *wantok* networks have become skewed towards these practices as has the liberal state, undermining the social and welfare roles that customary processes and roles also often provided.

As a result, Woods argues that a more communal form of democracy, indicative of Solomon's autonomy from the universal liberal democratic thesis, would have more resonance on the ground and would work with the grain of customary capacity rather than allowing elite predation.[191] He estimated that 80 per cent of the population had little to do with the modern state, given that custom and liberal norms are widely divergent. Engaging with the informal political system would rescue the state if it could find a way of incorporating both. Again, the assumption is that some form of territorial state is the answer to local conflict, and of course the Australian government has hinted at a long term, virtually trusteeship role via RAMSI to maintain this implausible arrangement. Even so, as the cash economy, on which rests the liberal state, reaches only about 3–5 per cent of the population, the reach of any state-wide institutions that develop will remain limited. Instead, these should recognise communalism, the *wantok*, communal property, and consensual customary values, if a localised state is ever to emerge.[192] Furthermore, this state must redistribute wealth, a role that the international community appears intolerant to but which most of the population expect. Woods argues that the state will eventually, given the demand for public services across the islands, emerge in a confederal or federal form allowing for high levels of contextualised hybridity and effective decentralisation and autonomy. In his view this needs to be based on a horizontal rather than hierarchical political system, enabling an informality that the liberal state currently does not envisage. This would connect with custom and the church at a village level, as also called for by many chiefs.[193] The *wantok* might then start to align with peacebuilding and statebuilding as the latter become far more sensitised, rather than being perceived to be antagonistic towards them. To be locally resonant and legitimate, this form of post-liberal peace probably would need to be skewed more to the local and the customary, rather than to the liberal and the neoliberal, though in practice the liberal peace framework may dominate superficially. Still, this may help in starting to resolve the many contradictions between the two especially if local-local actors are given full representation both in liberal and customary ways.

A realisation of this complex process has led to both RAMSI and outside actors directing more attention to the importance and role of informal processes and institutions in both positive and negative senses, and to a growing understanding that political community in the Solomon Islands may not be constituted by the post-colonial liberal state, but in fact to a large degree in these informal systems relating to power, land, social custom and cohesion, justice and welfare. The very existence of democratic and market institutions, chiefs, customary institutions, the state, councils, churches, RAMSI, and other internationals, as well as the tellingly named 'Ministry for National Unity, Peace and Reconciliation' testify to the hybridity that is emerging, as well as the necessity of a focus on local rather than state government. Customary institutions, conflict management and reconciliation practices are now being imported into the modern state, as in Timor Leste.[194] As Moore argues, late on in the statebuilding process, the location of the village, *wantok*, and churches remerged as the key site of politics and resilience, rather than the centralised, Western notion of the state.[195] (Indeed, he suggested that the Vanuatu model of an upper house of chiefs might be appropriate, perhaps helping with the problem that the 'modern' and the 'local' or 'indigenous' are not aligned).[196]

Yet this process is not merely a result of the ineffectiveness of liberal peacebuilding in attaining its prescriptive ideals, but is also representative of local attempts at peace formation, including elites and less visible actors, and to exercise agency in ways which renegotiate the state. Indeed, it is indicative of contextual agency, resistance, and of the emergence of a political project in which alternatives produce their own hybridity. This realisation has left many politicians, internationals, donors, and RAMSI in a difficult position – back-tracking in their faith in the liberal peace blueprint or in neoliberal economics, and trying to understand a political community which is relatively inaccessible because of its hidden praxis, unknown languages and informal cultures, yet also vital to social, political and economic stability. Effectively, they have become, late in the day, caught up in the search for the really-existing hybrid political order that Boege *et al.* have theorised in the region, and the hybridity that is already in existence, if hidden.[197] It is little wonder, as with an earlier phase in the Timor statebuilding process, that there is now a strong desire for the 'localisation' and decentralisation of the state,[198] and a fear that RAMSI has so far failed to address any of the conflict's underlying causal factors via its neoliberal statebuilding mission. Yet, at the same time, some local actors have realised the potential for profit from complying with liberal peace processes and have started to simulate compliance.[199] Such compliance is producing hybrid possibilities for peace and should not be taken as capitulation to the liberal model.

Conclusion: a really-existing hybridity, not virtually liberal states

Caution is needed in approaching, interrogating, and deploying culturally 'sensitised' approaches: culture should not be re-essentialised nor necessarily perceived as a benign site of agency. Emergent hybridities must be treated with caution, both in their liberal and local versions. Yet, they are very important, as are the often ignored emotional and spiritual aspects of conflict and peacebuilding, of politics, society and culture, as the above cases illustrate. The liberal peace system has failed to recognise the significance of these infrapolitical areas of peacebuilding – and of subsistence forms of peacebuilding – a failure which connects to broader theoretical and methodological failings in IR. As in many parts of Latin America where indigenous movements have emerged, claims are being made against it via such positions for the liberal peace to live up to its rhetoric; for special consideration for local culture and forms of political association; for special rights according to context, including over identity, land, and autonomous juridical spaces, distinct from those envisage within the liberal and neoliberal state.[200] The post-liberal peace emerges from these dynamics. It recognises that legitimacy is both international and local, and often based on perceptions. It recognises that local and international practices are evolving, and that the state should also.

In these case studies, over time internationals realised that they had to forge relationships with customary actors and elders, negotiate tradition, and traditional sites of power and social, political, and economic organisation (even the market, ownership, and land distribution issues). In the process they encountered acute alterity which challenged liberal values systems and norms, and institutional arrangements. Some internationals withdrew from this confrontation, others ignored it, and others engaged. Implicitly, these encounters challenge and modify local and international peace systems, though even now international actors have had great difficulty understanding, engaging with, and improving everyday life in both cases. Rather than international peacebuilding improving everyday life in a way that local actors, communities, and individuals recognise as significant, competition over the array of resources that internationals symbolise and provide has reshaped the politics of peacebuilding. Donor driven rather than context driven projects appear to determine this process. The shell of the states being produced appears externalised: the liberal peace model is out of kilter with local patterns of politics, which anyway tend to resist its strictures. Ironically, the liberal peace model tends to offer camouflage for local elitism, patriarchy, feudalism, and authoritarianism, because of its default bias towards already existing elite sites of power and knowledge in a state-centric setting. These are in open view to the very limited international gaze while local and contextual agencies remain hidden unless they fit preconceptions. Yet, there is growing evidence that they are as responsible for the 'crisis' of the liberal peace as are its own internal contradictions and 'inefficiencies'. Thus, emerging hybridity means context is modifying the liberal peace, reversing these processes to a degree.

This offers a powerful argument for hybrid political orders, which are the result of the renegotiation and integration of international peacebuilding practices with local traditional and customary processes of politics.[201] Of course, this approach rests on an assumption that there are compatible spaces where the liberal international praxis and the contextual local politics may meet and find resonance in each other rather than produce a malevolent hybridity. As Schmeidl points out, this might also see the warlord sitting at the table with the donor, official, or human rights activist, or see discriminatory practices regarding gender or justice co-existing with democracy and a rule of law – unlikely and problematic.[202] This is not the only dimension that hybrid political orders necessarily underline, however. Hybridity in its local and liberal interaction should not be taken necessarily to construct benign political orders – feudal and patriarchal patterns remain – but its test rests on local and international legitimacy. Thus, it offers the possibility of a more resonant form of peace formation, and state, and eventually, mutual transformation. Hybridity should also be seen as devised from a mixture of acceptance and resistance to the liberal model (especially to its neoliberal aspects). Customary governance tends to enhance rather than undermine community resilience and social welfare. Furthermore, it enhances order and security because of the respect for chiefs and elders from within communities, as opposed to the general lack of respect for security or police services.[203] However, social support, safety nets, and customary control of land are normally aimed at community subsistence rather than individual or state profit, meaning that the state project itself needs to be questioned in contexts where this is not the basis for social or political order. In contrast to the liberal peace, respect for elders or chiefs is often earned through normative validation rather than objective and rational professionalism. Liberal democratic practices' adversarial nature does not sit well with customary or respect-based forms of governance, nor with party politics and the concept of an opposition.[204] Of course, customary practices, tradition, and forms of governance also benefit specific sectors of society over others and can rarely be captured by liberal rationality.

Such dynamics mean some difficult compromises, at least in transition, but this should not be taken to mean a compromise over say human rights norms, post-conflict justice, or humanitarian law or democracy. Nor should it be taken to mean that warlords or patriarchy are conducive to an everyday peace in hybrid form. At the same time, it should not be assumed that the customary, the local, and the everyday, have few or no positive dynamics or potentials for peace, or lack the capacity to mobilise, organise, or indeed, institutionalise. Nor should it be taken to mean that institutional development and neoliberal reform are conducive to a broader peace. The local-liberal hybrid lays bare both local and international patterns of power, norms, needs, and rights, and induces an unscripted negotiation between them. Peacebuilding is now as much about creating a peace on the ground as it is about a process of negotiation between the local and the international paradigms of peace. This means much more focus on localised and decentralised forms of government and the residue of conflict which lies within them, as well as their potential for contributions to peace.

What has occurred in Timor and the Solomon Islands is a 'localisation' of international practice over time, and partly in response to the failure of the international peacebuilding package. It is of little surprise that this has coincided with the improved stabilisation of state and society. This has also occurred to some degree in the more significant examples of Iraq and Afghanistan, but Timor and the Solomon Islands are important because the full weight of international and regional liberal peacebuilding praxis has been employed in a 'minor' context, thus accentuating the agency of these minor registers and the infrapolitics of peacebuilding. This does not necessarily echo a 'real' historical practice because there may be no known past peace to reconstruct, but instead reflects the imagined political practices of the contemporary context, caught between modernity and tradition, between the liberal state and the pre-existing polity, in the context of local and global inequality. This liminal space of alterity has in both cases been reoccupied by a hybrid form of the liberal and the local, one which acts as an interface and a bridge, but also retains its own distinctive identity, and may act as a challenge to the liberal state and to the architecture of international peacebuilding and its centralised, modern tropes of power. It also may not closely resemble past patterns of politics. Indeed, it holds both to account. If broad legitimacy is to be returned to peacebuilding, then this process should be pursued. If there is a connection, it is with the construction of social resilience within the contemporary context. This may reflect a liberal social contract, but it is likely that it also reflects an older, feudal, and neopatrimonial exchange. However, there are also very positive aspects of local and customary agencies, not least in their resilience, long-term perspective, capacity to mediate external influences, and indeed to subtly renegotiate hegemonic discourses.[205] The dilemma of hybridity is that both local and international actors are forced to accept different and possibly mutually repulsive patterns of praxis in the name of order and are forced to moderate their claims that their order can be automatically related with peace. They both romanticise and mythologise each other in both negative and positive ways. What type of peace can emerge from this process?

There are several dimensions of peacebuilding: the liberal peace model; the resurgence of the local; critical agency, and resistance, often related to custom, to make up for the short-falls of this model, especially in terms of social support, dispute resolution, reconciliation, and local justice; and finally, the hybridisation of both to produce a polity that is both liberal and local, but not exclusively so. What are crucial are the local agencies this represents, both for resistance to conflict and an alien praxis of peace, and for 'liberation' from them both.

The next question is whether or not this liberal-local hybrid represents the local and the everyday in local or liberal terms. In answer to fears that a local-liberal hybrid might lead to a 'malevolent hybridity' in which liberal peacebuilders make deals with rights-deniers, corrupt politicians, and warlords, this has not generally been dominant (and isolated examples of malevolent practices do not indicate a broader trend). Yet, during the periods in both cases considered in this chapter such awkward expediencies were more likely to be the case (because internationals are contextually naïve). Later, internationals were forced to consider locality after the collapse of their state building endeavours, and they have been more successful.

In both cases there is an aspect of liberal peacebuilding that remains separate and solely in the domain of a nexus between state elites and the international civil service of peacebuilders and statebuilders. There is also a local domain that remains distinct from any intervention, and a nexus between the local and the international which produces hybrid and post-liberal forms of peace. It is here, perhaps, that a limited success for liberal and local peacebuilders alike might be gleaned. This is where local versions of liberal concepts such as human security, the rule of law, democracy, human rights, development and marketisation, civil society, and even a responsibility to protect, might emerge. This liminal space is where the de-romanticisation of the local and de-mystification of the international may occur, and where the everyday, the sacred house, the chief, the *wantok*, customary practices and land, customary/liberal constitutional frameworks, and the networks which exist around them may begin to enable individual and community agency and legitimate these emerging 'local-liberal' states. From these intersections a new hybridity and indeed a more grounded citizenship might arise. Hybridity emerges from critical agency, not subaltern voicelessness or post-colonial mimicry, and reiterates both the local and the international in their evolving and related complexity.

Conclusion
The birth of a post-liberal peace[1]

... poets of their own affairs, pathfinders in jungles of functionalist rationality ...[2]

Transformation is not contrary to resistance, but it reveals that the most effective strategies of post-colonial resistance have not become bogged down in simple opposition or futile binarism, but have taken the dominant discourse and transformed it for purposes of self-empowerment.[3]

A summary

From the liberal peace's metanarrative springs a range of consequences, whereby it has become clear that local agency is rewriting international relations. International actors and policies focus on local weakness from the liberal peace perspective. They romanticise and displace context and critical agency, expecting peace to arise through compliance, and often enable predatory elites to capture the state they endeavour to build. These dynamics emerge from the liberal peace's own internal contradictions, from its claim to offer a universal epistemological basis for peace, and to offer a technology and process which can be applied to achieve it. Much of this is crypto-idealism – the danger for all emancipatory theorising. But because of the governmentalising distance and biopolitical tendency of the metanarrative the liberal peace produces, when viewed from a range of contextual and local perspectives, these processes often appear to represent power rather than humanitarianism or emancipation.

Yet, much of this study has shown how different types of power arise from below and confront processes or institutions which do not represent context or critical agency: '[w]here there is power there is resistance'.[4] Such a critique is both an internal and an external challenge to hegemonic representations of peace, emphasising the need for autonomy even where peacebuilding, statebuilding, and development occur. On a more mundane level, liberal peace has not provided material benefit to its subjects, and has emphasised local and global inequalities.[5] Top-down approaches lack legitimacy, are unsuitable, coercive, undesirable, and indicative of external interests, contextually unfeeling and insensitive. The liberal peace's power and legitimacy appears to be fragmented and self-announced from the perspective of subjects who are under pressure not only to practice it but to make peace and produce a surplus (the latter perhaps for the first time). Many of the liberal peace's subjects challenge the nature of the inclusiveness it offers, and instead see it as exclusionary in terms of culture, identity, autonomy, land rights, and custom.[6] Indeed, it has become the basis of their challenge, providing them with registers, hidden and visible, to '... articulate a post-liberal challenge.'[7] This is being recognised now amongst some international actors, particularly in the UN system, where parallel institutions, the importance of working with them and not trying to convert them, has been noted, though they must also accept the significance of UN norms. Many in the UN system also recognise that local partners simulate partial compliance.[8]

Some subjects mobilise large networks, some do not, but either way their effects are notable. Conversely, placing the local at the centre of peacebuilding does not necessarily displace power, but it does enable contextual critical agencies in rights, needs, and institutional terms, rather than maintaining their peripheral status. This is also actually consonant with the liberal peace's focus on civil society and its emancipatory wing, but local alterity, identity, custom, culture – the site of much critical agency – as well as needs issues point further. Indeed, what has occurred to varying degrees across all the cases discussed in this book is that external and national agendas for peacebuilding have been accepted locally while still maintaining local contextual approaches via critical agency. This seems to represent a liberal dynamic of centralisation versus a post-liberal dynamic of decentralisation, meaning at both state and international levels, where autonomy from externalised states, territorial sovereignty, institutions and rights frameworks, and markets is both desired and reduced. Individualism, inflexible territoriality, statism, neoliberal forms of citizenship, and homogenisation are all targets of the post-liberal challenge, while also maintaining social justice, emancipatory forms of peace, and local tolerance.[9] The reach of the critical agency I have described is such that it is reforming the liberal peace and some of its protagonists are now becoming influential in the post-conflict states where it has begun to emerge realised, as well as amongst the internationals.

This has been expressed in a number of different ways. First, the standard international narrative about liberal peacebuilding relates to a lack of resources, local or international political will, coordination, overlap and inefficiency, as well as deviousness amongst local counterparts. This is a general theme across all peacebuilding operations. It does not question its underlying basis on international legitimacy as a rule. Secondly, local political elites have begun to resist the donor consensus openly in a number of countries, such as El Salvador.[10] Thirdly, they have called for more local ownership, as can be seen in the Kosovanisation, Timorisation, and Afghanisation campaigns.[11] In the former it was harnessed for a coordinated, though often hidden, campaign for sovereignty driven by ethnic affiliation, often through international institutional channels. In Timor, self-determination was a major issue, but critical agency was also driven by custom, religion, and issues relating to needs. In Afghanistan, it was partly driven by a local recognition of the need to accommodate opposing parties, including the Taliban. Fourthly, they have dragged their feet on implementation or resisted it, not often openly, though this has occurred in both Bosnia and Afghanistan. Fifthly, they have co-opted the missions into nationalist, liberation, or ethnic agendas, as can be seen in Kosovo, Mozambique, and Namibia to varying degrees, by a complex mix of co-option and resistance.[12] Often elites have accepted the neoliberal aspects of liberal peacebuilding, and expected internationals to draw a blind eye to nationalist pressures – often associated with predatory practices in the economic realm – in return. Sixthly, this dynamic can be extended to the 'authoritarian democracies' that have emerged in these aforementioned countries, and in Cambodia for example.[13] Seventhly, there often co-exists great social and economic inequality with these dynamics which indicates severe inequality in rights and opportunities, not just locally, but also globally (at least in terms of aspirations).

This indicates the establishment of a number of more localised and contextual, non-elite processes. Local–local responses to both elite agendas and liberal peace-building are even more significant in the challenges they raise for international actors, pointing to language, historical, cultural, and customary obstacles. In Timor, political elites mobilised against what they saw as an unaccountable and authoritarian statebuilding endeavour. In Bosnia, political elites have dragged their feet on reform and allowed internationals to make their difficult decisions for them. In Kosovo, local employees of international actors, as well as political and business elites, all placed their weight behind the notion that statehood would lead to peace in Kosovo.[14] In Guatemala, indigenous people do not regard the capital city as 'their' country, given it represents the dominance of an elite and an international ideology of peacebuilding not commensurate with local approaches. From the Solomon Islands, Timor, Mozambique, to Liberia there have been local attempts to bring customary forms of governance and law into the international blueprint for peacebuilding.[15] In Somalia, local institutional practices have long substituted for what internationals regard as a complete vacuum and anarchy.[16] In Afghanistan, the attempt to build a state without the Taliban has been against the advice of many local actors, not least the president, and the Taliban have made sure external strategies would fail.[17] In Iraq, local sectarian elites have struggled over the spoils of the collapse of the state after the US-led invasion, and exploit acute poverty to their ends. This is despite the fact that local elites had called for a social form of democracy in which welfare would be used to pacify the population.[18] Furthermore, in all of these locations there have emerged, or have long-existed, very many social, customary, labour, religious and civil society organisations and movements which have partially resisted and partially accepted state and donor led strategies. Behind all of this activity, there has also been the incalculable effect of individual, family, and community, approaches – forms of resistance and critical agency, which though fragmented, when seen as an aggregate are sources of legitimacy. Clearly, each context is different in the way in which local agencies engage with the international, but there are common threads that can be observed across such cases, as is increasingly becoming clear.

The notion of the post-liberal peace merely indicates a purposive transcendence of the rhetoric associated with the liberal peace in order to create contextual hybridity from social, political, economic, cultural, and historical experiences of peace in local, transnational, and international terms. Indeed, it might be said that such hybridity has always been present in the transversal and transnational relationship between the local and the international. It is an attempt to escape liberal enclosure and distant administration, to take a stake in a much broader discussion of peace where even fragmented collective action or mobilisation occurs inclusively rather than as an apparent dikctat from a distant international community. Politics re-enters peacebuilding and critical agency rather than external or elite power (even tastefully attired by normative claims) is key. In this way, agency is more clearly connected to the interactions and mediations of subjects upon states and international actors, governance, peacebuilding and statebuilding.

Such post-colonial and subaltern understandings of peacebuilding, understanding how it too might be subject to resistance (in constructive rather than merely reactive terms), enable a clearer comprehension of the possibilities rather than constraints of emancipation, empathy, and a move towards broadly legitimate emancipatory forms of peace in local contexts.[19] Peacebuilding would be constructed by its subjects, not merely by often well-intentioned external actors and internationals. We would also become aware of how peacebuilding (in liberal form even) has been influenced by its internal interests and its history, as well as its long-standing contacts with difference. Hidden, critical agencies have already modified it, either through material or cultural agency, or through empathetic relations. Liberal universal blueprints have had the unfortunate side effect of evacuating the local,[20] which has contradicted its humanitarian and empathetic claims of emancipation: local agencies have often responded to rectify and contextualise such failings. Sometimes this rests upon local contextual forms of subsistence peacebuilding where hidden actors, used to operating with few resources, develop their own approaches and institutions, drawing on contextual and liberal dynamics, while avoiding international conditionalities.

This enables critical positions to emerge which are very similar to post-colonial positions, in methodological and epistemic terms. From this tension the production and deployment of a range of 'local', transversal and transnational agencies emerges in context, through which the liberal peace is contested. Indeed the distance of the liberal peace from (or indeed blindness to) contexts (which include everyday life, citizens, identity, and subjectivity) allows these agencies to subvert it, modify it, or adopt it in unexpected ways. This process offers significant opportunities for the reconsideration of emancipatory notions of peace beyond the liberal peace framework, which have more contextual relevance, even while maintaining in modified forms international norms, institutions, law, and processes associated by liberal peacebuilding and with an emancipatory peace in liberal form. Even more significant is that this process involves the reconstruction of peace in both liberal and contextual forms so that neither seem necessarily to create binary oppositions or be in significant tension.

A hybrid form of peace emerges from this agonistic process, and as part of the normative and political project of peacebuilding the next step is to begin to identity the opportunities for peace inherent in the various localised processes I have described, as well international responses to these, and the new obstacles to peace that may emerge along with such hybridity. Rather than producing subjects, as does the liberal peace, a post-liberal peace enables subjects to produce peace. This retains aspects of emancipatory liberalism and of critical cosmopolitanism, but combines and displaces them with ways of knowing relating to peace that are inaccessible to them because of Enlightenment, rational, and individualistic biases. A post-liberal peace itself offers new opportunities, but it should also be acknowledged that a counter-critique of the post-liberal peace indicates that in the processes of the contextualisation of both the liberal peace and local peacebuilding agencies, dangers arise that the substance of peace even in its more sophisticated emancipatory terms could be diverted in very problematic ways.

The international apparatus for peacebuilding needs to find more representative and sensitised ways of negotiating with the range of agencies that exist in post-conflict environments. It should acknowledge the ethical and methodological basis of this process, or risk rejection and the continuing 'escape' of its subjects from its focus on governance over reconciliation, on elite power over citizens' rights and need, or producing merely scattered and fragmented 'spaces of peace'. Even more problematically, this may buttress exclusive projects which do not offer broad inclusion or emancipation and fail to enable an escape from the everyday and structural pressures which produce violence.

There is a need to connect post-liberal approaches to peacebuilding with contextual narratives of liberation, self-determination, self-governance, and autonomy, in cultural, social, economic, and political terms. Damaged by nationalism, liberation politics are often seen as a sign of impending humanitarian crisis, rather than the exercise of critical agency.[21] Yet, understanding discourses of liberation, whether from conflict, identity, poverty or oppression, in everyday terms would enable the redevelopment of international peace systems and norms. This might represent a 'decolonisation' of the liberal peace system and its various acts of 'enclosure', involving its main actors, from the UN to the World Bank and IMF, EU, other donors, and international NGOs or agencies. This does not mean an end to their relevance for peacebuilding/statebuilding, but a reconstruction of the normative legitimacy of their roles in contextual, everyday settings in parallel to the focus on Western perceptions of security, institutions, law, states, markets, and civil society. It is a response to the current crises of liberal peace and statebuilding, and the recognition of the legitimacy of local processes of peace formation.

These processes and dynamics are illustrated in the following diagrams, which depict how critical agency challenges the liberal peace model in everyday terms, and enables the birth of a post-liberal peace.

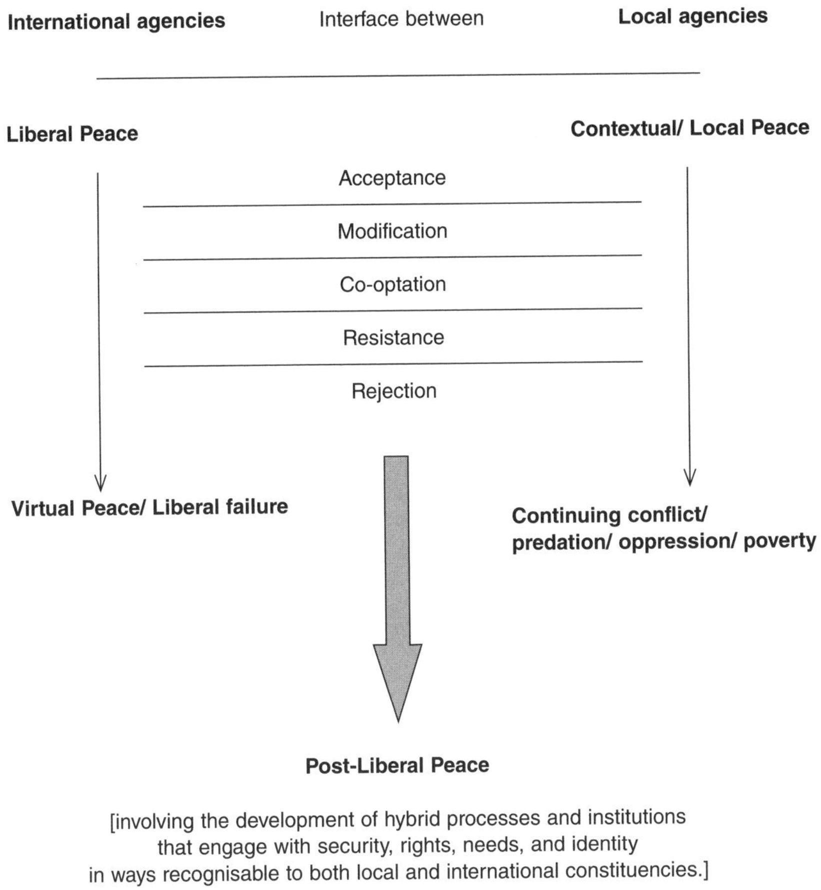

International agencies   Interface between   **Local agencies**

Liberal Peace   **Contextual/ Local Peace**

Acceptance

Modification

Co-optation

Resistance

Rejection

Virtual Peace/ Liberal failure   **Continuing conflict/
predation/ oppression/ poverty**

Post-Liberal Peace

[involving the development of hybrid processes and institutions
that engage with security, rights, needs, and identity
in ways recognisable to both local and international constituencies.]

Figure 3 A Post-Liberal Peace

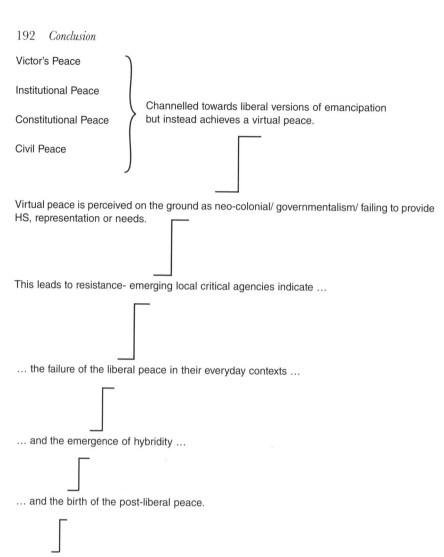

Victor's Peace

Institutional Peace

Constitutional Peace   Channelled towards liberal versions of emancipation
                         but instead achieves a virtual peace.

Civil Peace

Virtual peace is perceived on the ground as neo-colonial/ governmentalism/ failing to provide HS, representation or needs.

This leads to resistance- emerging local critical agencies indicate ...

... the failure of the liberal peace in their everyday contexts ...

... and the emergence of hybridity ...

... and the birth of the post-liberal peace.

This process raises the issues of:

➢ everyday peace formation and its requirements/ dynamics
➢ emerging hybridity- mutual remediation of and shifts in Liberal Peacebuilding and local peace projects
➢ non essentialising and non-instrumentalising engagements with local agency and contexts
➢ How local critical agency shapes the state and international policy for peace-building and statebuilding
➢ Emancipation beyond cosmopolitanism
➢ New methodologies and epistemologies
➢ Need for ethical and methodological development in peacebuilding and statebuilding

Figure 4 Processes of Liberal Peacebuilding/ Statebuilding

Actors
- Western/ Europeanised Political Elites
- Transnational NGOs
- Transversal Local Actors
- Identity, Customary, Religious Groups and Organisations
- Class actors, trade unions, etc
- Local counterparts of liberal peacebuilders
- Private individuals who act both publicly and privately

Issues
- Security
- Institutions
- Custom
- Culture
- Identity
- Religion
- Needs, class, inequality
- Subsistence frameworks
- Customary land use
- Modernisation/ liberalisation processes
- Modifications of the LP according to contextual politics and praxis

Processes
- Liberal processes- DDR/ SSR, institutional building, democratisation, rule of law, civil society, marketisation, development
- Customary processes/ institutions/ culture
- Transformation of identity, religious, labour and social movements/ institutions and organisations
- Transnational and transversal processes
- Critical agency: public organisation and mobilisation and hidden, small scale, infrapolitical mobilisation

Outcomes
- Acceptance/ Compliance
- Partial Reform
- Modification
- Co-optation
- Rejection
- Hidden resistance
- Explicit resistance

Figure 5 Everyday Peacebuilding

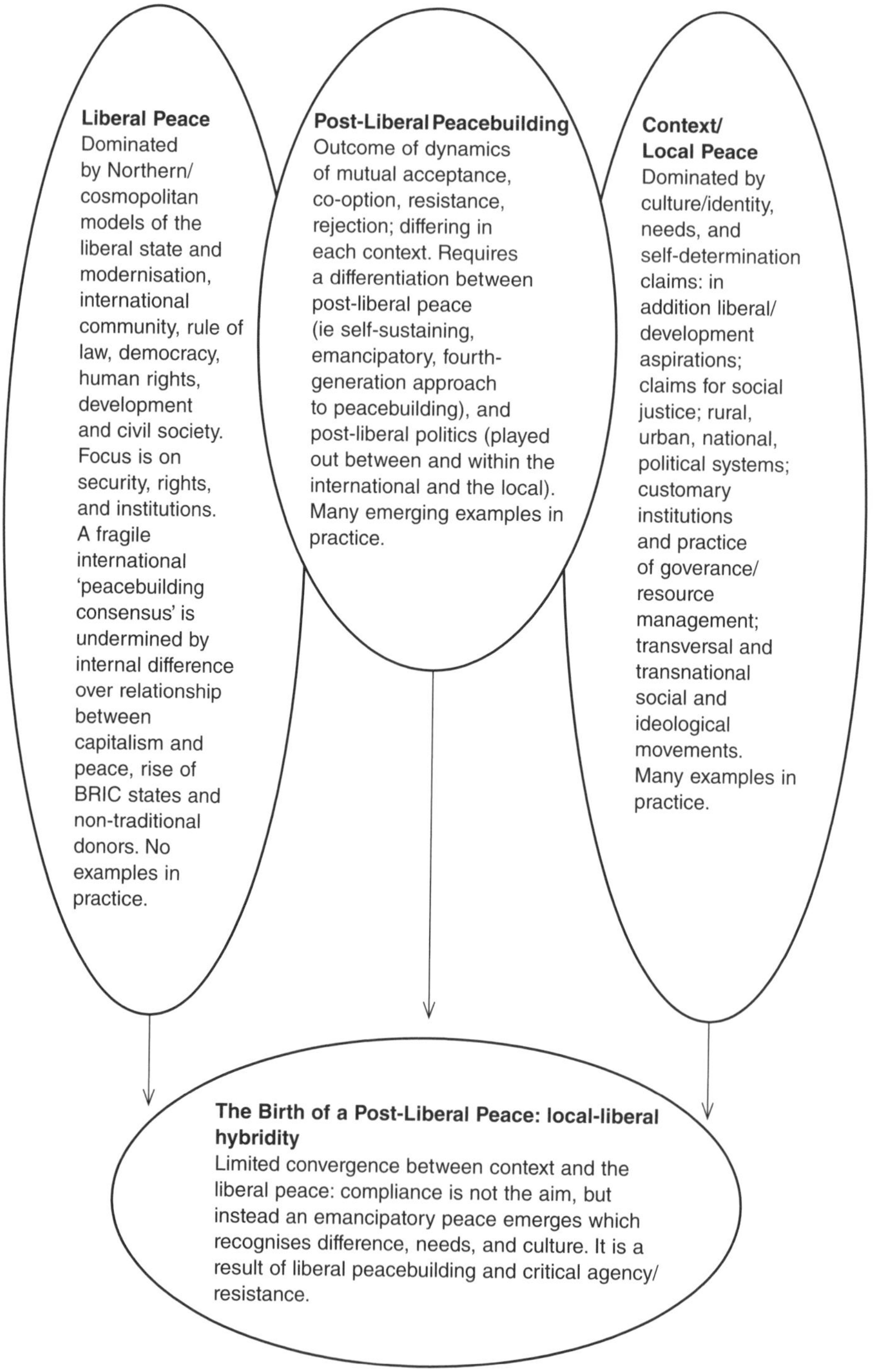

Liberal Peace
Dominated
by Northern/
cosmopolitan
models of the
liberal state and
modernisation,
international
community, rule of
law, democracy,
human rights,
development
and civil society.
Focus is on
security, rights,
and institutions.
A fragile
international
'peacebuilding
consensus' is
undermined by
internal difference
over relationship
between
capitalism and
peace, rise of
BRIC states and
non-traditional
donors. No
examples in
practice.

Post-Liberal Peacebuilding
Outcome of dynamics
of mutual acceptance,
co-option, resistance,
rejection; differing in
each context. Requires
a differentiation between
post-liberal peace
(ie self-sustaining,
emancipatory, fourth-
generation approach
to peacebuilding), and
post-liberal politics (played
out between and within the
international and the local).
Many emerging examples in
practice.

**Context/
Local Peace**
Dominated by
culture/identity,
needs, and
self-determination
claims: in
addition liberal/
development
aspirations;
claims for social
justice; rural,
urban, national,
political systems;
customary
institutions
and practice
of goverance/
resource
management;
transversal and
transnational
social and
ideological
movements.
Many examples in
practice.

**The Birth of a Post-Liberal Peace: local-liberal
hybridity**
Limited convergence between context and the
liberal peace: compliance is not the aim, but
instead an emancipatory peace emerges which
recognises difference, needs, and culture. It is a
result of liberal peacebuilding and critical agency/
resistance.

Figure 6 Post-Liberal Peacebuilding

From peacebuilding as resistance to peacebuilding as liberation

Peace processes, peacebuilding, and statebuilding are intensely political activities. They represent a contestation of power over resources, needs, class, rights, identities, and cultures. They require both a private and a public space of politics in which organisation and mobilisation to support any peace process occurs amongst its subjects. The liberal peace is itself a product of a rational, institutionalised and materialist culture encompassed by the modern state.[22] Even this needs grass-roots legitimacy in immediate terms as the concept of civil society and the associated civil peace illustrate, not merely in the long term, otherwise it will be resisted, modified, or co-opted, despite any international consensus over its value (this is partly why the liberal peacebuilding consensus is so weak).[23] This has been the fate of the liberal peace, and its romanticisation of the local has led to forms of resistance – critical agency – which have produced hybrid forms of peace, whether for social welfarism rather than neoliberal democracy, or for customary institutions, or even to reduce or avoid the power of the modern state (especially as the experience of statehood may so far have been very negative).[24] The concepts of local ownership and participation were introduced to combat this problem (but with very limited success).[25] This raises the question of the type of state peacebuilding lends itself to, whether centralised or decentralised, customary, hybrid, liberal, neoliberal, or in other form. But it also raises the bigger issue of whether the state as it is currently conceived, either internationally or local, enables or is an obstacle to emancipatory forms of peace.

This illustrates very significant local agency (even if it is exercised partly as resistance or escape),[26] in contradiction to the distant, liberal assumption that the local is without capacity, and very different political agendas to those that the liberal peace prescribes. These infrapolitical processes have shifted the peacebuilding process away from the simple objectives of the liberal peace into a terrain and via methodologies that are locally resonant rather than internationally compliant. As Foucault argued, a critical disposition implies that the reaction to governmentalism would be to find a mode of escape – the art of not being governed (or at least governed 'quite so much').[27] He identifies this as emerging in a cultural form in Europe in response to the post-Enlightenment governmentalism which emerged. This might also now be seen in local responses to the liberal/neoliberal peace. This is not an anarchist position, but relates to the critical complexities of subjects' consent and contextual legitimacy for political organisation whereby resistance reflects constructive agencies for peace not violence. It does not necessarily question the need for the state, but it does provide a good argument for its deterritorialisation, care in its claims for sovereignty, and for substantive rather than merely procedural or institutional engagements with rights and needs. Localisation and critical agency may also translate itself into acceptable language for liberal peacebuilders, without undermining the integrity of the localised process or institution, but modifying it in order to offer a parallel integrity. For example, in Liberia, the National Council of Tribal Elders use the language of the liberal peace, and in particular the rule of law, democracy, and human rights, provided for them in training by the Carter Centre, but also have preserved their own processes based on communality and indigenous processes of justice in which there is no division between criminal and civil cases (the Elders are only supposed to work on civil cases, referring criminal cases to the state justice system). This is partly an attempt by the Elders to remain relevant as the modern state is constructed, but also to shape that state and represent their communities in ways it cannot.[28]

That such issues are becoming apparent in the context of the interface between critical agency and international peacebuilding and statebuilding indicates that there has been significant mobilisation in terms of local agency, developing peacebuilding strategies in relation to the liberal peace but also, crucially, in opposition to it and in relation to local political forms and institutions. These may be defined in nationalistic terms or in localised, customary terms, so peacebuilding in infrapolitical terms may represent a national agenda, or it may represent a local agenda for decentralised forms of politics as in Kosovo, Timor, and the Solomon Islands. In either case, local actors have shift the terrain of peacebuilding into a conceptual and methodological space where local legitimacy makes it difficult to contest it, as was the case for example with Gandhi's campaign of passive resistance against the British.[29] The state is still often its focus, but the state is seen as a component of peacebuilding rather than the main prerequisite for peace as is the predominant international view.

Gandhi was not just against colonialism but was very suspicious of the modern state itself which he thought rationalised life rather than emancipated it though its involvement in war, ideological domination, and capitalism. He also appreciated the state's capacity for large-scale organisation if it led to prosperity[30] and thought that peace and social order for India should stem from cooperation, trusteeship over property, and 'ordered anarchy' with the minimum of institutional structures and no use of violence. In pedagogic terms, Gandhi implied that India's post-colonial order should stem from individuals' moral courage, reclaimed from empire, from autonomy, solidarity, and vibrant local communities and culture.[31] Democracy required the recognition of self-governance by fully capable individuals.[32] Gandhi thought that liberal democracy was restricted by its tendency to depend on a centralised state framework, although later in his life he also began to appreciate the state's role in large-scale mobilisation, industrialisation, and the redistribution of wealth.[33] Ultimately he came to realise that the state was necessary for development and for peace but may also be a threat to the types of local agencies (or awakening) crucial for resistance to oppression. Because of this tension, now being repeated in modern statebuilding approaches which veer erratically between centralisation to deal with security, institutions, rights, and public services issues, and decentralisation to respond to market, identity and territorial pressures as well as to provide closer and more locally legitimate forms of governance, the state cannot be the final arbiter of peace because it is pulled in too many directions. He saw this instead as emanating from local communities, united federally, whose critical agencies enabled forms of autonomous politics which determined rights, needs, and institutions. But Gandhi's citizens did not have much awareness of their responsibilities or connections further afield, and so his insights rest not on the construction of a radical alternative to the present international order but his mastery of 'indigenous ... symbolic discourse' which international actors could not comprehend. This enabled him to create a 'state' within a state, one which very quickly captured the formal state.[34]

Thus, the claim of modernity that peace should be created for others by those who have achieved a superior epistemology, which offers transformation and emancipation, is resisted and translated by the very local agencies it claims cannot create peace. They then set out to do just this, borrowing from, and supported by empathetic international actors and policies which are contextually viable or co-optable. A peace within the liberal peace is created via everyday strategies and critical agency. Indeed, this is partly the aim of the liberal peace even if the type of everyday peace that is arising is unexpected. Transformation and emancipation, themselves political, emerge from the negotiation between liberal and local forms of politics, and local agencies and capacities carry significant opportunities for both. This is where liberal peacebuilding meets everyday local resistance, and local applications of agency to exercise autonomy. This produces hybrid forms of peace, themselves indicative of new approaches to emancipation, transformation, and even liberation, but as Gandhi's political thinking illustrated, this hybridity must avoid relying on a nationalist/nation/and territorial state. Cooperation, consent, and local legitimacy were to be the basis of his state, not conditionality, domination, or fear, not a dependence on international sources of legitimacy. This state should not exist independently of its citizens[35] (as it does in many instances of liberal statebuilding where the virtual peace pertains). In Gandhi's description of the relationship between politics at the village level and the imperial power of Britain, and theoretically in the context of democracy and capitalism, he was predicting a post-liberal peace.[36]

Approaches to peacebuilding or statebuilding, and development praxis, have given rise to a need for a 'pedagogy of peace' spanning the dialogic relations of the most with the least marginalised, in humanist terms. This pedagogy might be as much aimed at the liberal international as it is the local, but more importantly it breaks down the dichotomy between the two which exists in traditional, problem-solving theory. Resistance to the liberal peace in post-colonial terms implies a hybrid form of peace with its own transformative qualities, which are resistant to exclusion. This critical agency does not negate the liberal peace necessarily but it resists its use as a universal blueprint.[37]

Resistance in these terms might stem from a range of uncoordinated activities in political, economic, social, cultural, identity, and customary spheres, with little hope of achieving emancipation or transformation, but actually they represent far more transformative potential than has often been recognised. This is especially so if they have an impact on informal and formal institutions, which preserves their intent for the future. The mobilisation of the 'weak', even if through small, surreptitious acts of resistance[38] is more than the atomised and fragmented phenomena it is often claimed to be. This is not to romanticise local agency or the capacity of the 'local' to act, identify agendas and objectives, to organise and mobilise on a large-scale, as is often claimed, but it is to connect local agencies to both the ongoing problems of liberal peacebuilding, and more appropriately to the transformatory project of peace itself. This cannot be overvalued, even if local critical agency might be overplayed. In a democratic, rights oriented transformation, thousands of minor resistances to externalised and uncontextual strategies of peacebuilding, statebuilding, or development, amount to a very significant obstacle for more 'efficient' and 'coordinated' international strategies. This is where the resources, capacity, and power deployed for the internationals' projects of peacebuilding, statebuilding, and development have disappeared to. They have been turned against themselves, co-opted, modified, or resisted and rejected, in a register that most international fail to comprehend, to their enormous frustration.

Thus, the hidden transcripts of peacebuilding – its infrapolitics – amount to meaningful agency in terms of preserving the integrity of local actors and social, historical, cultural, political, and economic realities, in their everyday contexts. A realisation of this requires the reconstruction of local ownership, consent, and legitimacy in contextual terms, and offer a critique of power which might add up to a platform for transformation of the self and the other (perhaps moving beyond the self and other), pertaining to both conflict dynamics, the liberal peace, and the negotiation of a post-liberal outcome in hybrid form. Critique in these terms infers a concern about peace which replaces governmentalism and its attempt to totalise and subjugate.[39] Sometimes this is achieved by connecting with national agendas, or other types of campaigns of a needs, ideological or identity nature, or perhaps against economic structures or interest groups or environmental degradation.[40] Cultural frameworks provide a crucial platform on which this agency develops, even if in transient forms.

This implies a contextual approach to peacebuilding, where context is local, state, regional, international, transnational, and transversal. It represents a praxis which occurs *with* its subjects in order to produce a synthesis, not *for* its subjects (or international actors) in order to produce an invasive form of peace. It is designed to increase their independence and their capacity for political, organised, and self-empowering processes for peace.[41] Thus peacebuilding, in dialogic and pedagogic terms, produces a form of action from this synthesis in which its subjects recognise their peace and its legitimacy as a contextual and international script rather than merely one or the other. In post-colonial terms this transforms the cultural capacity and ranges of infrapolitical agency by appropriating forms of domination for self-empowerment. This illustrates via local engagements with civil society, rights, and institutions, how needs, welfare, and culture, and identity are crucial parts of a more contextual peacebuilding. This should seek out and be connected to contextual, bottom-up dynamics of peace formation. From this emerges a post-colonial form of civil society, not predicated solely compliance with international views, and including a range of local-local actors, representing resistance and so hybridity. Instead of the current assumption that making peace requires cooperation between soon-to-be homogenous actors, this would enable a mediation between the most difficult and awkward actors whereby peace would be made between enemies rather than merely between friends.

To reconstruct a fourth generation of theory which recognises and enables agency in its localised senses, such theories and approaches need to recognise where oppression has arisen, whether from local political, social, economic, systems, whether strategic, feudal, patriarchal, customary, religious, or linguistic, tribal, clan, or class. But they also need to understand how they themselves become complicit in relations of power and oppression. The subjects of such violence also need to understand how they may have become embedded in local, regional, national, transnational, and international structures which silence them.[42] It is clear to them that liberal peacebuilding and statebuilding is contradictory: it aims to liberate them from conflict, poverty, and oppression, but it is also deeply biased against them. Thus, the next step is to transform this bias through resistance. The resultant birth of a post-liberal peace rests on the multiple and fluid critical agencies, mobilisation, advocacy, and accountably stemming from a post-colonial civil society, which offers multiple levels of legitimacy in the same way that the liberal peace was made legitimate both locally and internationally by its crucial civil peace component over the last century or more.[43]

A better understanding of the ways that agency is expressed amongst the subjects of peace should be the starting point for the transformative aims of a fourth generation of peacebuilding. This eirenist approach might then provide a basis for the mediation of the liberal peace paradigm in each context. Notions of hybridity do not mean peace will be comfortable or even mirror the progressive or transformative expectations of the liberal peace, however. It means engaging with the desire of local actors for autonomy and even national liberation – as in Kosovo, Timor Leste and the Solomons – rather than ignoring these dynamics and imposing the liberal peace. Thus the local agencies I have described, and its resistances and autonomies indicate that the local cannot be managed or even governed in the sense imagined in the liberal peace paradigm. Understanding the implications of this may then offer a basis for transformative forms of peace to emerge as a result of the politics of the local-liberal interface that liberal peacebuilding and the infrapolitics of peacebuilding indicate. This has broad implications for IR itself as well as the third generation praxis which has been widely institutionalised in the last twenty years or so.[44] In this sense, individuals have recovered the right to name themselves and their peace – the challenge is that their liberation should not be exclusive or violent, to re-erect sovereignty or exclusion.[45]

From peacebuilding as resistance, to expressions of agency and autonomy through peacebuilding, to the production of post-liberal forms of local-liberal hybridity through the recognition and realisation of the everyday and its dynamics, emerges a significant insight. This offers peacebuilding as liberation as well as the more well-known approaches to emancipation through social justice.[46] It expresses and engages with grass-roots agendas, politics, and capacities, and connects with the wide range of non-Western epistemologies, post-colonial, ethnographic, political, social, and other transnational and transversal movements and their theorists.[47] This has three main implications for thinking on peace. First, a liberation from the problem-solving methodology and quasi-colonial theories of elite oriented IR, which ironically have, in their complicity with power, sovereignty, territoriality, and liberal/neo liberal discourses of peace, seen their very projects of statebuilding undermine the models that have brought them about. There have been significant human costs for such experimentation. Secondly, the aspiration for liberation also confirms the drive of international peacebuilding and state-building actors to recognise and enable local ownership and agency, and pushes harder and further in the quest for emancipation; and finally and most crucially, peacebuilding as liberation arises on the part of its subjects according to their history, culture, identities, needs, rights, and forms of governance. Yet, in practice, as in the examples of Timor Leste and the Solomon Islands in the previous chapter and my other cases earlier in this study, the channelling by internationals, elites, and often by local actors of this project into that of a new or modified nation-state has contradictory effects. These return the discourse of peacebuilding to a third generation form, with all of its attendant problems. Thus, the frontier of the hybrid form of peace which is emerging lies in the connection between local agency, a 'national' local project, the state and international institutions and cosmopolitan norms of the liberal peace, and the form of transnational and transversal polity that develops. The challenge is now to understand how to construct localised, post-conflict polities, which mirror local agencies, international norms and rights, and reconciliation in a fourth generation form – where hybrid forms of peace are transformative rather than merely reconstructing old conflict dynamics.

In sum, my argument indicates that local agency, autonomy, and the many efforts to develop these in the everyday space of peacebuilding (left vacant by liberal peacebuilding/statebuilding's many blind spots and omissions) leads to peacebuilding as resistance. This, representing the infrapolitics of peacebuilding, in turn implies a form of peacebuilding as liberation, including everyday hidden agencies and capacities hidden from the liberal gaze. The production of a post-liberal peace, in its hybrid local and liberal forms, relies on a *via media* between both if peacebuilding as liberation is not to be conflict inducing (as is possible, say, in Kosovo). This *via media* might be the basis for a mutual acceptance or resistance, or the possibility of a liberation from conflict and its structures. It depends on transnational, transversal, liberal and local channels of communication that connect the most marginal to the most powerful in a transparent and putatively democratic manner.

The subjects of violence are crucial in the reconstruction of peace, or at least a fourth generation. They are the actors who can legitimise, name, understand, and develop pathways out of their violence, by which many or most have been affected or are complicit in. Thus the role of international actors, whether peace-builders, statebuilders, development specialists, a range of advisors or donors, or NGOs, is to facilitate this process, not supplant it. This reflects an older debate on peacemaking and peacebuilding. All must be wary of the oppressed becoming new oppressors, or of peace's facilitators supplanting peacebuilding with their own interests, assumptions, or knowledge systems, and of reiterating causal factors of conflict as if they were its solution (as appears to have arisen with the liberal peace).[48] Internationals, local peace actors, and constituencies all seek the rehumanisation of peace and politics based on a realisation that they cannot operate without each other (in conflict or peace). Prescriptive strategies tend to deny such requirements and replicate certain aspects of conflict.

A pedagogy of peacebuilding emerges as a result as multiple channels of cooperation and engagement between conflict and peace actors, local, elite, liberal, and non-liberal, in a rediscovery of local agency and humanity rather than a reassertion of interests and sovereignty.[49] Here a praxis of peacebuilding arise as a result of multiple local agencies and international praxis, both of which mediate the other in ways which may preserve liberal rights and institutions in modified form, but also modify them significantly to reflect local self-determination and autonomy as far as possible. Local patterns of governance, economy, and society are also modified but in ways which preserve their bottom-up and grass-roots legitimacy. International peacebuilding is merely a facilitation of this process. It should not project a *res nullius*, which it can 'fill' with liberal citizens and institutions according to Western interests, but instead should engage with everyday life, and how it may shape a peaceful polity in this respect. Peacebuilding is thus reframed as a dialogic and pedagogic process which reconstructs the everyday according to how its subjects need and want to live, perhaps in the broader liberal peace context, but in recognition that it arises out of multiple such everydays and their political engagements with each other.

This has four implications for a fourth generation peace project:

1 the early realisation of needs provision in local contexts beginning with the most marginal;
2 the development of rights and institutions reflecting context, needs and materiality, and their dialogics (identity, history, culture);
3 a local and contextual political debate over the nature of the polity to be brought into being in its local and international contexts;
4 the role of the internationals in ensuring the interplay of local agencies in situ with the liberal peace praxis to reduce rather than replay, conflict.

This is in contrast to the current late redressal of needs and the prior focus on the state, rights and institutions, beginning with elites (and in their mainly Anglo-American ethico-methodological forms), which replays conflict and fails to create reconciliation, a social contract, or a liberal state. This reconstruction of the agenda of peacebuilding shows how different a fourth generation approach to peacebuilding would be, and how significantly the third generation approaches needs to adapt.

The critique in practice

Increasingly, the question of how peacebuilding might lead to a state or polity built from the bottom up and commensurate with both local and international understandings of peace has become central, as outlined in Part I of this study. In this discussion, needs, civil society, local ownership, agency, and autonomy are crucial, but not in a romanticised manner which arises when they are described and transformed by distant actors. As Part II of this study illustrated, work on the everyday, 'networks of anti-discipline',[50] as well as work on how power projects knowledge, on agency and autonomy, and much post-colonial scholarship, both in early and late forms, demonstrate the dynamics of the everyday, which enables critical agency itself. There are many significant contributions to draw on in a range of related disciplines, which overcome the binaries produced by power, knowledge, structures and institutions, liberal and non-liberal modes of thinking, and highlight the effectiveness of what are normally regarded as marginal capacities. As disciplinary control, biopolitics, and governmentalism produce subordination the more they are resisted, though not necessarily overtly but in hidden registers, as much of Scott's work has shown.[51] Given that peace is often equated with one of the highest stakes of all – everyday emancipation, whether as part of a national project, or in the context of another form of polity – it should not be a surprise that contemporary peacebuilding displays such tendencies in its translation to local contexts, such as those I have examined in this study.

Various types and forms of authorship are emerging, however mundane, comprising the infrapolitics of peacebuilding. These, contrary to, or because of, their derivation from weak agency, have pushed the liberal peace into confrontation with itself and its others, producing hybridity, and post-liberal forms of peace in which there is no central authorial voice, and in which 'nomad thought' may be represented discussions of peace.[52] This, in the words of Bleiker – but in this case translated into a new perspective on peacebuilding – imbues '... discursive dissent with the capacity to exert human agency'.[53] From the Pacific, Timor, to Afghanistan, and across Central and South America, and in parts of Africa – such as in Mozambique – such dynamics have become visible in post-conflict sites when the necessary blinkers have dropped, as illustrated in Chapter 6.

Views of peacebuilding from the perspective of the everyday, incorporating a more nuanced understanding of the local, agency, autonomy, and of resistance, inevitably indicate that an important component of peace is in fact the support of forms of non-sovereign self-determination. Yet, as Bleiker and Barnsley have noted, self-determination claims are unresolved around the world in large numbers because of the way the international community and system focuses on territorial sovereignty as the basis for the liberal state and the international community it brings into being.[54] The notion of a local-liberal hybrid form of peace means that neither absolutely liberal nor local sovereignties can exist alone. Instead hybrids emerge, constantly reshaped by the interaction of alterity, and by the praxis of those actors who position themselves in their interfaces. In this way, within peacebuilding discourses '... power and knowledge articulate each other'.[55] This illustrates the parallel need for the recognition of alternative forms of self-determination, rather than the current denial of any alternative to the current restrained and rationalised forms of statehood.

Agencies might be constructive and accepting of external models, or they may be destructive and violent. Constructive types of agency might be expressed through opposition and resistance, expressed through demonstration, social or labour movements, NGOs, cooperatives, identity or religious groupings, the political process, democratic or customary, through co-option or reform and conversion, even through avoidance and silence in everyday and hidden terms. Agency in this context has to be expressed in the name of a specific project for order, peace, prosperity, territory, and identity, and also in opposition to those agendas of others, including progressive models brought in by external agents, whether peacekeepers, peacebuilders, development specialists, IFIs, and NGOs. Agency may be expressed to block or co-opt such agendas. These indicate stands based on principle, knowledge, and experience, which differ from others they identify as being in opposition. They represent a search for, and protection of, meaning, contrary to objectivisation, and in knowledge of competition over subjectivity and hegemony. This means organising a political, community, or individual, platform that is often disguised and hidden from which resistance arises, recreating conditions of power, or avoiding compliance as far as possible without compromising existence. Ultimately, it indicates a political agenda for agency, autonomy, self-determination, and liberation, via which peace is discursively constructed.

Where there are expressions of power, there will probably be resistance representative of conflicting agencies at different levels, from the international to the state, to the local. 'Power' is thus 'disrupted' through local or marginal agencies. It would be contradictory for any approach to making peace, or any actor engaged in doing so, to adopt a discourse of power, through knowledge, method, or ideology, because this ultimately disrupts peacebuilding, agonistically or violently. What is more, bringing into being such forms of resistance as a response to hegemonic forms of peacebuilding may lead to contradictions that are unlikely to be countermanded – even by discursive hegemony or naked power – because they are designed to resist hegemony and preserve something essential from the perspective of those engaging in such resistance. This type of critical agency is not insignificant even if hidden, but creates and adopts a platform on which it has similar tractability to that which it opposes on its own platform. It is particularly crucial as it is an important site of legitimacy for the state and for international peacebuilding, in the age-old struggle between particularism and universalism, and the immanent possibility of an emancipatory and empathetic peace.

Following on from Foucault's arguments about biopolitics and governmentality, and into the terrain of his work on the 'technology of the self'[56] it becomes clear that it might also be the very limitations of the liberal peace project that have sparked new forms of peace in reaction, response, or as resistance, by a repoliticisation of post-conflict subjects. This represents the inadvertent rediscovery or rebirth of post-liberal politics in infrapolitical terms. This does not represent the replacement of international norms and law, or state based order, institutions and market democracy by local critical agency as a form of populism. Instead it raises afresh, or even for the first time, issues of oppression, welfare, culture, and the interface between the liberal international and the liberal or local (the liberal-local hybrid) other, in this emerging everyday peace which a reborn politics of peace implies. This may overcome the culture/welfare paradox of existing liberal peacebuilding and open up a reflexive move away from liberal peacebuilding's tendency to romanticise the local.

More importantly, this has created space in various areas and domains relatively free of international designs, in which local actors, often hidden, have sought new ways of attaining liberal status, rejecting it, co-opting it, and most obviously hybridising it. These hidden registers, which collapse the public and private distinctions of Western modes of politics and the liberal (international) and local divide, and see political agency even in those actors it deems marginal, represent a new form of peacebuilding and peace formation, which transcends that of even a fourth generation approach. Here a new politics of peacebuilding is born.[57] What also then becomes possible is a new pedagogy of peacebuilding via the reconstruction of third and fourth generation approaches. This expression of local agency therefore becomes a platform for different forms of peacebuilding, even if not 'liberal', which are locally resonant and agential – even if normative, culturally, and technically unrecognisable to the liberal gaze. Of course it should be noted that not all contextual politics are necessarily indicative of hybrid forms of peace emerging.

Given that liberal peacebuilding might also be equated with imposition from above, it is clear that autonomy and agency are the crucial sites around which peacebuilding is centred and contested. If peacebuilding represents a removal of autonomous agency to be replaced with a shaped liberal agency, peacebuilding in the everyday aims at the development of autonomous agency, whether for resistance and liberation, reasons of nationalism, forms of identity, territoriality, or for more humanistic reasons (ie social justice), perhaps more easily associated with peacebuilding but without leading to new forms of exclusion. The political nature of peacebuilding in both international and local perspectives now moves into view and hybridity in this context prevents universality or homogenisation.[58] But at the same time, even while difference is crucial, an emancipatory project requires a common and political, social, economic, and cultural discussion about what transformation might entail amongst its subjects. It is important to note that hybridity itself should not become a new universal, nor should it privilege fragmentation, or those actors who benefit from a wider range of experiences or material resources. Yet, the liberal peace's universal and rights aspects have been, and are, empowering (e.g. at least in some of the work of IO, NGOs, and international donors/agencies), and increasingly have become less eurocentric as more voices have been included over time. This means a wider ranging concern about human welfare is gradually emerging.

Recognition of agency, autonomy, and identity, as well as material needs should form the focus of any discussion of peacebuilding, whether international or local, if they are to escape the post-colonial and culture-welfare trap, avoid mythologising the international or romanticising the local, or reverting to violence and force. Peacebuilding is therefore partly about the mediation of difference, whether of identity, of aspirations, material needs, rights, or capacities. The recent move to equate it with a *sui generis* liberal peace has been depoliticising towards local agency and autonomy. This is ironic given its focus on democracy, rights, and civil society. Instead, balancing critical agency and autonomy should be peacebuilding's *raison d'etre*, in the wider context of institutions, rights, needs, state, regional, and international dynamics.

Indeed, for much of the UN's existence, and for earlier generations of theory one might say it was. But once peacebuilding became a narrow positivist and problem-solving endeavour much of its importance faded from view; it slipped into a rejection of agency and autonomy while claiming to enhance them, and their replacement with neoliberal assumptions about states, constitutions, markets, and rights. Most theorists and many policymakers intuitively understand this, especially those who have had extended field contact, but so many dimensions of politics, development, and economic thought seemed to be converging after the end of the Cold War that opposition to the liberal peace, even if merely to sensitise it, seemed untenable. The venerable desire to help others turned into a diktat which for many reasons, lost sight of both 'help' and 'others'. Partly this was for physical or material reasons. Theory and policy has been made far away from the field, according to problem-solving methodologies and the interests of state power, and so has reflected the interests and biases of its makers.

Decentering this dynamic may not be that difficult, given that liberal emancipation was to a large extent the basis of the UN system. It requires changes in humanitarian thinking and development policy, as well as an ethnographic knowledge of and communication with the field in its everyday, political, social, economic, and cultural frames. Placing everyday relations and needs (as well as rights) at the centre of peacebuilding, to produce a more humanistic form, can be facilitated by a recognition of the liberal West's biases, making it difficult for these to be sustained. Then, the facilitation of mutual agency and autonomy becomes the goal of peacebuilding, in which differing normative standards, political systems, economic systems, societies, and cultural and customary systems engage, reject, mould, co-opt, and assimilate each other in full transparency and recognition of the power relations at play. Given the internationals' objectives for peacekeeping, peacebuilding, statebuilding, reconciliation, development, rights, and identity, it is possible to see a far more mediated, locally and internationally, resonant form of peace emerging. This would be a post-liberal form of peace for the West, and a localised and negotiated hybrid from the perception of those in other contexts. Indeed, this is not mere speculation. Many local contexts have modified their experience of liberal peace, and the liberal peace itself has been modified as a result.

Hybridising peace

Hybridity, in its negative and positive forms, represents more than the interactions of power and knowledge, however. It also represents local and international compromises and political arrangements which may lead to the co-existence of both international and local approaches, without being an apologist for the shortcomings of either. It indicates new ways of finding a solution to the self-determination trap that many find themselves in, and new foundations for international organisation, states and political organisation that do not necessarily rely on modernist and Western conceptions of territorial sovereignty, institutions, law, and ownership. These are perhaps deeply decentralised and reflect alternative forms of political action, while being focussed on rights, needs, and agency in democratic contexts, which are deterritorialised, whether 'post-Westphalia' or federal, confederal, and overlapping.[59] This has knock-on effects for pre-existing states, which currently rely on their territory being protected against such claims, of course.[60] Ultimately, local-liberal hybridity will have a significant impact on the international system, and its range of institutions. Indeed, this is already happening. Note the shifts in World Bank ideology, innovations in UN practice and policy (despite the failed reform of the UN system), the expansion from G8 to G20, the rise of the BRICs (Brazil, Russia, India and China), and their contribution to peacekeeping, peacebuilding and development, the innovative and expanding ways in which global forms of representation and communication are now making themselves felt, especially in terms of subaltern voices. Note also the sophisticated critiques and new approaches that are emerging in the wake of recent problems with democracy and capitalism in the West, and critical of their deployment in post-conflict and development sites.

Acknowledging local-liberal hybridity, its otherwise hidden agencies, and its implications for self-determination, reframes many of the foundational aspects of the liberal peace more generally. Democracy, human rights, the rule of law, development, as well as welfare, needs, and even security itself, need as a consequence to be seen partly as an expression of cultural predispositions[61] rather than merely facts, cold institutions, or distant policies. Here agency and autonomy are expressed in ways which make a peace-with-politics, rather than a peace-as-governance, possible. This also holds true to one of the earliest adages of peacebuilding: that engaging with the most marginalised enables a more viable, self-sustaining peace to emerge, and this in turn requires an engagement with non-Western, non-liberal modes of politics and peace.[62] This raises questions about representation, rights, needs, and agency, within peacebuilding, but not constrained by the liberal state. They need to be thought of in ways that span the local to the global.

It must of course be noted that both liberal and local voices are varied internally, ranging between those that focus on different aspects of liberalism – rights, needs, law, constitutions, security, development or civil society – or local actors which encourage outright rejection, acceptance, passivity, co-optation, or the modification for a range of identity related and political reasons. It may well be that the types of civil society, states, and of course, peace emerging from these discursive spaces do not conform to the vision imagined by international actors, that civil society and the local-local cannot be governed or managed in the way that they expect, and that many of the normative and institutional characteristics of the liberal peace are superficial. From the perspective of the state and the international actors engaged in peacebuilding, hybrid political orders, whether enabling space for customary governance and actors, engaging more distinctively with local civil society, or representing an unofficial bargain with rapacious elites perhaps over class issues,[63] will tend to settle on a hybrid form of clientelism, custom, authoritarianism, driven by security, democracy, needs, rights, and justice. The interplay between these dynamics and characteristics represent the political nature of the emerging peace. Even so as long as a contextual social contract, and an engagement with needs and rights, are priorities, it is probable that the peace that may emerge will be more sustainable and free standing in the longer term.

There are many other aspects to this interplay, some of which I have not treated in any sustained way in this study.[64] For example: the role of language and act of translation in liberal-local mediations of peace and politics; a more developed treatment of agency and autonomy from beyond Enlightenment orientations of rationality; the ways in which the state project is often hijacked against the thrust of the liberal peace for reasons of self-determination; the moral and ethical problems inherent in the liberal peace's confrontation with other normative systems, particularly those it rejects on grounds of feudalism, patriarchy and so forth, all merit further exploration. This is particularly necessary if the everyday is to be taken as a non-instrumental place in any discussions of peace, and even if some of the classically liberal aspirations for emancipation are to be achieved, or if the goal of emancipation and social justice is to be part of hybrid forms of peace that also maintain their contextual resonance. In such discussions, Western secular notions of rationality, and of sovereignty embodied in the Weberian state form, need to be once again challenged as antithetical to some or many aspects of these interlinked peace projects. There is also much more to be said on the question of whether the liberal peace project is at all capable of the sort of flexibility required to engage in the production of such hybridity openly, given the limitations of its problem-solving nature and its strategy of making ontological assumptions before it is exposed to its others. There is considerable scepticism whether Rawlsian liberalism or Habermasian approaches might be able, even in the context of the technology of the liberal peace constructed upon an abstract and universalised notion of the subject and of rights, to adjust to local needs, identities or traditions at all. This is perhaps a reason why so little effort has been made. Those supporters and administrators of the liberal peace tend to write off the local, context, and crucial agency without much thought. They might even argue that the crisis of the liberal peace does not stem from failure, but from its success (an argument which would have little support amongst most of its post-conflict subjects).[65] Success has been falsely called for peacebuilding and statebuilding on numerous occasions in the last twenty years, from Mozambique to Guatemala and Timor Leste. This represents liberal bias, influenced by power, partly that of liberal knowledge systems. It underestimates the local agencies that exist despite and perhaps because of liberal peacebuilding's unintended repro-duction of bare life.

It is from this bias that issues of agency, autonomy and resistance arise again. A key question is whether there might be an accommodation possible between liberal peacebuilding, even with its built-in bias, and local forms of agency even where they are expressed as resistance. Alternatively, does this mean that liberal peace and local context are now lined up in a confrontation with each, which may escalate into violence, as has been seen in Iraq and Afghanistan from the start of the Western (mainly US and UK) interventions there? Might this represent varieties of resistance, from the hidden and passive, non-cooperation to slow implementation, to avoidance, flight, or even Fanonian versions of anti- and de-colonisation resistance?[66] At the very least a recognition of such agency on the part of the local, also dawning in discussions of local ownership or participation, indicates a need to understand language, culture, custom, identity and history, without which international interventions may easily fall into the sorts of traps that will render them quasi-colonial in the eyes of local communities and elites. Thus, they unintentionally spark off political agency at the local level which engages in its own negotiation of peace and order, often in abrasion with the liberal peace model and not in keeping with its norms. This occurs as a way of preserving local identity, power relations, discriminatory practices, survival and subsistence strategies, and a range of methods that preserve order and even make peace which are unrecognisable to international actors. This means a recognition of culture is necessary for peacebuilding, but this does not necessarily make it a communitarian or cosmopolitan practice[67] because it instead leads to hybridity. It also implies, given that culture is a key site of agency, a recognition of needs issues, not just in terms of how internationals engage with them, but also in terms of how local actors mitigate them. In this hybridity are the seeds of the recognition of constant, though varying levels of local ownership of peace, war, and politics, welfare, and culture, despite international presence and intervention.

If the liberal peace now looks to have engendered a mimetic process of accepting power, or of resisting and hybridising it, it is necessary, to avoid the continuing concurrence with victor's or conservative notions of the liberal peace, to begin to explore the implications of the dynamics I have outlined above. As was widely noted during US 'statebuilding' in Iraq (and often by Iraqi officials) the issues of the use of force, political and economic experimentation, to bring 'peace' are illustrative of the dark side of attempts to make peace in problem-solving manner. They are easily debunked on intellectual, practical, ethical, and methodological grounds as a tragic wrong turn, which is strongly connected to the progressive development of liberal peacebuilding and statebuilding even in UN contexts elsewhere and earlier on. Their colonial dynamics are all too clear, as is their disregard for human life, agency, and autonomy. Even their participants exhibit a colonial anxiety about their ignorance of local context and need to make local alliances even so. It is not too much of a stretch to point to the constant ambiguity of the liberal project with colonialism, in the same way as experienced by John Stuart Mill, author of one of the seminal works on liberty and its relationship with government, who also ironically worked for the East India Company for thirty five years.[68] The liberal project that emerged from such situations was designed to set standards for the future attainment of liberal status, rights, and autonomy for the colonial subject, to reform the world while preventing a meaningful engagement with the subjects' indigenous standards, status or political systems. Thus, the liberal peace is as much about liberty and inclusion as it is about regulation and exclusion – both treated in different ways in the work of Mill, Locke, and Burke.[69] Liberal peace has followed liberal imperialism in asserting a superior moral order, knowledge, justice and freedom and devaluing, indeed discounting, local experiences of peace and politics and their relationship.[70] Partly, this is also aimed at concentrating legitimate power and knowledge in the hands of a certain global elite (often now doyens of narrow claims about unfettered globalisation) by discounting everyday issues, constituted and affected by dimensions of security, rights, needs, custom, culture, identity, religion, customary institutions and practices, as well as local norms, hierarchies, and economic and social systems, as insignificant.

As later generations of post-colonial theory have shown, however, it is not just the subjects who were victims, who suffered, or were socially engineered by colonialism.[71] As Nandy brilliantly has argued, British colonialism was run by a group of young, ambitious, but often relatively limited colonial administrators whose encounters with India perplexed them to the degree that they confronted the limits of their understandings of difference. With notable exceptions, this reflects my own experience of many, though not all of those who are engaged in the liberal peace-building project, often unknowing participants in such patterns. Nandy shows how they resorted to stereotypes supporting hierarchical and exclusive distinctions of their normative, intellectual, and military superiority, and often acted on them in order to reproduce imperialism. There could be no multiple identities, whether local or both British and Indian. But the colonial administrators themselves were also changed by their experiences, as was Britain, its government, and intellectual and cultural life. Nandy argues that the limitations of these trials of colonial rule forced the British government to effectively simulate the very martial order they did not want and that has been avoided by previous arrangements. Mehta has also shown how this project captured British business, schools, and universities, in its unlikely validation and perpetuation.[72] These strategies of coercion and legitimation were now needed to sustain colonialism where persuasion of local elites to cooperate was no longer sufficient. It led to an epistemology and methodology of problem-solving, positivism, and institutionalism to emerge in Britain and aspects of its institutions, policies, and schools of thought. It supported the denial of local agency in India, and of anything other than quaint historical forms of complicit governance (meaning a romanticisation of the local), a lack of engagement with needs and culture, overlooking or avoiding critical agency.

Yet it ultimately provided the ground for and supported the success of Gandhi in meeting British colonialism head on, but peacefully; de-legitimating it globally, forcing an internal reflection on Britain's role in the world; and ultimately created unforeseen expressions of local agency and identity, which led to independence (or rather, catastrophic multiple self-determination processes). Resistance to such practices did not just emerge amongst its colonial subjects, of course, but also in the wider Western world and in Britain itself. This was the far-reaching meaning of the post-colonial movements of the twentieth century. Thus, even the mimetic aspect of the hybridity that was produced was far from merely marginal and hidden resistance: it led to liberation though I do not want to romanticise what liberation meant for national struggles. Yet, liberal peacebuilding has been far from a liberation experience for many of its subjects, though in some cases such as in Namibia or Mozambique, where a liberation struggle was the basis for the new state, stability if not peace and justice has been more viable.

The discord of peace, liberal peace, progress, interests, and power, have thus reached a point where everyday resistance – intellectual, activist, material, normative, cultural, institutional, obvious or hidden, international, elite, or everyday, has begun to reshape the elitist and top-down liberal peace – a post-liberal moment is upon us. If the liberal peace sought to enable external sovereignty in various ways to tutor local actors away from their pathologies, it also seeks to endorse the territorial sovereignty of the liberal state system. The post-liberal moment, in which context and the local and the international recognise the tensions and attractions between them and embark on a mutual process of mediation, makes all of these issues questions worthy of political debate once again, allowing for a discussion of the nature of states, political organisation, and its goals, according to a broader range of contexts.

Understanding this involves dropping the realist notion of peace as an ontology, or that it emanates only from the state's control of the means of violence. It also involves moving away from the idea that institutional and rights-based processes of depoliticisation are necessary for peace, as the liberal approach appears to imply. The tendency towards metanarratives of peace via essentialisation and instrumentalisation erases the everyday lives of people, though they soon rewrite them as best they can and in ways which deny the attempted removal of politics and illustrate an agency that reframes the liberal subject and project. This occurs without liberalism recognising it, or when it does it appears as a dyfunctionality of the other, not a moderation of the self. So, though peace might seem to follow power at the surface, in practice it is also resistant to external power, especially where self or other implicate themselves in different types of politics, and even if they self-censor their expression of these alternatives. Thus, peace authorises antagonistic and agonistic politics from the grass roots upwards.

The liberal peace's gathering of power (as even in Kant's 'Perpetual Peace')[73] leads not to an end of history, but to agency, autonomy, and movements designed to protect these, often in forms designed to choose the weakest ground for a struggle with hegemonic actors, whether states, institutions, or empires. The 'weapons of the weak' turn out thus to be rather capable of producing forms of liberation which maintain at least a modicum of everyday integrity, even during or in the aftermath of war. The institutions of peace for many liberals (the state, international institutions, humanitarian intervention, the market, secularism, civil society) often appear to be the very dynamics these infrapolitics oppose, while also calling for peace, often couched as social justice, recognition, dignity, and resources, and not least self-determination. Indeed, in Afghanistan and Iraq, in large parts of South America – from Venezuela to Brazil – ideas of political, economic, and social equality have mobilised much grass-roots and indigenous, tribal, religious, and customary resistance to the liberal peace model, especially in its neoliberal form. Very recently, even the liberal peace framework has become more responsive to this shift towards local agency. Often this has resulted in very significant decentralisation, the emergence of new political voices and new accommodations, or normative compromises. These have produced more stable and less exclusionary polities and more practical and locally resonant forms of development and reconstruction – 'democracy in daily life', though still contained within a pre-existing form of state.[74]

Challenges

The last several hundred years of institution building and the last two decades of peacebuilding as statebuilding, have had mixed results. International apparatus for peace and the singular blueprints for states are now in tension with each other and often with local discourses of peace. Perhaps more significantly, the former are now in opposition to post-colonial struggles for autonomous agency at the local level, as well as for emancipatory forms of liberal and localism. Peacebuilding scholars have generally seen in these differing dynamics the capacity for peacebuilding, but have not clearly elucidated the role that critical agency and resistance plays in these dynamics. Furthermore, political philosophers and IR theorists have generally not prepared for the challenges that these dynamics have given rise to as new understandings of liberation emerge. Neither have political economists been prepared for calls for a neo-Keynesian approach in the light of the general valourisation of marketisation. Issues of identity, culture, custom, have now been raised in relation to building peace in a post-liberal context, beyond the liberal and Western international community. This raises a number of significant issues hinted at in a range of areas, from cosmopolitan theory, to peace and conflict studies, development studies, anthropology, and post-colonial theory and post-development studies. A post-liberal move requires that, for peace to be enabled for people and not just for states, markets or institutions, or the international system (in negative form), these are taken very seriously: it revives or makes more visible (given its continuing prevalence in certain contexts) discussions of liberation of both of the subjects of peacebuilding and the international peacebuilding community itself.[75]

Enabling a better and more ethnographically sensitised understanding of the everyday in peacebuilding is not sufficient for the attempt to develop a more sustainable form of peace. Indeed, just opening up this space runs the risk of enabling more technocratic forms of statebuilding, or of biopolitical engineering and governmentality to emerge. This is why, as Foucault showed along with later post-colonial theorists and anthropologists, it has become necessary to investigate forms of resistance and liberation in the everyday, whether civil or non-liberal, in order to understand how agency shapes contexts despite top-down material and intellectual predominance. Seeing agency in these forms, however small or hidden, as part of peacebuilding, enables a better understanding of local agencies for peace, and their relative autonomy, as well as allowing for difference to be expressed in parallel to liberal peace frameworks. If approaches can be developed to allow for this (necessarily interdisciplinary approaches, of course) this may preserve agency, autonomy, capacity, and context, providing for sustainability. They cannot be governmentalised (as the praxis of the last twenty years shows) as they merely retreat to hidden, but capable, spaces if challenged.[76] The marginal social contract that emerges thus also represents to some degree this resistance. Liberal co-option is inevitable to a degree but so is local co-option. Their combination leads to the local-liberal hybrid. The challenge will be to make such discursive connections positive and cooperative.

Yet, of course the fear of many of those involved in post-conflict issues is that local agency is applied to agendas and projects, or it represents identities and approaches, inimical to peace. Thus, the intense debates on political violence, spoiling, security, corruption, abuses of human rights, law, and democracy and so on. Discussions of agency tend to focus on an Enlightenment notion of agency for good, within the parameters of a liberal peace and state, rather than on its autonomy, authenticity, local resonance, and contingency. Discussions of resistance tend to focus on 'civil resistance' in terms of non-violent action by citizens and communities against bad governance and exclusive institutions (as with India's independence movement and other expressions of anti-colonialism, the US civil rights movement, against the Soviet Union during and at the end of the Cold War, or against Milosevic in 2000) constructed again within the liberal peace framework (and its emancipatory wing). They focus on reducing an oppressor's capacity and legitimacy ranging from the familiar tactics of labour movements, to those of anti-colonialists, anti-globalisation protesters, pro-democracy protesters, solidarity movements for peace, human rights, political prisoners, disarmament, or for indigenous communities, to the establishment of parallel societies, governments, states, and indeed parallel lives. In this way, liberation movements have also become tarnished by accusations of totalitarianism, nationalism, violence, or exclusion. Yet, in the sphere of peacebuilding and in addition to the cases I have already mentioned, in the cases of Nicaragua, El Salvador, Honduras, Guatemala, and Mozambique, a wave of popular organisations, civil society and student movements, along with trade unions, peasants cooperatives, and NGOs, as well as new political parties have emerged since the peace processes of the early 1990s. Similar dynamics have emerged to greater or lesser extends in the other cases I have examined in this study. These have become influential in national and local politics, despite (or perhaps because of) authoritarianism, corruption, anti-democratic practices, flimsy rights, and acute poverty, and sometimes despite the prescriptions of international actors. This has been especially in view of local rights and needs vis-à-vis both international prescriptions for peace and the often authoritarian behaviours of elites.[77] Local dynamics often respond to scripts of resistance and liberation couched in contextual modes, even in subsistence settings, rather than the international discourse of liberal peace. They are often transnationally and transversally connected, and foreshadow the dynamics I have outlined in my case studies. Liberation contexts and the protection of former national liberal movements also appear more capable of consolidating national level peace processes in the longer term, despite deep political, economic, and social problems – as the cases of Mozambique and Namibia illustrate in general terms.

Everyday patterns of hidden resistance offered by the supposedly most marginal post-conflict individuals and communities respond to external peace-building efforts in ways which ultimately reshape them. They operate because of and in spite of power, and often despite their proponents experiencing bare life.[78] Indeed, bare life might be an advantage ironically in that it creates a space for the infrapolitics of peacebuilding to emerge, and where political debate over the nature of peace can occur relatively free from international prescriptions.[79] This is whether it is locally constructed by warlords or elites or expressions of alien forms of peacebuilding, with varying degrees of effect, often mainly on everyday life and integrity but sometimes more directly. Indeed, in the cases I have presented in this study such dynamics have had an overall impact on the liberal peace agendas, pushing them into new terrains. The subject, however, marginal has shown both politics and capacity, especially to resist sovereign forms of structural domination, perhaps over generations, especially when it comes to developing a process and conception of peace as a response to conflict. From this we can observe how the politics of peace become the politics of liberation, with its attendant pressures for solidarity, social justice, empathy, and emancipation – and of a fourth generation of thinking about peace.

As conflict resolution, transformation, peacebuilding, statebuilding, development, and other related debates draw on social science disciplines, theories, and methods, this means a major challenge needs to be confronted if a move to a fourth generation approach – or beyond – is to be achieved. If post-liberal approaches are to infuse these areas, a very significant interdisciplinary and methodological challenge must be met: one which has long confronted the edifice of Western ontological assumptions and the epistemologies that mainstream approaches to the politics of others draws upon. This must also be carried out without resorting to new metanarratives of 'peace', including those often equated with resistance and liberation, designed to maintain control of others for reasons of order beyond their everyday lives. The post-liberal form of peace would be wary of sovereignty, whether of a state or an international actor, donor, agency, the UN, or of institutional prescriptions for the territorial, cultural, economic, social, political, historical, and aesthetic dimensions of a locally owned peace, whereby its subjects become 'poets of their own affairs'.

It should be noted that this does not undo the necessity of rights, liberal internationalism, or of institutions, especially for democracy, from which the rule of law may stem. Furthermore, this is not to represent the liberal peace as coherent and singular, or even that its rescue is fully plausible. It certainly should not be taken from the focus on the everyday that resistance or liberation imply a neoliberal claim about autonomy, rather than that context drives such choices. This requires the acknowledgement of the importance of political debate rather than closure/enclosure, and the implications of its own encounters with other's everyday experiences of peace and conflict. This radical move requires that the epistemology which has emerged for peacebuilding becomes more open to the everyday, difference, resistance, to agency, and the conditions of liberation, especially beneath the state.

It is from a much clearer understanding of the local-liberal interaction in peacebuilding, of the ways in which they interface and produce hybridity based on critical and cultural agency and the political agendas it brings into being in collective form, that critical knowledge about emancipatory versions of peace might then be deployed. This will have an influence on the nature of the state, the flexibility of boundaries, the nature of institutions, law, civil society, and mechanisms for development and redistribution. This enables a recognition of the politics of peacebuilding at local, national, and international level, of the reality of the hybridity that has been produced. Via the consequent deployment of more critical thinking on peace as representative of emancipatory and empathetic processes, the production of post-liberal forms of peace arises through its infrapolitics, resistances and liberations, in everyday form – a pedagogy for peacebuilding. In response to the many recent and rhetorical calls for an 'alternative' to the liberal peace, it has now become clear that alternatives are already in existence. If liberal peace were to be a 'gift' from internationals to locals, it is now necessary to engage with the demand for contingency and reciprocity that has emerged via critical agency – marked by its fragmented nature but also its small scale capacity and efficacy – rather than excluding it.[80] This is akin to the 'silent majority' that Baudrillard refers to.[81] The same applies to critical agency and everyday forms of peacebuilding and peace formation, which refuse to allow peace to be solely defined externally.

The next challenge is to address their many implications for peace, and particularly for the fraught issue of the local ownership of peacebuilding and the nature of the state or polity, and levels of reconciliation and citizenship, which may emerge under local ownership. Hybrid forms of peace, location agency, resistance, and liberation open up the politics of peacebuilding more fully, and require an engagement with the agonistic mediation of difference. It prevents apologist approaches to doing nothing or acting merely on interests via 'peacebuilding'. It reflects power and resources, but unsettles the notion that only internationals have these. Most of all it allows for an eirenist reconstruction of peace and peacebuilding itself to reflect more closely the politics, needs, rights, and institutions of its widely varying subjects, and especially its most marginal actors. It represents the creation of meaning and better, of disaggregated forms of representation, more inclusive versions of rights and institutions, and more open engagements with needs and culture.[82] The birth of such hybrid forms of peace – and the transformations they imply – make us aware of the dangers and opportunities of hybridity as well as of the liberal peace, and sets the scene for the reconstruction of more inclusive agendas for emancipatory forms of peace. This may include local critical agencies, resistance, and the emergence of a post-colonial civil society, which together enable the transformation of the liberal peace itself.

From this perspective, a fourth generation, post-liberal form of peace would avoid the conservative neoliberal model that has recently emerged, especially in transitional phases. It would probable focus on social forms of democracy, where local-local participant was foremost (as opposed to elite participation). Rights and needs would be intricately related both giving each other substance. These would be externally enabled and supported but locally developed and maintained, often in decentralised form. Human security, rights, needs, institutions, law, identity, culture and related critical agencies would both partly form and connect the local, contextuality, civil society, and the customary with the state, the regional, and the international, in an interwoven dialogue of peacebuilding in which the subject was foremost, also enabling a post-colonial and transnational civil society. From here a range of contracts emanate – the social, political, and economic contract between citizen and state, and a peacebuilding contract with the range of internationals, ensuring direct peace dividends for post-conflict citizens. The local, the state, regional and international forms of peace would be themselves transformed.

Epilogue

I conclude this study with a counterfactual version of an event that occurred during the liberation of Abyssinia during World War II from Mussolini's grip. George Steer, the famous British war correspondent, journalist and writer, who had previously reported the infamous Nazi chemical bombing of Guernica (commemorated by Picasso with his famous eponymous painting which became equated with peace) reported on the Italian occupation of Abyssinia and its brutalism as well as early bombing campaigns elsewhere. He eventually found himself responsible for Psychological Operations in Abyssinia for the British Intelligence Corps in 1940. He oversaw the dropping of pamphlets to persuade the people of the country, even if they had worked for the Italian occupation, to assist the returning Ethiopian forces and their allies in retaking the country from Mussolini's forces. Apparently, one such pamphlet, which had considerable effect, and was written by him on behalf of Haile Selassie (the Emperor who had made such a powerful entreaty to the League of Nations in 1936 to save his country from fascism), was dropped over the country at that time. It read in unashamedly propagandist style:

> 'The English wish to destroy the power of our common enemy and to complete our independence. They do not covet our territory. Whether you meet British officers or British soldiers, receive them as your friends and liberators ... Long live Ethiopia, free and independent! Long live Great Britain!'[83]

What if, in counterfactual vein, after the end of the Cold War, and during the era of conflict resolution, peacebuilding and statebuilding, development, and humanitarian intervention, any one of numerous peoples and their leaders who have been subject to these programmes had been rallied with a similar entreaty:

> 'The internationals wish to ... [help bring peace] and to complete our independence [as they have helped to do elsewhere. They respect our

culture, identities, rights and issues]. They do not covet our territory [or resources]. Whether you meet international peacekeepers, peacebuilders, administrators, advisors, or development specialists, receive them as your friends and liberators ... Long live [substitute the name of any place where peacekeeping, peacebuilding/statebuilding, mission has taken place], free and independent! Long live the internationals!'

Appendix 1: HDI and GINI data for post-conflict countries: from settlement to the present

HDI rank		Gini index according to UN Human Development Report 2009	HDI according to UN Human Development Report 2009	date of settlement	date of Gini Index closest to settlement
HIGH HUMAN DEVELOPMENT					
32	Cyprus	N/A	0.914		
45	Croatia	29.0	0.871	1995	1997–99
72	The former Yugoslav Republic of Macedonia	39.0	0.817	1991	1991
76	Bosnia and Herzegovina	35.8	0.812	1995	2001
MEDIUM HUMAN DEVELOPMENT					
89	Georgia	40.8	0.778	1995, reescalation	1996
102	Sri Lanka	41.1	0.759	2009	2009
106	El Salvador	49.7	0.747	1992	1997
122	Guatemala	53.7	0.704	1996	1998
127	Tajikistan	33.6	0.688	1996, but reescalation	1997–99
128	Namibia	74.3	0.686	no clear cut conflictand end	1993
135	Solomon Islands	N/A	0.610	2003	N/A
137	Cambodia	40.7	0.593	1991	1997
150	Sudan	N/A	0.531	2005	
LOW HUMAN DEVELOPMENT					
162	Timor-Leste	39.5	0.489	1998	
163	Côte d'Ivoire	48.4	0.484	2004	2002
167	Rwanda	46.7	0.460	1994	2000
171	Ethiopia	29.8	0.414	2000	1999
172	Mozambique	47.1	0.402	1992	1996-7
174	Burundi	33.3	0.394	2008	1998
180	Sierra Leone	42.5	0.365	2000	1989
Non or Limited UN Involvement					
	Afghanistan	no data		1990	1997
	Philippines	44	0.751		
	Democratic Republic of Congo	44.4	0.389	ongoing	
	Liberia	52.6	0.442	2003	not available
	Uganda	42.6	0.514	ongoing	
	Guatemala	53.7	0.704	1996	1998
	Bangladesh	31	0.543	2000	2000
	Zimbabwe	50.1	no data	ongoing	
	Nepal	47.3	0.553	2006	2003/04
	Papua New Guinea	50.9	0.541	1998	1996

* Thanks to Stefanie Kappler for compiling this data on my behalf

index st to ›ment	date of HDI closest to settlement	HDI closest to settlement	source for Gini index	source for HDI	year(s) of UN peace operation(s)	RESULTS	
						hdi	gini
\	1994	0.907		HDR 1997		marginal	
	1994	0.76	http://www.unicef-irc.org/publications/pdf/monee8/eng/2.pdf	HDR 1997	1995–96	improved	worse
/	1994	0.748	http://www.unicef-irc.org/publications/pdf/sm2004/sm2004.pdf	HDR 1997	1995–99	improved	worse
2	2001	0.777	HDR 2005	HDR 2003	1995–2002	improved	worse
	1994	0.637	HDR 2001	HDR 1997	1993–2009	improved	worse
	2009	0.759	HDR 2009	HDR 2009		na	na
3	1994	0.592	HDR 2001	HDR 1997	1991–95	improved	marginal
3	1997	0.624	HDR 2001	HDR 1999	1997	improved	worse
	1997	0.665	http://www.unicef-irc.org/publications/pdf/monee8/eng/2.pdf	HDR 1999	1994–2000	improved	improved
/	1992	0.425	HDR 2003	HDR 1994		improved	worse
	2001	0.632		HDR 2003		worse	no data
4	1994	0.348	HDR 2001	HDR 1997	1992–93	improved	marginal
A	2003	0.512		HDR 2005	2005-present, Darfur: 2007-present	improved	no data
	2002	0.436		HDR 2004	1999–2005	improved	no data
5	2003	0.42	HDR 2005	HDR 2005	2004-present	improved	worse
3	1994	0.187	HDR 07/08	HDR 1997	1993–94, 1993–96	improved	marginal
	1999	0.321	HDR 2005	HDR 2001	2000–08	improved	marginal
5	1994	0.281	HDR 2001	HDR 1997	1992–94	improved	worse
4	2001	0.337	HDR 07/08	HDR 2003	2004–06	improved	improved
9	1992	0.221	HDR 07/08	HDR 1994	1999–2005	improved	improved
2	1990	0.711	HDR 2001	HDR 1999		improved	improved
ilable	not available	not available					
3	1997	0.624	HDR 2001	HDR 1999		improved	marginal
3	2000	0.478	HDR 2003	HDR 2002		improved	marginal
2	2005	0.534	HDR 2007/08	HDR 2007/08		marginal	marginal
9	1998	0.542	HDR 2001	HDR 2000		marginal	marginal

Appendix 2: International versus local perspectives of peacebuilding in Bosnia[1]

	International	Local
Perspectives of Democratisation	-Are internationals 'democratic' and accountable in BiH? They are not, and do not need to be. -The Dayton peace agreement did stop the conflict, yet today there is disagreement as to its current role: does it help or hinder peace building? This debate feeds into a larger debate regarding whether it is appropriate or possible to re-write or amend the constitution. -Democracy is a holistic concept and could be described as a major component of peace building. -Discussions about democracy are contingent on the discrepancy between a short-term and long-term outlook and timeframe.	-The current problems in BiH are a result of the inadequacies of Dayton rather than of local participation. Dayton excluded the possibility of 'reaching' locals by not taking their experiences and 'political location' as a starting point. -Rather than promoting a holistic democracy internationals push for 'parliament' and 'voting' as benchmarks for achieving the former. This is seen to be hypocritical. -Dayton and the broader peace building should have been more process oriented. -Locally, there is historical precedent for democratic capacity. Locals arguably have understood their 'rights' (re. democracy) but some fail to recognise corresponding responsibilities; accordingly civil society is weak, which contributes to a poor security situation. -Democracy hasn't dealt with the roots of the conflict. It is questionable today whether politics has any capacity to stand alone, or, if it will be coupled to ethnicity in the long term. No independent political culture as of yet, has emerged. -The issue of education is important; where people remain uninformed they are easily manipulated. Individuals need educating about their democratic options.

	International	*Local*
Perspectives of Human Rights and Rule of Law	-Rule of Law design and implementation is making good progress. -Distinction between 1st/2nd Generation human rights and a focus on 1st generation. -There is a lack of clear local ownership over HR concerns and a resulting dependency upon the IC to dictate norms and action. -Furthermore; the IC itself is not united in goals or strategies, contributing to a broad confusion as to the nature of what is being promoted or how to do so.	-The national constitution enshrines discrimination, so that the foundational identity of the political community is formed in opposition to Human Rights. -The international community has little human rights focus: some argued it even consents to HR violations, this oversight often serves what the IC sees as more immediate aims, yet makes the IC appear hypocritical. -Consequentially, the rule of law within BiH often contradicts HRs. -The top-down and ethnicised nature of the constitution means it is very difficult to push for changes to make it more representative or responsive to locally understood notions of HRs. -It was suggested that HR have themselves become victim of an insensitive and inappropriate peacebuilding strategy, which has not protected HRs but contributed to their subjugation. -RoL and HR should be more clearly located in a more process-oriented, localised view of PB and democratisation which would be furthered by increased focus on local education.
Neo-Liberal Economics and Development	-Free market reform, marketisation, privatisation, FDI, competition in regional and globalised markets are essential. The welfare/national aspects of the state cannot survive. State, entity, federal levels of governance need to engage with this. -There is an obvious problem with inefficient, corrupt and decentralized state institutions, which largely fail to serve the interests of the population.	The ICs economic package is not seen to be a stand-alone phenomenon, but instead something that has brought with it ideological baggage which has been imposed on locals. -Controversially, the economic 'remedy' to post-conflict rebuilding being implemented by liberal internationals is a market which itself induces inequality and competition. -A centralised system

	International	*Local*
	-Some small and medium business enterprises are managing to develop and become competitive; there is hope that this success will snowball and provide the positive impetus lacking in the larger 'development' context. The big question is if this type of success will be widespread and large enough to unite the population and displace the prominence of identity politics (or that economic concerns would be prominent enough to challenge the primacy of ethnic issues as a voting issue).	(with more historical resonance) is denied to BiH, whilst within the ICs own systems, centralisation in actuality (if not name) is becoming increasingly prominent- suggesting the ICs own practices are not sustainable. Again this is seen to be hypocritical, further undermining the processes the IC promotes in BiH. - The economic burden of the conflict, even after its official 'end' is seen to fall upon ordinary individuals who continue to be victims of elites.
Civil Society	- The IC has created the majority of CS processes in BiH, making it an artificial realm. -There are reports of NGO abuse of positions, leading to mistrust in them, their agendas, and their means. -The larger question is who is responsible for the agenda of CS?	-IC promoted CS but has provided no structure for local/political access. -IC media has favoured simplicity in relating the situation of CS in BiH, the actual situation is very complex. -CS should be a cultural phenomenon, but it is difficult to see who/what locally to BiH is responsible for CS. -CS is weak, often seen to be nothing more than the NGO sector. -The lack of political options/ understanding of them – or how to create them, means that locals become dependent on IC knowledge, which further dislocates local sources of empowerment and knowledge which if promoted may have wider and deeper resonance with populations. -There is a lack of direct access to politics and democracy. -CS is a foreign concept that runs contrary to the reality that prior to the war large-scale protests occurred, which were ineffective against the driving nationalism and war-mongering of elites and politicians and failed to stop the war.

	International	*Local*
Welfare / Human Security / Culture	-IC promotes 'one size fits all' and universality, rejects a welfare state, and works for human security.	-A welfare system is necessary and internationals should contribute to its initial funding and design. -Human security is primary in all discussions, but IC is not committed beyond rhetoric. -(Disarmament and weapons control is still a widely unresolved issue in BiH today). -Cultural memory, history and customary dynamics are ignored.

Appendix 3: Universal welfare support in transitional states (very rough model)

Example:

Small post-conflict state of 12 million population. 40% of population need support, 20% are in employment and make contributions (these figure excludes the normal engagements with DDR, SSR, and emergency humanitarian assistance). This model roughly estimates costs of direct payments. Public services, such as reconstruction, infrastructure, schools, hospitals, etc, are not included, but of course would also be necessary.

- 5 million population at £1 per day per individual (or sum determined by basic needs and cultural/social functionality) = £1.9 billion per year multiplied by length of transitional period.
- Minus employed citizens' contributions @ 10% of wage of £300 pa from 2.4 million people = £72 million (though this might be better spent on infrastructure and public service, works/job creation).
- International personnel should pay local income tax at a higher rate: 5000 personnel, averaging £50k pa @ 20% income tax = £50m
- Plus costs of administering, roughly at £20 million p.a.

Cost to IC – equals £1.8 billion p.a. (potentially over a transitional period of 10 years) but reducing over time as economy develops.

Mechanism for delivery and standards

- Standards, rates, and recipients determined through local negotiation with reference to social democratic standards, in the context of rates viable in local economy.
- To deliver using an international institution in cooperation with local government, local mayors, local NGOs, aimed at supporting families and individuals in a socially and culturally appropriate manner. This provides liquidity to the state and local economy, but it is important to avoid significant inflation and dependency creation.
- These risks are, however, more than counterbalanced by the risk of reversion

to violence which will be lessened. Welfare assistance will stop the resort to violence, redirect corruption (perhaps by legitimating it) and stop grey/black market dependency.

- The model could be taken from Northern European social democracies rather than US neoliberalism, and experience at end of World War II rather than at end of Cold War with break up of Soviet Union (ie not structural adjustment Washington Consensus). Also factored in should be post-World War II style massive reconstruction projects funded through Marshall Aid and the Truman Doctrine, but run as far as possible by local labour and expertise (the problem with transferring this approach to contemporary peacebuilding is that for the most part it is dealing with non-developed countries, so reconstruction actually means starting from scratch from the ground up and labour/expertise is normally imported).

Notes

Introduction

1 Parts of this introduction draw on Oliver P. Richmond, 'Eirenism and a Post-Liberal Peace', Review of International Studies, vol.35, no.3, 2009, pp.557–580.

2 Michel Foucault, 'Two Lectures', *Power/Knowledge*, London: Pantheon, 1972, p.85.

3 Some confusion has arisen in the past by my use of the word 'liberal' in the context of different American and European understandings of the term. I use the term in reference to its genealogy in European, and later Western, political thought and theory, relating to peace.

4 For a discussion of this tendency of Western political philosophy, which underpins the liberal peace, see Bhikhu Parekh, *Gandhi's Political Philosophy*, Basingstoke: Macmillan, 1989, pp.1–3.

5 *The Economist*, 'No promised land at the end of all this', 6 March 2010, pp.27–9. The US has spent according to this article $800 billion to 2010.

6 I differentiate in this study between post-conflict and post-violence situations, the latter implying that structural violence has also been removed.

7 It should be noted that this study is concerned with post-violence situations, rather than those of ongoing violence. However, some of the dynamics I describe apply to both.

8 I hope to explore these dynamics in later publications. See in particular, D.J. Yashar, *Contesting Citizenship in Latin America: The Rise of Indigenous Movements and the Postliberal Challenge*, Cambridge: Cambridge University Press, 2005.

9 For one of the best critiques of liberalism, see Michel Foucault, *The Birth of Biopolitics*, London: Palgrave, 2008, esp. chapter 1.

10 See for example, *Human Security Brief*, 2006, http://www.humansecuritybrief.info/2006/contents/overview.pdf.

11 See among many others, David Chandler, *Empire in Denial: The Politics of Statebuilding*, London: Pluto Press, 2006; Michael Pugh: 'Corruption and the Political Economy of Liberal Peace,' chapter prepared for the International Studies Association annual convention, San Francisco (26–28 March 2008); Michael Pugh, Neil Cooper, and Mandy Turner, *Whose Peace?* London: Palgrave, 2008; Michael Pugh, 'The Political Economy of Peacebuilding: A Critical Theory Perspective,' *International Journal of Peace Studies*, vol.10, no.2, 2005, pp.23–42; Neil Cooper, 'Review chapter: On the Crisis of the Liberal Peace,' *Conflict, Security and Development*, vol.7, no.4, 2007, 605–16. Beate Jahn, 'The Tragedy of Liberal Diplomacy: Democratization, Intervention and Statebuilding,' *Journal of Intervention and Statebuilding*, vol.1, no.2, 2007, pp.211–29; Mark Duffield, *Development, Security and Unending War* (London: Polity, 2007); Roger Mac Ginty, 'Indigenous Peace-Making Versus the Liberal Peace,' *Cooperation and Conflict*, vol.43, no.2, 2008, pp.139–163; Roger Mac Ginty and Oliver P. Richmond (eds), 'Myth or Reality: The Liberal Peace and Post-Conflict Reconstruction', Special issue of *Global Society*, (2007).

12 The author has heard such criticisms in interviews and focus groups in several post-conflict peace operations, such as in Bosnia, Kosovo, Cambodia, and Timor Leste for the Liberal Peace Transitions project he directs. See Oliver P. Richmond and Jason Franks, *Liberal Peace Transitions: Between Statebuilding and Peacebuilding*, Edinburgh University Press, 2009.

13 See Chris Brown, *Sovereignty, Rights and Justice: International Political Theory Today*, Cambridge: Polity, 2002; Michael Howard, *The Invention of Peace and the Re-Invention of War*, London: Profile, 2002; Martin Ceadal, *Thinking About Peace and War*, Oxford: Oxford University Press, 1987.

14 Arthur S. Link *et. al.* (ed.), *The Papers of Woodrow Wilson*, vol.41, January 24–April 6, 1917, Princeton: Princeton University Press, 1983, p.525: Woodrow Wilson, Address to the Senate, 12 January 1917, in Arthur S. Link *et al.* (ed.), *The Papers of Woodrow Wilson*, vol. 40, Princeton: Princeton University Press, 1983, p.536–7.

15 *Report of the Secretary-General's High Level Panel on Threats, Challenges, and Change*, United Nations, 2004: Boutros Boutros Ghali, *An Agenda For Peace: preventative diplomacy, peace-making and peacekeeping*, New York: United Nations, 1992; *An Agenda for Development: Report of the Secretary-General*, A/48/935, (6 May 1994); 'Supplement to An Agenda for Peace' *A/50/60, S.1995/1*, (3 January 1995); *An Agenda for Democratization*, A/50/332 AND A/51/512, (17 December 1996).

16 For more on these strands of thought, and their relationship, please see my *Transformation of Peace*, especially conclusion. For supporters and critics of the 'liberal peace', see among others, Michael Doyle, 'Kant, Liberal Legacies, and Foreign Affairs,' *Philosophy and Public Affairs*, vol.12, no.3, 1983, pp.205–35: Michael Doyle and Nicolas Sambanis, *Making War and Building Peace*, (Princeton University Press, 2006); Charles T. Call and Elizabeth M. Cousens, 'Ending Wars and Building Peace: International Responses to War-Torn Societies,' *International Studies Perspectives*, vol.9, no.1, 2008, pp.1–21: Stephen D. Krasner, 'Sharing Sovereignty. New Institutions for Collapsed and Failing States,' *International Security*, vol.29, no.2, 2004, pp.85–120; Roland Paris, *At War's End*, Cambridge: Cambridge University Press, 2004): Jack Snyder, *From Voting to Violence*, London: W. W. Norton, 2000; David Rieff, *A Bed for the Night*, London: Vintage, 2002; Michael Mandelbaum, *The Ideas that Conquered the World*, New York: Public Affairs, 2002; Michael Pugh, 'The Political Economy of Peacebuilding: A Critical Theory Perspective,' *International Journal of Peace Studies*, vol.10, no.2, 2005, pp.23–42; David Chandler, *Bosnia: Faking Democracy After Dayton*, London: Pluto Press, 1999; Mark Duffield, *Global Governance and the New Wars*, London: Zed Books, 2001; Roland Paris, 'International Peacebuilding and the "Mission Civilisatrice"', *Review of International Studies*, vol.28, no.4, 2002, pp.637–56; Roger Mac Guinty, 'Indigenous Peace-Making Versus the Liberal Peace,' op. cit; Beate Jahn, 'The Tragedy of Liberal Diplomacy: Democratization, Intervention and Statebuilding (Part II),' op.cit.; Neil Cooper, 'Review chapter: On the Crisis of the Liberal Peace,' Conflict, Security and Development, 2007, op. cit..

17 For detailed empirical evidence see Oliver P. Richmond and Jason Franks, *Liberal Peace Transitions: Between Statebuilding and Peacebuilding*, op. cit. See also the many sources referred to in notes iv and vi. On the peacebuilding consensus, see Oliver P. Richmond, 'UN Peace Operations and the Dilemmas of the Peacebuilding Consensus', in *International Peacekeeping*, vol.10, no.4, 2004, pp.83–101.

18 On the ethics of care, see in particular, Kimberley Hutchings, 'Towards a Feminist International Ethics.' *Review of International Studies* vol.26, no.5, 2000, pp. 111–130.

19 See Roland Paris's 'Institutionalisation Before Liberalisation' strategy. Roland Paris, *At War's End*, p.188.

20 See for example the discussions of ownership and the local in Roland Paris, *At War's End*: Michael N. Barnett, 'Building a Republican Peace: Stabilizing States after War', *International Security*, vol.30, no.4, 2006, pp. 87–112; Jarat Chopra and Tanja Hohe, 'Participatory Intervention', *Global Governance*, vol.10, no.3, 2004, pp.289–305. These offer minor modifications to the liberal peace, but not alternatives.

21 This concept draws upon Michel Foucault, 'Two Lectures', op. cit., pp. 87–104. See also Kofi Annan, 'Democracy as an International Issue', *Global Governance*, vol.8, no.2, April–June 2002, pp. 134–42: Alex Bellamy and Paul Williams, 'Peace Operations and Global Order', Abingdon: Routledge, 2005; David Chandler, *From Kosovo to Kabul: Human Rights and International Intervention*, London: Pluto, 2002; Michael Pugh, 'Peacekeeping and Critical Theory', *Conference Presentation at BISA*, LSE, London, 16–18 December, 2002.

22 See the following essays: Shahrbanou Tadjbakhsh and Michael Schoistwohl, 'Playing with Fire? The International Community's Democratization Experiment in Afghanistan' *International Peacekeeping*, vol.15, no.2, 2008, pp.252–67; Astri Suhrke and Kaja Borchgrevink, 'Afghanistan – Justice sector reform', in Edward Newman, Roland Paris, and Oliver P. Richmond (eds.), *Beyond Liberal Peacebuilding*, Tokyo: UNU Press, 2009, pp.178–200; Richard Ponzio and Christopher Freeman, 'Afghanistan in Transition: Security, Governance and Statebuilding', *International Peacekeeping*, vol.14, no.1, 2007, pp.173–184. See for example, '*Speech of the Special Representative of the Secretary-General for Afghanistan*', *Opening of 55th Annual DPI/NGO conference, Rebuilding Societies Emerging from Confect: A Shared Responsibility, New York, 9 September 2002*.

23 Thanks to Tony Lang for distilling these points for me.

24 See the case studies in Oliver P. Richmond and Jason Franks, *Liberal Peace Transitions: Between Statebuilding and Peacebuilding*.

25 For an important contribution to this discussion in the context of Cambodia and Timor-Leste, see Caroline Hughes, *Dependent Communities: Aid and Politics in Cambodia and Timor-Leste*, Cornell University Press, 2009.

26 See in particular Shahrbanou Tadjbakhsh and Michael Schoistwohl, 'Playing with Fire?' pp.252–67

27 This might be seen to be in line with policy objectives also. See for example, Kofi Annan, *No Exit Without Strategy*, S//2001/394, UN: NY, 2001. Annan points to the need for 'comprehensive peacebuilding', which goes far beyond security and state-building but also leads to social transformation.

28 Michael Barnett and Christopher Zuercher, 'Peacebuilder's Contract: How External Peacebuilding Reinforces Weak Statehood', in Roland Paris and Timothy Sisk, *The Dilemmas of Statebuilding*, London: Routledge, 2008, pp.23–52.

29 United Nations, 'Report of the Secretary-General on Timor-Leste pursuant to Security Council resolution 1690', *UN Doc. S/2006/628*, August 2006, p.9.

30 Report of the Secretary-General, 'The situation in Afghanistan and its implications for international peace and security', *UN Doc. A/62/345–S/2007/555*, 21 September 2007, para. 24.

31 Ibid., parts V, VI, VII.

32 Ibid., part IX, para. 74.

33 Ibid., paras 74–84.

34 R.B.J. Walker, in discussion, Victoria, Canada, 14 July 2008.

35 Andrew Williams, *Liberalism and War*, p.215.

36 David Boucher, 'Property and Propriety in IR', in Beate Jahn (ed), *Classical Theory in IR*, Cambridge: CUP, 2006, p.157.

37 See the excellent collection of studies in Beate Jahn (ed.), *Classical Theory in International Relations*, Cambridge: Cambridge University Press, 2006.

38 Antonio Franceschet, 'One powerful and enlightened nation', in ibid., p.92.

39 John Macmillan, 'Immanuel Kant and the Democratic Peace', in ibid., p.71.

40 Beate Jahn, 'Classical Smoke, Classical Mirror', in ibid., p.203. See also David Chandler, *Empire in Denial*, London: Pluto, 2006, p.36.

41 Michel Foucault, *History of Sexuality*, vol.1, trans. Robert Hurley, London: Penguin, p.93.

42 Mark Duffield, *Development, Security and Unending War*, op. cit., p.27.

43 See for example, William E. Connolly, *Identity/Difference*, Minneapolis: Minnesota University Press, 1991, p.64.

44 Christine Sylvester, 'Empathetic Cooperation: A Feminist Method for IR', *Millennium*, vol.23, no.2, 1994, pp.315–334.

45 Timothy Donais, 'Empowerment or Imposition? Dilemmas of Local Ownership in Post-Conflict Peacebuilding Processes, *Peace and Change*, vol.34, no.1., 2009.

46 RBJ Walker, *Inside/outside: International Relations as Political Theory*, Cambridge: Cambridge University Press, 1992, p.ix.

47 Of course, most policymakers would deny that any such blueprint exists.

48 See Michael Dillon, 'A Passion for the [Im]possible: Jacques Ranciere, Equality, Pedagogy and the Messianic', *European Journal of Political Theory*, vol.4, no.4, 2005, pp.429–52.

49 See Arjun Appadurai, 'Grassroots Globalisation and Research Imagination' in Arjun Appadurai (ed.), *Globalisation*, Durham and London: Duke University Press, 2001, p.6.

50 Clifford Geertz, *Available Light*, Princetown: Princeton University Press, 2001.

51 Jahn Beate, 'One Step Forward, Two Steps Back: Critical Theory as the Latest Edition of Liberal Idealism', *Millennium*, vol.27, no.3, 1998, pp.613–41; Linda Bishai, 'Liberal Empire', *Journal of International Relations and Development*, vol.7, 2004, pp.48–72: Raymond Geuss, 'Liberalism and its Discontents', *Political Studies*, vol.30, no.3, 2002, pp. 320–338.

52 Michel Foucault, 'Governmentality', in: Graham Burchell, Colin Gordon, and Peter Miller (eds), *The Foucault Effect: Studies in* Governmentality, Hemel Hempstead: Harvester Wheatsheaf, 1991, pp. 87–104.

53 Oliver P. Richmond, *Maintaining Order, Making Peace*, London: Palgrave, 2002, Chapter 6.

54 Pierre Allan and Alexis Keller, 'The Concept of a Just Peace' in Pierre Allan and Alexis Keller, *What is a Just Peace?* Oxford: Oxford University Press, 2006, p.196.

55 Ibid., p.212.

56 Thanks to Roger MacGinty and Michael Pugh for making this point to me. See also Richard Gowan, 'Strategic context: Peacekeeping in Crisis', *International Peacekeeping*, vol.15, no.4, 2008, pp.453–69.

57 David Mosse, 'Global Governance and the Ethnography of the International Aid', David Mosse and David Lewis, *The Aid Effect*, London: Pluto, 2005, p.1.

58 Arjun Appadurai, *Modernity at Large*, University of Minnesota Press: Minneapolis, 1996, p.178.

59 Ibid, p.178.

60 On the local and its interconnections see Doreen Massey, 'A Global Sense of Place', in *Space, Place and Gender*, Minneapolis: Minneapolis University Press, 1994; see also, B. de Sousa Santos, 'Human Rights as an Emancipatory Script', *Another Knowledge is Possible: Beyond Northern Epistemologies*, London: Verso, 2007.

61 Dipesh Chakrabarty, *Provincialising Europe*, Princeton University Press, 2000, p.18: David Mosse, *Cultivating Development*, London: Pluto Press, 2005, p.4.

62 Michel Foucault, 'Governmentality', pp.87–104.

63 Michel Foucault, *History of Sexuality*, vol. 3, *The Care of the Self*, New York: Pantheon Books, 1986.

64 Arjun Appadurai, op. cit., p.133.

65 Gayatri Chakravorty Spivak, 'Foreword', in H. Schwarz and S. Rauy (eds), *Companion to Post-Colonial Studies*, London: Blackwell, 2000, p.xxi. Notably, the actual name of the 'subaltern' she writes about in her famous essay, Bhubanewari Bhaduri, has never been mentioned by critics since it was published.

66 Oliver P Richmond, 'Dadaism and the Peace Differend', *Alternatives*, Vol.33, No.4, 2007.

67 Oliver P. Richmond, *Maintaining Order, Making Peace*, London: Palgrave, 2002: Oliver P. Richmond, *The Transformation of Peace*, London: Palgrave, 2005. Here I must also make

a *mea culpa* about my own linguistic limitations which, even though English is now the international language of peacebuilding and development, is a serious obstacle for researching the everyday in post-conflict contexts in all of the case studies included in this study.

68 Here I am mindful of Lyotard's concern that even 'critical' work is about knowing and ordering 'better' and so carries assumptions of power. Jean Francois Lyotard, 'On theory: An Interview', *Driftworks*, (New York: Semiotext(e), 1984), p.13.

69 This term is adapted from the Greek word for peace (eirene/Ειρήνη).

70 For a fascinating discussion see Istvan Kende, 'The History of Peace', *Journal of Peace Research*, vol.26, no.3, 1989, pp.233–47. Erasmus believed that rulers were often responsible for war, and that a political system was required to prevent them from opposing the wishes of their subjects. He believed that rulers should not treat their territories as private property and should be concerned with the welfare of others. He believed speaking and praising peace and condemning war should be normal social practice as well as state practice.

71 Istvan Kende, ibid., p.236.

72 Oliver P. Richmond, *Transformation of Peace*, p.150.

73 Dipesh Chakrabarty, op. cit., p.43.

74 Michel Foucault, 'Governmentality', pp. 87–104.

75 Michel Foucault, *The Birth of Politics*, Graham Burchell (trans.). London: Palgrave, 2008 p.313.

76 Uday Singh Megta, *Liberalism and Empire*, Chicago University Press, 1999, p.11.

77 It should be noted that my focus in this study is on hybrid forms of peace, not on hybridising cultures.

78 De Certeau and Lefebvre have in a sociological framework, and in a historical and ideological context different to the contemporary setting have already sketched out the everyday and its agencies. See Henri Lefebvre, Critique of Everyday Life, London: Verso, 1991: De Certeau, Michel *The Practice of Everyday Life*, California University Press, 1984.

79 Michael Pugh, Peacekeeping and critical theory, International Peacekeeping, vol.11, no.1, 2004, pp. 39–58: Mark Duffield, *Development, Security, and Unending War*, Cambridge: Polity Press, 2007, p. 10.

1 Civil society, needs and welfare

1 For more on why I use this formulation, see Oliver P. Richmond, *Peace in IR*, London: Routledge, 2008.

2 J. Clifford, *The Predicament of Culture*, Cambridge MA: Harvard, 1988, p.10. Cited in Jonathan Spencer, *Anthropology, Politics, and the State*, Cambridge: CUP, 2008, p.13.

3 World Bank, *What is Civil Society*, 2002.

4 Michel Foucault, *The Birth of Politics*, London: Palgrave, pp.298–302.

5 See in particular, ibid., p.296.

6 Ibid., p.296.

7 Ibid., p.296.

8 Foucault argues that it is very easy for civil society to become seen as commensurate with nationalism, which is telling for the form of peace internationals envisage through civil society, ibid., p.296.

9 Gerhard Anders, 'Good Governance as Technology', in David Mosse and David Lewis (eds), *The Aid Effect: Giving and Governing in International Development*, London: Pluto Press, 2005, pp.37–60.

10 Ibid., p.297.

11 This study critiques 'liberal peacebuilding' and makes the assumption that it is assumed to be commensurate, if not the same as statebuilding. This most problematic attempt to elide peacebuilding and statebuilding is present in most mainstream literature. See,

to varying degrees, Francis Fukuyama, *State-Building: Governance and World Order in the Twenty-First Century*, London: Profile Books, 2004: Robert I. Rotberg, 'The Failure and Collapse of Nation-States: Breakdown, Prevention and Repair', in Robert I. Rotberg (ed.) *When States Fail: Causes and Consequences*, Princeton: Princeton University Press, 2004, pp.1–50; International Commission on Intervention and State Sovereignty (ICISS), *Responsibility to Protect*, Ottawa: International Development Research Centre, December 2001; Robert Keohane, 'Political Authority after Intervention: Gradations in Sovereignty', in J. L. Holzgrefe and R. O. Keohane (eds) *Humanitarian Intervention: Ethical, Legal and Political Dilemmas*, Cambridge: Cambridge University Press, 2003; James D. Fearon and David D. Laitin, 'Neotrusteeship and the Problem of Weak States', *International Security*, vol.28, no.4, 2004, pp.5–43; Jeffrey Herbst, 'Let Them Fail: State Failure in Theory and Practice: Implications for Policy', in Robert I Rotberg, op.cit.: Stephen Krasner, *Sovereignty: Organized Hypocrisy*, Princeton University Press, 1999.

12 *Fieldnotes, Interviews with donors*, including NORAD, DANIDA, and DFID, Maputo, Mozambique, 5–20 January, 2010.

13 See for example, Mehta's critique of liberal imperialism. Uday Singh Mehta, *Liberalism and Empire*, Chicago University Press, 1999.

14 Oliver P. Richmond, 'UN Peace Operations and the Dilemmas of the Peacebuilding Consensus', *International Peacekeeping*, vol.10. no.4, 2004.

15 As Lal has pointed out, culture has come to the forefront of debates about governance and development recently. Deepak Lal, 'Culture, Democracy, and Development', Paper presented at the *IMF Conference on Second Generation Reforms*, 20 September 1999.

16 Eric Herring, 'Neoliberalism Versus Peacebuilding in Iraq', in M. Pugh, R.N. Cooper, and M. Turner (eds), *Whose Peace?*, London: Palgrave, 2008.

17 See Ellen Meiskins Wood, *Empire of Capital*, London: Verso, 2003, p.72; David Harvey, *A Brief History of Neoliberalism*, Oxford: Oxford University Press, 2007.

18 Asa Briggs, 'The Welfare State in Historical Perspective', *European Journal of Sociology*, vol. 2, no.2, 1961, pp. 221–258,1961.

19 Seymour Martin Lipset, 'Some Social Requisites of Democracy: Economic Development and Political Legitimacy', *American Political Science Review*, vol.53, no. 1, 1959, pp. 69–105.

20 Richard Titmuss, *Universalism versus Selection, Commitment to Welfare*, London: Allen and Unwin, 1968, pp.128–37.

21 Nicholas Barr, *The Economics of the Welfare State*, Oxford: Oxford University Press, 1999.

22 Claus Offe, 'Some Contradictions of the Modern Welfare State', *Critical Social Policy*, vol.2, no.2, 1982, p7–14.

23 Ibid., p.8

24 See Michael Goldman, *Imperial Nature*, New Haven: Yale, 2005, p.57. See also, Arthur MacEwan, *Neoliberalism or Democracy*, London: Zed, 1999.

25 Freda Utley, cited in Ray Salvatore Jennings, 'The Road Ahead', *Peaceworks*, no.49, April 2003, p.14.

26 Christopher Coyne, 'After War: Understanding Post-War Reconstruction', *Global Prosperity Initiative Working Paper*, no. 40, Mercatus Center, George Mason University, 2005, p.22.

27 John W Dower, *Embracing Defeat: Japan in the Wake of World War II*, W. W. Norton & Company, 1999.

28 Coyne, op.cit., p.24.

29 See among others, John Maynard Keynes, *The Economic Consequences of the Peace*, London: Macmillan, 1920. Karl Polanyi, *The Great Transformation: The Political and Economic Origins of Our Time*, (Boston: Beacon Press, 1944). Karl Deutsch, *et al.*, *Political Community and the North Atlantic Area*, Princeton University Press, 1957; John Burton, *World Society*, Cambridge University Press, 1972. David Mitrany, *The Functional Theory of Politics*, London: Martin Robertson, 1975.

30 Adam Przeworski, Michael Alvarez, J.A. Cheibub, Fernando Limongi, *Democracy and Development*, Cambridge: Cambridge University Press, 2000, pp.269–70.
31 Anthony Giddens, *Positive Welfare, The Third Way*, Cambridge: Polity, 1998, pp.114–17.
32 Giuliano Bonoli, *The Politics of the New Social Policies*, Policy and Politics, vol.33, no.3., 2005, p.434.
33 This can be seen most clearly in the different versions of the 'Washington Consensus'.
34 Dirk Kotze, 'Implications of the Democracy-Development Relationship for Conflict Resolution', pp.70–1.
35 This is also exacerbated by the bias of the figures themselves, as they tend to be basis on a specific income range rather than the full range, thus not capturing the full dynamics of inequality. Nor can they account for informal income. This means that inequality is probably higher than my figures indicate.
36 Ha Joon Chang, *Bad Samaritans*, London: Random House, 2007, p.48.
37 Richard Sandbrook, Marc Edelman, Patrick Heller and Judith Teichman, *Social Democracy in the Global Periphery*, Cambridge: Cambridge University Press, 2007, p.5.
38 Ibid., p.6.
39 Ibid., p.11.
40 Ha Joon Chang, op.cit., p.176.
41 Adam Przeworski and Fernando Limongi, *Democracy and Development*, Cambridge: Cambridge University Press, 2000, pp.1–3.
42 Thomas Carothers, 'The End of the Transition Paradigm', *Journal of Democracy*, vol.13, no.1, 2002, pp.5–21.
43 Ibid., p.73.
44 Friederich von Hayek, 'The Meaning of the Welfare State', in *The Constitution of Liberty*, Routledge, 1959.
45 For more on these dynamics see, Ha-Joon Chang, *Bad Samaritans*, London: Random House, 2007.
46 See both Charles Murray, 'Two Wars Against Poverty', Lawrence Mead, 'The New Politics of the New Poverty', in Christopher Pierson and Francis Castles, *The Welfare State Reader*, Cambridge: Polity, 2000.
47 Claus Offe, op.cit., p.9
48 See in particular, Richard Sandbrook, Marc Edelman, Patrick Heller and Judith Teichman, op.cit.
49 Ibid., p.184.
50 For such an argument see, House of Commons International Development Committee, *Conflict and Development: Peacebuilding and Post–conflict Reconstruction*, Sixth Report of Session 2005–06, The House of Commons, London: The Stationery Office, 25 October 2006.
51 Mark Duffield, *Development, Security, and Unending War*, Cambridge: Polity, 2007, p.10. This reflects my arguments about 'peace as governance'. Oliver P. Richmond, *Transformation of Peace*, op.cit., p.192. Duffield argues that development discourses imply surplus and uninsurable populations and point to early practices of indirect rule and Native Administrations. Op.cit., p.30–1.
52 See Oliver P. Richmond, 'The Romanticisation of the Local: Welfare, Culture and Peacebuilding', *The International Spectator*, vol. 44, no.1, 2009, pp.149–69.

2   The culture of liberal peacebuilding

 1 See for example, the arguments of of Amilcar Cabral, (translated by Michael Wolfers), *Unity and Struggle*, London: Heinemann, 1980. It should be noted that the connection Cabral makes with a 'national' project of liberation is unlikely to be conflict reducing or lead to conflict resolution. But it is important to note his argument about how culture is a site of agency, for liberation in multiple forms.
 2 See *Oxford Dictionary of English Etymology*, Oxford: Oxford University Press, 1986, p.108.
 3 Ibid., p.9.

4 Clifford, Geertz, *The Interpretation of Cultures*. New York: Basic Books, 1973, p.5.

5 Ibid.

6 Jonathan Spencer, *Anthropology, Politics and the State: Democracy and Violence in South Asia*, Cambridge University Press, 2007, p.14. See also discussion of the US army's 'Human Terrain System', in *The Counter-Counterinsurgency Manual: Or, Notes on Demilitarizing American Society*, Network of Concerned Anthropologists. Prickly Paradigm Press, Chicago: Chicago University Press, 2009.

7 Kristoffer Tarp, *Personal Interview*, Peacebuilding Support Office, UN, New York, 4 June, 2010.

8 Ibid.

9 Jonathan Spencer, op. cit., p.47.

10 Giorgio Agamben, *Homo Sacer: Sovereign Power and Bare Life*, Stanford: Stanford University Press, 1998.

11 Benedict Anderson, *Imagined Communities: Reflections of the Origins and Spread of Nationalism*, Ithaca, NY: Cornell University Press, 1991.

12 James Clifford, *The Predicament of Culture*, Cambridge MA: Harvard University Press, 1998, p.10.

13 Confidential Sources, *Focus Group*, Human Security Unit, UN, New York, 4 June 2010.

14 Vivienne Jabri, *War and the Transformation of Global Politics*, London: Palgrave, 2007, p.267.

15 Ibid., p.267.

16 Michel Foucault, *The Birth of Biopolitics*, London: Palgrave, 2008, p.296.

17 Ibid., p.297.

18 Ibid., p.301.

19 Manuel Castells, *The Power of Identity*, Oxford: Blackwell Publishers, 2003.

20 Edward Said, *Culture and Imperialism*, London: Vintage, 1994.

21 Jacinta O'Hagan, *Conceptualising the West in IR*, London: Palgrave, 2002, p.232.

22 Arturo Escobar, *Encountering Development*, New Jersey, Princeton University Press, 1995, p.109

23 Ibid., p.113.

24 Michael Doyle, 'Liberal Internationalism, Peace, War, and Democracy', http://nobelprize.org/nobel _prizes/peace/chapters/doyle/index.html; See also Michael Doyle, *Ways of War and Peace*, NY: Norton, 1997.

25 Michael Doyle, 'Liberal Internationalism, Peace, War, and Democracy', op. cit., p.1.

26 See Oliver P. Richmond, *Peace In IR*, London: Routledge, 2008.

27 Oliver P. Richmond, *Transformation of Peace*, London: Palgrave, 2005, ch. 4 and 5.

28 Joseph Schumpeter, *Capitalism, Socialism and Democracy*, London: George, Allen and Unwin, 1943. pp.63–71.

29 Ellen Meiksins Wood, *Empire of Capital*, London: Verso, 2003, p.12.

30 See among others Christine Sylvester, 'Bare Life as Development/Post-Colonial Problematic', *The Geographical Journal*, vol.172, no.1., 2006, pp.66–77, p.66: J. Briggs and J. Sharp, 'Indigenous Knowledge and development', *Third World Quarterly*, vol.25, 2004, pp.661–76; Mark Duffield, 'Social Reconstruction and the Radicalisation of Development', *Development and Change*, vol.33, no. 5, 2002, pp.1049–71.

31 See Sylvester, op. cit., p.67. She draws upon G. Agamben, op. cit.

32 Ibid., p.7.

33 Ed Pilkington, 'Bush $1bn jobs plan to draw Iraqis into fold', *The Guardian*, 8 January 2007.

34 In an interview with a senior World Bank manager, I was assured that this was now taking place. Senior World Bank Official, *Personal Interview*, Washington, 23 April 2007.

35 UNCTAD, 'Doubling Aid: Making the Big Push work', *Report on Economic Development in Africa*, www.unctad.org, 2006.

36 Christopher, Coyne, 'After War: Understanding Post-War Reconstruction', *Global Prosperity Initiative Working Paper*, no.40, Mercatus Center, George Mason University,

2005: 'Timor Leste – Poverty Reduction Strategy Paper', *IMF Country Report no.05/247*, Washington, July 2005.

37 Nicholas Barr, *The Economics of the Welfare State*, Oxford: Oxford University Press, 1998.

38 *International Covenant on Economic, Social and Cultural Rights*, Adopted and opened for signature, ratification and accession by General Assembly Resolution 2200A (XXI) of 16 December 1966 (entry into force 3 January 1976, in accordance with chapter 27).

39 Rajeev Patel and Philip McMichael, 'Third Worldism and the Lineages of Global Fascism', *Third World Quarterly*, vol 25, no.1, 2004, pp.231–54, p.235.

40 Cited in ibid, p.239

41 I am indebted to Roger Mac Ginty's work for this critique. See his piece in J. Darby and R. Mac Ginty (eds), *Contemporary Peacemaking*, London: Palgrave, 2008.

42 William E. Connolly, *Identity/Difference*, Minneapolis: Minnesota University Press, 1991, p.94.

43 De Certeau, *The Practice of Everyday Life*, California University Press, 1984.

44 Arturo Escobar, op. cit., p.15.

45 Ibid., p.30 and p.45.

46 Ibid., p.57.

47 See my typology of the liberal peace in *Transformation of Peace*, London: Palgrave, 2005.

48 Frantz Fanon, *The Wretched of the Earth*, London: Penguin, 1967, pp.132–8.

49 A recent article by Roger MacGinty illustrates how successive British governments developed what he calls 'Liberal Peace lie' in Northern Ireland in response to such pressures. Roger Mac Ginty, 'The Liberal Peace at Home and Abroad: Northern Ireland and Liberal Internationalism, *BJPIR*, vol.11, 2009, pp.690–708.

50 See Stephen Chan, Peter Mandaville and Roland Bleiker, *The Zen of IR*, London: Palgrave, 2001.

51 Gayatri Chakravorty Spivak, *A Critique of Post-Colonial Reason*, Cambridge, Mass.: Harvard University Press, 1999, p.277.

52 Edward Said, *Orientalism*, London: Penguin, 1978, p.291.

53 Ashis Nandy, *The Intimate Enemy*, Delhi: Oxford University Press, 1983.

54 Roger Mac Ginty, 'Indigenous Peace-Making Versus the Liberal Peace,' *Cooperation and Conflict*, vol. 43, no, 2, 2008, pp.139–163.

55 See Michel Foucault, *Society Must be Defended*, trans. David Macey, London: Penguin, 2003.

56 David Chandler, *Empire in Denial*, London: Pluto, 2006, p.33

57 Uday Singh Megta, *Liberalism and Empire*, Chicago University Press, 1999, p.20.

58 Ibid., p.23 and 163.

59 Ibid., p.24.

60 Ibid., p.121.

61 Ibid., pp.173–4.

62 It become relatively common during the mid 2000s to hear in discussions between policymakers and academics, at least in the UK, a call for a re-examination of colonial archives to see how order was maintained in the colonial context as a direct parallel to contemporary liberal peacebuilding/statebuilding.

3   De-romanticising the local: implications for post-liberal peacebuilding

1 There are some notable exceptions, especially the work of Michael Pugh, including his 'Limited Survival and Economic Security', *Working Paper*, 2007. http://www.st-andrews.ac.uk/intrel/cpcs/chapters.htm

2 The following case studies draw partly on fieldwork conducted for *my Liberal Peace Transitions* project, 2007–8, as well as various other field visits by the author. See Oliver P. Richmond and Jason Franks, *Liberal Peace Transitions*, Edinburgh University Press, 2009.

3 Michael Doyle, *United Nations Peacekeeping in Cambodia: UNTAC's Civil Mandate*, Boulder, CO: Lynne Rienner. 1995.

4 Confidential Source, *Personal Interview*, World Bank Country Office, Phnom Penh, 10 November 2005.

5 Ibid.

6 Numerous international interviewees confirmed this version of events in Cambodia during my fieldwork.

7 *Phnom Penh Post*, November 2005.

8 Emma Leslie, *Personal Interview*, Alliance for Conflict Transformation/researcher, Phnom Penh, 11 November 2005.

9 Francis Fukuyama, *State Building: Governance and World Order in the Twenty-First Century*, London: Profile Books, 2004, p.55.

10 Grant Curtis, *Cambodia Reborn? The Transition to Democracy and Development*, Brookings institute Press, Washington, 1998, p.110–149.

11 Official Source, USAID, *Personal Interview*, Phnom Penh, 8 November, 2005.

12 See, Oliver P. Richmond and Jason Franks, Liberal Peace Transitions, Edinburgh University Press, 2009.

13 See, Adam Fagan, 'Civil Society in Bosnia Herzegovina Ten Years after Dayton,' *International Peacekeeping*, vol.12, no.3, 2005, pp.406–19.

14 Ibid., p.175

15 Confidential Source, Centre for Human Rights, *Personal Interview*, Sarajevo, 30 January 2007.

16 Ashis Nandy, *The Intimate Enemy*, Delhi: Oxford University Press, 1983, pp.30–3.

17 A range of such views were expressed during a meeting with MPs in Sarajevo. *Focus Group*, Halid Genjac, chair; House of Representatives; SDA – *Stranka demokratske akcije*, Party for Democratic Action, Milica Markovic, member; House of Representatives SNSD – *Savez nezavisnih socijaldemokrata* – Union of Independent Social Democrats, Bozo Ljubic, member; House of Peoples HDZ 1990; *Hrvatska demokratska zajednica 1990*; Croatian Democratic Union 1990, EU Accession Parliamentary Commission, Bosnia Herzegovinan Parliament, Sarajevo 3/09/09.

18 *UNDP National Human Development Report*, op. cit., pp.133–45.

19 Ibid., p.145.

20 One participant of a workshop I organised in Sarajevo in May 2007 described international peacebuilding as 'ambivalent building'.

21 Roberto Belloni, 'Civil Society and Peacebuilding in Bosnia Herzegovina and Herzegovina,' *Journal of Peace Research*, vol.38, no.2, p.169.

22 Ibid., p.170.

23 This view has has been mentioned to me several times in confidence by local and international staff in Bosnia Herzegovina.

24 Confidential Source, National Dialogue Centre, *Personal Interview*, Mostar, 2 February 2007.

25 See Peacebuilding Workshop, *Focus group* run for local peacebuilders, 14 March 2008, University of Sarajevo. This group was overwhelmingly negative about the liberal peace they were experiencing, the role of the internationals, the role of local political elites, their own agency, and of course, neoliberalism.

26 Confidential Source, National Dialogue Centre, *Personal Interview*, Mostar, 2 February 2007.

27 Confidential Source, SIDA, *Personal Interview*, Sarajevo, 1 February 2007.

28 Confidential Source, Council of Europe, *Personal Interview*, Sarajevo, 1 February 2007.

29 Program-Project Development Manager of NDC Sarajevo, Conference on 'Delivering Just and Durable Peace? Evaluating EU Peacebuilding strategies in the Western Balkans', Sarajevo, 04/09/09.

30 Michel Foucault, *The Birth of Politics*, op. cit., pp.313.

31 Michel Foucault, 'Governmentality', in: Graham Burchell, Colin Gordon and Peter

Miller (eds.), *The Foucault Effect: Studies in* Governmentality, Hemel Hempstead: Harvester Wheatsheaf, 1991, pp.87–104.

32 Paddy Ashdown, 'Europe needs a wake-up call. Bosnia Herzegovina is on the edge again', *The Observer*, Sunday July 27 2008.

33 Confidential Source, Council of Europe, *Personal Interview*, Sarajevo, 1 February 2007.

34 Catherine Gotze, 'Civil Society Organisations in Failing States: The Red Cross in Bosnia Herzegovina and Albania,' *International Peacekeeping*, vol.11, no.4, 2004, pp.664–81, p.679.

35 Deputy SRSG, *Personal Interview*, Sarajevo, 29, January 2007 and Ambassador Davidson, OSCE, Personal Interview, Sarajevo, 1 February 2007 and 15 March 2008.

36 Confidential Source, Centre for Human Rights, *Personal Interview*, Sarajevo, 30 January 2007.

37 *UNDP National Human Development Report*, p.70.

38 M. Pugh, 'Transformation in the Political Economy of Bosnia Herzegovina since Dayton,' *International Peacekeeping*, vol.12, no.3, 2005, pp.448–62.

39 *BHAS, Labour Force Survey* (preliminary data), Press Release no.1, 27 July 2006, Sarajevo.

40 Confidential Source, World Bank, *Personal Interview*, Sarajevo, 27 January 2007.

41 Ibid.

42 Confidential Source, Independent Economic Advisor, *Personal Interview*, Sarajevo, 30 January 2007.

43 Ibid.

44 The diagram in Appendix 1 outlines local responses to these critiques from the perspective of their perception of local and international discourses about peace-building, derived from a discussion on the liberal peace and at a workshop held for local peacebuilding personnel, at the Centre for Interdisciplinary Studies and Human Rights at the University of Sarajevo, 14 March 2008.

45 OSCE, *Assessing the Realisation of the Right to Social Assistance in BH*, December 2005.

46 Confidential Source, Personal Interview, Formerly with UNMIK, Brussels, 4 February 2010.

47 Recognition of the new state is accruing, with much of the EU having recognised it. In February 2009, on a visit to New York, I saw a convoy of cars celebrating the first anniversary of UDI. The KLA flag and the Albanian flag were on display but there was no sign of the National Flag of Kosovo. This may have just been coincidence, of course, though it seems to follow a broader pattern to me at least.

48 See, Florian Bieber, and Zidas Daskalovski (eds), *Understanding the War in Kosovo*, London: Frank Cass, 2003; Paul Latawski and Martin Smith, *The Kosovo Crisis and the Evolution of Post-Cold War European Security*, Manchester: Palgrave, 2003; Michael, Kyril Drezov, Bulent Gokay (eds), *Kosovo: The Politics of Delusion*, London: Frank Cass, 2001.

49 See, Miranda Vickers, *Between Serbs and Albanians, A History of Kosovo*, New York: University Press, 1998: Noel Malcolm, *Kosovo A Short History*, London: Macmillan, 1998; Julia Mertus, *Kosovo: How Myths and Truths Started a War*, California: University of California, 1999.

50 See, Julia Mertus, *Kosovo*, pp.231–34.

51 *UNDP Human Development Report – Kosovo 2004*, Pristina: UNDP, p.3.

52 79 per cent in 2000 to 54 per cent in 2002. *UNDP Human Development Report – Kosovo 2004*, Pristina: UNDP, p.57.

53 Confidential Source, OSCE – Democratisation Education Officer, *Personal Interview, Pristina, 5 April 2006.*

54 M. Llamazares, L. Reynolds, *NGOs and Peacebuilding in Kosovo*, University of Bradford, Dept. of Peace Studies, 2003, p.3.

55 Ibid., p.5.

56 M. Llamazares, L. Reynolds, op. cit p.2.

57 *UNDP Human Development Report – Kosovo 2004*, Pristina: UNDP, p.54.

58 Confidential Source, World Bank – Operations Officer, *Personal Interview*, Pristina, 3 April 2006.

59 Anne Holohan, *Networks of Democracy*, Stanford: Stanford Press, 2005, p.136.

60 Confidential Source, OSCE – Democratisation Education Officer, *Personal Interview*, Pristina, 5 April 2006.

61 www.unmikonline.org/2ndyear/unmikat2p4.

62 *UNMIK, Kosovo Economic Outlook 2006*, Economic Policy Office, March 2006, p.6.

63 The World Bank, *The World Bank Group in the Western Balkans*, Washington, August 2005, p.21.

64 *UNDP Human Development Report – Kosovo 2004*, Pristina: UNDP, p.19.

65 Confidential Source, NCSC – Programme Officer, *Personal Interview*, Pristina, 4 April 2006.

66 Jasmina Husanovic, 'Post-Conflict Kosovo: An Anatomy Lesson in the Ethics/Politics of Human Rights in Booth, K, (ed.), *The Kosovo Tragedy The Human Rights Dimension*, London: Frank Cass, 2001, pp.263–82.

67 W. O'Neill, *Kosovo: An Unfinished Peace*, London: Lynne Rienner, 2001, p.129.

68 Ibid., p.130.

69 Ibrahim Makolli, Council of the Defence of Human Rights, *Personal Interview*, Pristina, 6 April 2006.

70 See, P. Stubbs, 'Partnership or Colonisation? The Relationship Between International Agencies and Local Non Governmental Organisations in Bosnia Herzegovina-Herzegovina'. *Civil Society, NGOs and Global Governance*, B. Deacon, Sheffield: Globalisation and Social Policy Programme, 2000, p.24. Quoted in Llamazares and Reynolds, *NGOs and Peacebuilding in Kosovo*, op. cit., p.16.

71 Julia Mertus, op. cit., p.262.

72 For more on this conceptual issue, see among others, Oliver P. Richmond, 'States of Sovereignty, Sovereign States, and Ethnic Claims for International Status'. *Review of International Studies*. vol.28., no.2, 2002.

73 Ibid.

74 *UN Secretary General's Report on Timor-Leste pursuant to Security Council Resolution 1690*, 8 August 2006, esp. paras. 34–5.

75 Sidonio Frietas, *Personal Interview*, Programme Manager, Democracy and Governance Programme, USAID, 11 November, 2004.

76 Olav Ofstad, *Personal Interview*, Head of Delegation, International Federation of Red Cross and Red Crescent Societies, Dili 11 November 2004.

77 This was a constant complaint encountered during fieldwork in Timor Leste, amongst agencies, NGOs, the UN, and other internationals, in November 2004.

78 Jarat Chopra and Tanja Hohe, 'Participatory Intervention', *Global Governance*, vol.10, no.3, 2004, pp.289–305: Chopra, Jarat, 'The UN's Kingdom of East Timor', *Survival*, vol.42, no.3., 2000, pp.27–40.

79 Michael G. Smith, *Peacekeeping in East Timor*, Colorado: Lynne Rienner, 2003, p.63

80 President Xanana Gusmao, 'Peacekeeping and Peacebuilding in Timor Leste', *Seminar on the role of the UN in Timor Leste*, Dili, 26 November, 2004.

81 *Field Notes*, 1–15 September, 2007.

82 *Group Discussion* with staff at La'o Hamutuk, Dili, 4 November 2008.

83 Notable amongst these is Pat Walsh, *Personal Interview*, CAVR, Dili, 6 November, 2008.

84 *UNDP Monthly Newsletter*, February 2007, p.4.

85 Ibid., para. 91.

86 See UNDP, *Human Development Report: Timor Leste*, 2006, p.3.

87 Country Director, *Personal Interview*, World Bank, Dili, 6 November 2008.

88 'Poverty Reduction Strategy Paper', *IMF Country Report no.05/247*, Washington, July 2005, p.xvi.

89 Ibid., p.xvii.

90 Ibid., p.4. and p.11.

91 Ibid., pp.5–6, p.8.

4 De-romanticising the local: implications for post-liberal peacebuilding

1 Michel Foucault, *The Birth of Politics*, Graham Burchell (trans.), London: Palgrave, 2008 p.313.
2 Confidential Source, *Personal Interview*, DPA, UN, New York, 10 June 2010.
3 Confidential Sources, *Focus Group*, DPKO, UN, New York, 7 June 2010.
4 Deborah J. Yashar, *Contesting Citizenship in Latin America: The Rise of Indigenous Movements and the Post-Liberal Challenge*, Cambridge: Cambridge University Press, 2005, p.6.
5 Ibid., p.68.
6 Confidential Sources, *Focus Group*, DPKO, UN, New York, 7 June 2010.
7 Jean Baudrillard, 'Simulacra and Simulations' in Mark Poster (ed.), *Jean Baudrillard, Selected Writings*, Stanford; Stanford University Press, 1988, pp.166–84.
8 For example, even in the UN system those dealing with 'high-level' policy and politics often see the local context as dangerous. In an interview with one official in DPA I was told that many are afraid that their ignorance about context would undermine their legitimacy and that of the UN system more broadly in post-conflict environments. Of course such views are rare amongst humanitarian workers, or in UNDP for example. Confidential Source, *Personal Interview*, DPA, UN, New York, 10 June 2010.
9 See Mark Duffield and Nicholas Waddell, 'Security Humans in a Dangerous World', *International Politics*, vol.43, no.1, pp.1–23.
10 Arturo Escobar, *Encountering Development*, New Jersey, Princeton Univeristy Press, 1995, p.217.
11 David Chandler, *Empire in Denial*, London: Pluto, 2006, p.33 and p.56.
12 Mark Duffield, *Development, Security, and Unending War*, Cambridge: Polity, 2007, p.193.
13 Mike Pugh, 'Peacekeeping and Critical Theory', BISA, LSE, 18 December 2002, p.1.
14 Ashis Nandy, *The Intimate Enemy*, Delhi: Oxford University Press, 1983. My thanks to Phillip Darby for drawing my attention to this concept.
15 See Geoffrey Hull, 'The Languages of East Timor: 1772–1997: A Literature Review', in *Studies in Languages and Cultures of East Timor*, Macarthur, NSW: University of Western Sydney, 1999, pp.1–38: Agence France Presse, 11 December 2001.
16 David Held, *Global Covenant: The Social Democratic Alternative to the Washington Consensus*, Cambridge: Polity Press, 2004.
17 See, for a fascinating discussion of this, Richard Sandbrook, Marc Edelman, Patrick Heller, and Judith Teichman, *Social Democracy in the Global Periphery*, Cambridge: Cambridge University Press, 2007.
18 M. Pugh, Neil. Cooper, and Mandy Turner (eds.), *Whose Peace?*, London: Palgrave, 2008.
19 Caroline Hughes, *Dependent Communities: Aid and Politics in Cambodia and Timor-Leste*, Cornell, 2009, Chapter 4.
20 See Oliver P. Richmond, *Failed Statebuilding*, Yale University Press, 2013, forthcoming.
21 Jonathan Spencer, *Anthropology, Politics and the State: Democracy and Violence in South Asia*, Cambridge: Cambridge University Press, 2007, p.103.
22 Mark Duffield, Development, *Security, and Unending War*, op. cit., p.228.
23 See the pioneering research projects conducted by Sharhbanou Tadjbakhsh at the Centre for Human Security, Sciences Po, Paris, and in particular the recent conference held at this centre. Conference on *Liberal Peace: External Models and Local Alternatives*, Sciences Po, Paris, 17 June,2008.
24 Jonathan Spencer, op. cit., p.118 and p.172. See also Roger Mac Ginty, *No War, No Peace*, London, Palgrave, 2007.
25 See for the example of extra peacekeeping in Rwanda versus the costs of the 1994 genocide, Kofi Annan, *No Exit Without Strategy*, S//2001/394, UN: NY, 2001, p.6.

26 See also House of Commons International Development Committee, *Conflict and Development: Peacebuilding and Post–conflict Reconstruction*, Sixth Report of Session 2005–06 vol.I.

27 My recent engagement with US and European policymakers involved in peacebuilding suggests that they are beginning to take note of such argument especially in the light of the difficulties in Iraq and Afghanistan.

28 Mark Duffield, *Development, Security, and Unending War*, op. cit., p.176.

29 Oliver P. Richmond and Jason Franks, 'Co-opting the Liberal Peace: Untying the Gordian Knot in Kosovo', *Liberal Peace Transitions*, Edinburgh University Press, 2009.

30 See the content of a talk given by Dan Smith, Secretary General of International Alert, Centre for International Studies, University of Oxford, 23 October 2009.

31 Ashis Nandy, op. cit.

32 This argument was made in the early post-Cold War context, but has recently faded in the light of the many problems that have emerged with the liberal project. See Gene M. Lyons, and Michael Mastunduno, *Beyond Westphalia*, Johns Hopkins UP, 1995.

33 For an excellent discussion of this process, see Istvan Kende, 'The History of Peace', p.233–45.

34 Sadie Plant, *The Most Radical Gesture*, London: Routledge, 1992, p.157–8.

35 R.B.J .Walker, in discussion.

36 However, there are notable exceptions, particularly amongst PhD students, who increasingly appear to favour in-depth local studies as part of their research, along with a group of scholars working in development, and peace and conflict studies who increasingly are moving away from, or had little association with, the formal discipline of IR. In particular, see the often ground-breaking work of anthropologist, Carolyn Nordstrom, particularly, *Shadows of War*, Berkley: University of California Press, 2004.

37 Aturo Escobar, *Encountering Development*, op. cit., p.113.

38 Michel de Certeau, *The Practice of Everyday Life*, California University Press, 1984, p.xi

39 Ibid., Chapter II.

40 See for example, William Connolly, *Identity/Difference*, p.10.

41 Pierre Allan and Alexis Keller, *What is a Just Peace*, pp.16–17.

42 Alexis Keller, 'Justice, Peace and History', ibid., p.49.

43 Ibid., p.51.

44 Pierre Allan, Measuring International Ethics, ibid., p.91.

45 See Carol Gilligan, *In a Different Voice*, Cambridge, M.A.: Harvard University Press, 1993.

46 Pierre Allan, Measuring International Ethics, p.126.

47 Ibid., p.127.

48 Shahrbanou Tadjbakhsh, 'Human Security: Concepts and Implications', *Les Etudes du CERI*, no. 117–18, (September 2005), p.10.

49 'The Responsibility to Protect', Ottowa: International Commission on Intervention and State Sovereignty, December 2001.

50 For a development of this see Charles Taylor, 'The Politics of Recognition' in Amy Gutmann, ed., *Multiculturalism and the Politics of Recognition*, Princeton University Press, 1992, pp.25–73.

51 Fred Dallmayr, *Peace Talks – Who Will Listen?*, Paris: University of Notre Dame Press, 2004, p.100–101.

52 Cited in ibid., p.101. Michel Foucault, *History of Sexuality*, vol. 3, The Care of the Self, New York: Pantheon Books, 1986. See also William Connolly, *Identity/Difference*, p.10, and p.57. This is not to imply that Foucault's concept of the 'care of the self' is an alternative conception of ethics, but a position from which to engage in a constant critique of any attempt to establish order- even my own attempt to develop an everyday notion of peace. A post-liberal peace would therefore contained a feedback process and engage in constant adaption. Many thanks to Tony Lang for making this point to me.

53 Arpad Szakolczai, 'Thinking Beyond the East-West Divide: Patocka, Foucault, Hamvas, Elias, and the Care of the Self', *EUI Working Paper*, Florence: EUI, 94/2, (1994), p.9 and p.11. See also R.B.J. Walker, in discussion.

54 Zygmunt Bauman, *Postmodern Ethics*, Oxford: Blackwell, 1993.

55 Mark Duffield, *Development, Security, and Unending War*, p.234.

56 Carol Gilligan, *In a Different Voice*, p.2.

57 Fred, Dallmayr, *Peace Talks – Who Will Listen?*, p.110.

58 For more on such issues, see Christopher Freeman, 'Afghanistan in Transition: Security, Governance and Statebuilding'. The criticism of this might well be fair from the perspective of creating a centralised, liberal state, but a consideration of the local and everyday in the context of Afghanistan shows this to be both optimistic and 'eurocentric'.

59 See, for a range of views, David Chandler, 'Imposing the 'Rule of Law': The Lessons of BiH for Peacebuilding in Iraq', *International Peacekeeping*, vol.11, no.2, 2004, pp.312–33: USIP, Iraq, *Progress in Peacebuilding*, (March, 2008), http://www.usip. org/iraq/progress_peacebuilding_iraq.pdf; Carl Conetta, *Radical Departure: Toward A Practical Peace in Iraq*, Project on Defense Alternatives Briefing Report # 16. Cambridge, MA: Commonwealth Institute, 7 July 2004. http://www.comw.org/pda/0407br16. html

60 See Oliver P. Richmond and Jason Franks, *Liberal Peace Transitions: Between Statebuilding and Peacebuilding*, chapters 1–4.

61 David Chandler, *Empire in Denial*, p.36.

62 See among others Christine Sylvester, 'Bare Life as Development/Post-Colonial Problematic', *The Geographical Journal*, vol.172, no.1, 2006, pp.66–77: G. Agamben, *Homo Sacer: Sovereign Power and Bare Life*, Stanford: Stanford University Press, 1998.

63 Or see 'Critical Peace Research' (CPR) as conceptualised by Matti Jutila, Samu Pehkonen and Tarja Väyrynen, 'Resuscitating a Discipline: An Agenda for Critical Peace Research', *Millennium – Journal of International Studies*, vol.36, no3, 2008, pp. 623–40.

64 Vivienne Jabri, *War and the Transformation of Global Politics*, London: Palgrave, 2007, p.268.

65 Pierre Allan and Alexis Keller, *What is a Just Peace* pp.16–17.

66 Alexis Keller, 'Justice, Peace and History', ibid., p.49.

67 Ibid., p.51.

68 A good example of this can be found in documentation such as the Responsibility to Protect report, which operates to extend liberal norms and governance to non-liberal others, on the assumption that represents a universal process of conflict resolution. See William Connolly's idea of 'non-territorial democracy' as a possible way of overcoming the 'bordering' that occurs in the liberal peace. William Connolly, *Identity/ Difference*, p.218.

69 See in particular, Andrew Linklater, *The Transformation of Political Community*, University of South Carolina Press, 1998.

70 These points are a developed version of an agenda for peace I first presented in Oliver P. Richmond, *Peace in IR*, London: Routledge, 2008, conclusion.

71 Here the critique of Sadie Plant that Western liberalism has lead to a 'society asleep', where there are no politics, might be employed. Post-conflict zones are so intensely politicised that this situation is not particularly attractive. Sadie Plant, *The Most Radical Gesture*, p.12.

72 See the pioneering research projects conducted by Sharhbanou Tadjbakhsh at the Centre for Human Security, Sciences Po, Paris, and in particular the recent conference held at this centre. Conference on *Liberal Peace: External Models and Local Alternatives*, Sciences Po, Paris (17 June 2008).

73 Mark Duffield, *Development, Security, and Unending War*, p.234.

74 Michael Pugh, Neil Cooper, and Mandy Turner, *Whose Peace: The Political Economy of*

Peacebuilding, (London: Palgrave, 2008), conclusion. Permanent critique was of course a feature of 'revolutionary theory' aspired to by Marxist oriented sympathisers with the Dada and situationalist internationalist movements, which saw critique as a permanent practice of revolutionary theory. Sadie Plant, *The Most Radical Gesture*, p.87.

75 Ibid., p.114. Plant warns that metanarratives, as with Lyotard's celebrated arguments, relating to the 'real', to 'progress', and to 'emancipation', often deny the validity of events and voices (i.e. of the oppressed) that do not fit with their analyses.

76 See Mandy Turner and Mike Pugh, 'Towards a new agenda for transforming war economies', *Conflict, Security and Development*, vol.6, no.3, 2006, pp.471–7.

77 See also Michel Foucault, *The Birth of Biopolitics*, London: Palgrave, 2008, p.64.

78 Foucault describes this tendency as 'liberogenic', meaning the tendency of various liberal strategies to produce the opposite of what was intended. Ibid., p.69.

5 Everyday critical agency and resistance in peacebuilding

1 Article 21 (3), *Declaration of Human Rights*, 1948.

2 Homi Bhabha, *The Location of Culture*, London: Routledge, 1994, p.330.

3 Gayatri Chakravorty Spivak, 'Can the Subaltern Speak?', in C. Nelson and L. Grossberg (eds), Marxism and the Interpretation of Culture, Basingstoke: Macmillan, 1988, p.75.

4 This framework draws on Oliver P. Richmond, *Maintaining Order, Making Peace*, London: Palgrave, 2002. First generation approaches might be termed 'conflict management' in which a conflict was merely held in limbo (as with peacekeeping) in order to maintain the existing state. A second generation approach aimed at dealing with human needs or peacebuilding from the grass roots up and argued that conflicts could be resolved. A third generation approach attempted to achieve the latter through the construction of a liberal state. A fourth generation approach is concerned with emancipation and social justice beyond the state.

5 In conversation, University of Bristol, 30 July 2009.

6 For a fascinating discussion of such themes, see Phillip Darby, 'The Alternative Horizons of Ashis Nandy', Unpublished Paper, 2009.

7 Jaques Derrida, *Rogues: Two essays on reason*, Stanford: Stanford University Press, 2004, p.40.

8 The same might also be said of cosmopolitan forms of liberalism such as that of David Held, Marxist flavoured forms such as that of Andrew Linklater, and postmodern versions of liberalism as in Richard Rorty's work. See in particular, Richard Rorty, 'On Ethnocentricism', *Objectivity, Relativism, and Truth*, Cambridge: Cambridge University Press, 1991, p.209.

9 Ilan Kapoor, 'Acting in a Tight Spot: Homi Bhabha's Post-Colonial Politics', *New Political Science*, vol.25, no.4., 2003, pp.561–577.

10 Thanks to Necati Polat for pointing out that agency is an Enlightment concept, and my claim to facilitate it locally situates my work in this tradition. However, though I agree with his point, I am also interested in self-determination, the autonomy of the subject, and individual and community epistemes and so am not bound to the notion of universal agency. I intend to address the issue of the technology of the self and autonomy in peacebuilding in a later article. For key thinkers on everyday life see, Maurice Blanchot, *The Infinite Conversation*, Minneapolis: University of Minneapolis Press, 1993; Henri Lefebvre, *Critique of Everyday Life*, London: Verso, 1991: Guy Debord, *Society of the Spectacle*, London: Aldgate Press; Michel de Certeau, T*he Practice of Everyday Life*, California University Press, 1984.

11 L.H. Martin *et. al.*, *Technologies of the Self: A Seminar with Michel Foucault*, London: Tavistock, pp.16–49.

12 John Gerard Ruggie, 'Territoriality and Beyond: Problematizing Modernity in IR', *International Organisation*, vol.47, no.1, 1993, p.139–174.

13   This follows on from Agathangelou and Lings' argument that IR is a 'colonial household'. Anna M. Agathangelou and L.H.M. Lings, 'The House of IR', *International Studies Review*, vol.6, 2004, p.21–49.

14   This follows the well-known French tradition from Durkheim to Foucault, as well as the approaches of Geertz and Skinner among others. Cited in Ruggie, op.cit., p.157 and p.169.

15   Gayatri Chakravorty Spivbak, op cit., p.75.

16   Homi Bhabha, 'Freedom's Basis in the Indeterminate', in J. Rajchman (ed.), *The Identity in Question*, New York: Routledge, 1995, pp.47–61.

17   Partha Chatterjee, 'Beyond the Nation? Or Within', *Social Text*, no.56, 1998, p.57–69.

18   Thanks to David Chandler for alerting me to this danger.

19   I am indebted to Kristoffer Liden for this link with post-colonial theory.

20   'Leaning to learn' is how Kapoor puts it. Ilan Kapoor, *The Post-Colonial Politics of Development*, op. cit., p.56.

21   This section draws Randle's superb, and probably definitive, study to which I am indebted. Michael Randle, *Civil Resistance*, London, Fontana, 1994, p.198. For a recent contribution see Adam Roberts and Timothy Garton Ash (eds.), *Civil Resistance and Power Politics: The Experience of Non-violent Action from Gandhi to the Present*, Oxford University Press, Oxford, 2009.

22   Michael Randle, op. cit., pp.19–51.

23   Ibid., p.22 and p.55.

24   Bhikhu Parekh, *Gandhi's Political Philosophy*, Basingstoke: Macmillan, 1989, p.126.

25   Ibid, p.128.

26   Michael Randle, op. cit., pp.58–63.

27   Deborah J Yashar, *Contesting Citizenship in Latin America: The Rise of Indigenous Movements and the Post-Liberal Challenge*, Cambridge: Cambridge University Press, 2005, p.14.

28   Charles Tilly, Louise Tilly and Richard Tilly, *The Rebellious Century, 1830–1930*, London: JM Dent and Sons, 1975, pp.48–55.

29   Michael Randle, op. cit., p.86.

30   Ibid., p.113, citing Gene Sharp, *The Politics of Non-violent Action*, Porter Sargent, Boston, 1973.

31   Anders Boserup and Andrew Mack, *War Without Weapons : non-violence in national defence*, London : Francis Pinter, 1974, p.38.

32   David Chandler, 'Critiquing Liberal Cosmopolitanism? The Limits of the Biopolitical Approach', *International Political Sociology*, vol.3, 2009, p.56; Ilan Kapoor, 'Acting in a Tight Spot: Homi Bhabha's Post-Colonial Politics', op. cit., p.568.

33   Ibid., p.62.

34   See Eckl's review of ethnographic approaches, and reference to Malinowski in particular. Julian Eckl, 'Responsible Scholarship After Leaving the Veranda', *International Political Sociology*, vol.2, 2008, pp.187–90.

35   Ibid., p.196.

36   Ibid., p.197.

37   Homi Bhabha, op. cit., p.33.

38   Judith Butler, 'Universality in Culture', in Martha Nussbaum, *For Love of Country?*, J Cohen (ed.), Boston, MA: Beacon Press, 2002, p.52.

39   Partha Chatterjee, op. cit., p.59.

40   Oliver P. Richmond, 'Becoming Liberal, Unbecoming Liberalism', op. cit.

41   See, for a discussion of similar accusations aimed at Habermasian discourse theory, Andrew Linklater, 'Dialogic Politics and the Civilising Process', *Review of International Studies*, vol.31, 2005, pp.141–54.

42   See Barry Hindess, 'Not at Home in the Empire', *Social Identities*, vol.7, no.3, 2001, p.353.

43   Hindess cites Guha in his discussion of 'colonial anxiety' and liberalism's failure to

live up to its claims of offering freedom, but instead reverting to colonialism, despite its impacts on the sand colonisers, ibid., p.363.

44 Amity Acharya, 'How Ideas Spread: Whose Norms Matter? Norm Localization and Institutional Change in Asian Regionalism,' *International Organization*, vol.58, no.2, 2004, pp.239–75.

45 Among others, Jean Paul Lederach is well known for making such arguments, and Jarat Copra has made similar suggestions. J. Lederach, *Building Peace – Sustainable Reconciliation in Divided Societies*, Tokyo: United Nations University Press, 1997; Jarat Chopra and Tanja Hohe, 'Participatory Intervention', *Global Governance*, vol.10, no.3, 2004, pp.289–305. Such participatory approaches have been the subject of well-placed criticism, however, that they simply advocate international approaches at the local level rather engaging with local agency. Ilan Kapoor, op. cit., p.75.

46 Douglas Fry, *Beyond War*, Oxford: Oxford University Press, 2007, p.7.

47 Mikkel Vedby Rasmussen, *The West, Civil Society, and the Construction of Peace*, London: Palgrave, 2003, esp. p.13.

48 John Keane, *Global Civil Society*, Cambridge: Cambridge University Press, 2003, p.123: Mikkel Vedby Rasmussen, op. cit., p.16.

49 See Harvey among others for a discussion of this. David Harvey, *A Brief History of Neoliberalism* Oxford: Oxford University Press, 2005.

50 Michel Foucault, 'Governmentality', in: Graham Burchell, Colin Gordon, and Peter Miller (eds), *The Foucault Effect: Studies in* Governmentality, Hemel Hempstead: Harvester Wheatsheaf, 1991, pp.87–104.

51 See John Macmillan, 'Immanuel Kant and the Democratic Peace', in Beate Jahn (ed.), *Classical Theory in IR*, Cambridge: Cambridge University Press, 2006, p.71.

52 With thanks for this insight.

53 For early allusions, see Leonard Woolf, *The Framework of a Lasting Peace*, London: Allen and Unwin, 1917; Alfred Zimmern, *The League of Nations and the Rule of Law*, London: Macmillan, 1936.

54 Such analyses often draw on Geertz's understanding of culture as historically trans-mitted system of symbols, conceptions, knowledge, and attitudes. This is, of course, fluid and also plays out within and through politics. Clifford Geertz, 'Religion as a Cultural System', in Clifford Geertz (eds), *The Interpretation of Cultures*, New York: Basic Books, 1973, p.89. See also David Chandler, *Empire in Denial: The Politics of Statebuilding*, London: Pluto Press, 2006; Michael Pugh: 'Corruption and the Political Economy of Liberal Peace,' paper prepared for the *International Studies Association annual convention, San Francisco*, 26–28 March 2008; Michael Pugh, Neil Cooper, and Mandy Turner, *Whose Peace?* London: Palgrave, 2008; Michael Pugh, 'The Political Economy of Peacebuilding: A Critical Theory Perspective,' *International Journal of Peace Studies*, vol.10, no.2, 2005, pp.23–42; Beate Jahn, 'The Tragedy of Liberal Diplomacy: Democratization, Intervention and Statebuilding,' *Journal of Intervention and Statebuilding*, vol.1, no.2, 2007, pp.211–229; Mark Duffield, *Development, Security and Unending War*, London: Polity, 2007; Roger Mac Ginty and Oliver P. Richmond (eds), 'Myth or Reality: The Liberal Peace and Post-Conflict Reconstruction', *Special issue of Global Society*, 2007.

55 Volker Boege, M. Anne Brown, Kevin P. Clements, and Anna Nolan, 'States Emerging from Hybrid Political Orders – Pacific Experiences', *The Australian Centre for Peace and Conflict Studies (ACPACS) Occasional Papers Series*, 2008, p.4.

56 Arturo Escobar, *Encountering Development, The Making and Unmaking of the Third World*, Princeton University Press, 1995.

57 Michel de Certeau, op. cit., p.xi.

58 Michel Foucault, *History of Sexuality*, vol.3, *The Care of the Self*, New York: Pantheon Books, 1986.

59 See Carol Gilligan, *In a Different Voice*, Cambridge, M.A.: Harvard University Press, 1993.

60 Jurgen Habermas, 'Questions and Counter Questions', in R.J. Bernstein (ed.), *Habermas and Modernity*, Cambridge: MIT Press, 1985, pp.196–7.

61 Andrew Linklater, *The Transformation of Political Community*, University of South Carolina Press, 1998 p.31.

62 Homi Bhabha, op. cit., p.232.

63 Gayatri Chakravorty Spivbak, 'Can the Subaltern Speak?', op. cit.

64 Roland Bleiker, *Aesthetics and World Politics*, London, Palgrave, forthcoming 2009.

65 Roger Mac Ginty, 'Indigenous Peace-Making versus the Liberal Peace', *Cooperation and Conflict*, vol.43, no.2, 2008, pp.139–63.

66 Vivienne Jabri, 'Michel Foucault's Analytics of War', in *International Political Sociology*, vol.1, 2007, p.68.

67 Christine Sylvester, 'Empathetic Cooperation: A Feminist Method for IR', *Millennium*, vol.23, no.2, 1994, pp.315–34.

68 David Mosse, *Cultivating Development*, London: Pluto Press, 2005, pp.1–20.

69 Beatrice Pouligny, *Peace Operations See From Below*, London: Hurst, 2006.

70 Lisa Smirl, 'Building the Other, Constructing Ourselves: Spatial Dimensions of International Humanitarian Response', *International Political Sociology*, vol.2, pp.236–53.

71 Robin Luckham, 'Introduction: Transforming Security and Development in and Unequal World', *IDS Bulletin*, vol.40, no.2, March, 2009, p.3.

72 Jonathan Spencer, Jonathan Spencer, Anthropology, Politics, and the State, Cambridge University Press, 2008.

73 James C. Scott, *Weapons of the Weak: Everyday Peasant Resistance*, Yale UO, 1985.

74 Mark Mazower, *Inside Hitler's Greece, 1941 – 1945*, Yale University Press, 2001.

75 Alberto Melucci, 'Social Movements and the Democratisation of Everyday Life', in John Keane, (ed.), *Civil Society and the State*, London: Verso, pp.245–60.

76 Andreas Antoniades shows how many of its proponents see the everyday entering history, modernity, and opposed by bipolitics. Andreas Antoniades, 'Cave! Hic Everyday Life: Repetition, Hegemony and the Social', *British Journal of Politics and International Relations*, vol.10, no.3, 2008, pp. 412–28.

77 Ibid., p.416.

78 Ibid., p.424.

79 'Report of the Secretary-General's High Level Panel on Threats, Challenges, and Change', *United Nations*, 2004: Boutros Boutros Ghali, *An Agenda For Peace: preventative diplomacy, peacemaking and peacekeeping*, New York: United Nations, 1992; 'The Responsibility to Protect', *International Commission on Intervention and State Sovereignty*, December 2001.

80 Michel de Certeau, op. cit., p.xi: Sadie Plant, *The Most Radical Gesture*, London: Routledge, 1992, p.157–158.

81 Michel de Certeau, op. cit., Chapter II.

82 Ibid., Chapter II.

83 Ibid., p.48.

84 Again, I am indebted to Kristoffer Liden for the connection between post-colonial theory and peacebuilding.

85 Homi Bhabha, op. cit.

86 Ibid., pp.35–7.

87 Ibid., p.159 and p.163.

88 Ibid., p.245.

89 See for example, Ilan Kapoor, 'Capitalism, culture, agency: dependency versus postcolonial theory', *Third World Quarterly*, vol.23, no.4, 2002, pp.647–64.

90 Homi Bhabha, op. cit., p.274.

91 William Connolly, *Identity/Difference*, Minneapolis: Minnesota University Press, 1991, esp. conclusion.

92 As argued by Homi Bhabha, op. cit., p.56. Bhaba refers to ideological 'fixity' as a sign of colonialism, ibid., p.94 and p.101.

93   Ilan Kapoor, 'Capitalism, culture, agency: dependency versus post-colonial theory', op. cit., p.661.

94   Ilan Kapoor, 'Acting in a Tight Spot: Homi Bhabha's Post-Colonial Politics', op. cit., p.563.

95   Homi Bhabha, op. cit., p.33. This ambivalence has been widely criticised. Some have argued that material issues have been neglected by post-colonial scholars, and others have argued that their own transnational life-styles are reflected in their work, rather than the subaltern.

96   Homi Bhabha, ibid., p.49.

97   Wanda Vrasti, 'The Strange Case of Ethnography and International Relations', *Millennium – Journal of International Studies*, vol.37, no.2, 2008, pp.279–301.

98   Ibid, p.283.

99   Pierre Bourdieu, *Outline of a Theory of Practice*, Cambridge University Press, 1977: James C. Scott, op. cit.

100 Wanda Vrasti, op. cit., p.295.

101 Edward Newman and Oliver P. Richmond, *The United Nations and Human Security*, London: Palgrave 2001.

102 For conflicting views, see Roland Paris, '*Human Security: Paradigm Shift or Hot Air?*', *International Security*, vol.26, no.2, Fall 2001, pp. 87–102: Sharbanou Tadjbaksh, 'Human Security: Concepts and Implications', Les Etudes du CERI, no.117–118, September 2005.

103 Oliver P. Richmond, 'Emancipatory Forms of Human Security and Liberal Peacebuilding', *International Journal*, vol.62, no.3, 2007, pp.458–77.

104 For a similar argument see Endre Begby and J. Peter Burgess, *Human Security and Liberal Peace, Public Reason*, vol.1, no.1, 2009, pp.91–104.

105 Phillip Cerny, 'Some Pitfalls of Democratisation in a Globalising World', *Millennium*, vol.37, no.3, 2009, pp.767–90.

106 David Held, 'Democracy and Globalisation', *Global Governance*, vol.3, no.3, 1997, pp.251–67.

107 Mark Chou and Roland Bleiker, 'The Symbiosis of Democracy and Tragedy: Lost Lessons from Ancient Greece', *Millennium*, vol.37, no.3, 2009, pp.659–82.

108 Claudia Aradau and Jeff Huysmans, Mobilising Global Democracy, *Millennium*, vol.37, 2009, no.3, 2009, pp.583–604.

109 Cited in Saul Newman, 'Connolly's Democratic Pluralism and the Question of State Sovereignty', *British Journal of Politics and International Relations*, vol.10, 2007, pp.227–40.

110 Chou and Bleiker, op. cit., p.662.

111 Alexis De Tocqueville, *Democracy in America*, Vintage Books, 1945.

112 William Connolly, op. cit., pp.123–7; Chantal Mouffe, *The Democratic Paradox*, London: Verson, 2000:
     J Habermas, *The Inclusion of the Other*, Cambridge, MA: MIT Press, 1998.

113 Saul Newman, 'Connolly's Democratic Pluralism and the Question of State Sovereignty', op. cit., p.228.

114 See John Keane and Paul Mier, 'New Perspectives on Social Movements: An interview with Alberto Melucci', in Alberto Melucci (John Keane and Paul Mier [eds.]), Nomads of the Present: Social Movements and Individual Needs in Contemporary Society, Temple University Press, 1989,, p.196.

115 Ibid., p.197.

116 Volker Boege, M. Anne Brown, Kevin P. Clements, and Anna Nolan, 'States Emerging from Hybrid Political Orders – Pacific Experiences', op. cit., p.4.

117 See for example, J.C. Scott, op. cit.

118 J.C. Scott, *The Art of Not Being Governed*, New Haven: Yale University Press, 2009, p.x, p.7.

119 Ibid., p.20.

120   Michael Randle, op. cit., p.xvi.
121   Thanks to Necati Polat for pointing out this issue to me. See Hubert Dreyfus, 'Heidegger and Foucault on the Subject, Agency and Practices', http://ist-socrates. berkeley.edu/~hdreyfus/html/paper_heidandfoucault.html
122   For a fascinating discussion of these aspects of Foucault's development, see Roland Bleiker, 'Discourse and Human Agency', *Contemporary Political Theory*, vol.2, 2003, p.29.
123   Michel Foucault, '*What is an Author?*', Donald F. Bouchard and Sherry Simon (trans.), *Language, Counter-Memory, Practice*. Ithaca, New York: Cornell University Press, 1977, pp.124–7.
124   Hubert Dreyfus, op. cit., p.1.
125   Ibid., p.23.
126   Michel Foucault, *The Birth of Biopolitics: Lectures at the College de France*, 1978–79 Palgrave Macmillan, 2008.
127   See Carol Gilligan, *In a Different Voice*, Cambridge, M.A.: Harvard University Press, 1993.
128   See for example a range of work that reach 'beyond Westphalia' and for what Linklater called, a post-conventional morality. Andrew Linklater, op. cit.: Gene M. Lyons and Michael Mastunduno, *Beyond Westphalia*, Johns Hopkins UP, 1995.
129   See among other, my Transformation of Peace, op. cit., esp. conclusion: Laurent Goetshel, and Tobias Hagmann, 'Civilian Peacebuilding: Peace by Bureaucratic Means', *Conflict, Security, and Development*, vol.9, no.1, pp.55–73.
130   See among others, John Comaroff and Jean Comaroff, *Civil Society and Political Imagination in Africa*, University of Chicago Press, 1999; David Ucko, 'Militias, tribes, and insurgents: The Challenge of Political Reintergration in Iraq', *Conflict, Security and Development*, vol.8, no.3, 2008, pp.341–73; Susanne Schmeidl (with Masood Karokhail), 'Prêt-a-Porter States': How the McDonaldization of State-Building Misses the Mark in Afghanistan', Martina Fischer and Beatrix Schmelzle (eds), *Peace in the Absence of States: Challenging the Discourse on State Failure*, Berghof Handbook for Conflict Transformation Dialogue Series Issue no.8, 2009; Volker Boege, M. Anne Brown, Kevin P. Clements, and Anna Nolan, 'States Emerging from Hybrid Political Orders – Pacific Experiences', *The Australian Centre for Peace and Conflict Studies (ACPACS) Occasional Papers Series*, 2008.
131   *Field Notes*, Guatemala, July 2010.
132   R.B.J. Walker, *in discussion*, Victoria, Canada, 14 July 2008.
133   Ibid., p.118.
134   Oliver P. Richmond, 'Eirenism and a Post-Liberal Peace', op. cit.
135   Gene M. Lyons and Michael Mastunduno, Beyond Westphalia, op. cit.
136   William E. Connolly, op. cit., esp. conclusion.
137   Andrew Linklater, The Transformation of Political Community, op. cit
138   David Held, *Global Covenant*, Cambridge: Polity, 2004, p.3.
139   Homi Bhabha, *The Location of Culture*, op. cit.: Gayatri Chakravorty Spivbak, 'Can the Subaltern Speak?', op. cit
140   Claudia Aradau, 'Security and the Democratic Scene: desecuritization and emancipation', *Journal of IR and Development*, vol.7, 2004, pp.388–413.
141   Patrick Chabal and Jean-Pascal Daloz, *Culture Troubles*, London: Hurst, 2006, p.125, p.149 and p.173.
142   See for example, Barry Hindess, 'Not at Home in the Empire', *Social Identities*, vol.3, no.3, 2001; See also Spivak, op. cit.; Bhabha, op. cit.
143   Amitav Acharya and Barry Buzan, 'Why there is no non-Western international relations theory?, *International Relations of the Pacific*, vol.7, 2007, pp.287–312; Giorgio Shani, 'Towards a Post-Western IR', *International Studies Review*, vol.10, 2008, pp.722–34: Pinar Bilgin, 'Thinking past 'Western' IR?', *Third World Quarterly*, vol.29, no.1, 2008, pp.5–23.

144   Julian Eckl, op. cit.: Christine Sylvester, 'Bare Life as Development/Post-Colonial Problematic', *The Geographical Journal*, vol.172, no.1, 2006, pp.66–77: Christine Sylvester, 'Whither the International At the End of IR', *Millennium*, vol.35, no.3, 2007, pp.551–71; Nordstrom, Carolyn, *Shadows of War*, University of California Press, 2004.

145   Julian Eckl, op. cit., p.186.

146   Benedict Anderson, *Imagined Communities*, London: Verso, [1983] 2006, p.6–7

147   See for example, John Rawls, *Law of Peoples*, Harvard UP, 2001: John, Political Liberalism, New York: Columbia University Press, 1993.

148   David Mosse, and David Lewis (eds.), *The Aid Effect: Giving and Governing in International Development*. London: Pluto Press, 2005.

149   Jack Donnelly, 'The Relative Universality of Human Rights', *Human Rights Quarterly*, vol.29, May 2007, pp.281–306.

150   Richard Sandbrook, Marc Edelman, Patrick Heller, and Judith Teichman, *Social Democracy in the Global Periphery*, CUP, 2007.

151   Eric Herring, 'Neoliberalism Versus Peacebuilding in Iraq', M. Pugh, R.N. Cooper, and M. Turner (eds.), *Whose Peace?*, London: Palgrave, 2008.

152   For an interesting discussion, see Andrew Linklater, 'Dialogic Politics and the Civilising Process', op. cit., p.141–2.

153   Zaki Laidi, *The Great Disruption*, Cambridge: Polity Press, 2007 [2004], p.22.

154   Jonathan Spencer, op. cit., p.167 and p.181.

155   See James C. Scott, *Domination and the Arts of Resistance*, Yale University Press, 1990, p.xxii.

156   Ibid., p.41.

157   Ibid., p.72 and p.103.

158   Michel Foucault, cited in James C. Scott, op. cit., p.x. and ibid., p.29.

159   Rosemary E. Shinko, 'Agonistic Peace: A Postmodern Reading', *Millennium – Journal of International Studies*, vol.36, no.3, 2008 pp. 473–91.

160   James C. Scott, op. cit., p.301.

161   Michel Foucault, '*What is an Author?*', op. cit.

162   Hubert Dreyfus, op. cit., p.19.

163   This has certainly been very apparent in many of the field sites I have worked in myself over the years.

164   Vivienne Jabri, War *and the Transformation of Global Politics*, London: Palgrave, 2007, p.154. Jabri describes the politics of peace as local and rather invisible expressions of solidarity.

165   These categories draw on Sharp's work on non-violent resistance. See Gene Sharp, *Politics of Non-Violent Action*, Porter Sargent: Boston, 1973, p.705–776

166   Linklater, op. cit., p.154: William Connolly, *Identity/Difference*, op. cit., p.218.

167   Benedict Anderson, op. cit.

168   Patrick Chabal and Jean-Pascal Daloz, *Culture Troubles*, Chicago: Chicago University Press, 2006, p.327.

169   See my *Transformation of Peace*, op. cit.

170   See for a discussion of how Derrida develops such a position, Saul Newman, 'Derrida's Deconstruction of Authority', *Philosophy and Social Criticism*, vol.27, no.3, p.16.

171   S. Benhabib, *Situating the Self*, Cambridge: Polity, 1993.

172   Gayatri Chakravorty Spivbak, 'Can the Subaltern Speak?', op. cit., p.104.

173   I borrow this term from Scott. James C. Scott, *Domination and the Arts of Resistance*, op. cit., pp.183–4

174   Here I note Pinar Bilgin's argument that even mimicry can disguise subtle forms of agency. Pinar Bilgin, 'Thinking Past Western IR', *Third World Quarterly, vol.29, no.1, p.6.*

175 Frantz Fanon, *The Wretched of the Earth*, London: Penguin, 1967 [1963], p.147.

6 De-romanticising the local, de-mystifying the international: aspects of the local-liberal hybrid

1 J.S. Mill, On Liberty, p.87 in J.S., Mill: *Three Essays: On Liberty, Representative Government and The Subjection of Women*, Oxford: Oxford University Press. 1981, p.381.

2 Here I note Pinar Bilgin's argument that even mimicry can disguise subtle forms of agency and that it is problematic to draw lines between the West and non-West, liberal and non-liberal. Pinar Bilgin, 'Thinking Past Western IR', *Third World Quarterly, vol.29, no.1, 2008, pp.5–23.*

3 Confidential Sources, *Focus Group*, DPKO, UN, New York, 7 June, 2010.

4 Pinar Bilgin, op. cit., p.14.

5 Patrick Chabal and Jean-Pascal Daloz, *Culture Troubles*, London: Hurst, 2006, p.125 and p.149.

6 Ibid., p.173.

7 Action Aid Australia/Austcare, Deborah Leaver in *Discussion Group*, Sydney, 27 October 2009: R. Mac Ginty, 'Indigenous peacemaking versus the liberal peace', Cooperation and Conflict, vol.43, no.2, June 2008, pp.139–63.

8 UN Draft Declaration on the Rights of Indigenous Peoples, E/CN.4/SUB.2/1994/2/ Add.1:1994: UNITED NATIONS DECLARATION ON THE RIGHTS OF INDIGENOUS PEOPLES, Adopted by the General Assembly 13 September 2007.

9 Australian Aid, Identity Withheld, *Personal Interview.*

10 See James C. Scott, *Domination and the Arts of Resistance*, Yale University Press, 1990, pp.183–4

11 Homi Bhabha, *The Location of Culture*, London: Routledge, 1994, p.330.

12 Comaroff, J, and Comaroff, J, *Civil Society and Political Imagination in Africa*, University of Chicago Press, 1999, pp.4–7.

13 Peter Ackerman and Jack Duvall, *A Force More Powerful*, New York: Palgrave, 2000, p.4.

14 Volker Boege, M. Anne Brown, Kevin P. Clements, and Anna Nolan, 'States Emerging from Hybrid Political Orders – Pacific Experiences', *The Australian Centre for Peace and Conflict Studies (ACPACS) Occasional Papers Series*, 2008, p.5.

15 Henry David Thoreau, *On the Duty of Civil Disobedience*, New York: Signet, 1980 [1849], p.225.

16 See for example, Roland Paris, *At War's End*, Cambridge University Press, 2004. For a critique see my *Liberal Peace Transitions*, Edinburgh, Edinburgh University Press, 2009.

17 Boege *et al.*, op. cit., p.4.

18 Ibid., p.4.

19 Ibid., p.5.

20 Ibid., p.5.

21 Chandra Sriram, *Peace as Governance*, London: Palgrave, 2008.

22 Kristoffer Tarp, *Personal Interview*, Peacebuilding Support Office, UN, New York, 4 June 2010.

23 John Hummel, The Carter Centre, *Personal Interview*, Monrovia, 18 November 2009.

24 Carolina Enriquez Garcia, Coinde, *Personal Interview*, Guatemala City, 21 July 2010.

25 For example, see George Williams, *Personal Interview*, Democracy Watch, Monrovia, 19 November, 2009: Traditional Council, *Focus Group*, Monrovia, 25 November 2009; Carlton Cadeado, Personal Interview, Higher Institute, Maputo, 8 January 2010; *Focus Group*, Independent Peacebuilding Organisations, Ministry of Culture, Maputo, 10 January 2010: Confidential Source, *Personal Interview*, NEPRU, Windhoek, 14 January 2010; Phil YA Nangoloh, Executive Director, National Society for Human Rights, *Personal Interview*, Windhoek, 16 January 2010.

26 Bonaventura Zita, *Personal Interview*, Co-ordinator of 'Turning Swords into Ploughshares Project', Christian Council of Churches, 12 January 2010.

27 Bonaventura Zita, *Personal Interview*, op. cit.

28 Confidential Sources, Personal Interview, NEPRU, Windhoek, 15 January 2010.

29 Carlton Cadeado, Personal Interview, op cit.

30 Ibid.

31 Pat Johnson, *Local vs. National Peacebuilding: The Richness of Somali Peacemaking*, www.prio.no/peaceethics/PeacE-Discussions, 2010, p.1.

32 Ibid, p.2.

33 Ibid, p.2.

34 Ibid, pp.3–4.

35 Cleophas Toroi and Ismail Dodoo, *Personal Interviews*, UNDP, Monrovia, 21 November 2009.

36 David Ucko, 'Militias, tribes, and insurgents: The Challenge of Political Reintergration in Iraq', *Conflict, Security and Development*, vol.8, no.3, 2008, pp.341–73.

37 Ibid., p.365.

38 Ibid., p.366.

39 Susanne Schmeidl (with Masood Karokhail), 'Prêt-a-Porter States': How the McDonaldization of State-Building Misses the Mark in Afghanistan', Martina Fischer and Beatrix Schmelzle (eds.), *Peace in the Absence of States: Challenging the Discourse on State Failure*, Berghof Handbook for Conflict Transformation Dialogue Series Issue no.8, 2009.

40 See, for example, a series of articles written by Paddy Ashdown in the UK press in which he, somewhat ironically given his role as OHR in Bosnia Herzegovina, calls for the alignment of the modern state with customary governance, arguing this would be a simple and effective way of bringing peace. Paddy Ashdown, 'Afghanistan could be lost in the bars of Britain', *The Times*, 5th November, 2009.

41 Susanne Schmeidl, op. cit., p.70.

42 Ibid., p.71.

43 Laurent Goetshel and Tobias Hagmann, 'Civilian Peacebuilding: Peace by Bureaucratic Means', *Conflict, Security, and Development*, vol.9, no.1, 2009, pp.55–73.

44 Oliver P. Richmond and Jason Franks, 'Between Partition and Pluralism: The Bosnia Jigsaw and an 'Ambivalent Peace'' Journal of Southeast Europe and Black Sea Studies, vol.9, no.1, 2009.

45 See for example, Susan L. Woodward, 'A case of shifting focus: some lessons from the Balkans' in Martina Fischer and Beatrice Schmiezle, *Building Peace in the Absence of States*, op. cit., pp.47–56.

46 Numerous references to this abound in my field notes from a number of different visits over the years.

47 Boege *et al.*, op. cit., p.10.

48 Ibid., p.12.

49 This chapter will not deal with the formal attempts at statebuilding in either of these two cases. This topic has been dealt with at length elsewhere. See in particular, Clive Moore, 'External Intervention: The Solomon Islands Beyond Ramsi' in Anne Brown (ed.), *Security and Development in the Pacific Islands*, Boulder: Lynne Rienner, 2007 pp.169–196; Astri Suhrke, 'Peacekeepers as Nation-builders: Dilemmas of the UN in East Timor', *International Peacekeeping*, vol.8, no.4, 2001, pp.1–20; Ian Martin and Alexander Mayer-Rieckh, 'The United Nations and East Timor: From Self-determination to State-building', *International Peacekeeping*, vol.12, no.1, spring 2005, pp.104–20.

50 Jarat Chopra, 'Building State-Failure in East Timor', *Development and Change*, vol.33, no.5, 2002, pp.979–1000.

51 Arkanso De Silva, *Personal Interview*, GTZ, 5 November 2008.

52 Gunther Kohl, GTZ Director, *Personal Interview*, 5 November 2008.

53 Pat Walsh, *Personal Interview*, CAVR, Dili, 6 November 2008.

54 Referring to the 2007 'Living Standards Survey' and the 2004 Census. Rui A. Gomes, *Personal Interview*, UNDP, 5 November, 2008. 46 per cent of the population are 'food insecure'.

55 In 2004, World Bank personnel told me that these would reach $77m for that year, not allowing them to engage with public service or welfare support to a significant extent. During my latest field visit in 2008 it was clear that the picture had significantly changed. Chinese development engagement had also begun by this point.

56 Antonio S. Franco, *Personal Interview*, World Bank, Dili, 6 November 2008.

57 Ibid.,

58 This had not been raised as an issue however, according to local staff who pointed out that security was high for the HQ but not for field staff. USAID, Name withheld, *Personal Interview*, Dili, 5 November 2008. Despite the shift in World Bank policy towards a more 'Keynesian' approach, its security had been tightened since my last meetings there in 2004.

59 Ibid.

60 Michael Page, *Personal Interview*, UNMIT, Dili, 5 November 2008.

61 *Group Discussion* with staff at La'o Hamutuk, Dili, 4 November 2008.

62 Arkanso De Silva, op. cit.

63 See in particular USAID, *Personal Interview*, op. cit.

64 *Group Discussion* with staff at La'o Hamutuk, ibid.

65 Confidential Source, UNDP, *Personal Interview*, 6 November 2008.

66 Pat Walsh, *Personal Interview*, CAVR, Dili, 6 November 2008.

67 See my 'Co-opting the Liberal Peace: Untying the Gordian Knot in Kosovo' (with Jason Franks), *Cooperation and Conflict*, vol.43, no.1, 2008.

68 This was the case during fieldwork I conducted there in 2004 and remains so.

69 Rui Gomes, *Personal Interview*, op. cit:

70 UN Police, Confidential Source, *Personal Interview*, Dili, 3 November 2008: Confidential Source, UNDP, op. cit.

71 Confidential Source, *Personal Interview*, Dili, 4 November 2008.

72 *Law on Community Authorities*, N.5/2004: *Law on the Election of Suco Chiefs and Councils*, no.2/2004.

73 Francesco De Silva, *Personal Interview*, District Administrator and Village Elder, Viqueque, 8 November 2008.

74 Anne Brown, 'Towards Effective and Legitimate Governance' *ACPAC East Timor Report: Brisbane*, 2008, p.ii.

75 Jose Trindade, 'Rethinking Timorese Identity as a Peacebuilding Strategy', *EU/GTZ and EU Rapid Reaction Mechanism*, Dili, 6 June 2007, p.2.

76 Action Aid Australia/Austcare, op. cit.

77 Arkanso De Silva, op. cit.

78 Jose Trindade, op. cit., p.8.

79 Ibid., p.20.

80 Ibid., p.17.

81 Ibid., p.25.

82 Ibid., p.14.

83 Ibid., p.27.

84 Ibid., p.33.

85 Ibid., p.15 and p.17. *RDTL Constitution*, Section 59, 5. This refers to 'cultural enjoyment' and heritage.

86 Ibid., p.18.

87 Anne Brown, op. cit., p.ii.

88 Lisa Palmer and Demetrio do Amaral de Carvalho, 'Nation building and resource management: The politics of nature in Timor Leste', *Geoforum*, vol.39, 2008, pp.1321–32.

89   Many villages have mediation panels dispensing traditional forms of justice, but which also make villagers aware of the modern justice system that is slowly coming into being. Gunther Kohl, *Personal Interview*, op. cit.

90   Interview cited in Jose Trindade, op. cit., p.28.

91   Lisa Palmer and Demetrio do Amaral de Carvalho, op. cit., p.1324. and p.1331.

92   See for example, Damian Grenfell, 'Making Modernity in Timor-Leste', *Arena*, no.90, 2007, pp.9–12.

93   Jose Trindade, op. cit., p.24.

94   Country Representative, *Personal Interview*, World Bank, Dili, November 2008.

95   Ministry of Social Solidarity, *Community Dialogue in Suco Bahalara-ua'* in Press Release, 5 March 2009.

96   Andrew McWilliam, 'Houses of Resistance in East Timor: Structuring of Sociality in the New National', *Anthropological Forum*, vol.15, no.1, 2005, pp.27–44.

97   Ibid., p.34.

98   Andrew McWilliam, ibid., p.28.

99   Ibid., p.28.

100 Ibid.

101 Ibid., p.38.

102 Ibid., p.39.

103 See *Field Notes*, November 2004 and November 2008.

104 Ibid., p.39.

105 Ibid., p.40.

106 Ibid., p.40.

107 District Suco Commissioner, *Personal Interview*, Viquerque, November 2008.

108 GTZ Personnel, *Personal Interview*, Dili, November 2008.

109 Ibid., p.40.

110 Jose Trindade, op. cit., p.37.

111 Pat Walsh, Personal Interview, op. cit.

112 See my interviews and fieldnotes from 2004. See also Oliver P Richmond and Jason Franks, 'The Emperors' New Clothes? Liberal Peace in East Timor', (with Jason Franks), *International Peacekeeping*, vol.15, no.2, 2008, pp.185–200.

113 Pat Walsh, *Personal Interview*, op. cit.

114 'Poverty Reduction Strategy Paper', *IMF Country Report no.05/247*, Washington, July 2005, p.xvii.

115 Ibid., p.xvi.

116 Ibid., p.4. and p.11.

117 Ibid., pp.5–6 and p.8.

118 Country Director, *Personal Interview*, World Bank, Dili, 6 November 2008.

119 During my fieldwork I was at the District Commission in Viquerque and saw the queues of people waiting patiently for the first-ever payment. They looked anxious, and I was told this was because they perhaps did not really believe the money would arrive. *Field Notes*, 8 November 08.

120 Arkanso De Silva, op. cit.

121 Rui Gomes, *Personal Interview*, op. cit: Gunther Kohl, *Personal Interview*, op. cit.

122 Confidential Source, *Personal Interview*, Dili, 6 November, 2008.

123 Office of the Prime Minister, *On the Road to Peace and Prosperity*, Dili, 2010.

124 Anne Brown, op. cit., p.i.

125 Ibid., p.iii. and p.23.

126 Ibid., p.4.

127 Elsina Wainwright, 'Our Failing Neighbour?' Canberra: Australian Strategic Policy Institute, 2003.

128 *Focus Group Discussion* at Ministry for Reconciliation, op. cit. Complicating matters are the existing of British Colonial era land laws.

129 Clive Moore, op. cit., p.169.

130   Homi Bhabha. op. cit.
131   Mataiasi Lomaloma, *Personal Interview*, Special Coordinator, RAMSI, Honiara, 26 November 2008.
132   See *Focus Group Discussion* at Ministry for Peace and Reconciliation, including Father Philip Vanlusa, Betty Luvsia, and Andrew Adams, Honiara, 25 November 2008. Initially, it aimed at replacing the government even though the Australian government wanted a consent-based operation. Mary Louise O'Callaghan, *Personal Interview*, Public Affairs Unit, RAMSI, Honiara, 28 November 2008.
133   See the RAMSI website: http://www.ramsi.org
134   See ibid. for 'RAMSI Triumvirate Organisational Chart' Of course the word 'triumvirate' betrays a certain mindset, which undermines its apparent sensitivity.
135   Tom Woods, *Personal Interview*, Advisor, Constitutional Reform Unit, 26 November 2008.
136   This was a common theme reiterated amongst many of my local interviewees. See *Field Notes*, November 2008.
137   *Focus Group Discussion* at Ministry for Reconciliation, op. cit.
138   Confidential Source, *Personal Interview*, Ministry for Peace and Reconciliation, Honiara, 28 November 2008.
139   Ibid.
140   Chiefs' Meeting, *Focus Group*, Ministry of Peace and Reconciliation, Honiara, 4 December 2009.
141   *Focus Group* discussion with Malaita Group, Ministry of Peace and Reconciliation, Honiara, 29 November 2008.
142   *Focus Group Discussion* at RAMSI, 26 November 2009.
143   Clive Moore, op. cit., p.170.
144   Ibid., p.181.
145   Joy Fkere, *Personal Interview*, Ministry of Peace and Reconciliation, Honiara, 24 November 2008.
146   *Focus Group Discussion* at Ministry for Reconciliation, op. cit.
147   Ibid.
148   Many islanders do not know the welfare state or social democracy exists. ibid.
149   Paul Touva, *Personal Interview*, Ministry of Peace and Reconciliation, Honiara, 1 December 2008.
150   Ibid.
151   Ibid.
152   Tom Woods, *Personal Interview*, op. cit.
153   Clive Moore, *Personal Interview*, University of Queensland, Brisbane, 11 November 2008.
154   *Focus Group Discussion* at Ministry for Peace and Reconciliation, op. cit.
155   A common view was that a lease system might work better than the current modern neoliberal ownership system, but there are so many layers of land ownership that this would be very hard to negotiate, though less damaging that what is effectively a contemporary system of appropriation.
156   Ibid.
157   *Focus Group Discussion* at Ministry for Peace and Reconciliation, op. cit.
158   Ibid.
159   Ibid.
160   Joy Fkere, *Personal Interview*, op. cit.
161   See *Field Notes*, November 2008.
162   *Focus Group Discussion* at Ministry for Peace and Reconciliation, op. cit.
163   Anne Brown, 'Conflict and Resilience in the Pacific Islands Regon', in Anne Brown, (ed.), *Security and Development in the Pacific Islands: Social Resilience in Emerging States*, Boulder, Colorado: Lynne Rienner, pp.1–31.
164   Ibid., p.10.

165 *Focus Group Discussion* at Ministry for Reconciliation, op. cit.
166 One facilitator of this particular meeting asked me not to refer to democracy etc., in the discussion as 'the chiefs may not understand'. This was not the case, even if they had concerns about how such institutions or concepts would impact on their own positions. Chiefs' Meeting, op. cit.
167 Ibid.
168 *Focus Group Discussion* at Ministry for Reconciliation, op. cit.
169 Joy Fkere, *Personal Interview*, op. cit. It is also important to note that there is not just one but several Solomon Island contexts, in which different and complex forms of governance occur, from a chief to a matrilineal system, and that these remain the first point of contact for most individuals.
170 Alex Lokopio, *Personal Interview*, Ministry for Peace and Reconciliation, 2 December 2009: Chiefs' Meeting, op. cit.
171 Chiefs' Meeting, op. cit.
172 *Focus Group Discussion* at Ministry for Reconciliation, op. cit.
173 Boege *et al.*, op. cit., p.15.
174 Clive Moore, op. cit., p.189.
175 Francis Fukuyama, 'Statebuilding in the Solomon Islands', *Unpublished Paper*, July 9 2008.
176 Ibid., p.1.
177 Singh Mehta, Uday, *Liberalism and Empire*, Chicago University Press, 1999.
178 Morgan Brigg, *Wantokism and Statebuilding the Solomon Islands*, Unpublished Paper, 2009.
179 See Morgan Brigg, 'Wantokism and State Building in the Solomon Islands: A response to Fukuyama.' *Pacific Economic Bulletin*, vol.24, no.3, 2009, pp.148–61.
180 Chiefs' Meeting, op. cit.
181 RAMSI official, *Personal Interview*, Honiara, December 2008.
182 *Personal Interviews*, Constitutional Team, Honiara, December 2008.
183 *Focus Group* discussion with Malaita Group, Ministry of Peace and Reconciliation, op. cit.
184 Francis Fukuyama, op. cit. This report was later published as 'State-Building in Solomon Islands,' *Pacific Economic Bulletin* 23, no.3, 2008.
185 Stephen Krasner, 'Sharing sovereignty: new institutions for collapsed and failing states', *International security*, vol.29, no.2, 2004, pp.85–120.
186 Tom Woods, 'Informal Political System of Government in Solomon Islands', *Working Paper for the Constitutional Congress and the Eminent Persons Advisory Committee*, Honiara, 28 August 2008.
187 Ibid., p.8.
188 Ibid., p.10.
189 Tom Woods, *Personal Interview*, op. cit. This is often carried out in a customary manner, using 'red money' (custom money).
190 Ibid., p17.
191 Tom Woods, *Personal Interview*, op. cit.
192 Ibid.
193 Chiefs' Meeting, op. cit.
194 Chiefs' Meeting, op. cit.
195 Clive Moore, 'External Intervention: The Solomon Islands Beyond Ramsi', in Anne Brown, *Security and Development in the Pacific Islands*, op. cit., p.191.
196 Clive Moore, Personal Interview, op. cit.
197 Volker Boege, M. Anne Brown, Kevin P. Clements, and Anna Nolan, op. cit.
198 Clive Moore, op. cit., p.193.
199 *Focus Group Discussion* at Ministry for Reconciliation, op. cit.
200 Deborah J Yashar, *Contesting Citizenship in Latin America: The Rise of Indigenous Movements and the Post-Liberal Challenge*, Cambridge: Cambridge University Press, 2005, p.5.

201 *Focus Group Discussion* at Ministry for Reconciliation, op. cit.
202 Schmeidl, op. cit, p.71.
203 Volker Boege, M. Anne Brown, Kevin P. Clements, and Anna Nolan, op. cit., 26–7.
204 Ibid., p.31.
205 See also Rod Nixon, op. cit., pp.91–2.

Conclusion

1 Thanks to Roland Bleiker, Rob Walker, Roger MacGinty, and Audra Mitchell, for their contributions to this conclusion at various formative stages.
2 Michel de Certeau, *The Practice of Everyday Life*, Berkeley: University of California Press, 1984.
3 Bill Ashcroft (ed.), *Writing Past Colonialism: On Post-Colonial Futures*, London: Continuum, 2001, p.6.
4 Michel Foucault, *The Will to Knowledge*, London: Penguin, 1978, pp.94–5.
5 Confidential Sources, *Focus Group*, Human Security Unit, UN, New York, 4 June 2010.
6 For an excellent discussion of these dynamics in Latin America, see Deborah J. Yashar, *Contesting Citizenship in Latin America: The Rise of Indigenous Movements and the Post-Liberal Challenge*, Cambridge: Cambridge University Press, 2005.
7 Deborah J. Yashar, ibid., p.66.
8 See for example, Confidential Sources, *Human Security Unit*, UN, New York, 4 June 2010.
9 Ibid., p.298.
10 Carolina Enriquez Garcia, *Personal Interview*, Coinde, Guatemala City, 21 July 2010.
11 "Kosovanisation in action", *Quarterly Information Sheet*, Ombudsperson Institution In Kosovo, January–March 2006, http://www.ombudspersonkosovo.org/repository/docs/Informator09_final.pdf: Xanana Gusmão, 'Compatriots! Timorese!', *New Year's Message*, President of the CNRT/CN, Dili, 31 December 2000, http://members.pcug.org.au/~wildwood/JanNewYear.htm; Aljazeera, Is 'Afghanisation' possible? January 29, 2010, http://english.aljazeera.net/programmes/inside-story/2010/01/2010128132220903967.html.
12 See for more on some of these cases, Oliver P. Richmond and Jason Franks, *Liberal Peace Transitions*, Edinburgh: Edinburgh University Press, 2009. See also, Oliver P. Richmond, 'Resistance and the Post-Liberal Peace', *Millennium*, vol.38, no.3, 2010, pp.665–92.
13 Oliver P. Richmond and Jason Franks, 'Liberal Hubris: Virtual Peace in Cambodia', *Security Dialogue*, vol.38, no.1, 2007, pp.27–48.
14 Jason Franks and Oliver P. Richmond, 'Co-opting the Liberal Peace: Untying the Gordian Knot in Kosovo', *Cooperation and Conflict*, vol.43, no.1, 2008, pp.81–103.
15 Volker Boege, M. Anne Brown, Kevin P. Clements, and Anna Nolan, 'States Emerging from Hybrid Political Orders – Pacific Experiences', *The Australian Centre for Peace and Conflict Studies (ACPACS) Occasional Papers Series*, 2008, p.5; Tom Woods, 'Informal Political System of Government in Solomon Islands', *Working Paper for the Constitutional Congress and the Eminent Persons Advisory Committee*, Honiara, 28 August 2008; Traditional Council, *Focus Group*, Monrovia, 25 November, 2009; John Hummel, Carter Center, *Personal Interview*, Monrovia: 18 November 2009.
16 Pat Johnson, 'Local vs. National Peacebuilding: The Richness of Somali Peacemaking', Peace Ethics, 2010, http://www.prio.no/Peaceethics/PeacE-Discussions/
17 Astri Suhrkhe, 'The dangers of a tight embrace: Externally assisted statebuilding in Afghanistan' in Roland Paris and Timothy D. Sisk (eds), *The Dilemmas of Statebuilding. Confronting the contradictions of postwar peace operations*, London: Routledge, 2009.
18 David Ucko, 'Militias, tribes, and insurgents: The Challenge of Political Reintergration in Iraq', *Conflict, Security and Development*, vol.8, no.3, 2008, pp.341–73.
19 Dipesh Chakrabarty, *Provincialising Europe*, Princeton University Press, 2000, p.72.

20 Ibid., p.254.

21 See Alain Badiou, *Metapolitics*, London: Verso, 2005.

22 Bhikhu, Parekh, *Gandhi's Political Philosophy*, Basingstoke: Macmillan, 1989, p.112.

23 Oliver P. Richmond, 'UN Peace Operations and the Dilemmas of the Peacebuilding Consensus', in *International Peacekeeping*, vol.11, no.1, 2004, pp.83–101.

24 See for example, James C Scott, *The Art of Not Being Governed*, New Haven: Yale University Press, 2009, p.7.

25 Beatrice Pouligny, 'Supporting Local Ownership in Humanitarian Action', *Humanitarian Policy Paper Series*, Global Public Policy Institute, 2009: Timothy Donais, 'Empowerment or Imposition? Dilemmas of Local Ownership in Post-Conflict Peacebuilding Processes, *Peace and Change*, vol.34, no.1., 2009, pp.3–26. For my approach to local ownership see, Oliver P. Richmond, 'Beyond Local Ownership and Participation in the Architecture of International Peacebuilding', *Ethnopolitics*, forthcoming, 2011.

26 Ibid., p.165. According to Scott this means 'something like a homecoming' for the subject.

27 Michel Foucault, 'What is Critique', in *The Politics of Truth*, Cambridge, Mass.; MIT Press, 1997, pp.44–5

28 John Hummel, *Personal Interview*, Carter Centre, Monrovia, 18 November 2009: *Focus Group*, National Council of Elders, Monrovia, 25 November 2009.

29 Bhikhu, Parekh, op.cit

30 Ibid., pp.112–121, and p.130.

31 Ibid., p.113 and p.138.

32 Ibid., p.115.

33 Ibid., p.118.

34 Ibid., pp.205–7.

35 Ibid., p.123.

36 Ibid., p.196.

37 This mirrors the well-known critique of Foucault, which is that he needed liberal norms and rights in order to critique them as being potentially oppressive.

38 R.G. *Fox* and Starn, O. (eds), *Between resistance and revolution: Cultural politics and social protest*, New Brunswick, NJ: Rutgers University Press, 1997, pp.2–3.

39 See Judith Butler's interesting essay on Foucault and resistance for more on this notion of critique. Judith Butler, 'What is Critique: An Essay on Foucault's Virtue', in David Ingram (ed.), The Political: Readings in Continental Philosophy, London: Blackwell, 2002.

40 R.G. *Fox* and Starn, O, op.cit., p.4.

41 Paulo Freire, *Pedagogy of the Oppressed*, London: Penguin, 1996 [1970], p.48. and p.161. This also has methodological implications for a more action based approach to research, a more humanistic approach, researching for and with people rather than on then, being aware of bias, impact of the researcher on subjects, and reflexivity. See for example, Peter Reason and Hilary Bradbury (eds), *Handbook of Action Research*, London: Sage, 2001.

42 Richard Shaull, 'Foreword', Paulo Freire, op.cit., p.12.

43 Oliver P. Richmond, *The Transformation of Peace*, London: Palgrave, 2005, conclusion.

44 Oliver P. Richmond, *Maintaining Order, Making Peace*, London: Palgrave, 2002, conclusion.

45 Richard Shaull, 'Foreword', Paulo Freire, op.cit., p.15.

46 Mosse makes a similar argument in relation to aid. David Mosse, 'Global Governance and the Ethnography of the International Aid', David Mosse and David Lewis, *The Aid Effect*, London: Pluto, 2005, p.2.

47 For an early engagement with this discussion, see ibid.

48 Ibid., p.28.

49 Ibid., p.30.

50 Roland Bleiker, 'Discourse and Human Agency', *Contemporary Political Theory*, vol.2, 2003, p.34.

51 James C. Scott, *Weapons of the Weak: Everyday Peasant Resistance*, Yale UP, 1985, p.xvi

52 G Deleuze and M Guattari, cited in Roland Bleiker, 'Discourse and Human Agency', op.cit, p.39.

53 Ibid., p.40.

54 Ingrid Barnsley and Roland Bleiker, 'Self-determination: from decolonisation to derritorialisation, *Global Change, Peace and Security*, vol.20, no.2, 2008, pp.121–36.

55 Michel Foucault cited in Roland Bleiker, 'Discourse and Human Agency', op.cit. p.27.

56 L.H. Martin et al, *Technologies of the Self: A Seminar with Michel Foucault*, London: Tavistock, pp.16–49.

57 Michel Foucault, *The Birth of Politics*, Graham Burchell (trans.). London: Palgrave, 2008 p.313.

58 See Bruce Robbins, *Towards a New Humanist Paradigm*, in H Schwarz and S Ray, Companion to Post-Colonial Studies, London: Blackwell, 2000, p.565.

59 Michel Foucault, op.cit., p.130.

60 On *utis possidetis*- the principle that borders remain unchanged, see ibid., p.125. See also the 1992 Badinter Commission on Borders conclusions, which place human rights and self-determination in a problematic relationship with this principle during the collapse of Yugoslavia.

61 William E. Connolly, *Why I am not a Secularist*, Minneapolis: University of Minneapolis Press, 1999, p.155: See also Barnsley and Bleiker, op.cit., p.133.

62 Herman *Schmidt*, 'Politics and Peace Research', *Journal of Peace Research*, vol.5, no.3, 1968.

63 For the emergence of similar dynamics in Central America in the mid-1990s, known as '*democraduras*', see Terry Lynn Karl, 'The Hybrid Political Regimes of Central America', *Journal of Democracy*, vol.6, no.3, 1995, pp.72–86.

64 I am grateful to Roland Bleiker for the aspects I discuss in this and the next paragraph.

65 See G John Ikenberry for this argument, in 'Liberal Internationalism 3.0', *Perspectives on Politics*, vol.7, p 71–87, 2009.

66 Frantz Fanon, *The Wretched of the Earth*, Grove Press, 1965 [1961].

67 Timothy Donais, 'Empowerment or Imposition? Dilemmas of Local Ownership in Post-Conflict Peacebuilding Processes', *Peace and Change*, vol.34, no.1, 2009, pp.3–26.

68 Uday Singh Mehta, *Liberalism and Empire*, Chicago University Press, 1999, p.6.

69 Mehta argues that Burke has a more nuanced understanding of the contradictory claims of liberal empire, and preferred to distance himself from it, while other liberal thinkers saw it as part of their project at least in the short term. ibid., p.47.

70 Ibid., p.191.

71 Ashis Nandy, *The Intimate Enemy*, Delhi: Oxford University Press, 1983.

72 Uday Singh Mehta, op.cit, p.76. Mehta relates how Haileyburey College, where many academics who pioneered social science emerged from, apparently was started to help understand how to govern colonial peoples.

73 Thanks to Necati Polat for this point: 'Peace as War', *Unpublished Paper*, 2009.

74 For more on this, see the conclusion to the unapologetic, Naomi Klein, *The Shock Doctrine*, London: Penguin, 2007, esp. pp.454–6.

75 Paulo Freire, op.cit., p.26.

76 James C Scott, *Weapons of the Weak: Everyday Peasant Resistance*, Yale University Press,, 1985.

77 Terry Lynn Karl, op.cit., p.7.

78 See Jenny Edkins and Veronique Pin-Fat, 'Through the Wire: Relations of Power and Relations of Violence', *Millennium*, vol.34, no.1, 2005, pp.1–24: Giorgio Agamben, *Homo Sacer: Sovereign Power and Bare Life*, Stanford: Stanford University Press, 1998.

79 Andreja Zevnik, 'Sovereign-less Subject and the Possibility of Resistance', *Millennium*, vol.38, no.1, pp.83–106.

80 Sylyvere Lotringer, Chris Kraus, and H. El Kholti, 'Introduction' to Jean Baudrillard, *In the Shadow of the Silent Majority*, Cambridge, Mass.: MIT Press, 2007 [1978], p.9.

81 Jean Baudrillard, ibid, p.47. This is analogous to the discovery of 'dark matter' recently

by physicists, which represents most of the universe, is crucial in its construction, but has been largely invisible.

82 In this I appreciate, though disagree with David Chandler's argument that post-liberalism represents a loss of rights, meaning, and capacity to mobilise. David Chandler, *Hollow Hegemony*, London: Pluto, 2009, p.16.

83 Nicholas Rankin, *Telegramme from Guernica*, London: Faber and Faber, 2003, p.180.

Appendix 2

1 *Peacebuilding Workshop*, University of Sarajevo, 14 March 2008. Thanks to my students for facilitating this, and in particular to Deborah Johnson for helping to compile this diagram.

Bibliography

Acharya, Amitav and Barry Buzan, 'Why there is no non-Western international relations theory?, *International Relations of the Pacific*, vol.7, 2007, pp.287–312.

Acharya, Amity, 'How Ideas Spread: Whose Norms Matter? Norm Localization and Institutional Change in Asian Regionalism,' *International Organization*, vol.58, no.2, 2004, pp.239–75.

Ackerman, Peter, and Jack Duvall, *A Force More Powerful*, New York: Palgrave, 2000.

Action Aid Australia/Austcare, Deborah Leaver in *Discussion Group*, Sydney, 27 October 2009.

Agamben, Giorgio, *Homo Sacer: Sovereign Power and Bare Life*, Stanford: Stanford University Press, 1998.

Agathangelou, Anna M. and L.H.M. Lings, 'The House of IR', *International Studies Review*, vol.6, 2004, pp. 21–49.

Allan, Pierre and Alexis Keller, 'The Concept of a Just Peace' in Pierre Allan and Alexis Keller, *What is a Just Peace?* Oxford: Oxford University Press, 2006, pp. 195–215

Aljazeera, Is 'Afghanisation' possible? 29 January 2010, http://english.aljazeera.net/programmes/insidestory/2010/01/2010128132220903967.html.

Anders, Gerhard, 'Good Governance as Technology', in David Mosse and David Lewis (eds), *The Aid Effect: Giving and Governing in International Development*, London: Pluto Press, 2005, pp.37–60.

Anderson, Benedict, *Imagined Communities: Reflections of the Origins and Spread of Nationalism*, Ithaca, NY: Cornell University Press, 1991.

Annan, Kofi, 'Democracy as an International Issue', *Global Governance*, 8, 2, (April–June 2002), pp.134–42.

Annan, Kofi, *No Exit Without Strategy*, S//2001/394, UN: New York, 2001.

Antoniades, Andreas, 'Cave! Hic Everyday Life: Repetition, Hegemony and the Social', *British Journal of Politics and International Relations*, vol.10, no.3, 2008, pp. 412–28.

Appadurai, Arjun, 'Grassroots Globalisation and Research Imagination' in Arjun Appadurai, (ed.) *Globalisation*, Durham and London: Duke University Press, 2001, pp.1–21

Appadurai, Arjun, *Modernity at Large*, University of Minnesota Press: Minneapolis, 1996.

Aradau, Claudia, 'Security and the Democratic Scene: desecuritization and emancipation', *Journal of IR and Development*, vol.7, 2004, pp.388–413.

Aradau, Claudia and Jeff Huysmans, 'Mobilising (Global) Democracy', *Millennium*, vol.37, no.3, 2009, pp.583–604

Article 21 (3), *Declaration of Human Rights*, 1948.

Ashcroft, Bill, (ed.), *Writing Past Colonialism: On Post-Colonial Futures*, London: Continuum, 2001

Ashdown, Paddy, 'Afghanistan could be lost in the bars of Britain', *The Times*, 5 November 2009.

Ashdown, Paddy, 'Europe needs a wake-up call. Bosnia is on the edge again', *The Observer*, Sunday 27 July 2008.

Badiou, Alain, *Metapolitics*, London: Verso, 2005.

Barnett, Michael and Christopher Zuercher, 'Peacebuilder's Contract: How External Peacebuilding Reinforces Weak Statehood', in Roland Paris and Timothy Sisk, *The Dilemmas of Statebuilding*, London: Routledge, 2008, pp.23–52.Barnett, Michael N, 'Building a Republican Peace: Stabilizing States after War', *International Security*, vol.30, no.4, 2006, pp.87–112.

Barnsley, Ingrid and Roland Bleiker, 'Self-determination: from decolonisation to derritori-alisation, *Global Change, Peace and Security*, vol.20, no.2, 2008, pp.121–36.

Barr, Nicholas, *The Economics of the Welfare State*, Oxford: Oxford University Press, 1998.

Baudrillard, Jean, 'Simulacra and Simulations' in Mark Poster (ed.), *Jean Baudrillard, Selected Writings*, Stanford: Stanford University Press, 1988, pp.166–84.

Baudrillard, Jean, *In the Shadow of the Silent Majority*, Cambridge, Mass.: MIT Press, 2007 [1978].

Bauman, Zygmunt, *Postmodern Ethics*, Oxford: Blackwell, 1993.

Begby, Endre and J. Peter Burgess, 'Human Security and Liberal Peace', *Public Reason*, vol.1, no.1, 2009, pp.91–104.

Bellamy, Alex, and Paul Williams (eds.), *Peace Operations and Global Order*, Abingdon: Routledge, 2005

Belloni Roberto, 'Civil Society and Peacebuilding in Bosnia and Herzegovina,' *Journal of Peace Research*, vol.38, no.2, 2001, pp.163–180.

Benhabib, Seyla, *Situating the Self*, Cambridge: Polity, 1993.

Bhabha, Homi, 'Freedom's Basis in the Indeterminate', in John Rajchman (ed.), *The Identity in Question*, New York: Routledge, 1995, pp.47–61.

Bhabha, Homi, *The Location of Culture*, London: Routledge, 1994.

BHAS, Labour Force Survey (preliminary data), Press Release Nno.1, 27 July 2006, Sarajevo.

Bieber, Florian, and Zidas Daskalovski, (eds), *Understanding the War in Kosovo*, London: Frank Cass, 2003.

Bilgin, Pinar, 'Thinking past 'Western' IR?', *Third World Quarterly*, vol.29, no.1, 2008, pp.5–23.

Bishai, Linda, 'Liberal Empire', *Journal of International Relations and Development*, vol.7, 2004, pp.48–72.

Blanchot, Maurice, *The Infinite Conversation*, Minneapolis: University of Minneapolis Press, 1993.

Bleiker, Roland, 'Discourse and Human Agency', *Contemporary Political Theory*, vol.2, no.1, 2003, pp. 25–47

Bleiker, Roland, *Aesthetics and World Politics*, London: Palgrave, 2009.

Bleiker, Roland, *Divided Korea: Towards a Culture of Reconciliation*, Minneapolis: University of Minnesota Press, 2005.

Bøås, Morten. and Kathleen.M. Jennings, 'Insecurity and development: the rhetoric of the failed state', *European Journal of Development Research*, vol.17, no.3, 2005, pp.385–95.

Boege, Volker, M. Anne Brown, Kevin P. Clements, and Anna Nolan, 'States Emerging from Hybrid Political Orders – Pacific Experiences', *The Australian Centre for Peace and Conflict Studies (ACPACS) Occasional Papers Series*, 2008.

Bonoli, Giuliano, 'The Politics of the New Social Policies', *Policy and Politics*, vol.33, no.3, 2005, pp. 431–49

Boserup, Anders, and Andrew Mack, *War Without Weapons: non-violence in national defence*, London: Francis Pinter, 1974

Boucher, David, 'Property and Propriety in IR: the case of John Locke', in Beate Jahn (ed.), *Classical Theory in IR*, Cambridge: Cambridge University Press, 2006, pp. 156–177

Boutros Ghali, Boutros, *An Agenda for Democratization*, A/50/332 AND A/51/512, 17 December 1996.

Boutros Ghali, Boutros, 'Supplement to An Agenda for Peace' *A/50/60, S.1995/1*, 3 January 1995.

Boutros Ghali, Boutros, *An Agenda for Development: Report of the Secretary-General*, A/48/935, 6 May 1994.

Boutros Ghali, Boutros, *An Agenda For Peace: preventative diplomacy, peacemaking and peacekeeping*, New York: United Nations, 1992.

Brigg, Morgan '*Wantokism* and State Building in the Solomon Islands: A response to Fukuyama', *Pacific Economic Bulletin*, vol.24, no.3, 2009, pp.148–61.

Brigg, Morgan, *Wantokism and Statebuilding the Solomon Islands*, Unpublished Paper, 2009.

Briggs, John and Joanne Sharp, 'Indigenous Knowledge and development', *Third World Quarterly*, vol.25, no.4, 2004, pp.661–76.

Briggs, Asa, 'The Welfare State in Historical Perspective', *European Journal of Sociology*, vol.2, no.2, 1961, pp. 221–58

Brown, Anne (ed.), *Security and Development in the Pacific Islands: Social Resilience in Emerging States*, Boulder, Colorado: Lynne Rienner

Brown, Anne, 'Towards Effective and Legitimate Governance' *ACPAC East Timor Report:* Brisbane, 2008.

Brown, Chris, *Sovereignty, Rights and Justice: International Political Theory Today*, Cambridge: Polity, 2002.

Butler, Judith, 'Universality in Culture', in Martha Nussbaum, *For Love of Country?*, J. Cohen (ed.), Boston, MA: Beacon Press, 2002, pp. 45–53

Butler, Judith, 'What is Critique: An Essay on Foucault's Virtue', in David Ingram (ed.), *The Political: Readings in Continental Philosophy*, London: Blackwell, 2002, pp.212–26

Cabral, Amilcar, (translated by Michael Wolfers), *Unity and Struggle*, London: Heinemann, 1980.

Call, Charles T. and Elizabeth M. Cousens, 'Ending Wars and Building Peace: International Responses to War-Torn Societies,' *International Studies Perspectives*, vol.9, no.1, 2008, pp.1–21.

Carothers, Thomas, 'The End of the Transition Paradigm', *Journal of Democracy*, vol.13, no.1, 2002, pp.5–21.

Castells, Manuel, *The Power of Identity*, Oxford: Blackwell Publishers, 2003.

Ceadal, Martin, *Thinking About Peace and War*, Oxford: Oxford University Press, 1987.

Cerny, Phillip, 'Some Pitfalls of Democratisation in a Globalising World', *Millennium*, vol.37, no.3, 2009, pp.767–90.

Chabal, Patrick and Jean-Pascal Daloz, *Culture Troubles*, London: Hurst, 2006.

Chakrabarty, Dipesh, *Provincialising Europe*, Princeton University Press, 2000.

Chan, Stephen, Peter Mandaville, Roland Bleiker (eds.), *The Zen of IR*, London: Palgrave, 2001.

Chandler, David, *From Kosovo to Kabul: Human Rights and International Intervention*, London: Pluto, 2002.

Chandler, David, *Bosnia: Faking Democracy After Dayton*, London: Pluto Press, 1999.

Chandler, David, 'Imposing the 'Rule of Law': The Lessons of BiH for Peacebuilding in Iraq', *International Peacekeeping*, vol.11, no.2, 2004, pp.312–33.

Chandler, David, *Empire in Denial: The Politics of Statebuilding* London: Pluto Press, 2006.

Chandler, David, *Hollow Hegemony*, London: Pluto, 2009.

Chandler, David, 'Critiquing Liberal Cosmopolitanism? The Limits of the Biopolitical Approach', *International Political Sociology*, vol.3, no.1, 2009, pp.53–70.

Chang, Ha-Joon, *Bad Samaritans*, London: Random House, 2007.

Chatterjee, Partha, 'Beyond the Nation? Or Within', *Social Text*, no.56, 1998, pp.57–69

Chopra, Jarat, 'The UN's Kingdom of East Timor', *Survival*, vol.42, no.3., 2000, pp.27–40.

Chopra, Jarat, 'Building State-Failure in East Timor', *Development and Change*, vol.33, no.5, 2002, pp.979–1000.

Chopra, Jarat and Tanja Hohe, 'Participatory Intervention', *Global Governance*, vol.10, no.3, 2004, pp.289–305.

Chou, Mark and Roland Bleiker, 'The Symbiosis of Democracy and Tragedy: Lost Lessons from Ancient Greece', *Millennium*, vol.37, no.3, 2009, pp.659–82.

Clifford, James, *The Predicament of Culture*, Cambridge MA: Harvard University Press, 1998,.

Comaroff, John, and Jean Comaroff, *Civil Society and Political Imagination in Africa*, University of Chicago Press, 1999.

Conetta, Carl, *Radical Departure: Toward A Practical Peace in Iraq*, Project on Defense Alternatives Briefing Report # 16 Cambridge, MA: Commonwealth Institute, 7 July 2004. http://www.comw.org/pda/0407br16.html.

Connolly, William E., *Why I am not a Secularist*, Minneapolis: University of Minneapolis Press, 1999.

Connolly, William E., *Identity/Difference*, Minneapolis: Minnesota University Press, 1991.

Cooper, Neil, 'Review chapter: On the Crisis of the Liberal Peace,' *Conflict, Security and Development*, vol.7, no.4, 2007, 605–16.

Coyne, Christopher, 'After War: Understanding Post-War Reconstruction', *Global Prosperity Initiative Working Paper*, no. 40, Mercatus Center, George Mason University, 2005.

Curtis, Grant, *Cambodia Reborn? The Transition to Democracy and Development*, Brookings institute Press, Washington, 1998, p.110–149.

Dallmayr, Fred, *Peace Talks – Who Will Listen?*, University of Notre Dame Press, 2004.

Darby, John, and Roger Mac Ginty (eds), *Contemporary Peacemaking*, London: Palgrave, 2008.

Darby, Phillip, 'The Alternative Horizons of Ashis Nandy', unpublished paper, 2009.

De Certeau, Michel *The Practice of Everyday Life*, California University Press, 1984.

De Sousa Santos, Boaventura, 'Human Rights as an Emancipatory Script', in Boaventura de Sousa Santos (ed.), *Another Knowledge is Possible: Beyond Northern Epistemologies*, London: Verso, 2007.

De Tocqueville, Alexis, *Democracy in America*, Vintage Books, 1945.

Debord, Guy, *Society of the Spectacle*, London: Aldgate Press.

Derrida, Jacques, *Rogues: Two essays on reason*, Stanford: Stanford University Press, 2004.

Deutsch, Karl, *et. al.*, *Political Community and the North Atlantic Area*, New Jersey: Princeton University Press, 1957.

Dillon, Michael, A Passion for the [Im]possible: Jacques Ranciere, Equality, Pedagogy and the Messianic, *European Journal of Political Theory*, vol.4, no.4, 2005, pp.429–52.

Donais, Timothy, 'Empowerment or Imposition? Dilemmas of Local Ownership in Post-Conflict Peacebuilding Processes', *Peace and Change*, vol.34, no.1, 2009, pp.3–26.

Donnelly, Jack, 'The Relative Universality of Human Rights', *Human Rights Quarterly*, vol.29, May 2007, pp.281–306.

Dower, John W., *Embracing Defeat: Japan in the Wake of World War II*, W. W. Norton and Company, 1999.

Doyle, Michael, 'Kant, Liberal Legacies, and Foreign Affairs,' *Philosophy and Public Affairs*, vol.12, no.3, 1983, pp.205–235.

Doyle, Michael, *United Nations Peacekeeping in Cambodia: UNTAC's Civil Mandate*, Boulder, CO: Lynne Rienner, 1995.

Doyle, Michael, *Ways of War and Peace*, NY: Norton, 1997.

Doyle, Michael and Nicolas Sambanis, *Making War and Building Peace*, Princeton University Press, 2006.

Doyle, Michael, 'Liberal Internationalism, Peace, War, and Democracy', http://nobelprize. org/nobel _prizes/peace/chapters/doyle/index.html.

Dreyfus, Hubert, 'Heidegger and Foucault on the Subject, Agency and Practices', http:// ist-socrates.berkeley.edu/~hdreyfus/html/paper_heidandfoucault.html

Duffield, Mark, *Global Governance and the New Wars*, London: Zed Books, 2001.

Duffield, Mark, 'Social Reconstruction and the Radicalisation of Development', *Development and Change*, vol.33, no.5, 2002, pp.1049–71.

Duffield, Mark, *Development, Security and Unending War*, London: Polity, 2007.

Duffield, Mark, and Nicholas Waddell, 'Security Humans in a Dangerous World', *International Politics*, vol.43, no.1, 2006, pp.1–23.

Eckl, Julian, 'Responsible Scholarship After Leaving the Veranda', *International Political Sociology*, vol.2, no.3, 2008, pp.185–203.

Edkins, Jenny and Veronique Pin-Fat, 'Through the Wire: Relations of Power and Relations of Violence', *Millennium*, vol.34, no.1, 2005, pp.1–24.

Escobar, Arturo, *Encountering Development*, New Jersey: Princeton University Press, 1995.

Fagan, Adam, 'Civil Society in Bosnia Ten Years after Dayton,' *International Peacekeeping*, vol.2, no.3, 2005, pp.406–19.

Fanon, Frantz, *The Wretched of the Earth*, London: Penguin, 1967 [1963].

Fearon, James D. and David D. Laitin, 'Neotrusteeship and the Problem of Weak States', *International Security*, vol.28, no.4, 2004, pp.5–43.

Foucault, Michel, 'Two Lectures', *Power/Knowledge*, London: Pantheon, 1972.

Foucault, Michel 'Governmentality', in: Graham Burchell, Colin Gordon, and Peter Miller (eds), *The Foucault Effect: Studies in* Governmentality, Hemel Hempstead: Harvester Wheatsheaf, 1991, pp.87–104.Foucault, Michel, '*What is an Author?*', Donald F. Bouchard and Sherry Simon (trans.), *Language, Counter-Memory, Practice*. Ithaca, New York: Cornell University Press, 1977.

Foucault, Michel, *History of Sexuality*, vol.1, trans. Robert Hurley, London: Penguin, 1978.

Foucault, Michel, *History of Sexuality*, vol.3, *The Care of the Self*, New York: Pantheon Books, 1986.

Foucault, Michel, 'What is Critique', in *The Politics of Truth*, Cambridge, Mass.; MIT Press, 1997.

Foucault, Michel, *Society Must be Defended*, (trans.) David Macey, London: Penguin, 2003.

Foucault, Michel, *The Birth of Biopolitics: Lectures at the College de France*, 1978–79 Palgrave Macmillan, 2008.

Foucault, Michel, *The Birth of Politics*, Graham Burchell (trans.). London: Palgrave, 2008.

Fox, R.G., and Starn, O. (eds), *Between resistance and revolution: Cultural politics and social protest*, New Brunswick, NJ: Rutgers University Press, 1997.

Franceschet, Antonio, 'One powerful and enlightened nation', in Beate Jahn (ed.), *Classical Theory in IR*, Cambridge: Cambridge University Press, 2006.

Franks, Jason and Oliver P. Richmond, 'Co-opting the liberal peace: Untying the Gordian Knot in Kosovo', *Cooperation and Conflict*, vol.43, no.1, 2008, pp.81–103.

Freeman, Christopher, 'Afghanistan in Transition: Security, Governance and Statebuilding'.

Fry, Douglas, *Beyond War*, Oxford: 2007.

Fukuyama, Francis, *State-Building: Governance and World Order in the Twenty-First Century*, London: Profile Books, 2004.

Fukuyama, Francis, 'State-Building in Solomon Islands,' *Pacific Economic Bulletin* 23, no.3, 2008.

Fukuyama, Francis, 'Statebuilding in the Solomon Islands', *Unpublished Paper*, 9 July 2008.

Geertz, Clifford, *The Interpretation of Cultures*, New York: Basic Books, 1973.

Geertz, Clifford, *Available Light*, Princeton University Press, 2001.

Geuss, Raymond, 'Liberalism and its Discontents', *Political Studies*, vol.30, no.3, 2002, pp.320–338.

Giddens, Anthony, *Positive Welfare, The Third Way*, Cambridge: Polity, 1998.

Gilligan, Carol, *In a Different Voice*, Cambridge, M.A.: Harvard University Press, 1993.

Goetshel, Laurent, and Tobias Hagmann,, 'Civilian Peacebuilding: Peace by Bureaucratic Means', *Conflict, Security, and Development*, vol.9, no.1, 2009, pp.55–73.

Goldman, Michael, *Imperial Nature*, New Haven: Yale, 2005.

Gotze, Catherine, 'Civil Society Organisations in Failing States: The Red Cross in Bosnia and Albania,' *International Peacekeeping*, vol.11, no.4, 2004, pp.664–81.

Gowan, Richard, 'Strategic context: Peacekeeping in Crisis', *International Peacekeeping*, vol.15, no.4, 2008, pp.453–69.

Grenfell, Damian, 'Making Modernity in Timor-Leste', *Arena*, no.90, 2007, pp.9–12

Gusmão, Xanana, 'Compatriots! Timorese!', *New Year's Message*, President of the CNRT/CN, Dili, 31 December 2000, http://members.pcug.org.au/~wildwood/JanNewYear.htm

Gusmão, Xanana, 'Peacekeeping and Peacebuilding in Timor Leste', *Seminar on the role of the UN in Timor Leste*, Dili, 26 November, 2004.

Habermas, Jurgen, 'Questions and Counter Questions', in R.J. Bernstein (ed.), *Habermas and Modernity*, Cambridge, MA: MIT Press, 1985

Habermas, Jurgen, *The Inclusion of the Other*, Cambridge, MA; MIT Press, 1998.

Harvey, David, *A Brief History of Neoliberalism* Oxford: Oxford University Press, 2005.

Held, David, 'Democracy and Globalisation', *Global Governance*, vol.3, no.3, 1997, pp.251–67.

Held, David, *Global Covenant: The Social Democratic Alternative to the Washington Consensus*, Cambridge: Polity Press, 2004.

Herring, Eric, 'Neoliberalism Versus Peacebuilding in Iraq', Michael Pugh, Neil Cooper, and Mandy. Turner (eds.), *Whose Peace?*, London: Palgrave, 2008, pp.49–67.

Hindess, Barry, 'Not at Home in the Empire', *Social Identities*, vol.7, no.3, 2001.

Holohan, Anne, *Networks of Democracy*, Stanford: Stanford Press, 2005.

House of Commons International Development Committee, *Conflict and Development: Peacebuilding and Post–conflict Reconstruction*, Sixth Report of Session 2005–06 Volume I.

Howard, Michael, *The Invention of Peace and the Re-Invention of War*, London: Profile, 2002.

Hughes, Caroline, *Dependent Communities: Aid and Politics in Cambodia and Timor-Leste*, Cornell University Press, 2009.

Hull, Geoffrey, 'The Languages of East Timor: 1772–1997: A Literature Review', in *Studies in Languages and Cultures of East Timor*, Macarthur, NSW: University of Western Sydney, 1999, pp.1–38: Agence France Presse, 11 December 2001.

Human Security Brief, 2006, http://www.humansecuritybrief.info/2006/contents/overview. pdf.

Husanovic Jasmina, 'Post-Conflict Kosovo: An Anatomy Lesson in the Ethics/Politics of Human Rights' in Ken Booth (ed.), *The Kosovo Tragedy The Human Rights Dimension*, London: Frank Cass, 2001, pp.263–82.

Hutchings, Kimberley, 'Towards a Feminist International Ethics.' *Review of International Studies*, vol.26, no.5, 2000, pp.111–130.

Ikenberry, G. John, *After victory: institutions, strategic restraint, and the rebuilding of order after major wars*, Princeton: Princeton University Press, 2000.

Ikenberry, G. John, in 'Liberal Internationalism 3.0', *Perspectives on Politics*, vol.7, pp.71–87, 2009.

International Commission on Intervention and State Sovereignty (ICISS), *Responsibility to Protect*, Ottawa: International Development Research Centre, December 2001.

International Covenant on Economic, Social and Cultural Rights, Adopted and opened for signature, ratification and accession by General Assembly Resolution 2200A (XXI) of 16 December 1966 (entry into force 3 January 1976, in accordance with chapter 27).

Jabri, Vivienne, 'Michel Foucault's Analytics of War', *International Political Sociology*, vol.1, 2007.

Jabri, Vivienne, *War and the Transformation of Global Politics*, London: Palgrave, 2007.

Jahn, Beate, 'One Step Forward, Two Steps Back: Critical Theory as the Latest Edition of Liberal Idealism', *Millennium*, vol.27, no.3, 1998, pp.613–41.

Jahn, Beate, 'Classical Smoke, Classical Mirror: Kant and Mill in Liberal International Relations Theory' in Beate Jahn (ed.), *Classical Theory in International Relations*, Cambridge: Cambridge University Press, 2006.

Jahn, Beate 'The Tragedy of Liberal Diplomacy: Democratization, Intervention and Statebuilding (Part II)', *Journal of Intervention and Statebuilding*, vol.1, no.2, 2007, pp.211–29.

Johnson, Pat, *Local vs. National Peacebuilding: The Richness of Somali Peacemaking*, www.prio.no/ peaceethics/PeacE-Discussions, 2010.

Jutila, Matti, Samu Pehkonen, and Tarja Väyrynen, 'Resuscitating a Discipline: An Agenda for Critical Peace Research', *Millennium*, vol.36, no.3, 2008, pp.623–40.

Kapoor, Ilan, 'Capitalism, culture, agency: dependency versus postcolonial theory', *Third World Quarterly*, vol.23, no.4, 2002, pp.647–64.

Kapoor, Ilan, 'Acting in a Tight Spot: Homi Bhabha's Post-Colonial Politics', *New Political Science*, vol.5, no.4., 2003, pp.561–77.

Kapoor, Ilan, *The Post-Colonial Politics of Development*, London: Routledge, 2008.

Karl, Terry Lynn, 'The Hybrid Political Regimes of Central America', *Journal of Democracy*, vol.6, no.3, 1995, pp.72–86.

Keane, John, *Global Civil Society*, Cambridge: Cambridge University Press, 2003.

Keane, John, and Paul Mier, 'New Perspectives on Social Movements: An interview with Alberto Melucci', in Alberto Melucci (John Keane and Paul Mier [eds.]), Nomads of the Present: Social Movements and Individual Needs in Contemporary Society, Temple University Press, 1989

Kende, Istvan, 'The History of Peace', *Journal of Peace Research*, vol.26, no.3, 1989, pp.233–247.

Keohane, Robert, 'Political Authority after Intervention: Gradations in Sovereignty', in J. L. Holzgrefe and R. O. Keohane (eds) *Humanitarian Intervention: Ethical, Legal and Political Dilemmas*, Cambridge: Cambrudge University Press, 2003.

Keynes, John Maynard, *The Economic Consequences of the Peace*, London: Macmillan, 1920.

Klein, Naomi, *The Shock Doctrine*, London: Penguin, 2007.

'Kosovanisation in action', *Quarterly Information Sheet*, Ombudsperson Institution In Kosovo, January–March 2006, http://www.ombudspersonkosovo.org/repository/docs/Informator09_final.pdf

Krasner, Stephen, *Sovereignty: Organized Hypocrisy*, Princeton University Press, 1999.

Krasner, Stephen, 'Sharing sovereignty: new institutions for collapsed and failing states', *International Security*, vol.29, no.2, 2004, pp.85–120.

Laidi, Zaki, *The Great Disruption*, Cambridge: Polity Press, 2007 [2004].

Lal, Deepak, 'Culture, Democracy, and Development', Paper presented at the *IMF Conference on Second Generation Reforms*, 20 September, 1999.

Latawski, Paul, Martin Smith, *The Kosovo Crisis and the Evolution of Post-Cold War European Security*, Manchester: Palgrave, 2003.

Lebow, Richard Ned, *The Tragic Vision of Politics: Ethics, Interests and Orders*, Cambridge: Cambridge University Press, 2003.

Lederach, John, *Building Peace – Sustainable Reconciliation in Divided Societies*, Tokyo: United Nations University Press, 1997.

Lefebvre, Henri, *Critique of Everyday Life*, London: Verso, 1991.

Link, Arthur S. *et. al.* (ed.), *The Papers of Woodrow Wilson*, vol.41, January 24–April 6, 1917, Princeton: Princeton University Press, 1983.

Linklater, Andrew, *The Transformation of Political Community*, University of South Carolina Press, 1998.

Linklater, Andrew, 'Dialogic Politics and the Civilising Process', *Review of International Studies*, vol.31, 2005, pp.141–54.

Lipset, Seymour Martin, 'Some Social Requisites of Democracy: Economic Development and Political Legitimacy', *American Political Science Review*, vol.53, no.1, 1959, pp.69–105.

Llamazares, Monica, and Laina Reynolds Levy, *NGOs and Peacebuilding in Kosovo*, University of Bradford, Dept. of Peace Studies, 2003.

Luckham, Robin, 'Introduction: Transforming Security and Development in and Unequal World', *IDS Bulletin*, vol.40, no.2, March, 2009.

Lyons, Gene M. and Michael Mastunduno, *Beyond Westphalia*, Baltimore: Johns Hopkins UP, 1995.

Lyotard, Jean Francois, 'On theory: An Interview', *Driftworks*, New York: Semiotext(e), 1984.

Mac Ginty, Roger, *No War, No Peace*, London, Palgrave, 2007.

Mac Ginty, Roger, 'Indigenous Peace-Making Versus the Liberal Peace,' *Cooperation and Conflict*, vol.43, no.2, 2008, pp.139–63.

Mac Ginty, Roger, 'The Liberal Peace at Home and Abroad: Northern Ireland and Liberal Internationalism, *BJPIR*, vol.11, 2009, pp.690–708.

Mac Ginty, Roger and Oliver P. Richmond (eds), 'Myth or Reality: The Liberal Peace and Post-Conflict Reconstruction', Special issue of *Global Society*, (2007).

MacEwan, Arthur, *Neoliberalism or Democracy*, London: Zed, 1999.

Macmillan, John, 'Immanuel Kant and the Democratic Peace', in Beate Jahn (ed.), *Classical Theory in IR*, Cambridge: Cambridge University Press, 2006.

Malcolm, Noel, *Kosovo: A Short History*, London: Macmillan, 1998.

Mandelbaum, M.ichael, *The Ideas that Conquered the World*, New York: Public Affairs, 2002.

Martin, Ian and Alexander Mayer-Rieckh, 'The United Nations and East Timor: From Self-determination to State-building', *International Peacekeeping*, vol.12, no.1, spring 2005, pp.104–20.

Martin, L.H. *et. al.*, *Technologies of the Self: A Seminar with Michel Foucault*, London: Tavistock, 1988.

Massey, Doreen, 'A Global Sense of Place', in *Space, Place and Gender*, Minneapolis: Minneapolis University Press, 1994.

Mazower, Mark, *Inside Hitler's Greece, 1941–1945*, Yale University Press, 2001.

McWilliam, Andrew, 'Houses of Resistance in East Timor: Structuring of Sociality in the New National', *Anthropological Forum*, vol.15, no.1, 2005, pp. 27–44.

Mead, Lawrence, 'The New Politics of the New Poverty', in Christopher Pierson and Francis Castles, *The Welfare State Reader*, Cambridge: Polity, 2000.

Meiksins Wood, Ellen, *Empire of Capital*, London: Verso, 2003.

Melucci, Alberto, 'Social Movements and the Democratisation of Everyday Life', in John Keane, (ed.), *Civil Society and the State*, London: Verso, pp.245–60.

Mertus, Julia, *Kosovo: How Myths and Truths Started a War*, California: University of California, 1999.

Mill, J.S., On Liberty, in J.S., Mill: *Three Essays: On Liberty, Representative Government and The Subjection of Women*, Oxford: Oxford University Press, 1981.

Ministry of Social Solidarity, *Community Dialogue in Suco Bahalara-ua'* in Press Release, 5 March 2009.

Ministry of State, *Local Government Options Study*, Dili, 2003.

Mitrany, David, A., *The Functional Theory of Politics*, London: Martin Robertson, 1975.

Moore, Clive, 'External Intervention: The Solomon Islands Beyond Ramsi' in Anne Brown (ed.), *Security and Development in the Pacific Islands*, Boulder: Lynne Rienner, 2007, pp.169–96.

Mosse, David, and David Lewis (eds), *The Aid Effect: Giving and Governing in International Development*. London: Pluto Press, 2005.

Mosse, David, *Cultivating Development*, London: Pluto Press, 2005.

Mouffe, Chantal, *The Democratic Paradox*, London: Verso, 2000.

Murray, Charles, 'Two Wars Against Poverty', in Christopher Pierson and Francis Castles, *The Welfare State Reader*, Cambridge: Polity, 2000, pp. 96–106

Nandy, Ashis, *The Intimate Enemy*, Delhi: Oxford University Press, 1983.

Network of Concerned Anthropologists, *The Counter-Counterinsurgency Manual: Or, Notes on Demilitarizing American Society*, Prickly Paradigm Press, Chicago: Chicago University Press, 2009.

Newman, Edward and Oliver P. Richmond, *The United Nations and Human Security*, London: Palgrave 2001.

Newman, Saul, 'Connolly's Democratic Pluralism and the Question of State Sovereignty', *British Journal of Politics and International Relations*, vol.10, 2007, pp.227–40.

Newman, Saul, 'Derrida's Deconstruction of Authority', *Philosophy and Social Criticism*, vol.27, no.3, 2001, pp.1–20.

Nordstrom, Carolyn, *Shadows of War*, Berkley: University of California Press, 2004.

Office of the Prime Minister, *On the Road to Peace and Prosperity*, Dili, 2010.

O'Hagan, Jacinta, *Conceptualising the West in IR*, London: Palgrave, 2002.

O'Neill, William, *Kosovo: An Unfinished Peace*, London: Lynne Rienner, 2001.

Offe, Claus, 'Some Contradictions of the Modern Welfare State', *Critical Social Policy*, vol.2 no.2, 1982, p.7–14.

OSCE, *Assessing the Realisation of the Right to Social Assistance in BH*, December, 2005.

Oxford Dictionary of English Etymology, Oxford: OUP, 1986.

Palmer, Lisa, and Demetrio do Amaral de Carvalho, 'Nation building and resource management: The politics of nature in Timor Leste', *Geoforum*, vol.39, 2008, pp.1321–32.

Parekh, Bhikhu, *Gandhi's Political Philosophy*, Basingstoke: Macmillan, 1989.

Paris, Roland, '*Human Security: Paradigm Shift or Hot Air?*', *International Security*, vol.26, no.2, Fall 2001, pp.87–102.

Paris, Roland, 'International Peacebuilding and the 'Mission Civilisatrice', *Review of International Studies*, vol.28, no.4, 2002, pp.637–56.

Paris, Roland, *At War's End*, Cambridge: Cambridge University Press, 2004.

Paris, Roland, and Timothy D. Sisk (eds), *The Dilemmas of Statebuilding. Confronting the contradictions of postwar peace operations*, London: Routledge, 2009.

Patel, Rajeev and Philip McMichael, 'Third Worldism and the Lineages of Global Fascism', *Third World Quarterly*, vol. 25, no.1, 2004, pp.231–54.

Phnom Penh Post, November 2005.

Pilkington, Ed, 'Bush $1bn jobs plan to draw Iraqis into fold', *The Guardian*, 8 January 2007.

Plant, Sadie, *The Most Radical Gesture*, London: Routledge, 1992.

Polanyi, Karl, *The Great Transformation: The Political and Economic Origins of Our Time* Boston: Beacon Press, 1944.

Polat, Necati, 'Peace as War', *Unpublished Paper*, 2009.

Ponzio, Richard and Christopher Freeman, 'Conclusion: Rethinking Statebuilding in Afghanistan', *International Peacekeeping*, vol.14, no.1, 2007, pp.173–84.

Pouligny, Beatrice, *Peace Operations Seen From Below*, London: Hurst, 2006.

Pouligny, Beatrice, 'Supporting Local Ownership in Humanitarian Action', *Humanitarian Policy Paper Series*, Global Public Policy Institute, 2009.

Program-Project Development Manager of NDC Sarajevo, Conference on 'Delivering Just and Durable Peace? Evaluating EU Peacebuilding strategies in the Western Balkans', Sarajevo, 04/09/09.

Przeworski, Adam, Michael Alvarez, J.A. Cheibub and Fernando Limongi, *Democracy and Development*, Cambridge: Cambridge University Press, 2000.

Pugh, Michael, 'Peacekeeping and Critical Theory', *Conference Presentation at BISA*, LSE, London, (16–18 December, 2002).

Pugh Michael, 'Transformation in the Political Economy of Bosnia since Dayton,' *International Peacekeeping*, vol.2, no.3, Autumn 2005, pp.448–62.

Pugh, Michael, 'The Political Economy of Peacebuilding: A Critical Theory Perspective,' *International Journal of Peace Studies*, vol.10, no.2, 2005, pp.23–42.

Pugh, Michael, 'Limited Survival and Economic Security', *Working Paper*, 2007. http://www.st-andrews.ac.uk/intrel/cpcs/chapters.htm.

Pugh, Michael, 'Corruption and the Political Economy of Liberal Peace,' chapter prepared for the International Studies Association annual convention, San Francisco (26–28 March 2008).

Pugh, Michael, Neil Cooper and Mandy Turner, *Whose Peace: The Political Economy of Peacebuilding*, London: Palgrave, 2008.

RAMSI website: http://www.ramsi.org

Randle, Michael, *Civil Resistance*, London: Fontana, 1994.

Rankin, Nicholas, *Telegramme from Guernica*, London: Faber and Faber, 2003.

Rasmussen, Mikkel Vedby, *The West, Civil Society, and the Construction of Peace*, London: Palgrave, 2003.

Rawls, John, *Law of Peoples*, Cambridge, MA: Harvard University Press, 2001.

Rawls, John, *Political Liberalism*, New York: Columbia University Press, 1993.

Reason, Peter and Hilary Bradbury (eds), *Handbook of Action Research*, London: Sage, 2001.

Report of the Secretary-General's High Level Panel on Threats, Challenges, and Change, United Nations, 2004.

Report of the Secretary-General, 'The situation in Afghanistan and its implications for international peace and security', *UN Doc. A/62/345–S/2007/555*, (21 September 2007).

Richmond, Oliver P., *Maintaining Order, Making Peace*, London: Palgrave, 2002.

Richmond, Oliver P., 'States of Sovereignty, Sovereign States, and Ethnic Claims for International Status', *Review of International Studies*. vol.28, no.2, 2002.

Richmond, Oliver P., 'UN Peace Operations and the Dilemmas of the Peacebuilding Consensus', in *International Peacekeeping*, vol.11, no.1, 2004, pp.83–101.

Richmond, Oliver P., *The Transformation of Peace*, London: Palgrave, 2005.

Richmond, Oliver P., 'Critical Research Agendas for Peace: The Missing Link in the Study of International Relations', *Alternatives*, vol.32, no.2, 2007.

Richmond, Oliver P., 'Dadaism and the Peace Differend', *Alternatives*, Vol.33, No.4, 2007.

Richmond, Oliver P., 'Emancipatory Forms of Human Security and Liberal Peacebuilding', *International Journal*, vol.62, no.3, 2007, pp.458–77.

Richmond, Oliver P., *Peace in IR*, London: Routledge, 2008.

Richmond, Oliver P., 'Reclaiming Peace in International Relations', *Millennium: Journal of International Studies*, vol.36, no.3, 2008.

Richmond, Oliver, 'Eirenism and a Post-Liberal Peace', *Review of International Studies*, vol.35, no.3, 2009, pp.557–80.

Richmond, Oliver P., 'Becoming Liberal, Unbecoming Liberalism: The Everyday, Empathy, and Post-Liberal Peacebuilding', *Journal of Intervention and Statebuilding*, vol.3, no.3, 2009, pp.324–344.

Richmond, Oliver P., 'The Romanticisation of the Local: Welfare, Culture and Peacebuilding', *International Spectator*, vol.44, no.1, 2009, pp.149–69.

Richmond, Oliver P., 'Resistance and the Post-Liberal Peace', *Millennium*, vol.38, no.3, 2010, pp.665–92

Richmond, Oliver P., 'Beyond Local Ownership and Participation in the Architecture of International Peacebuilding', *Ethnopolitics*, forthcoming, 2011.

Richmond, Oliver P., *Failed Statebuilding*, Yale University Press, 2013, forthcoming.

Richmond, Oliver P., and Jason Franks, 'Liberal Hubris: Virtual Peace in Cambodia', *Security Dialogue*, vol.38, no.1, 2007, pp.27–48.

Richmond, Oliver P., and Jason Franks, 'The Emperors' New Clothes? Liberal Peace in East Timor', *International Peacekeeping*, vol.15, no.2, 2008, pp.185–200.

Richmond, Oliver P. and Jason Franks, Liberal Peace Transitions: Between Statebuilding and Peacebuilding, Edinburgh: Edinburgh University Press, 2009.

Rieff, David, *A Bed for the Night*, London: Vintage, 2002.

Roberts, Adam and Timothy Garton Ash (eds), *Civil Resistance and Power Politics: The Experience of Non-violent Action from Gandhi to the Present*, Oxford: Oxford University Press, 2009.

Rorty, Richard, 'On Ethnocentrism', *Objectivity, Relativism, and Truth*, Cambridge: CUP, 1991.

Rotberg, Robert I., 'The Failure and Collapse of Nation-States: Breakdown, Prevention and Repair', in Robert I. Rotberg (ed.) *When States Fail: Causes and Consequences*, Princeton: Princeton University Press, 2004, pp.1–50.

Ruggie, John Gerard, (ed.), 'Multilateralism' in *Multilateralism Matters*, NY, 1993.

Ruggie, John Gerard, 'Territoriality and Beyond: Problematizing Modernity in IR', *International Organisation*, vol.47, no.1, 1993, pp.139–74.

Said, Edward, *Orientalism*, London: Penguin, 1978.

Said, Edward, *Culture and Imperialism*, London: Vintage, 1994.

Sandbrook, Richard, Marc Edelman, Patrick Heller and Judith Teichman, *Social Democracy in the Global Periphery*, Cambridge: Cambridge University Press, 2007.

Schmeidl, Susanne (with Masood Karokhail), 'Prêt-a-Porter States': How the McDonaldization of State-Building Misses the Mark in Afghanistan', in Martina Fischer and Beatrix Schmelzle (eds), *Peace in the Absence of States: Challenging the Discourse on State Failure*, Berghof Handbook for Conflict Transformation Dialogue Series Issue no.8, 2009.

Schmidt, Herman, 'Politics and *Peace Research*', *Journal of Peace Research*, vol.5, no.3, 1968, pp.217–32.

Schumpeter, Joseph, *Capitalism, Socialism and Democracy*, London: George, Allen and Unwin, 1943.

Schumpeter, Joseph, *Sociology of Imperialism*, 1919.

Schwarz, Henry, and Sangeeta Rauy, *Companion to Post-Colonial Studies*, London: Blackwell, 2000.

Scott, James C, *Weapons of the Weak: Everyday Peasant Resistance*, New Haven: Yale University Press, 1985.

Scott, James C, *Domination and the Arts of Resistance*, New Haven: Yale University Press, 1990.

Scott, James C, *The Art of Not Being Governed*, New Haven: Yale University Press, 2009.

Shani, Giorgio, 'Towards a Post-Western IR', *International Studies Review*, vol.10, 2008, pp.722–34.

Sharp, Gene, *Politics of Non-Violent Action*, Porter Sargent: Boston, 1973.

Shaull, Richard, 'Foreword', in Paulo Freire, *Pedagogy of the Oppressed*, London: Penguin, 1996 [1970].

Shinko, Rosemary E., 'Agonistic Peace: A Postmodern Reading', *Millennium – Journal of International Studies*, vol.36, no.3, 2008, pp.473–91.

Singh Mehta, Uday, *Liberalism and Empire*, Chicago: Chicago University Press, 1999.

Smirl, Lisa, 'Building the Other, Constructing Ourselves: Spatial Dimensions of International Humanitarian Response', *International Political Sociology*, vol.2, pp.236–53.

Smith, Michael G., *Peacekeeping in East Timor*, Colorado: Lynne Rienner, 2003.

Snyder, Jack, *From Voting to Violence*, London: W.W. Norton, 2000.

Spencer, Jonathan, *Anthropology, Politics and the State: Democracy and Violence in South Asia*, Cambridge: Cambridge University Press, 2007.

Spivak, Gayatri Chakravorty, 'Can the Subaltern Speak?', in C. Nelson and L. Grossberg (eds), *Marxism and the Interpretation of Culture*, Basingstoke: Macmillan, 1988, pp.271–313.

Spivak, Gayatri Chakravorty, *A Critique of Post-Colonial Reason*, Cambridge, Mass.: Harvard University Press, 1999.

Sriram, Chandra, *Peace as Governance*, London: Palgrave, 2008.

Suhrke, Astri and Kaja Borchgrevink, 'Afghanistan – Justice sector reform', in Edward Newman, Roland Paris, and Oliver P. Richmond (eds), *Beyond Liberal Peacebuilding*, Tokyo: UNU Press, 2009, pp.178–200.

Suhrke, Astri, 'Peacekeepers as Nation-builders: Dilemmas of the UN in East Timor', *International Peacekeeping*, vol.8, no.4, 2001, pp.1–20.

Sylvester, Christine, 'Empathetic Cooperation: A Feminist Method for IR', *Millennium*, vol.23, no.2, 1994, pp.315–34.

Sylvester, Christine, 'Bare Life as Development/Post-Colonial Problematic', *The Geographical Journal*, vol.172, no.1, 2006, pp.66–77.

Sylvester, Christine, 'Whither the International At the End of IR', *Millennium*, vol.35, no.3, 2007, pp.551–71.

Szakolczai, Arpad, 'Thinking Beyond the East-West Divide: Patocka, Foucault, Hamvas, Elias, and the Care of the Self', *EUI Working Paper*, Florence: EUI, 94/2, (1994).

Tadjbakhsh, Shahrbanou, 'Human Security: Concepts and Implications', *Les Etudes du CERI*, no.117–18, September 2005.

Tadjbakhsh, Shahrbanou and Michael Schoistwohl, 'Playing with Fire? The International Community's Democratization Experiment in Afghanistan' *International Peacekeeping*, vol.15, no.2, 2008, pp.252–67.

Taylor, Charles, 'The Politics of Recognition' in Amy Gutmann(ed.), *Multiculturalism and the Politics of Recognition*, Princeton University Press, 1992, pp.25–73.

Thoreau, Henry David, *On the Duty of Civil Disobedience*, New York: Signet, 1980 [1849].

Titmuss, Richard, *Universalism versus Selection, Commitment to Welfare*, London: Allen and Unwin, 1968, pp.128–137.

Trindade, Jose, 'Rethinking Timorese Identity as a Peacebuilding Strategy', *EU/GTZ and EU Rapid Reaction Mechanism*, Dili, 6 June 2007.

Turner, Mandy and Michael Pugh, 'Towards a new agenda for transforming war economies', *Conflict, Security and Development*, vol.6, no.3, 2006, pp.471–79.

Ucko, David, 'Militias, tribes, and insurgents: The Challenge of Political Reintergration in Iraq', *Conflict, Security and Development*, vol.8, no.3, 2008, pp.341–73.

UN 'Speech of the Special Representative of the Secretary-General for Afghanistan', Opening of 55th Annual DPI/NGO conference, *Rebuilding Societies Emerging from Conflict: UN, A Shared Responsibility*, New York, 9 September 2002.

UN 'Report of the Secretary-General's High Level Panel on Threats, Challenges, and Change', *United Nations*, 2004.

UN Secretary General's Report on Timor-Leste pursuant to Security Council Resolution 1690, 8 August 2006

UN Draft Declaration on the Rights of Indigenous Peoples, E/CN.4/SUB.2/1994/2/ Add.1:1994: UNITED NATIONS DECLARATION ON THE RIGHTS OF INDIGENOUS PEOPLES, Adopted by the General Assembly 13 September 2007.

UNCTAD, 'Doubling Aid: Making the Big Push work', *Report on Economic Development in Africa*, www.unctad.org, 2006.

UNDP Human Development Report – Kosovo 2004, Pristina: UNDP.

UNDP Monthly Newsletter, February 2007.

UNDP, *Human Development Report: Timor Leste*, 2006.

United Nations, 'Report of the Secretary-General on Timor-Leste pursuant to Security Council resolution 1690', *UN Doc. S/2006/628*, (August 2006).

UNMIK, Kosovo Economic Outlook 2006, Economic Policy Office, March 2006.

USIP, Iraq, *Progress in Peacebuilding*, (March, 2008), http://www.usip.org/iraq/progress_peacebuilding_iraq.pdf.

Vickers, Miranda, *Between Serb and Albanian: A History of Kosovo*, New York: University Press, 1998.

Von Hayek, Friederich, 'The Meaning of the Welfare State', in *The Constitution of Liberty*, London: Routledge & Kegan Paul, 1959.

Vrasti, Wanda, 'The Strange Case of Ethnography and International Relations', *Millennium* –, vol.37, no.2, 2008, pp.279–301

Wainwright, Elsina, 'Our Failing Neighbour?' Canberra: Australian Strategic Policy Institute, 2003.

Walker, RBJ, *Inside/outside: International Relations as Political Theory*, Cambridge: CUP, 1992.

Waller, Michael, Kyril Drezov, Bulent Gokay (eds), *Kosovo: The Politics of Delusion*, London: Frank Cass, 2001.

Williams, Andrews, *Liberal War*, London: Routledge, 2006.

Wilson, Woodrow, Address to the Senate, 12 January 1917, in Arthur S. Link *et. al.* (eds), *The Papers of Woodrow Wilson*, vol.40, Princeton: Princeton University Press, 1983, p.536–7.

Woods, Tom, 'Informal Political System of Government in Solomon Islands', *Working Paper for the Constitutional Congress and the Eminent Persons Advisory Committee*, Honiara, 28th August 2008.

Woodward, Susan L, 'A case of shifting focus: some lessons from the Balkans' in Martina Fischer and Beatrice Schmiezle (eds), *Peace in the Absence of States: Challenging the Discourse on State Failure*, Berghof Handbook for Conflict Transformation Dialogue Series Issue no.8, 2009, pp.47–56.

Woolf, Leonard, *The Framework of a Lasting Peace*, London: Allen and Unwin, 1917.

World Bank Timor Leste Country Director, *Personal Interview*, World Bank, Dili, 6 November 2008.

World Bank, *The World Bank Group in the Western Balkans*, Washington, August 2005. Tilly, Charles, Louise Tilly and Richard Tilly, *The Rebellious Century, 1830–1930*, London: JM Dent and Sons, 1975.

Yashar, DJ, *Contesting Citizenship in Latin America: The Rise of Indigenous Movements and the Postliberal Challenge*, Cambridge: Cambridge University Press, 2005.

Zevnik, Andreja, 'Sovereign-less Subject and the Possibility of Resistance', *Millennium*, vol.38, no.1, 2009, pp.83–106.

Zimmern, Alfred, *The League of Nations and the Rule of Law*, London: Macmillan, 1936.

Interviews, Discussions, Focus Groups

Ambassador Davidson, OSCE, *Personal Interview*, Sarajevo, 1 February 2007 and 15 March 2008.

Cadeado, Carlton, *Personal Interview*, Higher Institute, Maputo, 8 January, 2010.

Confidential Sources, *Focus Group*, Human Security Unit, UN, New York, 4 June 2010.

Confidential Source, *Personal Interview*, NEPRU, Windhoek, 14 January 2010.

Confidential Source, Australian Aid, *Personal Interview*, 15 November 2008.

Confidential Source, Centre for Human Rights, *Personal Interview*, Sarajevo, 30 January 2007.

Confidential Source, Centre for Human Rights, *Personal Interview*, Sarajevo, 30 January 2007.

Confidential Source, Council of Europe, *Personal Interview*, Sarajevo, 1 February 2007.

Confidential Source, Council of Europe, *Personal Interview*, Sarajevo, 1 February 2007.

Confidential Source, Independent Economic Advisor, *Personal Interview*, Sarajevo, 30 January 2007.

Confidential Source, National Dialogue Centre, *Personal Interview*, Mostar, 2 February 2007.

Confidential Source, National Dialogue Centre, *Personal Interview*, Mostar, 2 February 2007.

Confidential Source, NCSC Programme Officer, *Personal Interview*, Pristina, 4 April 2006.

Confidential Source, OSCE Democratisation Education Officer, *Personal Interview, Pristina*, 5 April 2006.

Confidential Source, OSCE Democratisation Education Officer, *Personal Interview*, Pristina, 5 April 2006.

Confidential Source, *Personal Interview,* Dili, 4 November 2008.

Confidential Source, *Personal Interview,* DPA, UN, New York, 10 June 2010.

Confidential Sources, *Focus Group,* DPKO, UN, New York, 7 June 2010.

Confidential Source, *Personal Interview,* Formerly with UNMIK, Brussels, 4 February 2010.

Confidential Source, *Personal Interview,* Ministry for Peace and Reconciliation, Honiara, 28 November 2008.

Confidential Source, *Personal Interview,* World Bank Country Office, Phnom Penh, 10 November 2005.

Confidential Source, SIDA, *Personal Interview,* Sarajevo, 1 February 2007.

Confidential Source, UNDP, *Personal Interview,* 6 November, 2008.

Confidential Source, World Bank – Operations Officer, *Personal Interview,* Pristina, 3 April 2006

Confidential Source, World Bank, *Personal Interview,* Sarajevo, 27 January 2007.

Country Representative, *Personal Interview,* World Bank, Dili, November 2008.

Deputy SRSG, *Personal Interview,* Sarajevo, 29 January 2007.

De Silva, Arkanso, *Personal Interview,* GTZ, Dili, 5 November 2008.

De Silva, Francesco, *Personal Interview,* District Administrator and Village Elder, Viqueque, 8 November, 2008.

District Suco Commissioner, *Personal Interview,* Viquerque, November 2008.

Fkere, Joy, *Personal Interview,* Ministry of Peace and Reconciliation, Honiara, 24 November 2008.

Focus Group Discussion at Ministry for Peace and Reconciliation, including Father Philip Vanlusa, Betty Luvsia, and Andrew Adams, Honiara, 25 November 2008.

Focus Group Discussion at RAMSI, 26 November 2009.

Focus Group discussion with Malaita Group, Ministry of Peace and Reconciliation, Honiara, 29 November 2008.

Focus Group, Independent Peacebuilding Organisations, Ministry of Culture, Maputo, 10 January 2010.

Franco, Antonio S, *Personal Interview,* World Bank, Dili, 6 November, 2008.

Frietas, Sidonio, *Personal Interview,* Programme Manager, Democracy and Governance Programme, USAID, 11 November 2004.

Garcia, Carolina Enriquez, Coinde, *Personal Interview,* Guatemala City, 21 July 2010.

Gomes, Rui A, *Personal Interview,* UNDP, Dili, 5 November 2008.

Group Discussion with staff at La'o Hamutuk, Dili, 4 November 2008.

GTZ Personnel, *Personal Interview,* Dili, November 2008.

Hummel, John, *Personal Interview,* Carter Centre, Monrovia, 18 November, 2009.

Kohl, Gunther, GTZ Director, *Personal Interview,* 5 November 2008.

Leslie, Emma, *Personal Interview,* Alliance for Conflict Transformation/researcher, Phnom Penh, 11 November 2005.

Lomaloma, Mataiasi, *Personal Interview,* Special Coordinator, RAMSI, Honiara, 26 November 2008.

Makolli, Ibrahim, Council of the Defence of Human Rights, *Personal Interview,* Pristina, 6 April 2006.

Meeting with MPs in Sarajevo. *Focus Group,* Halid Genjac, chair; House of Representatives; SDA – *Stranka demokratske akcije,* Party for Democratic Action, Milica Markovic, member; House of Representatives SNSD – *Savez nezavisnih socijaldemokrata* – Union of Independent Social Democrats, Bozo Ljubic, member; House of Peoples HDZ 1990; *Hrvatska demokratska zajednica 1990;* Croatian Democratic Union 1990, EU Accession Parliamentary Commission, Bosnian Parliament, Sarajevo 3/09/09.

Moore, Clive, *Personal Interview*, University of Queensland, Brisbane, 11 November 2008.

Nangoloh, Phil YA, Executive Director, National Society for Human Rights, *Personal Interview*, Windhoek, 16 January 2010.

National Council of Elders, *Focus Group*, Monrovia, 25 November 2009.

O'Callaghan, Mary Louise, *Personal Interview*, Public Affairs Unit, RAMSI, Honiara, 28 November 2008.

Official Source, USAID, *Personal Interview*, Phnom Penh, 8 November 2005.

Ofstad, Olav, *Personal Interview*, Head of Delegation, International Federation of Red Cross and Red Crescent Societies, Dili 11 November 2004.

Page, Michael, *Personal Interview*, UNMIT, Dili, 5 November 2008.

Personal Interviews, Constitutional Team, Honiara, December 2008.

RAMSI official, *Personal Interview*, Honiara, December 2008.

Senior World Bank Official, *Personal Interview*, Washington, 23 April 2007.

Smith, Dan, Secretary General of International Alert, Centre for International Studies, University of Oxford, 23 October 2009.

Tarp, Kristoffer, *Personal Interview*, Peacebuilding Support Office, UN, New York, 4 June 2010.

Touva, Paul, *Personal Interview*, Ministry of Peace and Reconciliation, Honiara, 1 December 2008.

Toroi Cleophas and Ismail Dodoo, *Personal Interviews*, UNDP, Monrovia, 21 November 2009.

Traditional Council, *Focus Group*, Monrovia, 25 November 2009.

UN Police, Confidential Source, *Personal Interview*, Dili, 3 November 2008.

USAID, Name withheld, *Personal Interview*, Dili, 5 November 2008.

Walsh, Pat, *Personal Interview*, CAVR, Dili, 6 November 2008.

Williams, George, *Personal Interview*, Democracy Watch, Monrovia: 19 November 2009.

Woods, Tom, *Personal Interview*, Advisor, Constitutional Reform Unit, 26 November 2008.

Zita, Bonaventura, *Personal Interview*, Co-ordinator of 'Turning Swords into Ploughshares Project', Christian Council of Churches, 12 January 2010.

Index